To my beloved

husband-shepherd-friend
earthly head and king
my bridegroom

And to my Beloved

Savior-Shepherd-Friend
eternal Head and King
my Bridegroom

My beloved is mine, and I am his.

With great delight I sat in his shadow,
and his fruit was sweet to my taste.
He brought me to the banqueting house,
and his banner over me was love.

The Song of Songs

She's done it again! In *Adorned*, Nancy gives us another rich resource to help us become Titus 2 women. As I read this book I felt that I was sitting in Nancy's kitchen enjoying a cup of tea and a Titus 2 conversation. She invites us into her heart. She encourages and equips us to share the gospel and our lives with other women. This is a lovely book.

SUSAN HUNT
Author of *Spiritual Mothering—The Titus 2 Mandate for Women Mentoring Women*

I have seen firsthand and have benefitted personally from Nancy living out this message. I am so grateful for her as a sister in Christ, a mentor from afar, and a spiritual mother to many through True Woman/Revive Our Hearts!

LAUREN CHANDLER
Pastor's wife, worship leader, author

This is a beautiful book, written by someone who beautifully lives out its truths. Each chapter is chock-full of wisdom and faithful instruction to help you grow—woman to woman—into someone whose life adorns the beauty of the gospel. What a tremendous treasure for this generation!

MARY A. KASSIAN
Speaker, author of *Girls Gone Wise*

Adorned is a beautiful call to Titus 2 living—life on life, woman to woman, one generation to another. We need this book. Nancy shares with wisdom and insight the importance of female discipleship in the local church. Her words will inspire you to faithfully pick up the baton of truth and pass it on to others.

MELISSA KRUGER
Author of *Walking with God in the Season of Motherhood* and *The Envy of Eve*

I am so, so thrilled for you to experience this book! *Adorned* is beautifully written from beginning to end, and Nancy so thoughtfully reminds us how very much we women need each other. It blessed my heart and I know it will yours too.

JENNIFER ROTHSCHILD
Author of *Lessons I Learned in the Dark* and founder of Fresh Grounded Faith events

Nancy's practical insight, ageless wisdom, and warm fervor rang like bells through my spirit as I read this book. Both like an alarm waking me and a recurring melody inspiring me to understand again how my womanhood is beautified and can blossom in a multigenerational community of women following the Lord day by day together.

KRISTYN GETTY
Hymn writer/singer and mother of four daughters

Nancy is one of the women God has used to shape me into a better reflection of Himself. Her book *Adorned* crams a thousand coffee shop conversations about life, love, and godliness into a single, riveting book. Women in every season of life need to read it, reread it, and pass it along to the other women in their circle.

ERIN DAVIS
Women's ministry leader, wife, and momma who would be adrift without the encouragement and support of her sisters in Christ

This is truly Nancy's legacy work. Through what feels like a personal conversation, she takes women back to the Greek and Roman culture to grasp Titus 2, and urges us to rise up today to adorn the Bride of Christ. This book will influence the church and the personal lives of women in a way that few books ever have.

DANNAH GRESH
Bestselling author of *And the Bride Wore White*

Adorned is a Christ-exalting, mind-renewing, life-altering presentation of Titus 2 that will help women, young and old, embrace their call to learn from one another, to the glory of Christ our Savior.

JACKIE HILL PERRY
Writer, speaker, artist

Nancy's instruction, wisdom, and grace will challenge you to not only pray for a woman who you might call a spiritual mother, but you'll also desire to be the type of woman others might call on—for the good of the church and to the glory of God.

TRILLIA NEWBELL
Author of *Enjoy*, *Fear and Faith*, and *United*

Adorned is more than a book that articulates the virtues of the Titus 2 woman. You will be inspired to be biblically beautiful, adorned in the sound doctrine of God, and prepared for the kingdom work of God no matter your season of life.

KAREN LORITTS
Speaker and teacher

Nancy's new book is a call for all Christian women—young and old—to live out the Titus 2 command of life-on-life discipleship. More than ever, we need women to show us how to live out the gospel in our daily life. Older women, we need you!

CHRISTINA FOX
Licensed counselor, speaker, author of *A Heart Set Free: A Journey to Hope through the Psalms of Lament*

Nancy has penned her most significant work yet in *Adorned*! This delightful, fresh look at the biblical mandate in Titus 2 is profound, yet practical. You will sense the Holy Spirit calling you to live the life God has made you for and called you to.

REBECCA LUTZER
Retired RN and wife of Dr. Erwin Lutzer, pastor emeritus of The Moody Church

Adorned calls the women of the church to the vital and joyful work of cultivating real-life relationships centered on the gospel of Jesus. I am thankful for Nancy's work to develop a resource on Titus 2 that is substantive, faithful, and practical.

AMANDA BIBLE WILLIAMS
Chief Content Officer of She Reads Truth, author of *Open Your Bible*

. . . so that in everything they may adorn the doctrine of God our Savior.

TITUS 2:10

ned

Living Out the Beauty of the Gospel Together

NANCY DEMOSS WOLGEMUTH

MOODY PUBLISHERS | CHICAGO

Names and details in some illustrations have been changed to protect individuals' privacy.

Italics in Scripture references indicate author emphasis.

Published in association with the literary agency of Wolgemuth & Associates, Inc.

Edited by Anne Christian Buchanan
Interior design: Erik M. Peterson
Cover design: Faceout Studio
Calligrapher: Nicole Black of The Left Handed Calligrapher (thelefthandedcalligrapher.com)
Cover wedding photos: Photography by Britton (photographybybritton.com)

Library of Congress Cataloging-in-Publication Data

Names: Wolgemuth, Nancy DeMoss, author.
Title: Adorned : living out the beauty of the gospel together / Nancy DeMoss Wolgemuth.
Description: Chicago : Moody Publishers, 2017. | Includes bibliographical references.
Identifiers: LCCN 2016050148 (print) | LCCN 2017007377 (ebook) | ISBN 9780802412591 | ISBN 9780802492852
Subjects: LCSH: Christian women—Religious life. | Mentoring—Religious aspects—Christianity. | Bible. Titus, II—Criticism, interpretation, etc.
Classification: LCC BV4527 .W583 2017 (print) | LCC BV4527 (ebook) | DDC 248.8/43--dc23
LC record available at https://lccn.loc.gov/2016050148

ISBN: 978-0-8024-1900-2 (paperback)

We hope you enjoy this book from Moody Publishers. Our goal is to provide high-quality, thought-provoking books and products that connect truth to your real needs and challenges. For more information on other books and products written and produced from a biblical perspective, go to www.moodypublishers.com or write to:

Moody Publishers
820 N. LaSalle Boulevard
Chicago, IL 60610

3 5 7 9 10 8 6 4 2

Printed in China

Contents

Teach what accords with sound doctrine.

Older men are to be sober-minded, dignified, self-controlled,
sound in faith, in love, and in steadfastness.

Older women likewise are to be reverent in behavior,
not slanderers or slaves to much wine.

They are to teach what is good,
and so train the young women
to love their husbands and children,
to be self-controlled,
pure,
working at home,
kind,
and submissive to their own husbands,
that the word of God may not be reviled.

**. . . so that in everything they may adorn
the doctrine of God our Savior.**

TITUS 2:1–5, 10

CHAPTER 1

A Woman Adorned and Adorning

Beauty Secrets of Titus 2

Let us rejoice and exult,
and give him the glory,
for the marriage of the Lamb has come,
and his Bride has made herself ready;
it was granted her to clothe herself
with fine linen, bright and pure.
REVELATION 19:7–8

IT HAD BEEN A SHORT NIGHT OF SLEEP. But that didn't matter to me. I knew this day—Saturday, November 14, 2015—would be one I'd never forget. At the age of fifty-seven, I was about to be a bride for the first time. Today I would say "I do" before God and several hundred witnesses and become Mrs. Robert Wolgemuth. It was a day I had eagerly anticipated and for which I had been earnestly preparing for months.

My phone alarm woke me at 5:15 a.m. An hour later, a sweet young friend and her husband knocked on the door of my hotel room. Emerging into the predawn stillness, we drove twenty minutes through the western Chicago suburbs and finally pulled into a vacant church parking lot in Wheaton, Illinois.

Inside the church, we were directed to a small, sparsely furnished room, where over the next few hours a transformation would take place. I slipped on a robe and took a seat as first a hair stylist, then a makeup artist, quietly got busy. We had been through trial runs, so they knew just what to do.

My wedding gown, purchased months earlier, painstakingly altered and carefully steamed by a friend the night before, hung off to the side, ready for me to slip into. An elegant bracelet and "diamond" earrings sat out on a table along with sparkly silver shoes—which yet another friend would take to a shoe store as soon as it opened so they could be stretched. (They were brand-new and killing my feet!) Everything was ready to complete the ensemble.

Why was I going to all this trouble? Why was I getting more dressed up than I had ever been in my life? Why had I endured the seemingly endless attention to details that commandeered my life over so many months? Why did I enlist and gratefully accept the help of so many friends who had plenty of other important things to do?

I'll tell you why. All the time, thought, money, and effort expended for that one day were for a single purpose. I wanted to be *adorned*—beautiful, ready for my bridegroom. And I wanted to *adorn* my husband-to-be with my affection and attention. I wanted him to be honored and admired by others. I wanted our guests to see how much I loved this man and what a gift he was to me.

We had decided to take our photos prior to the wedding ceremony. So promptly at nine-thirty, arrayed in my dress, train, and white faux-fur wrap, I was carefully loaded into a car that would take me to an outdoor location nearby for our photo shoot.

Robert was already at the site, his back toward me. On cue, he turned around to get his first glimpse of the adorned bride he had only been able to picture in his mind till that moment. His response—the look in his eyes, his involuntary gasp—was priceless to me. It made all the effort worthwhile.

We walked the fifty feet or so toward each other, bracing against the brisk, late fall chill, our hearts warmed with each other's presence. Robert reached out to embrace me, and I fell into his arms.

Never had I felt more beautiful.

Woman to Woman

Back in the bride's room, just moments before the ceremony was to begin, as Robert and I and several others were tending to last-minute details, someone came in to let me know that one of our guests had asked to pray with me before the wedding.

Vonette Bright, a dear, lifelong friend, was like a second mother to me. Eighty-nine years old and widowed for a dozen years, she had been battling leukemia and had just been told she had only months to live. But she had been eager to be at my wedding if it was the last thing she did—and she'd made it. (As it turned out, she would be with the Lord just six weeks later.)

I was eager to see this beloved friend, so we invited her to join us for a few moments. Vonette's caregiver gently pushed her wheelchair into the room. Beautifully dressed in bright red, Vonette turned a radiant countenance toward us. We circled around her wheelchair as cameras flashed and video rolled and this venerable woman of God led us in prayer, blessing our marriage.

When she finished, Vonette turned to me and whispered, "I had hoped to be able to speak to you alone." In response, I quickly asked everyone to clear the room. Then she turned to me and spoke gently but forthrightly: "Honey, I'm a mama . . . and I'd like to know . . . Is there anything you'd like to ask a mama before you get married?"

No cameras or recorders were privy to the sweet exchange that took place in those next few moments, but that scene and our conversation will forever be etched on my heart.

A woman in the winter of her life imparting encouragement and exhortation to a woman in an earlier season who was eager to glean everything she possibly could.

A seasoned wife—having enjoyed a vibrant, loving marriage for fifty-four years— mentoring a novice in how to make much of Christ in her own marriage.

Two women, one older and the other younger, living out the beauty of the gospel—together.

Woman to woman.

The picture brings to mind another pair of women. I envision the elderly Elizabeth, after decades of infertility and unfulfilled longings, now supernaturally expecting a son . . . taking Mary of Nazareth into her heart and home . . . imparting faith and wisdom to the teenage virgin in whose womb was miraculously growing an infant who would one day be our Savior.

Precious little is recorded of their conversation, but what was preserved for us speaks to the beauty of the gospel being lived out by women walking in company with each other. Women whose lives are adorned by the presence of Christ and who adorn His gospel and make it believable for the next generation by their humble, joyful obedience.

After Vonette had shared with me what was on her heart, she took my hands in hers and once again prayed, praising our Father for the wedding about to take place and pleading for His blessing and favor on the marriage to follow. One could almost hear heaven whisper *Amen.*

That small, plain room, littered with hair and makeup gear, assorted clothing items, jewelry, and more, was transformed, through the Spirit of God knitting our hearts together, into a place of beauty, a temple adorned by and for the living Christ.

The Loveliness of Christ

As this modern-day Elizabeth and I exited that holy place, we could hear strains of the prelude flowing from the nearby sanctuary. Magnificent.

Not wanting to miss a moment of the celebration, Robert and I made our way to a secluded room just off the balcony, where we could see and hear the prelude and the first part of the worship service until it was time for the processional to begin.

The sanctuary with its colonial design was a visual feast. Tall, gleaming organ pipes lining the chancel wall. Gold banners proclaiming "Worthy is the Lamb" and "Unto Him be the glory." Massive arrangements of red roses and white calla lilies adorning the platform, with sprays of roses and ribbons at the end of the pews. Candles in elegant gold and silver stands. Exquisite.

And in the center of it all, prominently displayed on the platform, a twelve-foot, rough-hewn cross that made the whole setting even more striking.

For was it not at Calvary that our Savior took upon Himself the rags of our sin and shame, adorning us in exchange with the robes of His righteousness? Is not the cross the only source of any eternal beauty we may ever hope to experience or to offer other souls starved for love and loveliness?

> Jesus, Thy blood and righteousness
> My beauty are, my glorious dress.[1]

At the beginning of the ceremony, ten young girls whose families I have known and loved for years processed down the aisle ringing tiny bells. They were attired in darling dresses—some red, others white—with tights and fancy shoes, their hair curled and styled so sweetly.

A photo of the ten children surrounding the bride, all of us seated on steps at the front of the church, brought tears to my eyes the first time I saw it. For in these precious, beautifully dressed girls, I saw ten young women of God in the making.

I love the thought of inspiring those girls with a vision of what it means to be a bride who has experienced the love and grace of Christ and who radiates His beauty to others. I pray they will grow to have hearts that are adorned with grace and that their lives will adorn the gospel of Christ for their generation.

Children adorned. Guests adorned. A sanctuary adorned. A bride adorned.

All of it intended to fulfill the vision Robert and I had for our wedding from the time we announced our engagement—namely, *to showcase the loveliness of Christ.*

Or, as the apostle Paul put it in the second chapter of the book of Titus, to "adorn the doctrine of God our Savior" (v. 10).

Love and Beauty

Women love beauty. We enjoy the process of adorning ourselves and our environment.

Shopping for the clothes, makeup, or jewelry that will help us look our best.

Picking paint and accessories to make our homes more welcoming or comfortable or fashionable.

Carefully garnishing the food we put on the table.

Dressing our little ones in cute outfits.

Adding those special touches that make our surroundings, our relationships, and our activities a little more beautiful and personal and fun.

There's just something about assembling and creating beauty that's deeply satisfying.

And *feeling* beautiful—that's a longing deep in many women's hearts that has spawned and fueled countless industries.

I've never considered myself to be particularly beautiful in a physical sense. It's not that I think I'm unattractive or that I think there's something wrong with physical beauty. It's just not something I've focused on a whole lot. Mindful of the fleeting, deceptive nature of external beauty, I've tried to focus on cultivating the kind of beauty that can't be photographed (or photoshopped)—beauty of character and the heart.

Yet I can still remember how my heart skipped a beat the first time Robert told me I was beautiful.

I grew up in a loving home with a dad who adored me. I've been blessed to have many good, kind men in my life. It's possible my memory has failed me. But prior to that point, I cannot recall ever hearing a man say to me, "You're beautiful."

Robert kept telling me I was beautiful. He really seemed to mean it. And gradually I began to believe that he truly saw me that way—even when I had just finished working out at the gym, even on days when I hadn't taken time to apply makeup or fix my hair. As our courtship progressed, I told a friend, "I don't think there is anything I could do that would make him love me less or think I'm less beautiful."

But I also noticed that something even more significant was happening. As the persistent, gentle love of this man took root in my heart, it had a tenderizing, beautifying effect. In fact, to my amazement, people began to comment on my new "glow." Over and over again on my wedding day, friends said to me, "You're so beautiful!"

> *Our calling is to make His love and His truth visible, believable, and beautiful to skeptical observers.*

I say this not to shine a spotlight on myself, but to make the observation that to be adorned with another's love is to develop a greater capacity to reflect love and beauty to others.

You see, God has placed us here on earth as ambassadors of the gospel of Christ. And our calling as His followers is to make His love and His truth visible and believable—and beautiful—to skeptical observers.

Because they see it in *us*. Because they see it *changing* us.

His love making us beautiful. Adorning us.

And, through us, adorning His gospel.

Why We Need Each Other

It's a wonderful picture, isn't it?

But sadly—as you and I well know—it doesn't always work that way.

We may claim to love Jesus, but for some reason people don't always see His beauty reflected in our attitudes and actions. They don't always see in us the transforming power of His love.

Instead, too often, they see women who are just as overwhelmed, preoccupied, petty, or unloving as everyone else around us. If we're honest, that's the way we sometimes see ourselves.

But we long to do better. We really do want our lives to show the gospel in its very best light—even when we're

- up to our elbows in work and family life, with little time for personal prayer and Bible reading
- doubled over in worry and frustration because of a child who's running hard from God
- suffering through a lonely, loveless stretch of marriage with a husband who's pulled away
- retired to a shallow routine of crawling out of bed, making the coffee, watching television, and working the morning crossword puzzle
- or perhaps trapped in one of those tedious, one-foot-in-front-of-the-other seasons of life when the motivation to press on is almost more than we can muster.

But *how* do we do better? That's the question, isn't it?

How in the world do we manage to adorn the gospel and let it adorn us in the midst of our mundane or agonizing realities?

With help.

Lots of help!

The good news is that this task of being adorned by the gospel and enhancing the way it's perceived by others isn't something we're called to do alone. To help us accomplish what He has given us to do, God has graciously given us His Spirit and His church. And for us women, God has given us a community of other believing women for inspiration and support.

On my wedding weekend, a cadre of women friends, younger and older, banded together to provide personal and practical support in every way imaginable. The dear friend who took me to get my nails done (and secretly paid the bill). The young woman who accompanied me to the church for my makeup routine. Loving friends who baked and decorated cupcakes and others who managed guest lists and cared for administrative details for four different events. The sweet women who slipped away early from the reception to adorn Robert's and my hotel suite with an abundance of flowers, candles, and tasty snacks.

The love and combined efforts of these special women (along with many kind, helpful men) resulted in an indescribably lovely weekend. I couldn't have done it without the encouragement and help they provided. And in much the same way, I can't make it through life without walking in community with women who band together to support and beautify each other in Christ.

I need older women like my friend Vonette, who prayed for me from the time I was a child, watched me grow into a woman, often spoke into my life with wisdom, vision, and faith, and then, near the end of her life, endured the rigors of travel to be there for me and to share her love and wisdom when I got married.

I also need younger women in my life, even girls as young as those sweet little women-to-be who participated in my wedding. They help keep me from becoming narrow and brittle, and they bring me such joy and hope.

And I need women in my own season of life—like a small group of "sisters" I am a part of who gather periodically, on the phone or in person, for mutual encouragement, accountability, and prayer. I treasure the companionship and influence of these women in my life.

Older women, younger women, women who are peers—we all need each other if we are to adorn the gospel and show its beauty in our lives. And that reality brings us back to Titus 2 and the heart of this book. Because this important passage offers a primer for how and why this all works. It paints for us a picture of generational wisdom flowing downhill into inexperienced hearts, where it can cycle around and back up again in a continual process of godly care and counsel.

The biblical model of older women living out the gospel and training younger women to do the same is vital for all of us to thrive.

Woman to woman.

Older to younger.

Day to day.

Life to life.

This is God's good and beautiful plan. The biblical model of older women living out the gospel and training younger women to do the same, of younger women recognizing the value of older women in their lives—of women adorning the gospel together—is vital for all of us to thrive. Living our lives as Titus 2 women enables us to fulfill the purpose for which we were created. It helps our families and churches to flourish and the beauty of the gospel to shine forth in our world.

Together in the Race

We sometimes hear life compared to a marathon, the defining mark of which is *endurance*. And for sure, the race of life calls for endurance over the long haul.

But life is so much more than just staying the long course, gritting our teeth and enduring. We're also meant to grow, thrive, and celebrate. We're meant to enjoy beauty—awe-inspiring, life-enriching, God-exalting beauty.

And we're meant to experience the strength and encouragement that flow out of doing life together, helping each other live gospel-adorned lives that in turn adorn the gospel in the eyes of the world.

So I like to envision us Christian women participating in another kind of race. We're not just solo competitors slogging it out toward a distant finish line. Instead, we're a team. We run *together*.

Think of it as a *relay*—passing the baton from one person to another, each of us involved in the process, both giving and receiving as we press on toward our destination. It's teamwork, not just individual performance, that counts.

Or think of it as one of those charity runs where we all move forward in a group, helping one another, pooling our energies for the sake of a beloved cause. Knowing that our individual efforts count but that it's not entirely up to us to make it happen—and that the race itself has meaning, not just crossing the finish line.

Picture a vast field of runners—some older, some younger, some more mature, some less seasoned—and you and me, right there with them. We each need our own, personal relationship with God and His Word, of course, but we are not running by ourselves. God intends for our lives to intersect with one another, to carry each other forward under the strong, victorious, beautiful banner of Christ.

Now if all of this seems a bit too philosophical and esoteric, I assure you the practical implications will soon be clear. And they are huge, because this marathon, this relay, this race for a cause runs right through your living room. The baton passes directly over your kitchen table and through seemingly insignificant conversations and encounters.

When older women and younger women support each other in living out God's transforming love, the entire body of Christ grows more beautiful.

This is for you and me . . . real women living real, everyday lives.

And when it's working, believe me, it *works*. When older women choose to invest themselves in the lives of younger women, whole families and churches feel the blessing. When young moms and singles widen their close-knit groups to include women who have already run a few laps and lived to tell about it, both sides of the relationship are strengthened and grow. When older women and younger women support each other in living out God's transforming love, the entire body of Christ—the bride of Christ—grows more beautiful.

So if you're an *older woman* (and willing to admit it—as I am), the message of this book is for you.

And if you're a *younger woman* (as I still am to some), the message of this book is for you too. It's for all of us—because each of us is an older woman to somebody and each of us is a younger woman to someone else. And each of us, in different ways, in different seasons, can be on both the giving and receiving end of this life-to-life process.

Where We Begin

The heart of this powerful pattern can be seen in a single paragraph of Titus 2. And yet the rich, practical, gospel-drenched insight found in Titus 2:3–5 is sufficient to keep us nourished and growing for a lifetime.

These words were originally written by the apostle Paul to a young pastor named Titus, who was struggling to lead a church on the island of Crete. The Roman Empire, which ruled Crete, was just coming under the tyrannical reign of the ruthless emperor, Nero. Just imagine what Nero's maniacal threats felt like to the fledgling churches of his day, especially when his government officially outlawed Christianity throughout the empire.

Do you think it's hard being a Christian today? Try knowing you're a hunted species. Try thinking that if this young, revolutionary movement is to survive, plans must be put in place both to spread and to deepen its impact. It can't just be a religious order or a theological system; the gospel must soak through people's hearts and lives and families so pervasively that no emperor, no persecution, no reviling would be able to rock the church of Christ from its foundations. No amount of pressure, fear, or fatigue could dilute the church to the point that it would lose its light—its distinctiveness, vibrancy, and impact in the world.

Those were some of the concerns behind Paul's letter to Titus. Christians were wondering:

- How are believers supposed to think and act in such times?
- How can we keep from being deceived by false doctrine and teachers?
- How can we pass our faith on to the next generation, rather than seeing it become extinct?
- How can the church not just survive, but thrive, in a world that is hostile to our faith?
- How can we effectively fulfill our mission to reach a corrupt world with the beauty of Christ's gospel?

Sound familiar? Those questions are still with us.

Which is why we still need the book of Titus today.

We may not live in Nero's Rome, but we do live in a decadent, deceptive culture that threatens the church of Christ with its allure as well as its accusations and attacks. We need help to see how our lives can portray the gospel so beautifully that others see in us the transforming power of Christ and are drawn to know and follow Him. And (dare we say it?) we need help keeping His gospel attractive enough to *ourselves* that we—who claim to believe it—will actually trust Him, obey Him, and experience the power, peace, and joy He promises, even while living as exiles on this earth.

We all need to understand how to adorn the teaching of the gospel of Christ with the way we live—and to help each other do the same. And that's exactly what Titus 2 provides for us. With its succinct summary of the character qualities that delight God's heart and attract the hearts of those around us, this passage provides a timeless curriculum meant to be handed down from generation to generation. It lets older women know what is most important to share and younger women know what they're called to aspire to become.

Years ago, when I first began preparing to teach on this theme, I read this short book of the Bible scores of times—meditating on it, memorizing it, pondering individual words, letting my spirit soak in it.

I hope you'll do the same. Read it over and over again—all three chapters at first, to give you the overall setting, then narrowing down to chapter 2, with special emphasis on verses three through five. Immerse yourself in the text and its meaning because this is a passage you and I need to *get*. The more we let it define our lives and relationships, the more lovely Christ will be to us, and the more clearly the beauty of His gospel will shine through us to others.

Life, the Way It's Supposed to Be

Several years ago, I received an unforgettable email from a young woman in her early thirties, a single mom I had known since she was a little girl. The subject line said simply, "Happy Mother's Day."

Intrigued, I opened it and read on.

Her note brought back some memories that, while fuzzy in my mind, were still fresh in hers. She referenced a handful of activities I'd planned for her and several of her middle-school friends and a brief conversation here and there as she grew up—nothing particularly significant in my mind. But God had used these periodic connecting points as an enduring means of grace and encouragement in her life.

Her closing paragraph touched me deeply:

> Although you may not have biological children here on earth, your spiritual motherhood and its impact have been among the greatest blessings in my life. Thank you for being a shining example of Christ's likeness. Happy Mother's Day!

The note was signed, "From one of your many spiritual children."

It doesn't get much better than that.

I assure you that I fall far short of being the "shining example of Christ's likeness" I long to be. But how I thank God for the way He uses our lives and efforts—imperfect as they are—to accomplish His purposes here on earth.

My response to my young friend captures the essence of this book, as well as my heart for you—whatever your season of life—as we begin this journey together:

> I was pretty close to the age you are now when some of what you describe took place. I had no idea then how those simple things would impact the lives of you girls. I just wanted to love and encourage you. And God in His grace caused those seeds to take root and produce sweet fruit.
>
> Now God has given you a precious daughter to disciple, and undoubtedly has put others in your

sphere of influence. I pray your life will be a fragrance of Christ to them and that one day you will have the joy of receiving a note that will bless you as much as your note has blessed me.

Love,
Nancy

And so the race goes on. Each of us supporting others and encouraging them to press on. One generation passing the baton to the next, preserving and inspiring godliness and gospel witness. And, in the process, the beauty of Jesus shines forth and His kingdom is advanced in our world.

This is a joy you can experience. It's not about having a big platform or an official teaching role (though God may entrust one or both to you). More than that, it's about living the life He has made you for and called you to, right where you are.

Older women modeling holiness, obedience, and love, and investing intentionally in the lives of younger women.

Younger women seeking and receiving, with humility and gratitude, the blessings given to them from seasoned women, only to pass the treasure on to others down the line.

Women of all ages—growing ever more beautiful as the gospel of Christ adorns our lives.

Adorning that gospel by the way we live.

And doing it all, step by step, together—the Titus 2 way.

Making It Personal

Older women

1. Can you think of two or three younger women with whom you could share your life and experience—as Vonette Bright did for me? Who are they? How might you go about approaching them?
2. Older women are called to pass the baton to younger women. What have you learned or experienced that you would like to pass to the next generation?

Younger women

1. Does the note I received from my young friend inspire you to send a similar one to a spiritual mother in your life? If so, what specific things can you express gratitude for?
2. Name an older woman who speaks wisdom, vision, and faith into your life—as Vonette Bright did for me. If you don't have anyone like that currently, ask the Lord to direct you to a woman you could approach about investing in your life.

To get the most out of this book, invite a group of women—younger and older—to read through it together. You'll find a group discussion guide and lots of helpful companion resources at adornedbook.com. Connect there with other women about how to apply the Titus 2 calling in your life and relationships.

PART ONE

A Woman under God

Teach what accords with sound doctrine.

Older men are to be sober-minded, dignified, self-controlled,
sound in faith, in love, and in steadfastness.

Older women likewise are to be reverent in behavior,
not slanderers or slaves to much wine.

They are to teach what is good,
and so train the young women
to love their husbands and children,
to be self-controlled,
pure,
working at home,
kind,
and submissive to their own husbands,
that the word of God may not be reviled.

**. . . so that in everything they may adorn
the doctrine of God our Savior.**

TITUS 2:1–5, 10

CHAPTER 2

Doctrine, You, and Titus 2

The "What" and the "Now What"

Do not settle for a wimpy theology. It is beneath you.
God is too great. Christ is too glorious.
JOHN PIPER

MY HUSBAND IS A SELF-ADMITTED ACROPHOBIC. He has a fear of heights. Put him at the top of a ladder or peering over the balcony of a tall building, and he confesses that his heart pounds and his knees turn to Jell-O.

Robert is also a gifted handyman and amateur builder. Over the years, he has taken on some impressive building projects. I've seen the pictures. And some of these projects—building a thirty-foot chimney, painting a two-story house—have required him to do his work high in the air.

So how does he deal with his fear while perched twenty-five feet above the ground? "That's easy," he says. "I never climb a ladder or step onto scaffolding until I'm certain I have taken the time to level the legs of the ladder or plant the feet of the scaffolding on a perfectly solid place."

What Robert describes is a perfect metaphor for this chapter.

My heart's desire is to be a Titus 2 woman. Consistently. Contentedly. Beautifully. To be adorned with the gospel and to adorn the gospel in the eyes of others.

I hope that's your desire too.

But the starting point on the journey to get us there might not be what you expect.

Maybe you turned the page to this chapter ready to jump right into the heart of the noble calling and qualities Paul outlines for women. Like Robert scampering up the ladder or scaffolding to get started with his work, you're eager to get *on* with it. You're hoping for something useful, something you can put into practice in your day-to-day life.

Instead, you're about to run smack dab into one of those "church words" that doesn't seem to have much to do with how you live.

Doctrine.

That's right. This chapter is about doctrine.

It's a word that reminds me of my husband taking time to make sure his ladder is secure, that his scaffolding is built on solid, level ground before he climbs up.

I understand you may be tempted to skip ahead to the "good stuff," looking for "news you can use"—practical insights and tools to help you become a more godly, fruitful woman. And you'll find lots of that in Titus 2 and in this book. But Paul addresses doctrine before laying out specifics of our practice, and he does so for a good reason. Doctrine—what we believe—is foundational to how we live. And if you miss it, you'll never get to where you want to be.

Belief and Behavior

So what's your first reaction to the word *doctrine*? Sound dull? Dry? Divisive or disagreeable? Maybe you share the sentiment of a man who once told a friend of mine, "At our church we don't preach doctrine. We just love Jesus."

But the fact is, every one of us and every situation we encounter in life is fueled by some kind of doctrine. It is the ground we stand on as we build our lives.

Your kids may go to public schools—supposedly religion-free zones. But don't think for a minute that doctrine is not being taught in secular grade schools, high schools, and colleges. Every course taught in every school is informed by some sort of doctrinal framework.

The afternoon talk shows have a doctrine. The evening dramas and sitcoms have a doctrine. Books on the *New York Times* bestsellers list, just like the ones on the feature display at your local Christian bookstore, all contain doctrine. Even atheists have a doctrine. Not *good* doctrine, but a doctrine that leads them to certain conclusions and values and that determines the way they think and live.

Doctrine, you see, simply means teaching. It's the *content* of what we believe, the understanding of reality that shapes our faith. Like soil in a garden, doctrine provides the context for growing character.

The soil of doctrine in which we're planted can make us beautiful and help us point others to the beauty of Christ and His gospel.

But only if it's the *right* doctrine.

Even those of us who are longtime Christians can be misled by false or skewed beliefs we've picked up somewhere. If we aren't intentional about where our hearts and minds are planted and watered, we can't expect to end up with a healthy crop. Bad doctrine, bad fruit. Good doctrine, good fruit.

Let me give you an example: my longtime friend Holly Elliff is a pastor's wife, the mother of eight children. She has a vibrant ministry to her family and to other women. But there was a time in her late twenties when her experience of the abundant Christian life was hindered by a bad case of bad doctrine.

Early on, Holly, like many, had somehow picked up the belief that if she did her best to be a good Christian woman, if she prayed and read her Bible faithfully, if she loved her husband and children and checked off all the right religious boxes, then God could be counted on to return the favor by placing her in a no-trouble zone. Given this assumption—this incorrect doctrine of God—you can imagine how Holly's world was shaken when trouble started showing up.

After giving birth to her first two children, she had a miscarriage. Her next child had a birth injury that required months of therapy. In the midst of all this, her father-in-law, who had been a godly role model for many years, was unfaithful to his wife, resulting in her in-laws divorcing after forty-three years of marriage. Then her mother-in-law developed Alzheimer's disease, and Holly—now with four young children still at home—became the primary caregiver.

As if that wasn't enough, a loud, vocal faction began stirring up dissent in their church and targeting her husband, Bill, with their criticism. Something like that is hard enough to take when you're the object, but even harder when it's someone you love.

On Sunday mornings, one of Holly's jobs was to serve at the welcome table. This task, which she had always enjoyed, became uncomfortable during this season, when contentious conversations were taking place in the church hallways and meeting rooms, around dinner tables, and on phone calls. Nor did it help that the saccharine-sweet woman who sometimes shared Holly's hospitality duties was married to one of Bill's most outspoken critics.

Now, put yourself in Holly's place. If you were faced with this set of circumstances and were coming from the doctrinal standpoint Holly had embraced as a young woman—the one that says God shields obedient believers from overwhelming challenges or difficulties—what would your response be? Would you be "reverent" in your behavior, "self-controlled" in your demeanor, "kind" in your remarks, as Titus 2 urges you to be?

You see, belief affects behavior. Doctrine matters.

This whole experience forced Holly to examine what she really believed; it challenged her to build a solid foundation for her life by getting into the Word more seriously and getting to really know God. The fruit of that resolve, coming out of a difficult season in her life, has been extraordinary and beautiful.

So the starting place—the foundation—for becoming Titus 2 women is exactly where Paul begins—by calling us to a life that "accords with sound doctrine."

Desperate for Doctrine

The culture in first-century Crete, where Titus served as a pastor, was the furthest thing from good or godly. Quoting a contemporary philosopher of the day who had said, "Cretans are always liars, evil beasts, lazy gluttons," Paul added simply, "This testimony is true" (Titus 1:12–13). He described unbelievers there as being "detestable, disobedient, unfit for any good work" (v. 16).

As is invariably the case, rampant false teaching went hand in hand with the irreverent lifestyle that was so prevalent in Crete:

> There are many who are insubordinate, empty talkers and deceivers. . . . they are upsetting whole families by teaching for shameful gain what they ought not to teach. (Titus 1:10–11)

This false teaching was no small matter. That word translated "upsetting" means to "overthrow, overturn, destroy."[1] That's the kind of upheaval that unsound doctrine was causing for entire Christian families.

So what were those first-century believers to do in light of such pervasive unsound teaching and godless living? And what are we to do in similar circumstances today? Wring our hands in despair? Curse the darkness? Give up and just hold on for Jesus to come back?

"But as for you," Paul said to Pastor Titus, *"teach what accords with sound doctrine"* (2:1).

That's it? Teach God's people how to live according to truth?

That's it. That is God's plan—truth and light overcoming deception and darkness.

The Cretan culture was in desperate need of believers and churches that valued right doctrine. Our culture has the same need. Because where such doctrine is taught, believed, and put into practice, the gospel of Christ is put on display; it is proclaimed with power and becomes believable. That's why Paul urged Titus to appoint elders and overseers in each church who could "give instruction in sound doctrine" (v. 9) and whose example would back up their teaching.

The Greek word translated "sound" (as in "sound doctrine") is *hugiaino*. It's the term from which we get our English word *hygiene*.[2] Sound doctrine is a means of keeping us healthy. It's wholesome. It's life-giving. It helps make spiritually sick people well in every way that matters for eternity.

We hear a lot these days about clean energy sources and healthy lifestyle choices. Our activist culture is quick to fight the overuse of pesticides in the farming industry or in mosquito-infested neighborhoods. And we all know people who like to keep their friends close but their hand sanitizer closer.

But many who are fastidious about washing their fruits and vegetables are not nearly as careful about what they ingest in the form of doctrine. Contaminants don't seem to bother them when it comes to what they believe.

Sound, healthy doctrine is pure. It's hygienic. It's safe. It's free from poisonous error. As a result, it produces sound, healthy believers. Their lives show the difference good doctrine makes.

But too often, little if any such difference is evident in the lives of those who call themselves Christians.

Not long ago, I was struck by the results of a survey I read. Nonbelieving older teens and young adults were asked if they had a personal friend or acquaintance who was a Christian. Of the roughly 85 percent who said they did, only *15 percent* indicated they saw any lifestyle differences between their Christian and non-Christian friends.

Sound doctrine is radically transformational. Lived out it changes everything about us.

And it's not only students and young adults who see it that way. This problem applies to both older and younger generations.

It should not be this way. Believers should be noticeably different. True believers *will* be noticeably—beautifully—different.

And sound doctrine is what makes it so.

How Sound Doctrine Changes Us

Sound doctrine is radically transformational. Lived out, it changes everything about us. It counsels us. It corrects us. It's like an onboard guidance system, directing and determining our course. And ultimately it transforms the culture through us and around us.

The teaching of sound doctrine was so foundational to Paul's thinking that he actually included this phrase nine times in the three New Testament letters known as his "pastoral epistles" (1 and 2 Timothy and Titus). Five of those instances are in Titus alone.

Sound doctrine.

It mattered then. It matters now. It's the complete body of truth, revealed in Scripture, that explains and defines our faith. Among other things, it tells us:

- who we are
- who God is

- what it means to be a Christian
- what the gospel is
- who Jesus is
- why He came
- why He died
- why He lives again

Sound doctrine tells us that God is sovereign over all—over time, over nature, over us, over every minute detail in the universe. That means when everything in our world seems to be giving way, spinning out of control, we can trust that "He's got the whole world in His hands."

Sound doctrine tells us that we exist to bring glory to God and that every circumstance that comes into our lives can contribute to that end. If we could get just that one truth fixed in our hearts, we would never look at our circumstances the same way again.

That belief—that doctrine—would certainly change us.

Sound doctrine tells us that sin entered our world and infected it all the way down to the dust specks and the groundwater. It tells us that our natural tendency (going all the way back to Adam and Eve) is to try to remedy the situation on our own, apart from God, to hide from Him behind our hand-sewn fig leaves in hopes of avoiding notice and accountability. It also tells us that conflicts at home, at work, in our families, and in our world are evidence of what sin has done to us and to others.

Knowing this, our only hope is found in turning to the One who, while certainly within His rights to write us off, has chosen instead to introduce redemption and reconciliation into our world. In light of His truth, we see our sin and the sin of the world for what it is, and we recognize our utter dependence upon Him who is our righteousness and our life.

That, too, changes us.

Sound doctrine tells us that our personal opinions are inconsequential compared to God's, that individual rights do not trump eternal absolutes, that truth is not subjective and relative but consistent across all times and all places to all people—including us.

It tells us that the way things are is not the way they will always be, that the goal of the Christian life is not mere survival nor peaceful coexistence with a lost culture, but rather the ultimate triumph of Christ *over* culture.

Sound doctrine tells us that even as believers we can expect to struggle with indwelling sin, fleshly appetites, and self-centeredness. It reminds us that if we are not abiding in Christ and allowing His Spirit to do His sanctifying work in us, we may be capable of producing religious work but not of bearing spiritual fruit.

Yet sound doctrine also goes on to tell us that every time we say *yes* to Jesus and *no* to our flesh, allowing His love and power to flow through us, we become more and more like the King whose heavenly kingdom we represent here on earth.

It tells us that the cross is God's message of hope to the world and that the primary evidences of its present reality are lives in which His mercy and grace are actively at work.

And all that, my sister, should totally transform us.

The Gift of Sound Doctrine

Yes, sound doctrine changes us.

It is the *what* that leads to our *now what.*

"Give instruction in sound doctrine," Paul says to Titus (1:9). Lay a solid biblical and theological foundation in the hearts of your people. That's the *what.* It's the starting place.

Then "teach what accords with sound doctrine" (2:1)—that is, make personal and practical application of the truth. That's the *now what.* It's the practical application that follows. Sound doctrine is not just a collection of abstract theological concepts. It is always connected to duty. It requires, motivates, and enables us to live lives that are pleasing to the Lord.

Sadly, many believers and churches today seem to lack an appetite for sound doctrine. We live in a consumer culture. We want to be entertained. We want to be comfortable. We don't want to have to think. And we don't want outsiders to think we're narrow, exclusive, or boring. We've learned that "doctrine lite" often attracts bigger crowds than strong doctrinal teaching and preaching.

But the impact of the gospel in our world is inevitably weakened when our focus on programs, productions, marketing, and relevance outranks our emphasis on sound doctrine. When that happens, people are deprived of the very thing that gives the Christian message its greatest persuasiveness—the winsome witness of changed lives that reflect the beauty of Christ and His truth. To crave anything less than sound teaching is a dangerous place to be.

But this tendency is not unique to our era. Nor should it surprise us. Paul warned his young pastor friend Timothy of this very thing:

> The time is coming when people will not endure sound teaching, but having itching ears they will accumulate for themselves teachers to suit their own passions, and will turn away from listening to the truth and wander off into myths. (2 Tim. 4:3–4)

Paul was quick to point Timothy toward the timeless solution:

> I charge you in the presence of God and of Christ Jesus . . . preach the word; . . . reprove, rebuke, and exhort, with complete patience and teaching. (2 Tim. 4:1–2)

This is essentially the same message Paul gave Titus at the beginning of his letter, when he spelled out the qualifications for church leaders. Pastors and elders are responsible for providing spiritual *direction* and *protection* for the flock of God. An unswerving commitment to sound doctrine is central to that calling:

> He must hold firm to the trustworthy word as taught, so that he may be able to give instruction in sound doctrine [*direction*] and also to rebuke those who contradict it [*protection*]. (Titus 1:9)

If the pastors and leaders of your church love and live and teach sound doctrine, you have been given a huge gift. Be sure to let them know how blessed and grateful you are. If you're looking for a church home, make sure to choose one where you and your family will find a steady diet of solid, biblical teaching that encourages you to live out the implications of sound doctrine. And if your church is searching for a new pastor, pray that God will bring a man who will "teach what accords with sound doctrine" (Titus 2:1). He doesn't have to be a spellbinding orator or a superb administrator. He doesn't have to possess great charisma or the ability to build a megachurch. But he does need to be able to "preach the Word"—to "exhort and rebuke with all authority" (v. 15).

Dual Dangers

Without sound doctrine, we have no moorings, no firm footing for our lives. If we are not grounded in sound doctrine, we will be easily deceived and led astray—susceptible to false doctrine. We won't know how to discern truth from error when we hear a popular preacher or read a bestselling book that is not fully aligned with Scripture. Without sound doctrine, we can't know how to live in a way that pleases God.

That's why we so often see professing Christians falling prey to off-base teaching and justifying unbiblical and immoral choices—because they have fallen away from sound doctrine and its life implications.

Having said all of this, we need to acknowledge that it is possible to hold tenaciously to sound doctrine in a way that is cold, lifeless, and devoid of the Spirit. (Can you say Pharisee?) In fact, there are two dangers equally to be avoided when it comes to doctrine.

So far in this chapter we have emphasized the first danger—that of *life without sound doctrine*. On the other hand, those who value and promote sound Bible teaching can be in danger of having *doctrine without life*.

Doctrine that produces self-righteous, critical, contentious, dry-eyed defenders of truth is not truly sound—because sound doctrine is not only true and right; it is also beautiful and good.

This was Nicodemus' problem when he first came to Jesus. This Jewish spiritual leader was well versed in the Old Testament Scriptures. He observed their precepts meticulously. He had his doctrine down. But he didn't have the Spirit. He didn't have life. And when he came to talk with Jesus under cover of night, it quickly became clear that Nicodemus was missing the basics of life in the Spirit. This caused Jesus to marvel: "Are you the teacher of Israel and yet you do not understand these things?" (John 3:10).

Nicodemus was a prime example of the fact that it is possible to *know* right and *do* right and yet not *be* right.

Further, doctrine that produces self-righteous, critical, contentious, dry-eyed defenders of truth is not in accord with the heart and character of God. It is not truly sound—because sound doctrine is not only true and right; it is also beautiful and good.

Would people see that as they look at our lives? We may have the right answers to hard questions, but do we exhibit tenderness as we share those answers? We may be able to quote "chapter and verse" for our favorite doctrinal distinctives, but are genuine love and kindness—

the fruit of the Spirit—manifest in our theological correctness? We may have mastered the Word of God, but is it evident to others that our hearts are moved by the wonder of what we know?

As Paul told Titus, the goal is that "in everything," we would "adorn the doctrine of God our Savior" (Titus 2:10). As we live out His truth in the power of the Holy Spirit, our lives are made more beautiful. And that truth becomes more compelling and irresistible in the eyes of those around us.

The Only Difference

When Paul urges Titus to teach what accords with sound doctrine, that implies that some ways of life are *not* in accordance with sound doctrine. Throughout the book of Titus, Paul identifies ways that Christians' lives should differ radically from those of unbelievers.[3] Let's look at some of these distinctions:

- *Consistency of belief and behavior.* Unbelievers may "profess to know God, but they deny him by their works" (1:16)—whereas true believers' lives are expected to be consistent with what they claim to believe.
- *Purity.* Paul describes unbelievers as being "defiled" and lawless (1:15; 2:14), acting like "evil beasts" (1:12). By contrast, the doctrine of God's holiness calls us to be "above reproach" (1:6–7) in every area of our lives.
- *Self-Control.* Unbelievers are slaves to "various passions and pleasures" (3:3) such as drunkenness and laziness (1:7, 12). But believers in Christ are empowered by Him to be self-controlled.
- *Composure.* Unbelievers are sometimes "quick-tempered" and "violent" (1:7). But believers are to be "kind" and not "argumentative" (2:5, 9), "to speak evil of no one, to avoid quarreling, to

be gentle, and to show perfect courtesy toward all people" (3:2).

- *Relationships.* Paul describes unbelievers' attitude toward others as being full of "malice and envy" (3:3), whereas believers' relationships should reflect the "loving kindness of God our Savior" (3:4).
- *Truthfulness.* Paul describes unbelievers as scheming "liars" (1:12) and "deceivers" (1:10), he referred to believers, however, as having a "knowledge of the truth" (1:1) and a devotion to God, who "never lies" (1:2).

I could go on. But you get the point. The distinction between Christians and the world should be crystal clear. Not because we're better people or come from better upbringings. In fact, we're not inherently any different from anyone else. Our hearts would love to march to the same self-absorbed cadence that drives the rest of the world.

The only difference—the *only* difference—is Jesus. The gospel.

But what a difference that makes. What a difference *He* makes!

And the means by which the Spirit keeps loosening our grip on old patterns of behavior, releasing us from the bonds of cultural conformity, and awakening our hearts to the beauty of Christ and His ways, is through the implanted truth of His Word.

Through sound doctrine.

Don't think you can dress up your life with better behavior or become the beautiful woman you're hoping to grow into without grounding your life in biblical truth. If you're not willing to start there and stay there, saturating yourself in Scripture and receiving sound teaching from mature believers, your pursuit of a godly, fruitful life will always be an exercise in frustration.

And if you try to live without paying close attention to sound, biblical teaching, don't think you'll be avoiding an encounter with doctrine. You'll simply be choosing to live by a different kind of doctrine.

Because all of us live (and die) by doctrine.

The Gospel Truth

I have come to believe that every failure and flaw in our lives flows out of some sort of doctrinal deficiency.

Either we haven't been taught and really don't know the truth God has given that enables us to obey and enjoy Him.

Or (worse) we know the truth, but we aren't walking according to what we know.

It's one or the other. Because only sound doctrine, steadily applied, will keep our thinking and our living on the right track.

Sound doctrine is safe. It's hygienic. It's pure. And it's absolutely indispensable to a healthy heart and a godly life.

Our ultimate purpose is to make much of God. We do that as we experience, enjoy, and reflect the loveliness of Christ, making Him known to a world that is starved for true beauty.

Now, knowing and embracing sound, biblical doctrine doesn't candy-coat the spiritual warfare we face or guarantee we'll never blow it. But when we do fail, it tells us where to turn—it points us back to the cross, calls us to repent and to cast ourselves anew on Christ, and assures us of His mercy.

Again, it all comes back to the gospel. Our purpose for pursuing Titus 2 character, relationships, and ministry is not merely to be better wives, moms, and ministry leaders, to have a better reputation, or to be able to sleep better at night. Our ultimate purpose is to make much of God. We do that as we experience, enjoy, and reflect the loveliness of Christ, making Him known to a world that is starved for true beauty.

You may be concerned—as we all should be—about the rapid moral disintegration around us. Our reflexive reaction is to think the solution will be found in new and better laws, new structures and systems, an overhaul of schools and government. It's tempting to think that a different president, different legislators and judges, or more and better social programs will make the difference.

But what Paul argues in Titus is that what we need first and foremost are disciples who know and live in accord with sound doctrine. Men and women who are grounded in the Scripture and who live out what they believe. Believers who are godly, wise, good, and kind, who have loving, healthy families and relationships.

Our best intellectual arguments alone will never persuade the world at large about the existence of God, the uniqueness of Christ, the way to salvation, the moral rightness of a biblical worldview, or much of anything else. They are far more likely to be persuaded as they see the gospel lived out in our lives and relationships.

As the nineteenth-century German philosopher Heinrich Heine said: "Show me your redeemed life and I might be inclined to believe in your Redeemer."[4]

There simply is no more powerful tool of evangelism, no more effective means of bringing about social or systemic change, than for Christians to believe and demonstrate the doctrine and gospel of Jesus Christ.

That proposition might seem naïve and unsophisticated to some. What difference could a handful of regenerate Christ followers on the island of Crete possibly make in the far-flung, degenerate Roman Empire? What difference does it make if you and I live godly lives in our ungodly world?

You, your family, and your church may be tiny islands of godliness in a vast sea of wickedness. But don't underestimate what God can do to make the gospel desirable to lost souls through those outposts of grace and beauty. That's how the kingdom of God spreads.

So if you're a *younger woman* . . . get started now learning to pursue, grasp, and treasure the sound doctrine of God's Word, knowing it will shape the person you are today as well as the person you will one day become. And be sure you're connecting with godly, older women whose love for Christ and His Word will increase your appetite for sound doctrine and your understanding of the difference it makes in every area of your life.

And for those of us who are *older women*, let's be sure we never leave the basics—the pure, undiluted Word of God. Let's become living epistles of sound doctrine, both learned and practiced. Enough with the allurements and distractions of the world. It's time to show those coming behind us the beauty of God's truth and its sufficiency for the challenges of our day. I assure you, each time you're obedient to this calling, you'll be able to watch Him paint your life with bigger and bolder gospel colors than you ever imagined possible.

When God's Word is learned and lived out by older and younger women together, the outcome will be stunningly beautiful. A mirror reflection of Christ.

Doctrine is our *what*.

Its application is our *now what*.

And when both are put together, we'll have a strong, level foundation of truth on which to build our lives with confidence.

When God's Word is learned and lived out by older and younger women together, the outcome will be stunningly beautiful. Utterly captivating. A mirror reflection of Christ.

Making It Personal

Older women

1. If a younger woman were looking for a mentor who is solidly grounded in biblical truth and who makes truth beautiful, would she think of you? Why or why not?
2. What practical steps could you take to be better prepared to mentor a younger woman? (Remember you don't have to be perfect to be helpful!)
3. How could you encourage a younger woman in your life to be more intentional about "planting and watering" her heart in the soil of good doctrine?

Younger women

1. Where have you picked up the "doctrines" (teachings) that most influence your life—TV/movies, friends, family members, mentors, books, Scripture, church? Are these wise, godly sources? What is the fruit of these teachings in your life?
2. What qualities in a potential mentor would tell you she has a firm commitment to sound doctrine? What are some possible red flags?
3. What steps could you take to deepen your grasp of God's Word and to saturate your mind, heart, and life with sound doctrine?

Teach what accords with sound doctrine.

Older men are to be sober-minded, dignified, self-controlled,
sound in faith, in love, and in steadfastness.

Older women likewise are to be reverent in behavior,
not slanderers or slaves to much wine.

They are to teach what is good,
and so train the young women
to love their husbands and children,
to be self-controlled,
pure,
working at home,
kind,
and submissive to their own husbands,
that the word of God may not be reviled.

**. . . so that in everything they may adorn
the doctrine of God our Savior.**

TITUS 2:1–5, 10

CHAPTER 3

Don't Give Up on That Modeling Career

Aging Beautifully—at All Ages

Somebody old who has walked a long time in the path of righteousness is a treasure—a treasure of wisdom and a treasure of experience and a treasure of understanding.

JOHN MacARTHUR

NOT LONG AGO, A DOCTOR FRIEND INTRODUCED MY HUSBAND and me to a health supplement that has been developed to repair, rejuvenate, and restore the cells of the body at the molecular level. As we get older, these molecules tend to become imbalanced and depleted, and our bodies are no longer able to function at optimal levels.

As we listened to our friend explain the science behind the product and how it could result in increased energy, strength, and health, we looked at each other, both of us thinking: *How can we get it? When can we start?!*

You see, no one had to tell us those cells in our bodies are aging. We know it. We feel it. You do too. And who wouldn't love to slow down that process?

Robert and I are not looking for something that will bring back our twenty-five-year-old bodies. But we would like to have the physical strength to love and serve the Lord, each other, and others for as long as He gives us breath. Even more important, we want to remain spiritually vital—flourishing and fruitful—as we age.

And we're all aging—every one of us. Whether we're twenty or forty or eighty, the years keep ticking off at what seems to be a perpetually increasing rate of speed. None of us will ever be younger than we are now. Yet this reality, inevitable as it is, still somehow manages to surprise us.

Few of us are quite ready to see the characteristics we once noticed in our parents or grandparents now appearing on the skin of our own hands, in the shape of our own bodies, in the graying color of our own hair. When did this happen? Was that dark spot always there? Can I not read anything anymore without these glasses? (If this has not been your experience yet, trust me, it will—and sooner than you imagine!)

How quickly, they told us, the years would sail by.

How right they were.

But in our dismay over life's inexorable effects on our roots, our reflexes, and our recall, let's not lose sight of the fact that the Bible does not view aging as a bad thing. In fact, it *honors* those who have gleaned wisdom over the course of many years.

The aging process can actually be an opportunity for growth and—by eternal standards—for becoming more beautiful, not less.

That's why I love seeing a wide span of ages involved in the corporate worship and ministry of a local church or visiting together over a fellowship meal. We are sure to be diminished anytime the church becomes too homogenous, especially when older (or younger) people are pushed to the sidelines or are simply not sought out as part of the ideal demographic mix of a particular church.

The Lord said to the Israelites from earliest times, "You shall stand up before the gray head and honor the face of an old man" (Lev. 19:32). The Old Testament patriarchs were said to be "full of years," "full of days" (Gen. 25:8; 35:29). And many of the heroes of faith in Scripture flourished in the middle and latter portions of their lives. Job himself pointed out that

> wisdom is with the aged,
> and understanding in length of days. (Job 12:12)

Even the structure of Titus 2 implies deference toward older believers. Paul spoke first to the older men, then to the older women, followed by his instructions to the younger women and men in turn.

In general, Western culture doesn't think this way anymore. We tend to devalue people as they age, much as we tend to depreciate our own sense of worth as we grow older, becoming unhappy with our appearance and our slower pace and the effort required to stay limber and fit. But the aging process can actually be an opportunity for growth and—by eternal standards—for becoming *more* beautiful, not less. It can lead to increased fruitfulness and a changing but vital role in the body of Christ, contributing to the advancement of the kingdom even as we advance in age.

Please hear me. I'm not suggesting that it's necessarily sinful to be bothered by unattractive changes we see in the mirror or to think back to earlier days with fondness and a fleeting desire to return there.

What I'm saying is that our common experience of getting older, like every other experience in life, should be defined by a biblical paradigm rather than the perspective promoted by the world. Instead of pinning our expectations on what we see in the commercials or hear in conversation or even on research published in scientific and medical journals, we are called to frame our present and our future around the ageless model for aging found in Scripture.

Yes, we are getting older, whether "older" to you means thirty-five or sixty-five or ninety-five.

And, yes, each of these ages brings new challenges, some more acute than others.

But even if you find yourself in the biblical category of "older women" (somewhere beyond the child-rearing years, perhaps far beyond them), your best days as a vital, vibrant model of godliness can still be ahead of you. Each day of life God gives you is an opportunity to continue growing in Christlike character and to recognize in these new lines and creases the makings of a Titus 2 woman.

To Aging Women of All Ages

I've already introduced you to my friend, the late Vonette Bright. I knew Vonette from the time I was a little girl. On numerous occasions, I had the privilege of traveling and ministering with this accomplished woman, the cofounder (with her husband, Dr. Bill Bright) of Campus Crusade for Christ (now Cru). For me, she was one of those people who captured so much of what is beautiful about a godly woman—full of the Word, full of faith, full of spiritual vitality—all the way to the finish line.

Well into her eighties, even long after being widowed, this amazing woman was still traveling worldwide, serving the Lord and others with vigor and joy. Her pastor told me how, busy as she was, she offered to host a weekly small-group meeting in her home. She refused to settle back and live for herself.

In her late seventies, Vonette even took an online course to become a full-fledged member of the Christian Motorcyclists Association—she passed the online test and then went for a ride!—because she loved what they were doing to spread the gospel and wanted to encourage them. One of the most moving moments the day of her funeral was watching an escort of a dozen bikers lead the motorcade of family, close friends, and the hearse that was carrying her casket. What a sight that was—men on Harleys, honoring the memory of an eighty-nine-year-old woman who loved Jesus and loved them.

What came through in Vonette's public ministry was equally evident in her private demeanor and lifestyle. She was a Titus 2 woman all the way through. And it showed.

Vonette and I talked often in the final months of her life, sometimes at length. It gave me great hope to witness the still-full-of-life spirit and the never-ending growth and devotion of this woman more than three decades my senior and to realize, "Yes, this *can* be done!" She offered living proof of what God's grace can bring about in us—in me—as we continue to run the race He has set before us.

But here's the thing we have to remember: Vonette Brights don't just happen. Women don't just wake up at eighty-nine and suddenly find themselves spiritually fruitful and blossoming. This isn't something we can put off thinking about until after we're menopausal.

The challenge for older women may be to think of themselves as still being spiritually vital and relevant. As Vonette faced mounting health issues and her body weakened, she lamented that she was not able to do more for the Lord and for others, and longed to go home to heaven. She needed to be reminded that she had not outlived her usefulness or her calling.

> *When you see an older woman who is wise, winsome, grateful, kind, and filled with the Spirit of God—you are looking at character that most likely has been formed over the course of many years.*

There's a challenge for younger women as well: to make good use of these years when physical strength and beauty and energy come more naturally, so you'll be prepared for the day when your clothes don't quite button the same way and your joints begin to stiffen—and your modeling career can still go on.

Becoming "a godly older woman" has been one of my goals in life for as long as I can remember. I know that may sound a little strange. But even as a young teen I began to realize the choices I was making then would contribute to my life as a college student and a young adult and a middle-aged woman and, eventually, the little old lady who one day will live at my mailing address. I sensed then, and I know now, that there are no shortcuts to acquiring the traits of a godly, older woman. They must be cultivated over time and slowly seasoned to acquire their taste and savor.

They take life. They take experience.

They take failing, confession, and repentance.

They take intentionality and sacrifice.

They take a lifetime of practice.

I'm not trying to put the pressure of your whole life on top of your social plans for this weekend. Nor am I saying that God can't do anything with you if you fail to be spiritually intentional from a young age. But when you see an older woman at church who is wise, winsome, grateful, kind, and filled with the Spirit of God—a model in every way—you are looking at character that most likely has been formed over the course of many years. And when you notice those older women who appear whiny, narrow, petty, or bitter, they almost certainly became that way over the course of decades.

Here's the truth of it: the most amazing, godly older women you know likely were serious about being godly *younger* women as well.

So the message of Titus 2 is for all of us, older and younger. And as we dig more deeply into its treasures, we'll see how older women in the church thrive by staying attached to the younger and how younger women can find a compelling vision for their long-term character and fruitfulness in the lives and faces of their older spiritual sisters.

That's not to say there are no differences between the various stages of life. Each has challenges and experiences that make Paul's words to each group appropriate. And yet all of us can benefit from reading and applying all of what he wrote.

Including, oddly enough, his opening remarks to the older men.

All-Around Maturity

As we take our first dip into verse 3 of Titus 2, where Paul's instructions regarding older women begin, you'll notice almost immediately a word that causes us to pause before moving on.

"Older women," the verse begins, "*likewise . . .*"

Likewise?

This word leads me to believe that what Paul wrote to older *men* in the previous verse was meant to apply to an older *woman's* character as well. So we need to step back to verse 2 to see what kind of character qualities are in accord with sound doctrine—for both men and women:

> Older men are to be sober-minded, dignified, self-controlled, sound in faith, in love, and in steadfastness. (Titus 2:2)

These are not cafeteria-style qualities we can pick and choose. No, these are trademarks of all spiritually mature believers. None of them is optional if we are to become Titus 2 models. So let's take time to unpack them briefly.

"Sober-minded"

The most literal application that comes to mind when we hear this term is being free from the intoxicating influence of alcohol. But being sober-minded in a biblical sense has broader implications. It involves not becoming drunk on *any* of the various excesses that are available to us in the world.

It could be a gluttonous appetite for food, medicating your emotions with mindless munching on your favorite snacks, living for the hour when you can go out for dinner and indulge your craving.

It could be a fever for spending money, even if you justify it as a grandma's right to spoil her grandkids with toys and trinkets.

It could be a habit of mindlessly scanning the Internet or binge-watching the newest television series.

From this distance, we can easily see activities like these (and others) as being extravagant, wasteful, self-absorbed, senseless. And yet in a tempting moment, under circumstances that lend themselves toward seeking escape or emotional relief, any of us can fall into overindulgence and excess, stuffing ourselves on short-lived, empty-calorie pursuits that never give us quite enough and always draw us back for more.

A sober-minded woman, by contrast, has learned the soul-satisfying difference between temporary pleasures and eternal pleasures. She recognizes she'll never be entirely immune to the demanding cry of unmet needs and the tug toward fleshly appetites, whether they take the form of extravagant purchases or highly addictive computer games. But maturity has taught her what really matters in life.

And so through a pattern of practiced obedience and surrender to the Spirit, she's experienced the freedom of saying no to indulgences that could eventually leave her defeated, discouraged, and demoralized. And younger women who crave this kind of discernment and strength for themselves will find her example of temperance and moderation—her sober-mindedness—to be appealing and worthy of imitation.

"Dignified"

The NIV translates this term as "worthy of respect." It's the quality of being honorable, reverent, and appropriately serious about life.

Our lives include plenty of opportunities for appropriate fun and laughter, moments that lend themselves to lightheartedness. But not all moments are like that. In fact, I'd say *most* of them are not. Life is to be taken seriously—not gloomily, not unhappily, not devoid of joy and cheer, and yet not flippantly or carelessly either.

That's why Paul urged all believers to "walk properly" (Rom. 13:13), "making the best use of the time" (Col. 4:5). We are called to live in a way that is fitting for those who belong to our God, "who is high and lifted up, who inhabits eternity, whose name is Holy" (Isa. 57:15).

One of the benefits of getting older is a rising awareness of eternity, which ought to color everything about our daily life.

One of the benefits of getting older is (or *should* be) a rising awareness of eternity, which ought to color everything about our daily life. Things look different when we adopt that long view. We have reason for being less ruffled, less hurried, less dramatic, less inclined to call everything an emergency. We can be more at peace and settled, better able to determine how to handle a given dilemma or dynamic or disagreement. Heaven is near and nearer—enabling us to carry ourselves with quiet confidence and grace and to walk in awe of the One in whose presence we live. And far from making us morose or prudish, this way of thinking and living leads to the highest, purest joy.

Older women are in the best position to model this kind of dignity and poise to younger women, who regularly encounter situations that feel too big for them to handle and who need the calming influence of wisdom and maturity.

Dignity is a beautiful thing to watch.

"Self-controlled"

We're going to devote a chapter to this subject later, since Paul returns to it several times. But let's take a brief look at this important word.

"Self-controlled" comes from the Greek word *sophron*, which derives from two words, one meaning "saved" or "sound," and the other meaning "mind." To be self-controlled is to operate from a "saved mind," a sound mind—to be living in one's right mind.

Interestingly, the last portion of the word—*phron*—is related to the modern Greek word for car brakes. The self-controlled person knows when to stop, when to say no. She knows how to curb her desires and impulses. She is self-restrained under the control of the Holy Spirit. She governs herself and disciplines her mind, her passions, her affections, her behavior.

There are no shortcuts to acquiring this trait. Each of us knows from hard experience how insistent and resistant our human wills can be. We naturally resist not only others' attempts to manage and direct us, but our own efforts as well. That's why younger women need older models who have experienced the challenge of becoming *sophron*, but who can also show by their lives what this quality looks like and how it's cultivated.

"Sound in faith"

Paul ends this list of character qualities in verse 2 with three traits that demonstrate the fruit of sound doctrine in an older believer's character: sound in faith . . . sound in love . . . sound in steadfastness.

The word translated "sound" implies health and wholesomeness, which makes it all the more encouraging when directed to believers in their later years, when health issues tend to worsen. Even while the body may be slowing and sputtering and sagging in various places, spiritually speaking we should be in the best shape of our lives.

"Sound in faith" means to be sound in *the* faith—grounded in the truth of God's Word. And able to affirm from experience the trustworthiness of God's promises.

I think of Joshua, standing before the people of Israel near the end of his life, declaring, "Now I am about to go the way of all the earth, and you know in your hearts and souls, all of you, that not one word has failed of all the good things that the Lord your God promised concerning you" (Josh. 23:14).

These are not the words of a man whose faith was merely intellectual. They reveal a seasoned faith, a faith that's been tested and proven, an unshakable confidence in God and His Word. Even in old age—in fact, *because* of his old age—Joshua could declare his faith with confidence. Having experienced God's reliable track record over many years and in countless desperate situations, he wasn't merely speaking of something he'd heard, but testifying to something he knew firsthand.

How inspiring such a testimony can be to those who are still running the first laps of their race.

The soundness of your faith is based on the soundness of the One in whom you've placed it, not on your perfect record in walking out that faith.

And yet you may be an older woman who doesn't *feel* "sound in faith." You may not feel qualified to inspire the generation coming behind you. The fact is, we're all still learning. Still growing. Still in need of daily grace. Soundness of faith is not a mountaintop, a finish line. It is a journey. And we each travel imperfectly.

But I promise you, what you have gleaned of God's nature and ways throughout the course of your life, however inadequate you may feel, is worth passing on to others, particularly to those following behind you. Wherever you've seen God prove Himself faithful, wherever His Word has sustained you in weakness and provided needed direction, and yes, even wherever you have experienced the consequences of *failing* to walk according to His Word—there's your story to share.

The soundness of your faith is based on the soundness of the One in whom you've placed it, not on your perfect record in walking out that faith.

"Sound . . . in love"

While sound biblical doctrine is crucial, it can also be complex or even overwhelming. And in the process of trying to get it all straight in our heads, we can miss the heart.

The heart of Christian love.

Increasing age for the believer is to be marked by an ever-increasing capacity for love. Genuine love. Sacrificial love. Patient love. God's kind of love.

I have attended many funerals of people who were well-known for their professional accomplishments or their courageous stand on moral issues or their remarkable public ministry. And I always find it touching to hear these "greats" remembered more for their personal, often unseen demonstrations of love and concern for others.

This character quality can show itself in countless ways, but nowhere does it radiate more beautifully through a person's life or more clearly adorn the doctrine of God than when it is expressed through *genuine forgiveness.*

How many families and family histories and once-close relationships have been destroyed through years of unresolved anger, bitterness, deafening silence, and misunderstanding? A colleague was experiencing this when she wrote and asked me to pray for her mother, who had terminal cancer:

> While I continue to hope that God will do a miracle in her physical body, my main prayer is that He will work in her heart and that she will forgive my father's sister, who has deeply hurt her and my father. She knows she needs to forgive, but she feels like she just can't do it.

Oh, what scars can be left by betrayal and broken trust. But love can help heal those wounds, even years after they were inflicted. Forgiveness in the heart of an older person is among the most compelling modeling performances of all. A person who is sound in love will be familiar with the words, "I forgive you" and "I was wrong, will you forgive me?"

Forgiveness is just one example of the kind of love Paul calls us to model as we grow older. Here are some good questions to ask ourselves periodically:

- Is my love growing—abounding "more and more" (Phil. 1:9)?
- Am I more focused on the needs of others than on my own needs?
- Is my love deeper, richer, healthier than it was a year ago, a decade ago?

"Sound . . . in steadfastness"

Two elderly, godly believers told me recently they are in the midst of the most difficult circumstances they've ever faced. I've been pondering their words, reminded of the sobering biblical observation that

> the years of our life are seventy,
> or even by reason of strength eighty;
> yet their span is but toil and trouble. (Ps. 90:10)

That's not the cynical opinion of a depressed pessimist; it's simply the truth. Life in this fallen world is hard, and it often gets harder as we age. No matter what difficulties we may have encountered already, the worst (in this life) may still be ahead of us.

As older women, we know this. Our own experience confirms it, as does the testimony of others we know. So what kind of people do we want to be for the rest of our lives, realizing that hardship is inevitable and life may get even more difficult?

If our future is to be shaped by the Scripture, then we know what our answer should be: to become sound (healthy and strong) in "steadfastness."

This Greek word is a compound of two shorter words that could be translated literally "abiding under." The idea is that of bearing up under a heavy load—not caving in under the pressure, not being flattened by it, but keeping on despite its weight. And not just surviving, but facing life's circumstances triumphantly, allowing God to use them to mold and shape us, bearing up in a way that glorifies the God we trust.

I love the way one of my heroines of the faith, Dr. Helen Roseveare, put it. In that eloquent British accent of hers, she explained why she preferred the word *perseverance* to *endurance*: "The word *endurance* has a sort of connotation of gritting your teeth, stiff upper lip, getting through somehow. The word *perseverance* refers to steadily going on, refusing to give up, no matter what comes."[1]

This kind of character is found in those who recognize and submit to God's providences. They view even their trials as coming from His hand, which enables them to press on with courage and faith.

That's the kind of woman I want to be.

People who are hurting and those facing trouble ahead need models like that. Younger women with their lives still before them need models like that.

Models of sober-mindedness. Of dignity. Of self-control. Of faith, love, and steadfastness.

And yes, this can be you. It *should* be you. According to the Bible, God *expects* it to be you. And me.

The more we age, the more we can allow God to mold and shape us, to beautify and refine us, to exfoliate the dead, dry skin of impurity and self-centeredness, and to radiate through us with the glow of His workmanship.

Shine On

Everyone is included in the pattern for Christian living found in Titus 2. Older men. Older women. Younger men. Younger women. Each of us has a role to play in adorning the doctrine of God. Whether you're *young* and aging or *not* so young and aging, you can be a vibrant, thriving, fruitful model for as long as God gives you breath—provided you stay sound and constant in your walk with God as your birthdays add up. That's the expectation: chronological maturity accompanied by continual spiritual growth and increasing spiritual health. It's the same vision painted by one of my favorite Scripture verses, one I often include on birthday greetings:

> The path of the righteous is like the light of dawn,
> which shines brighter and brighter until full day.
> (Prov. 4:18)

You're not doomed to crest and start heading downhill when you reach your fifties, sixties, seventies, eighties, or beyond. That is the world's perspective on aging, not God's. As we age, our physical bodies and our minds may deteriorate, but our inner spirit (Christ in us) can shine brighter and brighter until we reach high noon—that Day when we enter the endless, shadowless light of His presence and He "transform[s] our lowly body to be like his glorious body" (Phil. 3:21).

One commentator has said, "Old age strips the body of its glamour in order to emphasize the beauty of the soul."[2] It's true. When we're young, we may be able to gloss over some of those pesky character defects with the natural blush of our energy, good looks, and personality. But as we get older, our physical sparkle begins to fade. And those same character shortages, if not dealt with and sanctified, will only become more pronounced and visible.

But if we persevere in the Titus 2 prescription for adorning the gospel, we'll become more and more like the "righteous" people described in Psalm 92, the ones who

> flourish like the palm tree
> and grow like a cedar in Lebanon. . . .
> They shall bear fruit in old age;
> they are ever full of sap and green,
> to declare that the Lord is upright . . . (Ps. 92:12, 14–15)

Don't you love that? It's a compelling picture of believers who are flourishing, growing, and fruitful—renewed within day by day, to proclaim the beauty of Christ.

Older woman, don't listen to what your feet and fatigue are telling you. Listen to what your faith in God and His Word are telling you. You were destined to be a model, to live a life worthy of respect that is worth following. To become a person of whom others say, "That's what I want to be like when I'm her age." To model the heart and character of Christ.

And *younger woman*, whether you're sixteen or twenty-six or whatever "younger" means in your case, the godly older woman I hope you want to become is not as far removed as you think from the young woman you are now. Begin now cooperating with the Holy Spirit to cultivate these qualities in your life.

Whatever your age, remember we're all aspiring models, following Christ and making others long to know and follow Him. Women of all ages adorned—made beautiful—by the indwelling Christ. And women whose lives adorn the doctrine we claim to believe, making what is already beautiful even more attractive to everyone we encounter.

Making It Personal

Older women

1. Vonette Bright refused to settle back and live her life for herself. She continued to grow and to serve and encourage others until she passed into eternity. How does her life inspire you to be a Titus 2 model until the Lord calls you home?
2. As we get older, many women have a "rising awareness" of eternity. Is this true for you? How does Colossians 4:5–6 encourage you in this area?
3. What can you do to include more of the younger, hungry-hearted women in your church in your times of worship, fellowship, and ministry?

Younger women

1. Have you ever seen age-defying beauty modeled in an older woman? Describe what you see in her.
2. How might the choices you are making today affect the older woman you will someday be? If you can, list some specific examples.
3. What can you do to include more of the wise, older women in your church in your times of worship, fellowship, and ministry?

Teach what accords with sound doctrine.

Older men are to be sober-minded, dignified, self-controlled,
sound in faith, in love, and in steadfastness.

Older women likewise are to be reverent in behavior,
not slanderers or slaves to much wine.

They are to teach what is good,
and so train the young women
to love their husbands and children,
to be self-controlled,
pure,
working at home,
kind,
and submissive to their own husbands,
that the word of God may not be reviled.

. . . so that in everything they may adorn
the doctrine of God our Savior.

TITUS 2:1–5, 10

CHAPTER 4

Grow Up and Step Up

Teaching and Learning—Life-to-Life

Here is the challenge to you spiritual mothers:
Will you allow God to use you to help others learn from your knowledge and experience, your mistakes and your victories?

CATHE LAURIE

PASTOR TOM NELSON TELLS A STORY ABOUT A WOMAN in his Denton, Texas, congregation. Joy Brown,[1] who at the time was already in her seventies, was known as a godly woman whose life exhibited many of the characteristics we discussed in the last chapter. She had received Christ at an early age and had personally been in attendance to hear some of the greatest preachers of the twentieth century. She had also been an eager student of the Word for years and, through its sanctifying influence, had matured into a true lover of God as well a loyal wife, mother, and friend.

"But Joy," the pastor asked her one day, "are you making disciples?"

"Me?" she answered. "I don't know if I'm ready."

Hearing this, we might wonder, *Ma'am, if you're not ready, who is?* But how many of us, whatever our age or experience, could be asked the same thing and feel the same way?

"Me? I don't know if I'm ready."

Not long after hearing this response, Pastor Nelson pulled aside the church's director of women's ministries. "I don't want Joy Brown enrolled in any more Bible studies. She already knows more than anybody there." He wanted this enormous wealth of knowledge, experience, and perseverance to be shared with a younger generation who could use what a woman like Joy could teach them.

"Get ready," he told Joy. "You're about to go into the ministry."

He assigned her to teach a small group of teenagers. She was scared to death. What would those young people possibly want to hear from an old lady like her? But she dived into the assignment by studying Scripture—filling up notepad after notepad and developing detailed lesson plans.

Six months into her meetings with those girls, Joy had hardly touched her pages of notes. The teens were so full of questions—about life, parents, sex, sin, school, marriage. Joy drew from her knowledge of the Word and the experience of her long life (including her weaknesses, imperfections, and struggles) to respond to their questions, seeding those young hearts with biblical wisdom and perspective.

She continued teaching that way until she was well into her *nineties*. The generations of young women who had sat under her teaching became known around church as the "Brownies," and they tagged around behind her like ducklings following their mother.

Inspiring, right?

But as special as this story is, it shouldn't be all that unusual.

I have watched many friends send the last of their "brood" out of the nest. As their children finish their formal education, get jobs, marry, and start their own families, these moms who have spent so many years caring for their families begin to wonder, *What am I supposed to do now? What is my purpose? My identity?*

Maybe you have asked these questions. Fortunately, Titus 2 tells you exactly what you're supposed to do now:

> Older women . . . are to teach what is good, and so train the young women . . . . (vv. 3–4)

In a part of this passage we'll explore later, Paul says that older women are not to be slanderers. That is, we are *not* to use our tongues to spread lies or evil or to wound or tear others down. But here we're told how we *are* to use our tongues: "to teach what is good." We are to speak words that are true and good, words that bless and build others up. And in the process, we train younger women in the life of faith.

That phrase, "teach what is good," translates one Greek word that could also be rendered "teachers of good things." Proverbs 31 puts it this way:

> She opens her mouth with wisdom,
> and the teaching of kindness [faithful instruction—NIV] is on her tongue. (v. 26)

If you're an *older woman*, teaching good things to younger women is part of your job description. God has a purpose for you in this season of life that is vital and that no one but you can fulfill. The assumption is that you have learned how to apply the sound teaching of God's Word to your behavior, affections, relationships, priorities—everything—and that you are committed to take what you have learned and pass it on to others. This should be the norm, not the exception.

And if you're a *younger woman*, this passage raises important questions for you: Who are you learning from? Who are your teachers? Are they mostly your peers? What online communities are saturating your thinking and shaping your relationships? What celebrities are influencing your values, your sense of identity and purpose?

You see, Titus 2:4 is not just a call for older women to teach what is good. It's also a call for younger women to *learn* what is good from their older, more experienced sisters. As we will see, this mandate is a great gift for women of every age.

A Vision and a Calling

If you qualify as an older woman, there's a reason you've been learning about life all these years. More than one reason, actually. One is to help you accumulate godly wisdom—from your mistakes as well as your triumphs—and apply that wisdom to the hurdles you encounter. But equally important is the ability to share that hard-won wisdom with others, especially those who aren't as far along in their journey as you are.

Women who by God's grace have cultivated the fruit of the Spirit in their lives are to come alongside other women who need help developing self-control, kindness, and well-ordered priorities.

Wives who have learned how to love and respect their husbands well over the long haul—"for better, for worse"—are to teach younger women how it's done.

Mothers who have faithfully raised and trained their own children are to use the wisdom they've gained in the classroom of experience to teach younger women who are in the child-bearing/child-rearing years.

This is our job whether we're forty, sixty, eighty—whatever. Our job is to embody the wisdom of God's Word in such a way that we can effectively teach it to others—not just out of our notebooks, but out of our lives.

Our job is to embody the wisdom of God's Word in such a way that we can effectively teach it to others—not just out of our notebooks, but out of our lives.

This vision and calling is not just for some supposed class of spiritual superstars or for those among us who possess special teaching gifts. And it's not just for women who are wives and mothers. We are all called to cultivate godly character—to model what it looks like to live out the gospel in every area of our lives. Then we are to teach those women coming behind us how to do the same. As we do this—with our lives, our lips, our labors, our love—our own growth in grace is furthered, the baton of authentic faith is passed on to the next generation, the health of the church is preserved, and its witness to the world is enhanced.

This is a call to grow up and step up. "By this time, you ought to be teachers," God's Word says to believers who have had ample time and opportunity to learn sound doctrine and put it into practice (Heb. 5:12).

But this mandate is not intended to weigh us down with one more obligation, one more burden to be borne. Far from it. God is offering us the incredible privilege and joy of engaging with Him in molding lives (including our own) into the likeness of Jesus, adorned by sound doctrine and ultimately making the gospel beautiful in the eyes of all around. And as anyone who has said yes to this challenge knows, the process itself provides great satisfaction. Unlikely friendships form. Sweet seasons of prayer, Bible study, and spiritual growth are shared.

Why would we not want to be part of that?

Always Teaching

You may struggle to see yourself as a teacher. Perhaps you envision a classroom, PowerPoint slides, two nights every week with commentaries spread out on your kitchen table—a picture that is daunting to you. Perhaps the thought of standing up in front of a group to speak makes you a little queasy.

If so, take heart. I thank the Lord for women He has gifted and equipped to teach the Word to other women in structured settings. I hope your church has women like that. But I don't believe that's the only (or even the primary) kind of teaching the apostle Paul had in mind when he called us to be teachers.

The truth is, you're *always* teaching, simply by the way you live. Your conversation in unguarded moments teaches. Your response to gossip teaches. Your reaction to an unexpected problem teaches. The question is not whether you're teaching; it's whether you're teaching (as Paul says) "what is good."

Many of a younger person's peers, not to mention advertisers who determine what we can't live without, constantly communicate their definition of what's good—good to have, good to do, good to know, good to strive for, good to be involved in.

And most of it, unfortunately, is *not* good.

The younger women in our lives need something to counter those constant messages. They need the voice of someone who teaches them what is truly good. And as a rule, they won't learn the most about goodness—at least not in a way that resonates in their hearts and is reflected in their choices and behavior—by hearing it in a classroom or from some well-known speaker at a conference. They'll hear it and see it best from you, with a cup of spiced tea in front of them, with your hand close enough to reach over and touch theirs, with your wisdom, experience, biblical perspective, and love connecting—one-on-one, life-to-life—with their specific questions and needs.

This is the gift I received from Leta Fischer (or "Mother Fischer," as she was called affectionately) during my last two years of college. I was still in my late teens; Leta's children were all grown. In the church where I worshiped, she was legendary for meeting one-on-one with younger women across a small kitchen table—turning pages in her well-marked Bible, loving, listening, caring, sharing, praying, pouring practical wisdom into open hearts. And today, I have the joy of pouring into the lives of younger women the gifts I received at Mother Fischer's kitchen table more than forty years ago.

A Desperate Need

I find it interesting that Paul didn't assign to Titus this responsibility to teach the younger women. The task of the young pastor was to teach sound doctrine to the church, to keep the gospel and its implications front and center. But the personal discipleship and nurture of younger women was (and is) wisely assigned to the older women. And their ministry is every bit as necessary to the health of the church and to the living out of the gospel as the pastor's ministry is to the whole congregation.

The older women are "to teach what is good," Paul said, "and so *train* the young women" (vv. 3–4). Other translations render this "*admonish* the young women" (NKJV) or "*encourage* the young women" (NASB).

This verb with the complex meaning—which is why one English word can't quite express it—is the Greek word *sophronizo.* It appears only here in the New Testament, and yet it's related to a word we've already seen and will see again: *sophron.* As you may recall, this word carries the idea of a "saved mind" or a "sound mind." Similarly, *sophronizo* means "to make of a sound mind . . . to instruct or train someone to behave wisely and properly."[2] It has to do with bringing someone to his or her senses, so they will live a sensible, self-controlled, sober, spiritually disciplined life.

Sadly, many women today are living lives that are far from self-controlled and sensible. And that's not just true of women you see on reality TV. A lot of women within the church seem to make one foolish, destructive choice after another—choices that result in chronically troubled relationships. Many live shallow lives, spending their time on empty pursuits and vain conversation, carried along by the values of this world.

However, if our reflexive reaction is to regard these women with disapproval or exasperation, we have to ask ourselves: *Have we fulfilled our responsibility as older women?* Have we modeled the beauty of an ordered life, lived under the control and lordship of Christ? Have we been faithful in reaching out to our younger sisters, teaching what is good, and training them to live a life that honors Him?

In some cases, these younger women have never been adequately parented. They have little idea of how to make a marriage work or how to raise kids or how to lead fruitful single lives. Amid the pressures and exhaustion of raising children or building a career, it is easy for resentment, depression, and wrong thinking to creep in. With all the false teaching out there, they are easily deceived, tempted to buy into the world's philosophies.

They need older women in the church to get involved in training them to live self-controlled, wise lives, to show them what that looks like in every area of life and how to fulfill their duty to God, family, and others. They need mothers in the faith to take them by the hand, to encourage and instruct them, and to help them keep their eyes on Christ and maintain spiritual and emotional equilibrium.

They need older women to lovingly teach them what is true and good.

A Ministry of Mentoring

As we've seen, this kind of training usually doesn't happen so much in a formal teaching environment as it does through intentional, nurturing relationships—often called discipleship or mentoring. At times that discipleship may take place in a small-group meeting or a scheduled appointment. More often, however, it takes place organically, in the laboratory of life.

Just this morning I sent a young mom a link to a blog post about her season of life that I thought would be encouraging. Within an hour she wrote back and thanked me for sharing it: "Loved the great reminder of having a Godward focus in my never-ending, mundane, daily responsibilities!"

I also heard this morning from a mom of teens expressing what a lot of moms of teens experience: "I feel like things are moving at warp speed, and I just want everything to slow down." That gave me another chance to encourage a younger woman with a personal testimony of the grace of God I have received in my own harried seasons of life.

But what such mentoring may not require in platform speaking skills, it does require in time. The cultivation of new thinking patterns is not the result of a single get-together. It is the fruit of an ongoing process, a commitment. *I'll be there. You call me. I'm with you. I'm praying for you.*

My sweet friend Sarah recently had her fifth child. She homeschools her three older children. And though she does a wonderful job as a wife and mother, as with every mom, there are times when she loses perspective and thinks she is going over the edge. Sarah's own mother died when she was a teen, and she lives far from family. But she has intentionally cultivated rich relationships with older women like myself—women who have invested in her life and to whom she can turn for wisdom or encouragement when things get crazy in her world.

I got to know Sarah when she and her husband were first married, and I invited them to live in my home. We thought it might be six months or so till they could settle into their own home. Three and a half years and two babies later, they moved out. In the years since, we have remained connected, mutually blessing and encouraging each other as we have opportunity. And now I'm watching with joy as the baton is being passed and God is using Sarah to speak into the lives of women in the generation coming behind her.

I've heard of a church where a group of older women (and their husbands!) throw a bridal shower for couples who are getting married. The main gift they give this young bride and groom is an evening of conversation in which couples who've been married for thirty, forty, fifty years or longer share from their experience what makes a marriage sweet and enduring. How many newlywed women would look back on such an occasion as a defining moment in their preparation for marriage—and would likely find in that group an older woman who could be a great resource down the road?

There are so many other ways this kind of mentoring ministry can play out—in the neighborhood, in the workplace, in gyms and coffee shops. Older women teaching from their lives, investing in those who come after them, training them in what is good. Young women soaking up the help and the advice and learning to reach out in turn to those who come after them.

And no, this kind of mentoring is not easy—for the older woman or the younger.

It requires discipline and planning.

Time and patience.

Willingness to commit to a relationship.

Honesty in opening up our lives to one another.

Nor are we likely to see dramatic results overnight. It's not as formulaic as saying, "Come take my six-week class on how to be a woman of God." This is more a matter of getting next to someone, walking alongside her, going over to see her when you might rather be reading a magazine or watching a movie or taking a long bath. It's costly—the same way anything worthwhile is costly.

But who doesn't want, looking back, to see a legacy of fruitful relationships rather than just a shelf full of used books or a well-worn DVD collection?

Out of Our Failures

"But I've blown it in my relationships."

"I've made so many bad choices."

"I still struggle with this besetting sin."

A sense of personal failure keeps many older women from embracing this kind of ministry and relationships. Your marriage, for example, may still be a battle of wills. Some of your children may be making foolish choices, contrary to what you tried to teach them. An ongoing struggle with anger or addiction or some other issue may leave you feeling disqualified to teach anyone, especially as you look at other women your age who seem to be such models of Christian virtue.

I know. I sometimes look at the inconsistencies and battles in my own life and think, *How in the world could God use me to make a difference in anyone's life?*

None of us measures up to what we long to be. But don't let that stop you. Teach out of your failures. Use them to point others to the amazing grace of God and to a Savior who came to redeem sinners.

Teach out of your failures. Use them to point others to the amazing grace of God and to a Savior who came to redeem sinners.

Teach out of what God showed you when you messed up and didn't trust Him—where you ended up, where God found you. Teach from the addictions you've battled, the choices you should have made, the pain you could have avoided. Open the Word, open your heart, share the hard questions you've wrestled with, and watch God create beauty from ashes right before your eyes.

Perhaps you've experienced a broken marriage. But if you've allowed God to heal, restore, and forgive whatever wounds and failures were involved in the breakup of your relationship, are you not in a prime position to reach out to a woman who sometimes wonders if it's worth hanging in there with her own marriage?

Perhaps you were not sexually pure as a teenager or young adult. Are you not uniquely qualified to counsel a high school girl in your church who doesn't have godly parental support in her life? She needs to know—not from the Internet, the latest cultural icon, or her own best guesses, but from someone who has been where she is—what kind of emotional, physical, and spiritual damage can be done by not treasuring the gift of purity.

Let's admit it: this life-to-life model from Titus 2, the sharing of relationship between older and younger women, would be neither effective nor needful if each of us—if *any* of us—had it all together. The truth is, if we are going to invest ourselves in others or receive the wisdom offered to us by others, some of the most significant encounters will occur within the context of human weakness and inadequacy. Yes, even failure and sin. Because even while we're still in the process of being changed into the image of Christ, He can use us as a means of grace in others' lives.

We're sinners, yes. We're still far from where we ought to be and want to be (and one day will be, praise God!). But this is part of the story we have been given to share with others. Even our failures—humbly acknowledged and redeemed by His mercy and grace—can become a path to a more fruitful life and ministry.

We can't afford to allow past (or current) failures and foolishness to deprive us of the blessings God inevitably multiplies when women come together to draw from one another's wisdom and experience. This is where God makes valuable use of the things we've learned to help others avoid mistakes we have made and to encourage each other to become faithful, fruitful followers of Christ.

Bottom line: God is able to use everything about us—our victories and our defeats. By being open and transparent with the women we influence, we increase our impact in their lives.

No One on the Sidelines

You may be convinced you're too busy to dedicate this kind of time to somebody else, no matter how important the idea sounds in theory. You just can't imagine how to fit it in to an already overcrowded life.

To this, I would gently respond: if you're too busy to do this—to commit to even a single mentoring relationship either as the older or younger woman—perhaps you need to ask yourself if you're too busy with less important things. This generational sharing of life is actually a basic requirement of the Christian lifestyle. It's among the "one anothers" of Scripture—loving one another, serving one another, bearing one another's burdens.

I can't underscore enough how vital this is. In fact, I'm convinced there would be far less need for crisis counseling and treatment if these kinds of woman-to-woman relationships were the norm in the church.

And keep in mind that "older" and "younger" are relative terms. You may only be twenty-three years old, but you're older than that sixteen-year-old in the youth group who has caught your attention because of the things you've heard her say and the way she flirts with the boys. How about approaching her as an older friend who cares enough to teach her what is good? Who knows what tragedy and heartache the Lord might use you to help prevent in that teen's life?

The roles of older woman—lovingly teaching what is good—and younger woman—humbly learning—are for all of us. These connections are not optional for believers. They're what Scripture calls us to. None of us belongs on the sidelines.

Reaching Out—in Both Directions

One summer evening I gathered a group of about twenty younger women in my home; they were all in their late teens or early twenties and serving together in a ministry. After dinner, we arranged our chairs into a circle on the deck, and I asked each of the girls to share a short synopsis of her spiritual journey. As you might imagine, a wide variety of life experiences and issues was represented in that circle. At points I interjected words of encouragement or insight, sometimes sharing out of my own journey. But mostly I listened, my heart warmed by their openness to share their stories and their eagerness to receive the seasoned perspective of the oldest woman in the circle.

Afterward, several of those young women expressed gratitude for the interest I had shown in them and the investment (small as it was) that I had made in their lives. One of them commented how helpful this night had been to her because, as she said, "Our generation is so prone to think we have all the answers, that there's nothing an older person could tell us that we really need to hear."

I believe this sense is a major reason why many older women tend to back away from their role in younger women's lives. *The younger women don't want us*, they think. *If they did, they'd ask.*

So, *younger woman*, let me ask you: How willing are you to seek out and receive the involvement of older women in your life? Do you have a teachable spirit? Or do you leave the impression that you can figure life out on your own?

In His wisdom, God has made a gracious provision that you can't afford to do without. So my challenge to you is to take the initiative. Seek out an older woman who seems to possess the qualities you'd like to embody one day. Ask if she'd be open to visit with you on occasion, fielding your questions and allowing you to learn from her experiences and—together—from God's Word.

Don't be surprised if she says she doesn't know what she could really offer you. But don't be surprised either if she's delighted that you asked.

When you meet, it might help to ask her questions like,

- "Have you ever struggled with ____?"
- "How have you handled _____?"
- "Would you pray with me about ____?"

Don't expect perfectly formulated answers. But do expect to learn from and be encouraged by the experience and hard-earned wisdom of this older sister/spiritual mom.

I believe I can guarantee that, as your relationship grows, you will glean so much from this older woman that you'll wonder how you ever got along without her friendship, prayers, and input. Hopefully you will be inspired to become the older woman in another woman's life—and to never stop pouring yourself into others as long as you live.

I would offer a challenge as well to those who, like me, have reached that *older-woman* season of life. It's easy (and tempting) for us to sit around with our little circle of like-minded friends, talking disapprovingly about how the young women in our church are dressing or behaving. But how much more productive (and biblical) would it be for us to roll up our sleeves and get involved in the life of one or more of those younger women.

I've always realized that younger women need older women in their lives. But now, as an older woman, I've come to realize how much we need younger women in our lives. (One practical perk for me, among many others, has been help with my wardrobe!) You just don't know what you're missing if you don't have these kinds of intergenerational relationships.

These younger women challenge my thinking. They inspire me to press on when I'm weary in the race. They keep me from getting cold-hearted and crusty. They motivate me to believe God for more than I can see or imagine. Today marks another birthday for me. My phone is lighting up with sweet texts, many of them from precious young women I have known and walked with over the years—thanking me for my friendship, encouragement, and influence in their lives. They cannot know how deeply I feel the same way about them.

I assure you, few things in life are more satisfying than watching God work in another's heart through the example of your life, your thoughtful, biblical wisdom, even your humble acknowledgment of regret and lessons learned the hard way.

I realize you may be busier than you ever thought you would be at this stage of life. Many women I know in this post-child-rearing season are working hard to help cover college costs or supplement retirement savings. Others find themselves caught in a whirlwind of volunteerism—activities they always wanted to try but never had time for, as well as new expectations placed on them "now that you have the time."

But these years—when our circumstances and commitments

begin to change and we face new decisions about how to fill our days—can also bring rich opportunities to lean in to our Titus 2 calling. So before dusting off your résumé as an empty nester or filling up your calendar with new commitments, why not at least consider whether you could be of greater kingdom usefulness by freeing up more of your time for a different kind of responsibility?

I sometimes want to say to those moms who are trying to figure out what's next now that their kids are out of the nest: "Look around! You are needed now more than ever. There are younger women who desperately need your love, your time, your encouragement, and your wisdom!"

And what if no one is coming out of the woodwork to sit at your feet for training? Why not begin asking God to bring a hungry-hearted younger woman across your path? Ask His Spirit to show you how to fulfill this biblical mandate. And as He works—He will!—be obedient to follow through, confident that He's paired you with someone who needs what you and your love and life experiences can provide her.

The Power of Availability

I can't emphasize enough that this kind of mentoring ministry does not require advanced degrees or unusual skills. More often than not, it looks quite simple—lingering after a church service, at the kitchen table, over coffee, on the phone, throughout the week. It happens in casual but meaningful conversations that start with showing interest and asking questions and proceed by listening, caring, saying, "Let's pray about that." With even the tiniest bit of intention—a reassuring email or text, a shared link or Scripture verse—relationships grow. Teaching happens. And all it takes is being available, sometimes on the spur of the moment . . .

Several years ago a woman approached me after hearing me speak in another city. She began to pour out her heart about some intense challenges she was facing in her marriage and family. I knew she needed more than what I could offer in the few minutes we had available to talk. Just then, I saw my friend Bonnie out of the corner of my eye. Bonnie was an older woman who lived in that city, a woman I knew to be wise, compassionate, and biblically grounded. I beckoned to Bonnie, introduced her to the younger woman, and encouraged the two to get together in the days ahead.

A short time later, the younger woman and I had occasion to reconnect, and I asked how she was doing. She couldn't say enough about how helpful Bonnie had been to her in the three times they had met. "I've never had anyone do this for me before," she said. "This has been more valuable than nine months of counseling!"

Another woman shared similar feelings with me in a recent email:

> I am twenty-five and have only been a Christian for two and a half years. My mentor's name is Carole. She is always seeking the Lord, and when she talks about the Lord you can see the joy on her face. She has taught me so much, been patient, caring, and loving. She loves her husband and family, and it is just beautiful. She has been a godly example and seeks to do the will of God. I was so lost. No one ever taught me about Jesus or took time to show me God's love. I will be thankful for her as long as I live. *Hopefully I can be a Carole to someone some day.*

And that's the goal of these mentoring relationships. As the apostle Paul said to his young disciple Timothy, "What you have heard . . . entrust to faithful men [and women] who will be able to teach others also" (2 Tim. 2:2).

Over the years, I have watched my friend Holly Elliff become an incredibly effective mentor and discipler of younger women. She has never advertised her services. But younger women flock to her side, eager to learn from the insight she has gleaned through decades of knowing God and walking with Him through a wide variety of seasons and life experiences.

Holly has often shared out of her life and wisdom on the daily broadcast of Revive Our Hearts, the ministry where I serve. Some time ago, one of our listeners—a younger woman—wrote a moving letter, thanking Holly for teaching her what is good:

> When Nancy first had you as a guest on her program, my soul was so famished for help that your calm, seasoned advice brought me out of a deep, dark place.
>
> What helped was my sense that your knowledge wasn't theoretical. It sounded like the words from someone who learned it in the trenches—marrying, raising a family, cooking meal after meal, raising each child, and glorifying the Lord in it.
>
> *Thank you* for giving warm words of godly counsel, for standing on the Lord's commands to us instead of compromising. You cannot know how that has made a real impact on a life and soul so marred and scarred by sin and without any godly women to turn to.
>
> I'm sure when you were changing diapers, or listening to the same story . . . again . . . you could not have known that those were the very things that would make your advice so weighty and true for me—a single woman. When you speak, it's from the point of view of someone who's lived it, who has raised a family and had to work out the Scriptures in close quarters. The Lord's Word has molded you so your life is sending out such riches.
>
> Please let older women know that the most valuable thing they can do is to develop in *righteousness*, not the

> career or beautiful home. It is the life of righteousness that *alone* can help redeem broken lives. I never thought I would come to value God's ways above the world's or actually *see* how beautiful holiness is, but I have, and I thank you for being part of the Lord's way of revealing Himself and His loveliness and the beauty of living a godly life to me.

Older woman, you may never be asked to stand on a platform to speak or to teach from behind a mic on a national radio broadcast, as Holly does at times. But never underestimate the impact your life can have on other women—life-to-life, adorning the gospel, wherever He may have planted you.

And *younger woman*, this is something for you to aspire to—beginning now. As you learn what is good and are trained in righteousness, your life in turn will put the loveliness of Christ on display for those younger women who are coming behind you.

The words Paul wrote to Titus some two thousand years ago are timeless in their impact and relevance. More important, they are God's recipe for the thriving and fruitfulness of His women, essential for the successful passing of truth to the next generation and to our world.

And it starts with you and me—imperfections and all—available to teach and to be taught what is good.

Making It Personal

Older women

1. What does the story about Joy Brown, the older woman in the beginning of this chapter, teach you about what young women really want and need today?
2. Have you ever felt that no one would ever want to learn from your life? What are some of the life experiences you might be able to share to encourage or teach a younger woman more about the ways of God?
3. God's Word calls older women who are not acting as spiritual moms to "grow up and step up." Paraphrase Hebrews 5:12 for these reluctant women. If you are one of these, include your name in the paraphrase.

Younger women

1. Who are you learning from these days? Who are your teachers? Are they mostly your peers? What online communities are saturating your thinking and relationships? What older women are influencing and speaking into your life?
2. A young woman told me, "Our generation is so prone to think we have all the answers, that there's nothing an older person could tell us that we really need to hear." Do you think this is true? What part does humility play in a mentoring relationship? A teachable spirit? The willingness to ask an older woman to invest in your life?
3. What are some questions you could ask to strike up a conversation and encourage a possible mentoring relationship with an older woman?

Teach what accords with sound doctrine.

Older men are to be sober-minded, dignified, self-controlled,
sound in faith, in love, and in steadfastness.

Older women likewise are to be **reverent in behavior,**
not slanderers or slaves to much wine.

They are to teach what is good,
and so train the young women
to love their husbands and children,
to be self-controlled,
pure,
working at home,
kind,
and submissive to their own husbands,
that the word of God may not be reviled.

**. . . so that in everything they may adorn
the doctrine of God our Savior.**

TITUS 2:1–5, 10

CHAPTER 5

Revival of Reverence

Living in Sacred Service

This older woman sees life, all of life, from God's viewpoint
and understands that even the mundane routines of life are important to God. . . .
Watch her walk through her day in order to see what is next to God's heart.
Her life revolves around things that matter to Him.

ROCHELLE FLEMING

THERE AREN'T MANY PLACES YOU CAN GO THESE DAYS without being watched. Consider:

- Traffic cameras monitor your morning commute and stand guard at major intersections, taking careful notice of the precise moment when yellow lights turn red.
- Enormous databases keep tabs on your Internet activity, storing a digital record of every tap or click.
- Street-level images of your home and neighborhood are available for online viewing, all the way down to the cars in your driveway and the doghouse in your backyard.
- And the next time you walk into Walmart or Costco, take a quick look up at the ceiling—and see from the number of

camera portals up there if they can't immediately locate every mother who's scolding her impatient four-year-old somewhere in the store.

I'm not trying to make you paranoid. I'm simply observing that whatever anonymity earlier generations may have enjoyed is no longer available to us. No longer can we control what other people know about us merely by being nice, friendly church ladies and keeping the rest of our lives to ourselves.

And while this erosion of personal privacy is unsettling, I can't help but think it also comes with at least one positive, something we could turn to our advantage. Perhaps the pervasive presence of security patrols, online monitoring, and cellphone cameras can serve as a reminder that as Christians, our lives are always on display. Always. As a colleague of mine sometimes says, "Live like the mic is on—because it is."

Whether we like it or not, as Paul said, we are "a spectacle to the world, to angels, and to men" (1 Cor. 4:9). People are watching. More important, God is watching. This awareness should deepen our motivation to honor and represent Him well at all times.

I recall being at a women's conference where I'd been invited to speak. At one point I was seated in the back row, listening to the speakers who preceded me on the program, when a brightly attired woman was introduced to the stage. I recognized her as a comedian whose routines I had heard before. And though her brand of comedy is advertised as being Christian and family friendly, I knew from experience that she could also drift off-color.

Two men who were part of our ministry team that weekend were seated along with the rest of us. As the speaker made her entrance—to loud hoots and applause—I leaned over to the gentleman nearest me and whispered, "I think you may be uncomfortable with some of this." He nodded and motioned to his colleague and they quietly slipped out.

Unfortunately, I was right. The presentation included lots of body humor and coarse subject matter meant for easy laughs. From my perspective it stretched way beyond the limits of good taste. And yet the women in the audience, who just moments earlier had been praying and worshiping together, were now convulsed in laughter over the crude banter that was being offered up as Christian entertainment.

It saddened me greatly—not that I couldn't see what made the woman's delivery so engaging (she was an exceptionally gifted communicator), and not that I was out to spoil anybody's good time. But we are women who profess to know and love a holy God. We are women redeemed by a Savior's costly sacrifice. We are older women training younger women in what is good. We are younger women desiring to grow in grace and truth, becoming dignified, self-controlled, and steadfast in the faith.

Aren't we?

So with those goals in mind, let's delve more deeply into the nuts and bolts of Paul's challenge to the women of God in Titus' day as well as our own. The ideals contained in verses 3–5 of Titus 2—reverence, love, purity, kindness, and all the rest—are qualities we hope to see cultivated in our lives as God's Spirit works through our surrendered hearts. But they also form a practical discipleship plan for those we're teaching and training in our woman-to-woman, heart-to-heart relationships.

There's a lifetime of wisdom and growth to be gleaned from these few verses, and there's no time like today to begin walking it all out.

Beginning with reverence—the fountainhead from which springs the other graces to which we are called and to which we aspire.

"Older women likewise are to be reverent in behavior," Paul wrote. What does that mean? And what difference should it make in our daily lives?

A Sacred Existence

Various translations capture this exhortation from Paul as instructing us "to live in a way that is appropriate for someone serving the Lord"

(NLT 1996) and to be "reverent and devout in [our] deportment as becomes those engaged in sacred service" (AMP).

Commentator William Barclay's rendering of this verse is similar: "Charge the older women to be in demeanor such as befits those who are engaged in sacred things."[1]

The Greek word translated "reverent" in this passage is a compound word that combines the idea of being sacred, holy, or consecrated to God with that of behaving in ways that are fitting, right, or appropriate. Its root meaning has to do with being "priest-like."[2]

That's supposed to be us! A reverent woman understands that she has been set apart by God for sacred service, and she acts like it.

To be reverent means living with the constant, conscious awareness that we are in the presence of an awesome, holy God. God's presence isn't a place of dullness and drabness, with no dessert on the table.

At all times, day and night, whether on or off the clock, wherever she may be—at church, at work, at home, or online—in public and in private, whether with family, friends, colleagues, or total strangers, she is an example of holiness. It shows in the way she carries herself, in her attitudes and the way she interacts with others. Her daily lifestyle, like that of priests in the temple, is always consistent with her high and holy calling.

Now don't misunderstand this. Being a reverent woman doesn't mean always talking in hushed and somber tones, walking through life as if we were tiptoeing through a European cathedral. It doesn't mean being dour and downcast, always deathly serious, unable to crack a joke with a clear conscience. And it certainly doesn't imply being legalistic and fault-finding. That's not at all what true reverence is about.

To be reverent means living with the constant, conscious awareness that we are in the presence of an awesome, holy God. And God's presence isn't a place of dullness and drabness, with no dessert on the table. Rather, it's a place of abundance, of soul-satisfying pure delight. A place, as the psalmist declared, where there is "fullness of joy" (Ps. 16:11).

And this is where we are to live 24/7—as sacred people in sacred places. Recognizing that all day long we're handling sacred moments and sacred duties.

A young mom and I talked about this the other day. She was feeling stretched, stressed, and scrambled by the demands pulling at her from every direction. When I tried to encourage her by reminding her that she is engaged in sacred service and sacred things, she protested, "But so often all this doesn't *feel* holy!"

I get that. The interruptions, irritations, and interminable tasks that occupy so much of our time and attention don't feel holy—until we recalibrate our focus and remind ourselves that we are in the presence of a holy God.

Wherever we are at this moment is a sacred place, and whatever He has given us to do is sacred service. That means:

- If you're a wife, serving your husband is a sacred duty to be carried out with devotion and intentionality, out of reverence to God.
- If you're a mom, tending to your children's needs is a sacred duty, a daily offering to the Lord in whose presence you serve.
- If you work outside your home, the performance of your responsibilities, however insignificant they may seem in the big picture, is a sacred duty, carried out in plain view of the Lord as an act of worship.
- If you're a student, applying yourself to your coursework is a sacred duty, as is your participation in class, your commitment to integrity, and the sacrifices necessary to make the most of your training.

- If you're retired or unemployed, single or widowed or childless, your daily tasks and relationships are your sacred duty, to be carried out as a woman who lives and breathes and walks in God's presence.

There is simply no hard dividing line between the sacred and the secular in our lives, no special compartment for those pieces and parts of our lives that pertain to our faith, with everything else in another, separate compartment.

No, it's all a sacred exercise. Each of us, in whatever season of life we find ourselves, is to live in a way that is fitting for "those engaged in sacred service." We each possess a holy calling, a high calling, one worthy of our awe-inspired devotion to God and His will. And we flesh out this calling each day by honoring Him with lives that reflect His character and exemplify our grateful, loving surrender to Him.

Being a Titus 2 woman—and training others to be the same—is not a way of life we can turn off and on. We don't hang up our reverential demeanor in the closet when we come home and change clothes at the end of a long day. We are always serving in His presence, whether we are at home or in church or elsewhere, in our downtime as well as during our tightly scheduled appointments. Yes, we can still have our fun and make the most of each other's company. We can enjoy a good laugh, be silly, celebrate. But the most satisfying enjoyment of all will only come by being aware that we live each moment in His sweet, holy presence.

We become the women we truly want to be by practicing reverence.

Never Out of Style

The prophetess Anna, who appears in one of the earliest scenes of Jesus' life, His presentation at the Temple, provides a lovely example of reverence in action. In the brief biblical snapshot of her life we're allowed to view in Luke's gospel, we see that she was an older woman, a widow for many years. (Her husband, whom she had married as a young virgin, had passed away after only seven years of marriage.) And Anna, even at eighty-four, remained devoted to a reverent lifestyle. "She did not depart from the temple, worshiping with fasting and prayer night and day" (Luke 2:37). Her daily habit, strengthened through years of faithful practice, was just to be with God without distraction, without itching to hurry on to something else more exciting.

Here was a woman with every temptation to slack off in her efforts—a history of aloneness, the onset of advanced age, perhaps the flagging fatigue of unfulfilled dreams. If we were to fast-forward her situation into our day, she might have become someone who spent one mindless evening after another in front of the television, someone who poured forth woe-is-me details of her doctor visits whenever the phone rang, someone who assumed her church didn't really need her anymore except for filling the same seat every Sunday morning.

Anna, however, still spent her hours productively worshiping God. She was prayerful and disciplined, watchful and expectant. Her reverence involved not just camping out for long periods of time in her favorite physical location—the temple—but also an active, everyday awareness that she existed to be in His presence.

I can't imagine Anna turning into a whole other person when she ventured out beyond the temple walls. Can you? And I don't believe her reverence was a recent development either. I see her living this way not just at eighty-four, but even back in her younger days, when she might still have had an active social life and a taste for celebrating and living large.

Reverence wasn't limited to a certain place or time for Anna. It wasn't a certain mood, a certain spiritual routine. It had become the fabric of her life—fashioned over a lifetime of loving and fearing God, trusting Him and savoring His goodness. Whatever else may have competed to occupy her time and attention, she had found her fullness as a woman by recognizing that she was constantly engaged "in sacred service."

That kind of woman is able to experience Christ in ways few others ever enter into. No wonder Anna recognized her infant Messiah so quickly. I love the image of her breaking out in amazed and thankful praise, joyfully announcing the good news to others throughout the city who had long been keeping vigil with her, waiting for God's promised redemption: "He's here! He's here!"

But does this kind of woman appeal to you? Would she fit in well among your circle of friends? Would they admire her brand of perpetual reverence and want to be like her? Or would she be the object of condescending comments and rolled eyes—just a bit too serious about her faith?

I'm concerned that we've lost our appreciation and appetite for a reverent lifestyle—not in theory perhaps, but for sure in practice. I'm troubled by the flippant manner in which so many professing Christian women live today, declaring their *affection* for God but with little if any *fear* of God. Claiming mental assent to His Word but not to the point of actually restraining their impulses and appetites and behaving appropriately before Him. I'm bothered by how prone we are—how prone *I* am—to forget Whose presence we're in, how willing we are to live with a gap between our calling and our character, acting and reacting without recognizing that the moments of our morning quiet time are no more sacred than *this* moment. Than *any* moment.

We need a revival of reverence.

And from what Paul said to Titus, older women in particular need to be mindful of this. As we transition into those stages of life where we are the most tempted to let off the gas, having expended so much energy on conquering the various challenges of young to middle age, we need a reminder that now is not the time to coast.

These days are for yielding ourselves more fully than ever to worship and prayer. To examined lifestyles and consecrated thinking. To God-honoring friendships. To sanctified habits and topics of discussion. To everyday choices that reflect our relationship with this One we revere.

Yes, the house may be a little quieter these days, but not so we can repopulate it with crime-drama characters and Facebook "friends." The body may be more stiff and unresponsive than in our nimbler years, but not so we can spend days on end with our feet propped up. There might be a bit more breathing room in the bank account, but not so we can indulge whatever pleasures and appetites we can afford.

It is not only for our own sakes that we are called to lives of reverence. We are models, remember—for our daughters, our granddaughters, and the other young women we influence. And they desperately need models of reverent living.

You may think they're drawn to those older women who somehow manage to maintain a youthful air of coolness about them, who enjoy playing around the edges of a coarsened culture. But I promise you, what younger women desire most from you as a mentor and model is the fruit of a genuine relationship with God. They're constantly surrounded by coolness, worldliness, and shallowness. What they don't see enough of—what they are suffering from lack of—are mature women who have been with Jesus, what one Bible commentator has described as "life in the presence of the holy."[3]

Young women don't need your perceived relevance as much as they need your reverence.

Young women may laugh loud and long at irreverence, but what they actually long for and need is its polar opposite. They may be enamored of popular trends, but deep down they desire to be rescued from the trivial identities they're experiencing as a result.

They don't need your perceived relevance as much as they need your reverence.

Everyday Reverence

We sometimes reduce reverence to a physical posture: heads bowed, eyes closed, hands folded. But I want to draw you back to the more active meaning of *reverent* that Paul employs in his letter to Titus. He speaks of being "reverent in behavior"—that is, reverent in *everyday actions*, in practice, in our overall character and deportment.

Teachers used to give grades for "deportment" on students' report cards. It's an old-fashioned term for the way we act and carry ourselves. And the way we act, Paul reminds us, is a key indicator of how reverent our hearts truly are. He touched on this same idea in a few instructive passages written to another pastor, Timothy. These passages give us several practical examples of how a heart of reverence shows itself in our choices and our actions.

Reverent in Appearance

> Women should adorn themselves in respectable apparel, with modesty and self-control, not with braided hair and gold or pearls or costly attire, but with what is proper for women who profess godliness—with good works. (1 Tim. 2:9–10)

Yes, a spirit of reverence should affect the way we dress and present ourselves. Now, Paul isn't placing a ban on jewelry or makeup or trying to look our best. His point is that these things—the hair, the earrings, the latest cuts and colors and styles—are not meant to be our obsession or to occupy our time inordinately. A woman's physical appearance is only a part of who she is—and not the primary part. So she doesn't need to put excessive energy into adorning her external self. She has more important forms of adornment to focus on.

Also found here is an appeal to "modesty"—which, to take a look around, seems to have gone the way of the wall-mounted kitchen phone. I'm not advocating a rigid and unhealthy preoccupation with measuring necklines and hemlines. But let's at least say that godly reverence should inspire each of us to personal standards of reserve and respectability.

Our selection in clothing and our fixation with the mirror can tell us what our heart is hoping to accomplish through our appearance. Who are we trying to please? Does our appearance draw attention to ourselves? Does it distract others from being drawn to Christ? Or does it cause them to be attracted to Him? These are the kinds of questions that matter to a woman who has a reverent heart.

Reverent in Attitude

> Let a woman learn quietly with all submissiveness. I do not permit a woman to teach or to exercise authority over a man. . . . She will be saved through childbearing—if they continue in faith and love and holiness, with self-control. (1 Tim. 2:11–12, 15)

This passage, admittedly, has flummoxed countless commentators and can make women bristle. It's not my intent to explore its full meaning here. But don't miss the timeless principle that speaks to the attitudes of Christian women.

We cannot afford to pick and choose what situations call for a reverent attitude and behavior. They all do.

No, we women are not confined to vows of silence, but reverence toward God and His Word does make us teachable and responsive to God-ordained authority. It restrains us from asserting ourselves beyond divinely appointed bounds. And it makes us willing and eager to carry out His sacred calling for our lives.

As for that statement about being saved through childbearing, it needs to be understood in light of the rest of Scripture. Clearly we are not saved eternally from our sins or justified before God by being mothers and bearing children. And *not* bearing children certainly does not cause us to miss out on salvation. In the context of this verse, I believe Paul is saying women can be "saved" (or as some translations put it, "preserved") from wasted, useless years, simply by being faithful to what God has called us to do, behaving with reverence in whatever season and situation of life we may find ourselves.

Reverent in Lifestyle

> Let a widow be enrolled if she is not less than sixty years of age, having been the wife of one husband, and having a reputation for good works: if she has brought up children, has shown hospitality, has washed the feet of the saints, has cared for the afflicted, and has devoted herself to every good work. (1 Tim. 5:9–10)

This passage is part of a discussion about women who qualified for financial care by the church. It paints a portrait of an older woman who, even during her younger years, lived with purpose and intentionality before God and others. She served and gave faithfully and sought to bless those around her. She was reverent in her behavior, faithful to her sacred calling. She didn't waste her life on what doesn't matter. And as a result, her life reflected the beauty of the gospel.

That's true for us, too, whether we're older or younger women. We cannot afford to be frivolous or careless with our time, to pick and choose what situations call for a reverent attitude and behavior. They all do.

That's not to say it's wrong to take a break or a vacation. But wherever we go, a reverent heart must travel with us—not just to church, but also to the coffee shop, the gym, the beach, wherever we go. It's who we are. It's the hallmark of the way we live, informing every choice and interaction.

Where Reverence Begins

A nineteenth-century English clergyman, reflecting on what he had witnessed in his childhood home, remembered this:

> My mother's habit was every day, immediately after breakfast, to withdraw for an hour to her own room, and to spend that hour in reading the Bible, in meditation and prayer. From that hour, as from a pure fountain, she drew the strength and sweetness which enabled her to fulfill all her duties, and to remain unruffled by the worries and pettinesses which are so often the trial of narrow neighborhoods.
>
> As I think of her life, and all it had to bear, I see the absolute triumph of Christian grace in the lovely ideal of a Christian lady. I never saw her temper disturbed; I never heard her speak one word of anger . . . or of idle gossip; I never observed in her any sign of a single sentiment unbecoming to a soul which had drunk of the river of the water of life, and which had fed upon manna in the barren wilderness.[4]

That, my friend, is a picture of reverence. And it focuses on where reverent behavior begins—with spending regular time alone with God.

"Yeah, but that's just not practical," you may say. "I just don't have room for one more thing in my life."

I know your little ones may be awake and demanding your attention—one needing a diaper change, another needing help finding the shoes he kicked off somewhere the night before, all clamoring to be fed. I understand the phone won't stop ringing and your boss is impatient for you to finish that project and dinner won't make itself.

No matter where you find yourself on the older-younger continuum, life can feel overwhelming.

But ask yourself, *younger woman*: What do your children most need from you as they grow up? What do you want your relationship with God to look like when you're fifty, sixty, seventy, or eighty years of age? And *older woman*, what do the younger women around you most need from you as you teach and train them?

I'm not talking about losing ourselves in prayer and Bible reading every waking minute. That's not the definition of a reverent lifestyle. I just mean staying aware of God, realizing He's here, devoting our worship and attention to Him, until we begin to adjust our thinking, planning, scheduling, and lifestyle to match this glorious, eternal reality.

Until we become what God, through Paul, calls us to be.

Reverent in behavior.

Reverent in worship.

Reverent in lifestyle.

Reverent in what we read and listen to and how we entertain ourselves.

Reverent in where we go, what we do, and who we admire.

Reverent in what we wear and what we love, what we say and what we don't say.

Reverent in a way that adorns our lives and the doctrine of Christ.

Reverent all the time—not just because God's cameras are rolling, but because He is worthy of our wholehearted devotion and obedience. And because He has made pleasing Him the most pleasurable life on earth.

Making It Personal

Older women

1. Christians' lives are always on display—and that's a good thing if we're living to glorify Christ. Is there any attitude or behavior you wouldn't want people to see because you know it wouldn't please the Lord? Something that does not reflect His character? Ask God's Spirit to give you strength to change.
2. Older women are sometimes tempted to sit back and take it easy when it comes to serving the Lord and others. In what ways do you recognize this tendency or desire in your life? Why is this not a time to coast spiritually?
3. Younger women need friendships with older women who model the fruit of a genuine relationship with God. How does your life evidence that you're spending time with Jesus? What could help you grow in this area?

Younger women

1. Is there any attitude or behavior you wouldn't want people to see because you know it wouldn't please the Lord? Something that does not reflect His character? How would an awareness of the presence of God make a difference in that area of your life?
2. What part can friendships play in our desire to live a reverent, holy life—both negatively and positively?
3. What friends (younger or older) inspire you to be "reverent in behavior"?

PART TWO

A Woman under Control

Teach what accords with sound doctrine.

Older men are to be sober-minded, dignified, self-controlled,
sound in faith, in love, and in steadfastness.

Older women likewise are to be reverent in behavior,
not slanderers or slaves to much wine.

They are to teach what is good,
and so train the young women
to love their husbands and children,
to be self-controlled,
pure,
working at home,
kind,
and submissive to their own husbands,
that the word of God may not be reviled.

**. . . so that in everything they may adorn
the doctrine of God our Savior.**

TITUS 2:1–5, 10

CHAPTER 6

You Don't Say

Abstaining from Slander

We are stewards of the treasure of each other's good names. Let us seek to silence the . . . slanderer within and graciously give and receive others' help when one of us slips, perhaps unaware, into slander.

JON BLOOM

"REVERENT IN BEHAVIOR." AS WE'VE JUST SEEN, this should characterize older women in the church. But what exactly does reverent behavior look like? The apostle Paul makes practical application in two specific areas: "Older women . . . are to be reverent in behavior," he says, "*not slanderers or slaves to much wine*" (Titus 2:3).

Sound doctrine in a woman's life produces reverence for God. And that reverence shows itself in a careful use of her tongue and in a temperate lifestyle.

Older woman, this is how we adorn the doctrine of God and make it beautiful and desirable. If we don't have these qualities, we won't have credibility to "teach what is good." We will discredit our own message. We will cause younger women to stray from what "accords with sound doctrine." And the church will fail to reflect the gospel to our world in a compelling way.

Younger woman, this is a portrait of the kind of older woman you want to become; these are the qualities to which you are to aspire. They are worthy of your attention, time, effort, and lifelong pursuit. This kind of Spirit-produced, Christlike character is what will make you truly beautiful.

So let's start with this matter of slander—something God takes seriously for all believers, and, as Paul indicates, for women in particular.

Words That Hurt

Some time ago a listener to our daily broadcast emailed our ministry expressing grave concern about a recent guest on the program. The email included a link to a website she said would provide information to support her concern.

Because I feel responsible for our programming, I decided to check out the site.

What I found behind that single click was a host of online sites, each linked to others, all seemingly devoted to exposing Christian ministries and individuals. I'm talking about reams of personal accusations and biting commentary, including private documents that never should have been made public—church disciplinary proceedings, leaked memoranda, and the like. Most of the material on those pages consisted of petty hearsay related in sensational, scandalous, "he said/she said" fashion, leaving readers to fill in the blanks with their own suspicions.

The site was like a maze of mole tunnels, the kind that run beneath the soil in some of our backyards. Each one that popped up seemed to implicate another person—a pastor, author, speaker, ministry head, or church leader of some sort. It was insidious and ugly—all laid bare in cyberspace for the world to see (and "like" and "share").

The radio guest whose character had been called into question by our listener's email was among those targeted in the feeding frenzy.

Few were left out, it appeared. But when I dug a little deeper into the charges that had been brought to my attention, I discovered a common thread that explained a lot.

The whole thing seemed to trace back to one woman with a vendetta against the spiritual leaders of her local church. They had attempted to confront her about a pattern of disobedience. Unbroken, unrepentant, she had apparently set out on a mission to bring down the people who dared to speak truth into her life, and she had drawn many others into the fray.

If the exposé I was reading had ever been a genuine effort to uncover the truth, it no longer was anything of the sort. It was a hateful, vindictive campaign of division and destruction. And it had all started with one woman whose anger and bitterness gave birth to slander.

Our unleashed words can be every bit as damaging and destructive as any other kind of aggressive outburst.

As, sad to say, it often does.

In his characteristically blunt way, Martin Luther makes this point in his commentary on the Sermon on the Mount:

> It is especially among womenfolk that the shameful vice of slander is prevalent, so that great misfortune is often caused by an evil tongue.[1]

These words are not easy to hear. But if we're honest, we have to admit that women often seem to have particular trouble with this issue. This is not to suggest that men are not just as capable of instigating revenge against others, of getting bent out of shape and wanting to settle their personal scores. But when we hear Paul specifically exhorting Titus to remind the *women* in the church not to be "slanderers" (2:3), we do well to sit up and pay attention.

When men have a dispute with another man, they may resort to getting physical. But we women are more likely to let our tongues do the fighting. When we feel threatened, we can be vicious with our words.

(Do you wonder, as I have, why Paul addresses *older* women about this issue of slander? Perhaps this is a particular temptation for women whose families are grown and who have more time to sit around talking, sharing hearsay and stories about others, without pausing to think: Is this true? Is it benefiting those who are listening? Is it building up those we're talking about?)

As we press into the practical heart of Titus 2, a good place to begin is by realizing that our unleashed words can be every bit as damaging and destructive as any other kind of aggressive outburst.

Sometimes, in fact, they can be worse.

Devil in the Details

Paul's admonition in Titus 2 against slander and sins of the tongue hits close to home for me. Just moments ago, while working on this chapter, I caught myself starting to say something to a close friend about a third party—a report that was unnecessary and would not have put the other person in a good light. This is the very thing Paul says older women who revere the Lord should *not* do. How grateful I am for His Word and His Spirit that restrained me in this instance from passing along the potentially harmful information. I think back with regret to many times when I have not heeded that restraint.

And so I take this seriously.

I hope you do too.

As a clue to how serious this matter of slander should be to us, the word translated as "slanderers" in Titus 2:3—which other translations render as "malicious gossips" (NASB) or "false accusers" (KJV)—is the Greek word *diabolos,* from which we derive our English word *diabolical.*

This word—*diabolos*—appears thirty-eight times in the New Testament. And in all but four of those occurrences, it's used to refer to Satan.

Give that a moment to sink in.

Diabolos. Slander is devilish.

This connection between slander and Satan shouldn't surprise us. The first time we meet him in Scripture, he is slandering God's nature and character to Eve in the garden of Eden. "You will not surely die" for eating fruit from the forbidden tree, he told her (Gen. 3:4). You can almost hear the sound of a snicker in those words. *God said that? No He didn't. If He did, He wasn't telling you the whole truth. Because the truth is . . . well, let's just say there's something He doesn't want you to know . . .*

Slandering God to humans—that's one of Satan's trademark tactics. I'm sure at times he's tried selling you on the notion that "you can't trust God; His Word isn't true; He doesn't care anything about you. If He did, then why did *this* happen? And why didn't *that* happen? God is clearly not on your side, so . . ."

We also know from Scripture that Satan actively persists in *slandering believers to God*. He famously did it in the early chapters of Job, declaring that righteous man's behavior to be the easy response of an easy life. "Stretch out your hand and touch all that he has," Satan said to God, "and [Job] will curse you to your face" (Job 1:11).

See what this Job character is like when You're not paying him to love You, the slanderer sneers.

To be a slanderer is to be like the devil, doing his bidding and fulfilling his purposes.

Diabolical. Do you hear it? And Satan has been slandering us ever since. "The accuser of our brethren"—that's what the apostle John called him in the book of Revelation (12:10 NKJV). He constantly brings slanderous accusations about us before the throne of God, refuting what Christ's sacrificial death has accomplished in declaring us holy and righteous in the Lord's sight.

He's a liar. An accuser.

Satan (*diabolos*) is a slanderer (*diabolos*).

And to hear Paul tell it to Titus, we should immediately get the connection. To be a slanderer is to be diabolical—to be like the devil. It is to participate in the works and character of Satan himself. When we slander others, we are doing his bidding and fulfilling his purposes.

Interestingly, in two of the three instances where *diabolos* is employed in Scripture to communicate the idea of slander, it is specifically addressed to women. Titus 2:3 is one of these; 1 Timothy 3:11 is the other. In the 1 Timothy passage, the word *diabolos* appears three times between verses 6 and 11, referring to Satan twice and to slanderers once.

As if there's not a lot of difference between the two.

So lest we think of our runaway mouths as inconsequential in the grand scheme of things, let's remember whose acrid, smoke-filled company they place us in. Let's remember, too, that Jesus Himself included the sin of slander in the same list as murder, adultery, and sexual immorality (Matt. 15:19). Are we as concerned and shocked over the sin we commit with our tongues as we are over the evil behavior of others?

May the Lord open our eyes to see how sinister our bent toward slanderous, stinging talk really is.

What Is Slander?

When Paul says, "Let no corrupting talk come out of your mouths" (Eph. 4:29), one of our reactions is to think we'd probably be better off if we never said anything at all.

Yet in that same verse we're exhorted to speak those things that are "good for building up . . . that it may give grace to those who hear."

So before we go off the deep end, taking vows of silence to avoid saying things we shouldn't, let's clarify just what is included in slander (plus some related sins of the tongue) and explore what we need to model and learn in this regard as both older and younger women growing into conformity with Christ.

1. Slander can involve giving a false report.

Saying something that's not true about someone is slander. But this is tricky because we may not intentionally be lying. Perhaps we're just misinformed, or at least *under*informed. We can't know everything that can be known about people's hearts, backgrounds, and circumstances. We rarely have all the facts. And so our version of the truth may be a far cry from what actually happened or what the person really meant. We can give a false report merely because we're not privy to all the information.

So when we're aware of a situation that puts someone in a negative light, we need to be careful not to assume we know all there is to know. If we choose to share what we think we know, we could be passing along lies and misleading conclusions without even realizing it.

And God takes this seriously. It's one of the Ten Commandments: "You shall not bear false witness against your neighbor" (Ex. 20:16). And Proverbs 6 names "a false witness who breathes out lies" among the "six things that the LORD hates" (vv. 19, 16). We must not take lightly what God despises.

2. Slander can involve the spreading of harmful information.

The King James Version uses the quaint but descriptive term *talebearer* to describe one who specializes in this activity. "The words of a talebearer are as wounds," Proverbs 18:8 says—intended to hurt, disparage, malign. In our heart, we know how our harmful words make the other person look. And we'd hate to think people would say similarly unkind things about us. But all too often, to our shame, we go ahead and say them anyway.

3. Slander can include the reporting of truth with harmful intent.

Be sure you don't read too quickly past this one because it's an oft-neglected member of the slander family, one we can easily pass by and rationalize. In order for a word or a story to be slanderous, it need not be concocted out of thin air or delivered inaccurately in the telling. What we say could be 100 percent true and still be a type of slander. So even when we're right, we need to ask ourselves: *What's my purpose in adding this into a conversation? Am I intending to hurt someone? To get back at someone? To put someone down or cast him or her in a bad light? To draw attention to myself as someone in the know?*

"Whoever goes about slandering reveals secrets," Solomon said, "but he who is trustworthy in spirit keeps a thing covered" (Prov. 11:13).

"It is his glory to overlook an offense," he added in Proverbs 19:11.

Just because we know something doesn't mean we need to share it. If part of our motive in telling it is to tarnish what others think about another person, then who cares how true it is? The Lord Himself will bring the truth to light in His own good time without our help.

That is not to say that we should never discuss negative truths with anyone. There are certainly times we need to confront painful realities and perhaps hold someone accountable. But we need to be careful when we do so—praying about the matter, seeking dependable counsel if necessary, and examining our motives. There's a big difference between thoughtful, necessary confrontation about an issue and using that issue to build ourselves up or tear someone else down.

4. Slander is not the same as gossip, but gossip makes slander easier.

By definition, gossip means spreading rumors or revealing personal information about another person. It's not precisely the same as slander, which generally means spreading *harmful* information or lies about the other person. But in the chatty comfort of a gossip session, it's easy to cross the line into speculation, false information, outright lies, or malicious rumors—in other words, slander. Avoiding gossip will help us avoid slander.

Slander Hurts

Slander can be a lie. Slander can be the truth.

But slander always hurts somebody.

That's what makes it slander.

I realize, of course, that our intent is not always malicious. Sometimes the hurtful comment just slips out. It comes to mind, and we can't seem to control ourselves. Before we even know what we're doing, we've already said something slanderous.

Looking back, we see why we did it. People were laughing, our guard was down, and we just went along with the mood around the table. How odd or self-righteous would we have appeared if we'd tried changing the subject?

But that's why James gives this watchword: "Do not speak evil against one another" (James 4:11).

Period.

The Greek word that is translated "speak evil" in this verse contains the idea of "thoughtless words."[2] Casual conversation. Offhand comments. We didn't really mean anything by it—we were "just saying."

But what difference does it make how lightly we say it if reputations are smeared, if trusts are broken, if leaders are trashed and churches maligned, if our children are hardened or our relationships damaged? Are we not still playing into the hands of the Enemy? Is not our fellowship with the Father being hindered? Are we not undoing the unity of the Spirit that is to be a hallmark of God's people?

It may feel good at the moment to make a catty or hurtful comment about someone else. But does anything good come from our having done that? I think we all know the answer to that.

Not only does slander hurt others; it also reveals contaminants in our own hearts such as

- *Pride*—the desire to make ourselves look better, smarter, more together, and superior, if only by making another person look worse by comparison.

- *Envy*—resenting another's position, connections, success, family, talents, possessions, or reputation. We may not be able to speak or sing or entertain guests or quote Scripture like that person can, so we want to bring them down a notch.
- *Critical spirit*—the tendency to be judgmental, to jump to conclusions, to secretly hope others will fail. We can downplay whatever others have achieved by questioning or cheapening how they did it and making them appear "less than."

Scripture warns us that slander divides; it breaks up relationships (Prov. 16:28; 17:9). And slander destroys. Someone has called it a form of "verbal homicide." Proverbs associates it with the imagery of "a war club, or a sword, or a sharp arrow" (25:18). It is heinous. It is vicious. It claws at old wounds. It opens new ones.

Slander hurts.

Unchecked, it will only keep on hurting more.

But you and I can make the hurting stop.

A Plan for Rooting Out Slander

"The bitterness is gone," she told me. "It's all gone!"

I've often witnessed visible relief on people's faces when they are set free from the lies of the devil, from the bondage of sin. That look in their eyes when the weights fall off, when they step into the freedom of surrender, honesty, and forgiveness—there's no feeling quite like it.

And that's what I saw on my young friend's face that day.

She had called and asked if I'd be willing to meet with her that afternoon. I could tell right away something was really disturbing her. She hadn't been sitting there for more than a few minutes before she started sobbing.

It had been a tough season for this young woman and her family. Through no fault of her own, some deeply regrettable things had happened. A conflict had arisen. Several people she trusted and respected had acted and reacted badly. Though she was not responsible for what had taken place, she had picked up an offense for someone she loved and had allowed her heart to become infected with resentment and disgust. Then she had caused the wound to fester even further by talking about it to others. She had let them know what certain people had done and how she felt about it. How she felt about *them*.

But over time, my friend had become saddened and ashamed at how her anger had turned into slander. And now she was broken—right there in my living room. She couldn't have taken her role in the fallout any more seriously.

I listened carefully. We talked and we prayed. And then, sensing a prompting from the Lord, I asked if she'd like me to call the person she felt she had wronged the most—a local pastor. "What if he were to come over here," I said, "and you could talk with him right now?"

Less than an hour later, my friend was pouring her heart out to this man who had been an object of her anger and venom: "I've sinned against you. I've said unkind things about you to others. I've undermined your leadership, and I hope you can forgive me. I'm truly sorry." More tears. More prayers all around.

What took place that day was so beautiful. So redemptive. Exactly what God instructs us to do when we've caused harm to another person.

That's the kind of thing that happens when we get before the Lord and discover how *He* feels about what's going on in our lives. Instead of being stuck with how we feel and what we want, we can begin to face and confess what our own words have done—how they've injured other people, poisoned others' opinions. And then, with all our pride and envy and criticism and contention pulled up by the roots, we also might be able to say, "The bitterness is gone. It's all gone!"

As God does His healing work in your heart (and mine), let's take advantage of the opportunity to root slander out of our lives. As repentant people, as women who know we've been loose with our tongues and are serious about not inflicting verbal damage on our homes, our relationships, and the body of Christ, let's turn to the Word for our way out.

Here are seven practical helps to putting a halt to slander.

1. Humble yourself.

Breaking free of the diabolical grip of slander in your life begins with facing your own involvement—acknowledging that you have spoken falsely or passed along hurtful "news"—even under the pretense of a prayer request or personal concern. Then, once you've admitted it to yourself, confess this hurtful behavior and ask forgiveness.

Start with God because, first and foremost, you've sinned against Him (Ps. 51:4). Confess your sin in speaking rashly as well as the root issues behind it, those hidden attitudes that have been like silent partners in the process. Receive and begin to rest in the forgiveness He's purchased for you by His saving grace.

But you've not only sinned against God. You've also sinned against other people. So if you truly want to experience release, you may also need to confess your slander to others—those to whom you've spoken words of slander as well as those you've slandered—and seek their forgiveness.

There are times, of course, when the act of apologizing for what you've done might injure the victim further, especially if they aren't already aware of what you've said. But if we would purpose in our hearts to humble ourselves and confess and ask forgiveness for the negative things we say about other people, we'd think twice about saying them in the first place.

2. Stop it!

Scripture tells us, "Let all bitterness and wrath and anger and clamor and slander be put away from you, along with all malice"

(Eph. 4:31). All of it. Impose a zero-tolerance policy concerning the sharing of unkind, untrue, unhelpful information about others.

Notice the first sin listed in this verse—*bitterness.* Think how often our divisive words are fueled by a bitter spirit. If you are harboring resentment in your heart, if you can hardly think of this person or of certain people without reeling off your list of charges and accusations, realize you will never be able to control what crosses your lips until you've crimped off the oxygen line that feeds life to it. Bitterness, wrath, anger, clamor, slander, malice—get rid of it all. Do whatever is necessary to stanch the flow at the source.

I understand you may be dealing with situations where people have truly sinned against you. They may still be doing things that harm you or others. Your husband may be passively delaying decisions and not seem to care how you're affected by his procrastination. Someone you considered a friend may be undercutting you at the office. Name a relationship, name a setting, and you can probably find a good reason for commiserating with someone about what's going on.

But before you air your grievances, take a minute to check your motivation. Is it to see the offender exposed? To punish him or her? To gain an outside ally who'll sympathize and feel sorry for you? Are you as concerned about the people you're criticizing as you are about how their actions are affecting you?

And then consider: have you prayed for the person who is hurting you? And have you gone to that person directly, not in a shouting match but in a genuine appeal for his or her personal welfare and restoration?

Some situations—I'm thinking in particular of abusive relationships, or perhaps a rebellious teen, something involving criminal behavior—do call for outside intervention. You need to report what is happening to the appropriate authorities and seek guidance from a pastor or wise counselor. But whatever you share in such an instance ought to be meant as a salvage operation, not sabotage. When it becomes necessary to expose the sin of another, be sure the exposure comes from a heart that is genuinely concerned for the other person and wants to see him or her restored to a right relationship with God. And be sure to pick your confidants carefully. A good rule of thumb I heard many years ago has been helpful to me: If the person with whom you're sharing this concern is not part of the problem or the solution . . . don't say it.

3. Speak well of others.

Commentator William Barclay rightly observes, "It is a curious feature of human nature that most people would rather repeat and hear a malicious tale than one to someone's credit."[3]

Perhaps the best way to curb our bent for picking at others' faults is simply to go out of our way to say *good things* about them—not by being insincere or buttering people up, and not by being blind to their imperfections, but simply by paying attention and making the effort to voice what we notice.

You might be surprised how many opportunities present themselves to pay a compliment, brag on the good work someone else has done, or express gratitude for a lesson you've learned from observing the other person's demeanor and character. If you're married, you might be amazed how taking the time to express admiration to your husband or tell a friend what you admire about him can enrich your relationship.

How much slander could we displace if we were more intentional about speaking words of grace and encouragement?

As the wife of an intense, busy pastor and the mother of eleven children, Sarah Edwards (1710–1758) certainly faced temptation and opportunities for slander. But she was known for just the opposite:

> Sarah made it her rule to speak well of all so far as she could. . . . She was not [prone] to dwell with delight on the imperfections and failings of any; and when she heard persons speaking ill of others, she would

> say what she thought she could with truth and justice in their excuse or divert the [slander] by mentioning those things that were commendable in them.
>
> Thus she was tender of everyone's character, even of those who injured and spoke evil of her. . . . She could bear injuries and reproach with great calmness, without any disposition to render evil for evil; but on the contrary, was ready to pity and forgive those who appeared to be her enemies.[4]

What a commitment—to speak well of all. And what a calling—to reflect the kind, gracious heart of Christ to those around us.

4. Rein in your thoughts.

Much of what eventually becomes slander is born and nourished when our unbridled thoughts are given free rein. That's why we need to be careful what we choose to let our minds dwell on. We need to squelch that unholy curiosity of ours, the kind that loves hearing dirt about others and then adds our own commentary as we reflect on it later in the day.

A commitment to "take every thought captive to obey Christ" (2 Cor. 10:5) requires conscious, disciplined effort. And it takes time spent at the feet of Jesus—fixing our eyes on Him, being "transformed by the renewal of [our minds]" (Rom. 12:2) as we meditate on His Word.

When we bring our thought life under the control of the Spirit, we can enjoy the sweet fruit of words that are acceptable to Him and nourishing to others.

We would all do well to make the psalmist's prayer our own:

> Let the words of my mouth and the meditation of my heart
> be acceptable in your sight,
> O LORD, my rock and my redeemer. (Ps. 19:14)

When we bring our thought life under the control of the Spirit, we can enjoy the sweet fruit of words that are acceptable to Him and nourishing to others.

5. Talk less.

How often do we engage in conversations we just don't need to be part of? We inject ourselves into a discussion. We impulsively reach for our phone. We ask questions that probe more deeply than we ought to go. Cutting back on the quantity of our words lessens the opportunity for and temptation to slander.

Again, I'm not saying we need to go stoically silent or feel guilty for being friendly. But there is wisdom in the words of Proverbs 10:19:

> When there are many words, transgression is
> unavoidable,
> But he who restrains his lips is wise. (NASB)

For several years I had a walking partner. Over the course of that time, we walked some 1,500 miles together. And while we enjoyed the chance to chat and catch up, even to pray and quote Scripture and encourage one another in the Lord, we also had to guard against idle talk, sharing gossip, and even slandering others with our words.

It's so easy. It comes so naturally. It breeds in constant conversation and can quickly grow into slander.

Of course, we ought to speak *more* words that bless and encourage and strengthen others. But if there's nothing needful to say at the moment, nothing kind, uplifting, encouraging, or helpful . . . *fewer* words may be just what is needed.

6. Think before you speak.

Are you one of those people who doesn't really know what you think until you've said it aloud? Do you tend to blurt out your thoughts and impressions? If so, you may be in greater danger of falling into slander than a more reflective person—although quiet folk are not immune from sinning with their tongues.

If the person being talked about were here in the room with us, would I say the same thing?

I'm not trying to inhibit effervescent, spontaneous speech, but I do think this is something to consider, especially for those of us who possess a quick and eager tongue. How often do we get ourselves in trouble by failing to think about what we're saying while we're saying it?

When people ask our opinion, sometimes the best answer we can give is, "I don't really know enough to have an opinion." And when we find ourselves in the middle of a group discussion, sometimes the wisest thing we can do is say nothing at all. Do the people we're talking to really need to know what we think—especially if our assessment of another person is less than positive?

I try to ask myself: if the person being talked about were standing or sitting right here in the room with us, would I say the same thing? In the same way? Would I be willing to say it to his or her face? If not, I likely shouldn't be saying it behind their back.

7. Don't even listen to it.

I don't mean making a big show about leaving the room whenever talk turns to other people. That's pride of another color. But where gossip and slander are starting to flow, we can graciously try to steer the conversation to another topic or to say something positive about the one who's being talked about. In some situations, we may need to gently ask our companions if we really ought to be talking this way.

You may remember that the apostle Paul—before he became an apostle—once watched over the coats of those who stoned the Christ follower Stephen to death. Although he may not have thrown the rocks, he was as much a part of the scene as those who did. And so are we, whenever we listen greedily to slanderous conversation.

Just as we have an "advocate with the Father, Jesus Christ the righteous" (1 John 2:1), we as beneficiaries of His unmerited mercy should be quicker to advocate for our brothers and sisters than to debase them—or to *hear* them being debased.

Bookends

Humble ourselves. Stop speaking ill of others and speak well of them instead. Control thought patterns. Talk less. Think before we speak—in fact, don't even listen when others are speaking slander. Doing these things will go a long way toward eliminating slander from our lives. Better yet, as women joined together in this commitment, we'll adorn the gospel by keeping slander out of the church. And in the process, we'll help each other develop the hallmarks of an abundant life spelled out in Galatians 5:

> The fruit of the Spirit is love, joy, peace, patience,
> kindness, goodness, faithfulness, gentleness, self-control;
> against such things there is no law. (vv. 22–23)

Did you notice the two bookends of Paul's famous list? *Love* and *self-control.* Between these two lie all those other qualities that characterize a fruitful life—joy, peace, patience, kindness, goodness, and faithfulness. I'm convinced the order of this listing is no accident. Wherever we lack love and self-control, we invite all manner of breakdown and discord to take up residence in our midst. Bitterness and anger in our hearts, expressed in evil speaking, vengeful words, malicious gossip, and talebearing—these are the telltale signs that love and self-control are in short supply among us.

I imagine that Satan watches and cheers as we bite and devour one another, rather than being like our reconciling, life-giving Father. So let's join together as women in shutting down the slander machine—the one we've used to chew up far too many people, damaging reputations, wounding spirits, and fracturing relationships (even entire churches) in the process.

Instead, "let us pursue what makes for peace and for mutual upbuilding" (Rom. 14:19). And let's pray earnestly with the psalmist:

> Set a guard, O Lord, over my mouth;
> keep watch over the door of my lips! (Ps. 141:3)

If you and I will adopt a "don't say it" policy when the Spirit tries to restrain us or we're not sure what's motivating our drive to speak, we will be in a position to make peace and to make a difference where we live. People will know from experience, "That woman can be trusted with my heart, my vulnerabilities, my confessions, and my imperfect story, because I know she would never slander me to others."

The groom in the Song of Solomon praises his bride for how she blesses him and others with her words:

> Your lips drip sweetness like the honeycomb, my bride.
> Honey and milk are under your tongue. (4:11 HCSB)

This woman doesn't babble on and on like a flowing brook. She doesn't gush everything she thinks. Her words, like honey, are measured. They are thoughtful and sweet. Her tongue has a filter. It has a governor—much like the safety mechanism that limits the speed on a car or boat. And her words strengthen and encourage the hearts of those who hear them instead of causing harm and contention.

I want to be like that woman, don't you? I want my words to minister grace to others, starting with my heavenly Bridegroom.

With God's help, let's use our tongues to build up those around us rather than tearing them down. Above all, let's speak words that make much of Christ. Words that adorn His gospel and put His loveliness on display. Words worthy of women whose hearts have been won by His amazing grace.

Making It Personal

Older women

1. What kinds of speech and behavior evidence the quality of reverence in our lives? Why is this especially important for mature Christian women? Are there any changes you need to make in this regard?
2. Jesus included the sin of slander in the same list as murder, adultery, and sexual immorality (Matt. 15:19). Do you tend to be as concerned about the sin you commit with your tongue as you are about the evil behavior of others?
3. Which of the seven practical steps from this chapter do you especially need to put into practice? Which are the most challenging for you?

Younger women

1. How does social media contribute to sins of gossip and slander? Why is it easier to share hurtful information on social media?
2. Much of what eventually becomes slander is "born and nourished" when our thoughts are unbridled, unrestrained, not under the control of Christ. How can Psalm 19:14 help you train your heart against gossip and slander?
3. Which of the seven practical steps from this chapter do you especially need to put into practice? Which are the most challenging for you?

Teach what accords with sound doctrine.

Older men are to be sober-minded, dignified, self-controlled,
sound in faith, in love, and in steadfastness.

Older women likewise are to be reverent in behavior,
not slanderers or **slaves to much wine**.

They are to teach what is good,
and so train the young women
to love their husbands and children,
to be self-controlled,
pure,
working at home,
kind,
and submissive to their own husbands,
that the word of God may not be reviled.

**. . . so that in everything they may adorn
the doctrine of God our Savior.**

TITUS 2:1–5, 10

CHAPTER 7

At Liberty

Experiencing Freedom from Bondage

Looking this addiction straight in the eye
has brought me to my knees—
To the cross.

RENEE JOHNSON

IF EXCESSIVE DRINKING ISN'T AN ISSUE FOR YOU, you may be inclined to skip this chapter.

Finally (for once!) a Titus 2 directive that doesn't step squarely on your toes.

Well . . .

Regardless of whether you drink or not, I hope you'll hang in with me here, because this is not just about alcohol—though we will definitely touch on that in this chapter.

It's not just about older women, either, although I believe there's a reason Paul specifically cautions older women about this issue. We will touch on that as well.

In this passage, Paul specifically pinpoints the issue of alcohol abuse—a warning that was needed by Christian women in his day and is no less needed in ours. But I believe the heart of this text goes beyond dealing with a single behavioral issue. It seeks to plumb and expose the hidden depths of our hearts, the chains that keep us from being free to portray and proclaim the gospel.

We live in a highly addictive culture. At some level, most of us struggle with some kind of enslavement or sinful bondage. The prohibition against being "slaves to much wine" could more broadly include any behavior, practice, or craving that we have allowed to enslave us.

Indulgence and Excess

We've seen the apostle exhort older women to be "reverent in behavior"—to live in a way that "accords with sound doctrine," as those who are engaged in sacred service (because we are!).

And what does that look like? What are the implications for everyday life? Paul identifies two marks of reverent behavior in older women: we are not to be "slanderers," and we are not to be "slaves to much wine" (Titus 2:3). Our reverence for God is to be reflected through our tongues and our temperate lifestyles. We looked at the first mark in the previous chapter; now we turn our attention to the second.

At one level, being "slaves to much wine" represents a mindset of overindulgence that leads invariably to bondage. It is the natural, human bent that is perpetually in pursuit of whatever brings us pleasure or eases our pain. It's the "eat, drink, and be merry" mentality. The tendency to pursue a life of ease and comfort, pampering the flesh and—whenever the flesh experiences physical or emotional discomfort—doing whatever is necessary to make that discomfort go away. Now. At any price.

Are older women the only ones who fall into such a mindset? Of course not! But apparently the apostle Paul, under the inspiration of the Spirit, knew that older women particularly needed this word of exhortation. And indeed, as I grow older, I find I'm often tempted to seek pleasure and ease in excess. It can be a subconscious, unspoken attitude: "I've paid my dues. I deserve a break today. I'm going to do something that makes me feel good. And if it makes me feel good . . . maybe I'll do it some more."

Note that emphasis on *more*. Paul tells us not to be slaves of "*much* wine." That's an important part of this all-too-human tendency. If we have a little of something, even something good, we tend to want a *lot* of it. Indulgence turns to *over*indulgence. In particular areas of our lives, we may find ourselves wanting more and more of something until we reach the point that we depend on it—we must have it.

Being "slaves to much wine" (or "slaves to much" of anything else other than Jesus) is the opposite of being sober-minded—temperate, self-controlled—a virtue Paul upholds repeatedly in this short epistle (1:8; 2:2, 5, 6, 12).

So in considering what the Spirit is saying to us through this phrase, we might begin by asking whether there are any areas where we are given to indulgence and excess. Are we driven to have too much of anything?

Is our life temperate? Is it fruitful and productive and bounded by godly ways of thinking? Or are we just taking our ease, indulging ourselves, mindlessly doing whatever brings us pleasure or numbs our pain?

Can't Get Away

But Paul is speaking about something even deeper than overindulgent lifestyles. He's concerned about our tendency to become *enslaved* to certain substances or habits or activities—anything—that we deem essential to our happiness, sanity, or survival.

That word *slave* in Titus 2:3 means "to be held and controlled against one's will."[1] And that's exactly what happens when we are enslaved by a substance or a behavior. We can't stop. We can't do without it. We cannot get away.

We call such slavery by many names—habit, obsession, compulsion, dependency, addiction, stronghold. Each term has a specific nuance, but they're all about slavery—and we're all prone to it. It's hardwired into our human nervous system—the brain's tendency to create habits out of repeated actions and its drive to seek pleasure and avoid pain. It's part of our spiritual DNA as well—our natural propensity for turning even good gifts or neutral activities into opportunities for sin.

Consider some of the common compulsions that enslave many women today—including Christian women:

- *Food.* Binge eating is the most common eating disorder in the US. A CNN.com report called it "a way to numb feelings."[2] Research suggests that while one in ten women who attend church is likely to have a problem with drugs or alcohol, as many as one in four possesses an abusive relationship with food.[3]
- *Diet and exercise.* Have you ever spoken to someone who talked of nothing but carbs, calories, heart rates, and repetitions? It really is possible to get hooked on being healthy!
- *Shopping.* According to one report, compulsive shopping affects up to 8 percent of the U.S. population, and 90 percent of those shopaholics are women.[4] What starts as a way to meet legitimate needs becomes a relief from pent-up pressure. And before we know it we're hiding credit card receipts and paying exorbitant interest rates on overdue bills.
- *Television.* American households overall watch far more TV each day than families in thirty-four other countries surveyed.[5] Soap operas continue to be a popular "drug of choice" among women. Author Shannon Ethridge writes, "It's no coincidence that I was experiencing the most extramarital temptation during the days that I watched *All My Children*, *One Life to Live* and *General Hospital* while my children were napping."[6]
- *Screen time.* The panic you feel if you lose or break your

phone is evidence enough that phone use can have addictive qualities. That goes for other forms of "screen obsession"—computer games, social media, or the like.

- *Work.* Workaholism is sometimes thought of as primarily a male addiction, but women can also become obsessed with either paid or unpaid "productivity."
- *Romance novels.* A woman writing under the pseudonym Lindsay Roberts describes a time in her life when she became "addicted to romance." "Feeling trapped," she remembers, "I escaped by reading romance novels. . . . Since I worked only in the mornings, I'd spend afternoons reading one or two novels before the children came home from school. In the evenings, after the kids went to bed, I even progressed to a third. But . . . after a while it wasn't enough to just read about romance. Long, solitary walks or drives blocked out the real world, enabling me to conjure up my own fantasies."[7]
- *Sex.* Whether it involves illicit sexual activity, marital infidelity, or pornography, a compulsive desire for sex (even legitimate sex) can be deeply destructive and especially hard to shake. A woman who ministers to college students wrote to me: "During our recent women's retreat, I was up till 4 a.m. talking to young women addicted to Internet porn and self-stimulation. Help!"
- *Prescription meds.* Abuse of prescription drugs such as stimulants, painkillers, sedatives, and tranquilizers is the fastest-growing category of substance abuse among women. Beyond that, millions of women are dependent on psychotherapeutic drugs to function.

Masters and Minions

Some experts reserve the term "addiction" for the abuse of substances such as alcohol and narcotics. However, so-called behavioral addictions (most of the items on the above list) share some common characteristics with chemical dependencies.

First, they all involve something that lifts our mood or changes the way we feel. Desiring God's Jon Bloom observes that it is this good feeling that initially lures us in:

> At the moment of indulging, it doesn't feel like an enemy. It feels like a reward that makes us happy. And it feels like a relief from a craving that insistently begs for satisfaction."[8]

Second, all such dependencies can eventually compromise our physical health, our emotional and spiritual well-being, and our relationships—sometimes all three. They're bad for us and for others.

And third, they are extremely difficult to stop, even when we desperately want to.

Slavery indeed. And it happens so easily.

Whether it's so-called innocent pleasures (the kinds that aren't likely to send us into rehab for treatment) or the more destructive habits of drug use, pornography, gambling, and alcohol addiction, they all begin with a choice. Then the body's mechanisms and our sinful desires kick in, and before we know it we're hooked.

If you don't believe me, I challenge you to an experiment.

Over the next thirty days, why not intentionally abstain from anything you think *might* be controlling you? See if you can say no to it for just those few short weeks. If you find that you can't, then ask yourself who's in charge here. Who's the master, and who's the minion?

More likely, though, you don't need any convincing that your heart has been hijacked by one or more controlling passions or habits. You may have given up hope that your life could ever be different. Maybe you've concluded you're just going to have to live with this.

Or maybe you're fed up to the point where you're ready to take any action you can to break free.

Either way, when the Scripture says we should not be "slaves to much wine" (or anything else that might enslave us), implicit in this text is an invitation to be set free from addictive cravings and lusts. That should give us hope. And it should motivate us to pursue deliverance from anything and everything that controls us apart from Christ.

Not just for our own sakes, but for those who may be patterning their lives after ours.

And for the sake of adorning the gospel in their eyes.

A Worship Issue

Paul reminds us that prior to being saved by the grace of God, we were all "slaves to various passions and pleasures" (Titus 3:3)—that is, to sinful desires and satisfactions. By contrast, he writes, godly women are to be known for *not* being slaves to much wine or by implication, to any other substances or practices that do not honor God.

Because we can't do both.

We cannot be servants of God while at the same time bowing and scraping to the demands of some other substance or influence. Jesus Himself said it is impossible to serve two masters (Matt. 6:24).

So we have to choose.

And how do we choose? By obeying. As the apostle counsels in another place, "You are slaves of the one whom you obey, either of sin, which leads to death, or of obedience, which leads to righteousness" (Rom. 6:16).

In other words, we are either slaves to ourselves, to our sin, to Satan and his deceptions, or we are slaves to our loving God, trusting that His "wages" are "eternal life in Christ Jesus" (Rom. 6:23). I think we'd all agree this beats the payback we get for hiring ourselves out to other masters.

Another way of putting this is that addiction is a worship issue.

We are slaves to what we worship.

Now, admittedly, a lot of factors come into play when we feel powerless to stop engaging in harmful or unhealthy activities. There's guilt, there's history, there's a desire to meet what we feel to be unmet needs and to dull or anesthetize our pain. There's the urge to escape our relational problems or financial pressures or other unsolvable issues. There may be anger toward God, toward life, toward others who have contributed to the difficulties we face and the ways we instinctively react to stress and adversity. And even when there are no chemical substances (such as drugs or alcohol) involved, physiological factors or changes in our bodies can render us more susceptible to dependency.

And yet . . .

Our addictions reflect our heart's inclination to kneel before other gods that can do nothing for us, dissatisfied with the one true God.

Above and underneath it all, when we become dependent on a substance or an activity, we're yielding our willing *worship* to it. We are offering it the firstfruits of our time, our love, and our energy. We are saying through our actions—the most telling language of all—that we choose sin's rule over us rather than that of our wise, loving, heavenly Father.

So we more accurately describe our addictions when we think of them as what they truly are: *idolatry*. They reflect our hearts' inclination to vacillate in our allegiances, voluntarily kneeling before other gods that can do nothing for us, dissatisfied with the one true God to whom we owe our lives.

That's the exact opposite of what we're called to be as Titus 2 women. Our mission and our privilege is to yield ourselves fully in service of the Lord Jesus. To turn from our idolatrous habits and experience together the joy, the freedom, and the pure, sweet worship that flow from being wholly His.

Freedom Fighters

"But it's not that easy!" you might say.

And of course you're right.

I hear from so many women—younger, older, married, single—who feel enslaved to sinful habit patterns and destructive compulsive behaviors. They thought their faith in Christ would be enough to drive these intruders away. They hear stories and testimonies of people set free from horrible lifestyles by the rescuing power and mercy of Christ, but that's not been *their* experience. Instead they keep giving in, keep going back, keep falling under the weight and pressure, surprised at how they can still feel so pulled toward something that leaves them feeling so guilty, hurt, ashamed, and unhappy.

Those unrelenting obsessions feel to them like the enemies David describes in Psalm 59:

> Each evening they come back,
> howling like dogs
> and prowling about the city.
> They wander about for food
> and growl if they do not get their fill. (vv. 14–15)

They may have experienced seasons of victory, hoping that perhaps they'd put this thing away for good: this indulgent escape, this private embarrassment, this sexual sin. But then one day, under a certain alignment of circumstances, with their guard down and their emotions on edge, a familiar temptation came sneaking back in. It seemed

Our enemy would have us believe we can't be free, that we'll always be prisoners to our habits and addictions. The Word of God declares that no matter how enslaving your sin has been, it is no match for the overcoming power of the Spirit of God.

so harmless. So deserved, in fact. And before they knew it, they were enslaved again.

And that's just what life is like for them now. Even when they work hard to resist the temptation—gritting their teeth and sitting on their hands—they still don't feel free. Just tired. Torn. Like they're trudging through.

Our enemy, of course—*diabolos*—would have us believe we *can't* be free, that we'll always be prisoners to our habits and addictions, that even God Himself is not strong enough to help us conquer what we've obviously not been able to overcome in all these years of trying.

But, let me remind you, the Word of God is filled with promises intended to fuel hope, expectation, perseverance, and triumph. Repeatedly it declares that no matter how enslaving your sin has been (and can sometimes continue to be), it is no match for the overcoming power of the Spirit of God.

Now, this doesn't mean that God will wave some cosmic wand and instantaneously remove all desire for every harmful practice that calls to us. Of course, He is able to do that—and sometimes chooses to do so. But our experience will likely be more like that of the Israelites in relation to their enemies in the Promised Land:

> The LORD your God will clear away these nations before you little by little. You may not make an end of them at once, lest the wild beasts grow too numerous for you. (Deut. 7:22)

God could have supernaturally wiped out all the opposition His people would face in Canaan. But He knew that would cause more difficult circumstances, so in His mercy He promised to give them victory "little by little"—the same way He helps us conquer our idolatrous, enslaving dependencies.

We know from His Word that our fight against sin will not be completely won until we are at Home with the Lord. And what He wants us to learn through the sometimes grinding battle is that this gospel that saved us can also *keep on saving us*, delivering us moment by moment, even as the daily war between flesh and spirit wears on. This onslaught can keep us continually turning to Christ, His cross, His power, and His grace. And when we do, we discover that He is actively at work within us "both to will and to work for his good pleasure" (Phil. 2:13).

It is actually His love for us, then, that causes God to lead us down this long, hard road, putting to death all our unwholesome substitutes one obedient choice at a time. He enlists us in the battle so we can learn to fight His way.

After all, we were the ones who made the choices that led us into this bondage in the first place. We played an active part in our enslavement. And now we can play an active part in our liberation—by choosing to set our affections on Christ, believing that we've been set free "from the law of sin and death" (Rom. 8:2) and taking "every thought captive to *obey* Christ" (2 Cor. 10:5). As we persevere in these spiritual tactics, we begin to experience a richer, more satisfying, more enduring victory over our habits and addictions than any divine snap of the fingers could provide.

That's because our goal is not merely to get better, to be able to say we've quit doing this or that or whatever thing we've done a thousand times before. The goal is to draw near to our God, who is more desirable, attractive, and fulfilling than any excess of food or drink. Than any forbidden relationship. Than any pleasurable, exciting, yet enslaving enticement.

Than anything.

Fighting Together

Part of the beauty—and the power—of a Titus 2 lifestyle is that we're not in this battle alone. We tend to think of our compulsions and addictions as a personal issue—something that's mainly about our individual health, growth, and desire for change. But the directives we're exploring in this book—such as not being "slaves to much wine"—are not just about us as individuals, but also about how we live out the beauty of the gospel—*together*.

God has given us each other, remember. We do this in community with others, and we do it for the sake of others. What a joy—and responsibility—it is to fight together for grace and freedom in Christ and to take others with us into a place of victory where together we can worship in full surrender at the feet of Christ.

This Titus 2 mandate is about sharing and receiving from one another the gifts of transparency, accountability, mercy, and encouragement, reminding one another who our Master really is.

And it's about teaching one another as well—which brings us back to why Paul addressed his "not slaves to much wine" admonition to older women in the church.

In much the same way that a pregnant mother is said to be eating for two—and should view her daily choices in that context if she wants her child to be healthy—we cannot think of our secret sins and excesses as being mere private indulgences. They are not. If left unchanged and unchallenged, they will not only continue to discourage and defeat us personally, but will also hinder what God has called us to do for others.

By God's grace, being a slave to "much wine" has not been an issue in my life. However, as I have shared elsewhere, I have faced a recurring battle with being a slave to "much food." I am committed to keep pursuing freedom in this area—and in *every* area of my life that threatens to enslave me—for the sake of my own walk with God, yes, but also for the sake of my sisters and daughters in Christ.

I know that being enslaved to anything other than Him makes it more difficult for me to speak words of encouragement and hope to other strugglers in the battle. It diminishes my confidence in the gospel and my ability to proclaim it passionately. It causes me to shy away from certain topics of discussion, leaving younger women to fight their battles alone and thus perpetuating the shame and defeat into the next generation.

I've tried to stress that we don't have to conquer every weakness before we can speak into the lives of other women. We'd all be disqualified if this were the case. But we'll be far more effective in leading them through struggles similar to ours when we are experiencing freedom in our own lives.

Just think what life could be like with all of us running together, fighting together—rather than shadow boxing all alone with such stubborn opponents.

And Now . . . About the Wine

Thus far, our consideration of this portion of Titus 2 has focused on the need for vigilance in the battle against all kinds of overindulgence, excess, and anything that enslaves us. But Paul's challenge to the older women of the Cretan church specifically addresses the issue of being "slaves to much *wine*."

You may wonder if this issue affects enough women to warrant giving it more than a passing mention. The fact is, this is a significant and growing issue among women. Journalist/author Gabrielle Glaser sheds light on the little-known epidemic of female drinking in her book *Her Best-Kept Secret*. She points out that

> by every quantitative measure, women are drinking more. They're being charged more often with drunk driving, they're more frequently measured with high

> concentrations of alcohol in their bloodstreams at the scene of car accidents, and they're more often treated in emergency rooms for being dangerously intoxicated. In the past decade, record numbers of women have sought treatment for alcohol abuse.[9]

And it's not just a concern outside the walls of our churches, as I was reminded when a mature Christian woman confided in me recently that she had found herself returning to some destructive patterns that had plagued her before coming to know Christ, including "a super unhealthy coping mechanism of relying on alcohol at certain times and in response to certain emotions."

So I think we would be remiss not to address more specifically the use and abuse of alcohol, as Paul does in Titus, and to examine what the Bible as a whole has to say about it. Three recurring admonitions in Scripture can serve as a starting place.

1. The Bible condemns drunkenness.

There's not a positive word in Scripture about the overuse or abuse of alcohol. To the contrary, drunkenness in the Bible is associated with sensuality, immorality, carousing, violence, works of darkness, and sinful, pagan behaviors.

That, of course, raises the question of when drinking crosses the line into drunkenness. People I've known who have battled alcoholism confess they were the last ones to recognize they'd had too much. They generally couldn't tell when they were heading out of bounds. And, as there is no standard consumption level that defines being "drunk,"[10] it is difficult if not impossible to know how much is too much until that line has been crossed.

2. The Bible counsels us regarding the consequences of abuse.

Cautions regarding alcohol use and warnings against its abuse are frequent in Scripture. Proverbs 20:1 pulls no punches about this:

> Wine is a mocker, strong drink a brawler,
> and whoever is led astray by it is not wise.

And Proverbs 23 expands on the theme, describing the symptoms and effects of excessive drinking:

> Who has woe? Who has sorrow? [*emotional effects*]
> Who has strife? Who has complaining? [*relational effects*]
> Who has wounds without cause?
> Who has redness of eyes? [*physical effects*]
> Those who tarry long over wine;
> those who go to try mixed wine. (vv. 29–30)

So what are the wise to do? How can these destructive effects be avoided? The writer's counsel (at the very least, for the person described in the preceding verses) is straightforward:

> Do not look at wine when it is red,
> when it sparkles in the cup
> and goes down smoothly. (v. 31)

This passage, which continues through the end of the chapter, paints the picture of a person who takes a dangerous moral path and ultimately reaches the point where he wakes up each morning saying, "I must have another drink" (v. 35). He (or she) is enslaved. His drink of choice may look good, and it may feel good as it goes down. But he is urged to carefully consider the consequences (the ones the ads don't mention) and to stay away from the intoxicating substance (vv. 31–35).

3. The Bible charges those with greater responsibility to exercise greater restraint.

Several chapters later, the royal mother who gave us the description of the Proverbs 31 woman instructs her son, who will one day rule the land, with these words:

It is not for kings, O Lemuel,
it is not for kings to drink wine,
or for rulers to take strong drink,
lest they drink and forget what has been decreed
and pervert the rights of all the afflicted. (Prov. 31: 4–5)

Knowing how strong drink can dull the senses, slow the mind, and cloud good judgment, this mother warns the young prince about anything that could render him ineffective or cause him to become an oppressive, insensitive leader.

"Remember who you are," she says in effect. "You're destined to be a king! You can't govern others if you're a slave to your appetites, passions, and lusts."

She acknowledges that, for some, "strong drink" might be a means of dulling physical or emotional pain or drowning out problems, and it might be helpful as an end-of-life palliative:

Give strong drink to the one who is perishing,
and wine to those in bitter distress;
let them drink and forget their poverty
and remember their misery no more. (vv. 6–7)

But the royal son needed to be clear-headed, in full control of all his faculties, able to focus on his responsibilities and to be a wise, good leader.

And who were the people Paul challenged to a temperate lifestyle in his letter to Titus? The elders of the church (1:7) as well as, of course, the older women—groups of people who were particularly influential and whose example would be closely watched and followed.

Considerations for Titus 2 Women

So the Bible makes clear that the *abuse* of alcohol is to be avoided. However, before leaving this subject, I feel constrained to raise the question of the *use* of alcohol. I do so, with the realization that sincere believers who love God's Word hold quite different positions on this topic. After all, there are some verses that represent wine as a gift from God intended for our enjoyment (for example, Ps. 104:15; Isa. 55:1; John 2:1–11), while others, some of which we've just seen, focus on the potential dangers of drinking.

I believe this is one of those gray-area issues on which Scripture gives no explicit command. That means Christians have freedom in this matter. No one position necessarily makes us more spiritual than another. Neither do we have license to tear down those who disagree with us. Paul, in fact, addressing a similarly contested subject from the first century, warned specifically against passing judgment on a brother who is "convinced in his own mind" that he is staying true to the Lord in his thinking and practice (Rom. 14:5–12).

That said, here are several questions I have found to be helpful in determining our practice in this matter—considerations which can and should be applied to other potentially enslaving behaviors as well:

1. Is it harming my body?

Scripture declares that the body—the corporal, flesh-and-bone part of us—is a "temple of the Holy Spirit" (1 Cor. 6:19). In the context of this verse, Paul was warning specifically against sexual immorality, but the same warning could be applied to any misuse of our physical bodies.

The physical risks associated with drinking too much—whether on a single occasion or over time—are well documented. According to the National Institute on Alcohol Abuse and Alcoholism, these potential effects include interfering with the brain's communication pathways, heart damage (strokes, high blood pressure), liver damage (fibrosis, cirrhosis), increased risk of certain cancers, weakened immune system, and more.[11] Pregnant and nursing women are warned against any consumption of alcohol because its presence in the bloodstream elevates the risk of physical or mental birth defects in their unborn children as well as spontaneous abortion.

This is not to say that occasional or moderate drinking will ruin your health. Still, in light of its potential for abuse and addiction, I believe it's a mistake to downplay the physiological risks of excessive alcohol consumption—which leads us to the next, more important, question.

2. Does it—or could it—enslave me?

One woman told me that in her drinking days she would call her husband before leaving work and promise to come straight home, which she fully intended to do. But a local bar was also on her way home, and "I couldn't drive past it without stopping," she told me. "I tried. I just couldn't."

Obviously, this woman was not free. She was a slave.

Drinking, of course, is not the only habit that can have this kind of effect on a person. But the nature of alcohol—which the American Medical Association classifies as an addictive drug—is that it can take us and hold us. Ironically, many people who drink to escape some sort of pain in their life, all too often end up imprisoned by their habit.

In 1 Corinthians 6, Paul quoted the popular slogan, "All things are lawful to me," as a way of establishing common ground with his audience in the city of Corinth. But though "all things are lawful to me," he added, "not all things are helpful." Sure, he was at liberty to enjoy earthly blessings with a clear conscience. But he would not allow himself—even in his freedom—to "be dominated by anything" (v. 12).

Here's what I gather from these words of Paul. When choosing whether or not to drink, we must consider what alcohol can do to challenge the limits of our self-control and take away our freedom.

As a young man, prior to coming to faith in Christ, my dad demonstrated a propensity toward addictive behavior as a gambler and in his use of alcohol. That history, coupled with knowing my natural bent toward compulsive patterns when it comes to simple pleasures, has caused me to suspect that if drinking were a part of my life, I could well be among those who have a predisposition toward excess. So years ago, I decided that was a risk I would rather not take.

3. Is alcohol an idol in my life?

We hear sometimes of people being "driven to drink," perhaps by the stress of marriage problems, work difficulties, depression, or other challenges. God wants to use such eye-opening bouts with adversity to teach us just how fully we can rely on Him—how faithful, caring, and redemptive He is. But when things aren't going the way we want, our hearts often go searching for substitutes. And the calming, diffusing effects of alcohol can seem like exactly what we need to help us cope.

Liquor is quicker, in other words. (Or so we think.)

And it does something for us that prayer can't do. (Or so we think.)

And what do we call a substitute for God?

An idol.

As you think about your drinking habits, ask yourself whether you're turning to alcohol for comfort He wants you to seek from *Him*. In processing how you respond to life's hardships and disappointments, consider: Are they driving you to drink, or are they driving you to Christ? Are you trying to fill a place in your heart that was made for God? Are you looking to alcohol (or anything else) to provide relief and answers to problems such as anxiety, guilt, boredom, rejection, or loneliness? Have you embraced a false, substitute god in your life?

Of course, the "bad guy" here is not alcohol (or food or whatever), but our own, sinful hearts that are bent to seek substitutes for God. You may never touch alcohol and yet have other false gods in your life. It's wise, however, to consider how any substance or thing could become an object of false worship.

4. Could my drinking cause spiritual damage to others or lead them into sin?

This question invokes the law of love—our responsibility to love others more than we love ourselves and our liberty.

In Romans 14 and 1 Corinthians 8 and 10, Paul addresses various lifestyle issues that are not clearly spelled out in Scripture—issues in which some believers feel they have liberty and in which others cannot partake in good conscience. The apostle lays out two principles for how we should deal with such matters, the first of which we've already talked about. Both of these principles are applications of the law of love:

- Don't pass judgment on others when debating questionable topics. (Rom. 14:1–12)
- Don't place a stumbling block or hindrance in the way of a Christian brother or sister. (vv. 13–23)

This second principle is a key checkpoint in thinking about such matters as alcohol use. Which trumps the other—my freedom to drink, or the possible negative effect my example of drinking may have on others? What does the law of love require?

You may have heard it said, for example, that what parents tolerate in moderation, their children often excuse in excess. I have seen this illustrated by women who've shared with me about their nightmarish ordeals with alcoholism. Many could trace their first taste of liquor back to the readily available stock in their childhood homes. I'm not talking about parents who were alcoholics, but those who simply enjoyed a beer with their football games or a glass of wine with dinner.

Were the parents doing anything wrong? Not necessarily. Did they have a personal drinking problem? Maybe not. But did their example help ignite the spark that set a curious teenager on the path to becoming a forty-year-old alcoholic? All too frequently, yes.

I watched one husband's eyes fill up with tears of regret as he realized—too late—that in the exercise of his liberty to drink socially and moderately, he had failed to consider the weakness (and the family history) of his wife, who along the way had fallen prey to a dependency on alcohol.

To limit your liberty for the sake of others who may be led into sin as a result is not to capitulate to legalism, as some would suggest. It is to exercise a greater liberty—to live by the law of love.

There are many devoted followers of Christ who believe they are being faithful to Scripture by exercising the liberty to drink in moderation. And that may be where you land in good conscience before the Lord.

However, in our day—and in a culture where addictions are so epidemic and destructive—my personal opinion is that it is the better part of wisdom to voluntarily choose to limit rather than exercise our liberty to drink.

Admittedly, my thinking has been influenced by seeing the horrific toll taken on the lives of men, women, and young people—including many believers, even pastors—by the intemperate use of alcohol. It has always struck me as unwise (at best) that some Christian leaders would be so keen to celebrate the liberty to drink without being equally earnest about stressing the potential physical and spiritual dangers of excessive drinking, for the sake of those who are less mature in their faith or who battle strong temptation in this area.

Once again, however, this is an issue each of us must decide thoughtfully and prayerfully, with a sincere desire to honor the Lord and to bless and serve others.

In fact, I would encourage you to read or listen to a trusted Bible teacher who has a different view than mine. Then ask God for wisdom and clarity about your own life, considering your circumstances and proclivities, seeking to walk in the Spirit.

For Love's Sake

After reading a draft of this chapter, my husband came up to my study and (ever the encourager) said, "This is terrific, honey! And so greatly needed." Then he wondered aloud if I should include "our story" about this issue. So with his blessing I share a personal, unforgettable account of a conversation we had that gave me an important glimpse into the heart of the man I would marry nine months later.

One evening, on one of our first dates, when we were just getting to know each other, Robert asked, "Would it be okay with you if I were to have a glass of wine before dinner?"

"Of course, feel free," I responded.

He apparently suspected or assumed that I don't drink. So he pressed, to be sure I would not be offended by his having a drink. "That's totally between you and the Lord," I assured him. "But at some point I would love for us to discuss this further so we can hear each other's hearts on it."

We added it to our growing list of "things to talk about." He brought the subject up when we were together again later that week.

Robert shared with me that for years he and his first wife had enjoyed a glass of wine each evening after work. It was a way of relaxing and transitioning into the evening. He knew of others who had struggled with drinking to excess, but that had never been a temptation for him.

When he asked about my thoughts on the matter, I explained that I did not see this as a matter of clear-cut right or wrong or a measure of spirituality. But I also shared about my dad's issues with addictive behaviors before he came to Christ. He knew from firsthand experience both the attraction and the potential risks of drinking. So after he became a Christian, he resolved to abstain from alcohol. He was not self-righteous about his position or condemning of those who did not share his views. But we did not have alcohol in our home, and we knew he believed it was, at best, unwise to drink.

As I grew to adulthood, this is one of many areas where I took to heart the exhortation of Hebrews 13:7—I remembered the way my parents had taught me the Word of God, considered the outcome of their way of life, and set out to imitate their faith. It was not a hard decision for me not to drink. I saw it as a way of honoring my parents, as a protection from any genetic predisposition to dependency I might have inherited from my dad, and as an opportunity to find my soul's greatest satisfaction in Christ.

I shared all this with Robert, as well as my desire as a ministry leader not to exercise any liberty that could possibly cause spiritual harm to others.

Our conversation on this topic was not a long one. He listened intently, and within a matter of minutes said, "This is a no-brainer. If alcohol is something I have to have, then I have a problem. And if it means more to me than you do, how foolish would that be? You're worth far more to me than the freedom to drink could possibly be."

He thanked me for sharing my heart and then said tenderly, "This is not a big deal to me. I'll never drink again."

End of conversation.

In that moment, my heart was touched at a level Robert could not possibly have realized at the time. The issue wasn't really about alcohol—to drink or not to drink. Far greater than that, I knew this was a man who loved the Lord supremely and who was willing to surrender any pleasure or habit for the sake of another.

For love's sake.

And isn't that to be the driving force behind all our decisions? Love . . . and the true liberty Jesus offers from our self-indulgent and addictive tendencies.

Liberty for Captives

It happened on a sleepy Sabbath in Nazareth. Jesus, fresh from His experience of being tempted in the wilderness, had stopped by His hometown and decided to visit the synagogue. He stood up to read from the Scriptures, and someone handed Him a scroll. There was a pause while Jesus found His place. Then He read this passage from the prophet Isaiah:

> "The Spirit of the Lord . . . has sent me to proclaim liberty
> to the captives
> and recovering of sight to the blind,
> to set at liberty those who are oppressed,
> to proclaim the year of the Lord's favor." (Luke 4:18–19)

The words were familiar. Everyone in that Nazareth synagogue had heard them before. But something seemed different this time. Nobody spoke as Jesus rolled up the scroll, returned it to the synagogue attendant, and then sat down. Every eye was fixed on Him.

Then came the words that transport the writings of an Old Testament prophet right into the living rooms and bedrooms and other places where we've all experienced the chafing restraints of sin's enslavement.

"Today," the Lord Jesus said that afternoon in Galilee, "this Scripture has been fulfilled in your hearing" (v. 21).

And on this day—today—wherever you happen to be reading, know that this Scripture can be fulfilled for you too. Through the presence and power of Christ in your life, you can be free from whatever holds you captive.

Free from the "innocent" pastimes that have you hooked.

Free from the substances and behaviors that have lured you into idolatry.

Free from bondage to (so-called) pleasures that can never truly satisfy.

That freedom comes not by willing yourself to obedience, but by yielding yourself to your Master.

It probably won't happen in an instant. In fact, escaping your enslavement may be the hardest thing you've ever done—though God's deliverance is available to you on a moment-by-moment basis. And chances are it won't happen in a vacuum, without the help of other Christians who know you well and pray for you and hold you accountable—especially other Christian women who have experienced the liberating power of the gospel and are eager to help you know the same.

Jesus came to earth to set the captives free. May one of those captives be you. And another, me. And being liberated from every earthly enslavement, may we become wholehearted, grateful, adoring slaves of Christ. There is no greater liberty.

But it can happen. It does happen. And that's the word we all need to hear when we're struggling with our temptations and our obsessions.

Jesus came to earth to set the captives free.

May one of those captives be you. And another, me.

And being liberated from every earthly enslavement, may we become wholehearted, grateful, adoring slaves of Christ. There is no greater liberty.

Making It Personal

Older women

1. In what areas of your life do you tend toward indulgence and excess? Are you driven to have *too much* of anything?
2. How could your transparency about your own struggles with areas of bondage encourage a younger woman and give her hope? How much "victory" do you think an older woman needs in one of these areas to be helpful to a younger woman?

Younger women

1. Are there any substances, habits, or activities that you consider essential to your happiness, sanity, or survival? What lies are you believing about these issues?
2. How might seeking out a godly, older accountability partner help you in your struggles with habits that enslave you? Can you think of some precautions that should apply in doing so?

Teach what accords with sound doctrine.

Older men are to be sober-minded, dignified, self-controlled,
sound in faith, in love, and in steadfastness.

Older women likewise are to be reverent in behavior,
not slanderers or slaves to much wine.

They are to teach what is good,
and so train the young women
to love their husbands and children,
to be self-controlled,
pure,
working at home,
kind,
and submissive to their own husbands,
that the word of God may not be reviled.

. . . so that in everything they may adorn the doctrine of God our Savior.

TITUS 2:1–5, 10

CHAPTER 8

A "Sophron" State of Mind

Developing Self-Control

Without self-control, we become the slaves of all our enemies (the world, the flesh, and the devil) and become incapacitated, unable to serve God and one another or even our own best interests. We end up not only serving ourselves, but we become slaves to our appetites.

J. HAMPTON KEATHLEY III

IT WASN'T THAT BIG AN ERUPTION, AS VOLCANOES GO. But the disruption it caused was unbelievable.

It started in March of 2010. Seismic activity around the Icelandic volcano Eyjafjallajökull began to spike. Fire fountains spewed from a dozen or more vents along its rocky surface, but those slender openings could not accommodate the vast amount of raging magma underneath. By April 14 the lava had boiled its way toward the summit, melting the glacial ice before finally blasting out an explosive plume of ash that mushroomed to a height of more than thirty thousand feet.

The event continued for six days. Falling debris threatened farming and livestock operations in the surrounding areas, contaminating water sources and coating everything in its path under a gray-black layer of ash. More notably, the massive cloud of particles in the atmosphere grounded air traffic in twenty countries across northern Europe. Hundreds of thousands of travelers were stranded, and the delays cost an estimated billion dollars. It was the greatest disturbance of its kind on the European continent since World War II.

As I followed the news reports about this event, I began to realize that something all too similar had been taking place a lot closer to home.

My emotional gauges had been spiking for a number of months. Organizational and financial pressures in the ministry. The stress of an unsettling move. Hormonal changes. Just a lot of things. And over time, the pressure building inside had pushed its way to the surface.

I had grown increasingly tense and tightly wound. I often found myself on edge, reacting instead of responding to circumstances, snapping at people who were trying to be helpful, micromanaging our team, and being generally uptight, negative, and difficult to please. I felt out of control—like an emotional pressure cooker threatening to explode. And though I was aware that I was demoralizing even my closest friends and coworkers, I couldn't seem to stop myself.

But all the hubbub about that eruption in Iceland strangely exposed me. In its angry, fuming face, I could see the cauldron of my own heart. And in the swath of volcanic ash that spewed out across the European continent, I could see something of the damage my erupting spirit was doing to those around me.

Early one morning I confessed to the Lord in my journal that I had "spread a toxic, ashen cloud over the lives of countless people, among them dear staff and friends," and had "caused the light to go out from the eyes and souls" of some of my closest ministry colleagues. I had been allowing my emotions to dictate my behavior—to the detriment of my friends, my ministry, and my own soul.

That's just one of many personal examples I could share. I'm definitely a "work in progress" when it comes to the difficult challenge of becoming a woman of godly self-control. I suspect you've faced it as well.

The single word from Titus 2 we're looking at in this chapter represents a daunting requirement—an impossible one, apart from the gospel of Christ. It is this gospel and this Savior we seek to adorn; and it is the same gospel and Savior that empower us to "live *self-controlled*, upright, and godly lives in the present age" (Titus 2:12).

A Life of Self-Control

Lest we become so immersed in these individual chapters regarding slander and enslavements—or, later, in chapters dealing with our homes and family relationships—that we lose sight of the big picture, let's remind ourselves of Paul's reason for giving us this character curriculum.

To older women, Paul is saying that the grand goal of our lives on earth is not to reach some point of sit-back, feet-up ease. We're called to know, love, and serve Christ our entire lives, even when confronted with joint stiffness or back pain or the nagging fear that our best days might be behind us. This calling requires us to keep ourselves spiritually healthy. It also involves investing in younger women and serving as mentors and friends, as women who have a track record with God and know what it is to be recipients of His amazing grace.

And to younger women, his message is that a beautiful, blessed, bountiful life begins *now*, not decades from now. The woman you will be in ten or twenty or fifty years is being determined by the woman you are this week. And by joining hands with older women who model truth and encourage and guide your growth, you can become a mature, fruitful follower of Christ who will do the same for the women coming behind you.

Put it all together, and we're becoming what God intended His people to be. We're adorning the gospel by living out His Word—together—in dependence on His Spirit.

And in few places do we need the Spirit more consistently than in cultivating self-control.

Self-control is both a lifetime need and a lifetime pursuit.

The idea of "self-control" is a thread that runs through Paul's message to Titus. Paul mentions it six times in this short pastoral epistle and applies it to all varieties of people in the church.

Elders, he wrote, are to be self-controlled (1:8). The older men are to be self-controlled (2:2). Older women are to train the younger women to be self-controlled (2:5)—something they can't do effectively if they themselves aren't self-controlled! Younger men, too, are told (in the only line that's written specifically to them): "be self-controlled" (2:6).

The clear implication is that self-control is both a lifetime need and a lifetime pursuit.

We're all in this together.

And we're in it for the long haul.

What I hope we *don't* take away, however, is that this lifelong battle is a perpetual breeding ground for discouragement, defeat, and weariness. Constantly beating ourselves up. Living with that scolding voice of shame and inferiority in our heads.

For while self-control is indeed hard work, it's not God's plan to torture us with this lofty demand from Scripture. When seen rightly, against the backdrop of His grace and His gospel—by which, we're told, we are *still* "being saved" (1 Cor. 15:2)—the rewards of self-control become a sweet, soul-satisfying experience. And they make us instruments of goodness and grace in the lives of those around us.

There is *hope* for us, in other words. You and I can actually be self-controlled women in a world that is spinning wildly out of control, in a way that beautifully adorns both our own lives and the doctrine of Christ as we share it with others.

To help us begin moving together in that direction, I want you to let a strong but beautiful Greek word start rolling off your tongue and into your life. We've already introduced it briefly, back in chapter 2.

The Beauty of Sound Thinking

Sophron. (Pronounced *so-phrone*.)

What does that word sound like to you? Maybe it brings to mind the aromatic, orangey spice saffron, which is prevalent in much Indian and Mediterranean cuisine. You may think exotic. Earthy. Colorful and flavorful. Hold on to that association because we need a fresh appreciation of the beauty and fragrance of *sophron* in our lives.

Sophron, as we have seen, comes from two other Greek words—*soos*, meaning either "sound" or "saved," and *phren*, meaning "outlook" or "mind." When we put the two together, it means to have a "sound mind" or a "saved mind."

It's tough to come up with one English word that conveys the full meaning of this word. In many modern translations it's translated "self-controlled." Other translations render it as "discreet" (NKJV) or "sensible" (NASB). In a few instances it is rendered "sober" or "temperate."

Here's what some Bible dictionaries and commentators have to say about *sophron* and related words in this Greek word group:

- "the exercise of that self-restraint that governs all passions and desires, enabling the believer to be conformed to the mind of Christ"[1]
- "habitual inner self-government, with its constant rein on all the passions and desires"[2]
- "one who has a sound mind; a person who limits his own freedom and ability with proper thinking, demonstrating self-control with the proper restraints on all the passions and desires; one who voluntarily places limitations on his freedom"[3]
- "that cleansing, saving strength of mind which has learned to govern every instinct and passion until each has its proper place and no more"[4]

As I mentioned in chapter 3, the second part of this word is related to the modern Greek term for car brakes—conveying the idea of being able to slow down or stop. If you're headed down a steep mountain incline or zipping along on the freeway when a truck pulls in front of you, you want to know that your brakes work. If they don't, you're going to be in trouble. And that's exactly the reason a lot of women are in trouble today: their "brakes" don't work. Their thoughts, their attitudes, and their tongues are always racing full speed ahead with no way of stopping.

A *sophron* lifestyle begins with a *sophron* state of mind—a way of thinking that affects everything about the way we live. A sensible, sound, self-controlled mindset will result in sensible, sound, self-controlled behavior.

By the same token, irrational, impulsive, undisciplined, out-of-control behavior is evidence of thinking that is not *sophron*.

Now, I understand the language lesson can get a little confusing here. But I don't want you to miss the huge meaning compressed inside this handful of letters. Learning to be *sophron*—self-controlled, sensible, sober, able to "put on the brakes" when appropriate—is vital to the process of becoming an adorned and adorning woman.

As I've pondered this word and its meaning, I've come to see it as one of the most practical and vital aspects of my personal walk with the Lord. My reactions to everyday or unexpected circumstances can often be explained simply by asking one basic question:

"Is it *sophron*?"

Are my words, actions, or reactions excessive, compulsive, or unstable? That's a dead giveaway that, at least in that moment, I am not *sophron*. I lack the self-control that flows out of having a "sound mind." My thinking is not in accord with "sound doctrine" as found in God's Word.

And that's true for all of us. When we consider some of the foolish, destructive, out-of-control choices we've made in life—or when we hear others trying to figure out how they've gotten themselves into some of the fixes they're currently experiencing—most of them can be traced back to times when we weren't thinking or reasoning clearly, when we were basing our actions on faulty thinking or simply reacting without any thought at all.

In other words, when we weren't operating from a sound mind. When we weren't *sophron*.

The devil delights in perpetuating the kinds of unsound thinking we addressed in the last chapter, the kind that leads us to excesses and indulgences and eventually to compulsion and addiction:

- "That box of Christmas candy will make it all better."
- "I just need one drink to settle my nerves."
- "I can't help myself. He makes me so mad!"
- "Just one more handful of chips. I'll fast tomorrow." (Or "I'll run an extra mile tonight.")
- "Just one more computer game and I'll get back to work."
- "But it was on sale!"

On and on it goes—giving in to excuses, distractions, substitutes, and temporary idols, all because a lack of sound thinking leads to out-of-control actions.

The ramifications of self-controlled, sound thinking and living (or the lack thereof) are deep and wide. Notice how Paul's reference to self-control sits right in the middle of his curriculum for young women:

"Train the young women," he says, "to love their husbands and children, *to be self-controlled* [*sophron*], pure, working at home, kind . . . that the word of God may not be reviled" (Titus 2:4-5).

In other words, if you don't have a self-controlled, sound mind,

- You won't be able to *love your husband* when he's not lovable.
- You won't be able to *love those children* of yours amid all the laundry and lunches and trying to get everybody to bed on time.
- You won't be able to sustain *purity* in your habits and relationships.

- You won't be able to see the value or the necessity of *caring for your home.*
- You won't be able to show *kindness* toward those who are unkind to you.

You'll storm out and check out and flame out and wimp out on every bit of resolve you can muster. And ultimately your life will cause others to reject the very gospel you claim to believe.

Unless you're *sophron.*

The Goal Is Transformation

Too often, I believe, we focus on trying to change or stop our behavior—"I won't," I'll quit," "I promise"—without understanding the real trigger behind our actions. That's because those actions originate not in our wills or our stressful circumstances, but rather in our minds.

In what we're thinking—or *not* thinking.

The reason you lashed out at __________ again (insert name of husband, child, mother-in-law, coworker) is not that he or she did something to hurt you. Not really. It's because in that moment when the frustration and anger erupted in impatient, fiery words, you weren't operating from a sound mind.

The reason you polished off that whole bag of chips or went out and bought six new pairs of shoes or couldn't stop checking your Facebook page every five minutes—even though you were telling yourself the whole time to quit—was that you weren't thinking sensibly about what you were doing.

You thought you'd never hear such nagging and venom coming out of your mouth. You never *dreamed* you could act the way you've been acting.

Or you look up one day, sick from the bitter consequences of a reckless, shortsighted decision, and you wonder, "Why did I *do* that? Why didn't I stop before it came to this?"

Here's why.

It's because you weren't *sophron*. You weren't self-controlled. Your thinking wasn't sound.

This is a grid that can be applied in countless situations in the laboratory of life:

- The way I talked to that person—was it *sophron*?
- The way I ate today, or exercised today, or managed my time today—was it *sophron*?
- Was that a *sophron* response?
- Was I *sophron* in that situation?

We're talking about a virtue that is as foundational for living the Christian life as are the ABCs and times tables for a child's education. If we don't master this, we will struggle with every other virtue and spiritual discipline. To be self-controlled—to have a *sophron* mind—is basic to every believer in every season of life.

The Sophron *Woman*

To help you understand the impact that a sound—*sophron*—mind has on every area of our lives, I'd like to paint a portrait of two kinds of women. The chart on pages 170–171 lists tendencies and characteristics that indicate a woman is *not sophron*—that she doesn't have sound thinking and is not self-controlled. On the right side are corresponding qualities that characterize a woman who *is sophron*.

Of course, no woman falls entirely on one side or the other. Within the course of a single day, we may demonstrate qualities from both lists. But thinking about these characteristics has helped consider whether I am being a *sophron* woman in any given moment or situation. I hope it will help you do the same.

I would encourage you to set aside some time to go through the chart prayerfully, with a pen or highlighter in hand. Make a notation next to those qualities that are often characteristic of your life. Then ask yourself:

- Am I generally a *sophron* woman?
- What are the areas of my life where I need greater *sophron* thinking and living?

Godly examples and personal encouragement can be a great help in becoming more *sophron*. *Older woman*, are you a model of self-control? We can't lead others where we've not been ourselves. How could you use your personal experience and what you have learned about developing a *sophron* mindset and lifestyle to help the younger women in your life cultivate greater self-control?

And *younger woman*, is this something to which you aspire? Then don't wait until you're sixty years old and your lack of discipline and self-control have worn deep ruts in your character that are oh, so tough to change. The time to start developing this kind of thinking and lifestyle is now. Find an older woman who demonstrates self-control in her attitudes, emotions, words, and behavior. Ask her to pray for you, encourage you, and walk with you as you seek to cultivate the kind of sound thinking and self-control that result in sound living.

If I could somehow wind the clock back thirty years or so, this is one area where I wish I could have a do-over.

Please hear my heart on this. *If I could somehow wind the clock back thirty years or so, this is one area where I wish I could have a do-over.* There are areas of my character and my walk with God today that would be more fruitful and blessed, battles I might not have to fight so vigorously, if I had been more intentional about developing a *sophron* mind as a younger woman. How I would love to be an older woman in your life who helps you make those choices now.

Now, perhaps this self-controlled, sober-minded woman sounds to you like someone who never has any fun. Someone who is boring, rigid, uptight. You've probably known some women like that. I've been that kind of woman more often than I care to admit.

But the woman with Spirit-produced, grace-enabled self-control is anything but boring. Unlike other women around her, she is not a slave to her passions and impulses. She is free to love and serve God and others, free to enjoy His greatest gifts. Her life is a winsome, compelling reflection of the goodness and loveliness of Christ.

Or maybe this way of thinking and living sounds exhausting to you—always struggling to rein in your flesh—kind of like playing whack-a-mole at the county fair. No sooner do you strike one "mole" down into its hole than two more pop up.

But thankfully, God hasn't left us to acquire *sophron* by sheer willpower and determination. As Paul makes clear in his letter to Titus, this *sophron* mindset is initiated, produced, and enabled by His Spirit and His grace.

> For the grace of God has appeared, bringing salvation for all people, training us to renounce ungodliness and worldly passions, and to live self-controlled, upright, and godly lives in the present age . . . (Titus 2:11–12)

That said, to be a *sophron* woman does require effort and vigilance on our part. And we tap into the enabling grace of God as we take advantage of the means He has provided for our transformation and growth.

Renewed by His Word

Consider how you've felt at times after you've lost control, after your emotions rose up and sloshed over their banks like a river at flood stage.

Are you *Sophron*?[5]

	Non-*sophron* Woman	*Sophron* Woman
	HER MINDSET AND ATTITUDES	
1.	Impetuous, impulsive	Exercises restraint and self-government
2.	Easily taken in by unbiblical ways of thinking and ungodly philosophies	Brings every thought captive to the obedience of Christ; processes everything through the grid of Scripture
3.	Overly concerned about what other people think	Fears the Lord; lives for His approval
4.	Lacks discernment; not careful about what influences her; lets anything in	Careful/discerning regarding what she reads, watches, listens to
5.	Feeds the flesh; flesh controls the spirit	Feeds the spirit; restrains the flesh; spiritually/mentally/morally vigilant—heart and mind are grounded and guarded
6.	Seeks escape from pressure and problems	Willing to endure hardship for the sake of ultimate gain/reward
7.	Victim of her circumstances and past	Uses her past as a stepping-stone to greater fruitfulness
8.	Self-centered—"How does this affect me?"	Others-centered—"How does my behavior affect others?"
9.	Consumed with externals	More concerned about being godly than looking fashionable, beautiful, or youthful
10.	Mentally unstable	Healthy, stable; mind fixed on the Lord
11.	Has good intentions but doesn't follow through; commitments are short-lived	Follows through on commitments; develops godly disciplines
12.	Discontented; entitlement mindset: "I deserve better"	Contented, humble, grateful; gives thanks in all things
13.	Manipulative; takes matters into her own hands	Surrendered; waits for the Lord to act
14.	Focuses on the here and now; little or no thought for eternity	Has an eternal perspective; views the here and now in light of eternity
	HER EMOTIONS	
15.	Emotions controlled by circumstances; lives on emotional roller coaster	Emotionally stable; remains calm/doesn't lose it under pressure
16.	Choices driven by feelings, external pressure, circumstances	Choices driven by the Word of God
17.	Falls apart in a crisis	Heart is steadfast, trusting in the Lord; responds in faith rather than fear when facing challenges; confident in the Lord; has presence of mind and knows what to do in a crisis
18.	Easily provoked/irritated; flies off the handle quickly	Slow to get angry; not easily provoked
19.	Fearful	Trusts in the Lord
20.	Moody, sullen, temperamental	Peaceful, joyful; the joy of the Lord is her strength
21.	When life doesn't work, becomes angry, resentful, depressed, loses hope	Hopes in the Lord; trusts Him to write her story; waits on Him to right all wrongs
22.	Fretful, anxious	Prayerful, trusting

	Non-*sophron* Woman	*Sophron* Woman
	HER TONGUE	
23.	Says whatever comes to mind without hesitating	Slow to speak; words are measured; thinks first
24.	Talks too much	Good listener
25.	Quick to vent frustration/anger	Quick to praise, give thanks
26.	Wounds/belittles/tears down others with her words	Words minister grace/blessing/encouragement to the hearer
27.	Exaggerates	Careful with the truth
28.	Speaks roughly, uses profane or crass talk	Gracious, pure words
29.	Argumentative—has to get the last word	Humble; yields the right to be right
30.	Excessive shyness; fearful to talk	Blesses others by speaking good words in due season
	HER BEHAVIOR	
31.	Life is out of order—chaos, confusion, perpetual drama; out of control	Well-ordered, peaceful life; controlled by the Spirit and convictions vs. circumstances and emotions
32.	Instant gratification—must fulfill cravings now!	Willing to delay gratification; can say "no" now for future benefits
33.	Impulsive spender; buys things she can't afford or doesn't need; temporal values	Wise, restrained spending—doesn't spend money she doesn't have; lays up treasure in heaven; generous
34.	Eats whatever she feels like eating when she feels like eating it; lives to eat	Temperate, balanced eating—eats to live versus living to eat
35.	Unpredictable	Consistent
36.	Rash—acts without thinking about the consequences or impact	Stops and considers the potential consequences of her choices before acting
37.	Morally careless—lacks discretion; flirtatious, sensual, easily led astray; seductive; leads others astray	Modest in dress and behavior; morally chaste/pure
38.	Yields easily to temptation; in bondage to fleshly, sinful desires	Resists temptation; servant to God and righteousness
39.	Frivolous; lover of vain pleasures; lives for temporal pleasure	Eternal values; finds joy in the things that bring God pleasure
40.	Procrastinates—puts off hard or unpleasant duties; play now, work later	Diligent and faithful in her responsibilities—worship and work first, play later
41.	Struggles to maintain consistent disciplines and routines	Develops and maintains healthy, consistent disciplines and habits
42.	Given to excesses and extremes	Temperate, moderate lifestyle
43.	Makes foolish decisions; lacks wisdom to deal with difficult issues	Shows good judgment; has the ability to solve difficult problems
44.	Wasteful	Wise steward of the resources God has entrusted to her
45.	Silly, vain, trite, foolish	Sober-minded, wise
46.	Loves mindless entertainment; life's a party	Enjoys wholesome recreation for the glory of God
47.	Fritters away time; lives for the moment	Uses her time purposefully; considers long-term results of her choices
48.	Easily distracted—flits from one thing to another; inability to focus, concentrate, or finish a task	Focuses on what God has given her to do at the moment; brings tasks to completion
49.	Makes decisions based on personal feelings or what is easiest or most comfortable	Makes decisions based on biblical principles, even if that requires difficult choices

You were desperate to stop, to change, to get yourself back under control.

But what you and I are *most* desperate for in such moments is not just more restraint and self-control, but more of Jesus. More of His Spirit. More of His power to live with a saved and sound mind.

It is the Word that will restrain your flesh, renew your mind, strengthen your resolve, and give you an appetite for those things that bring God pleasure.

And to get more of Him, we need more of His Word. I think most of us underestimate just how much we need it. This is why Paul's exhortation in Romans 12 is so vital:

> Do not be conformed to this world, but be transformed by the renewal of your mind, that by testing you may discern what is the will of God, what is good and acceptable and perfect. (v. 2)

That's the goal—being transformed by the renewal of our minds. And the proven means of this renewal is time spent in the Word. Reading it. Studying it. Discussing it. Meditating on it. And obeying it.

It is the Word that will restrain your flesh, renew your mind, strengthen your resolve, and give you an appetite for those things that bring God pleasure. It is His Word that will fortify and prepare you for troubles that may lie around the corner.

Many years ago my longtime friend Susan gave birth to a son with multiple, serious, life-threatening defects, including having no esophagus. Susan hardly slept for the first four years of her son's life because she had to watch through the night to make sure he did not choke or stop breathing. But during that season this young mom was driven to the Word. When some might understandably have gone crazy with sleep deprivation and worry, Susan developed a sound mind, grounded in the Word, the character, and the ways of God. That is where she found perspective, comfort, and strength; this daily manna from the Word became her sanity and her sustenance.

Years later, when another one of her children was facing a prolonged health crisis with a child of her own, Susan (now the older woman) was able to walk her daughter through that difficult season with wisdom and grace—taking the younger woman to the Word, helping her cultivate a *sophron* mind. In God's providence, Susan has also been used to minister to and mentor hundreds of other young moms, passing on to them what God taught her in that stressful season years ago.

This is the dynamic Paul had in mind when he wrote Titus 2. *Older woman*, the younger women in your life need your example. They need your encouragement and your prayers. And they need you to help them get into the Word and get the Word into them.

There is no substitute.

There are no shortcuts.

By choosing to let Scripture reshape our thinking and redirect our choices, we can become *sophron* women of God.

Inspired by Eternity

A little later in Titus 2, Paul gives us another important key to cultivating a *sophron* lifestyle. He calls us to

> live self-controlled, upright, and godly lives in the present age, waiting for our blessed hope, the appearing of the glory of our great God and Savior Jesus Christ . . . (vv. 12–13)

In other words, our ability to have godly self-control in the here and now is tied to our *future* hope. Those who look forward to the return of Christ can say no to their flesh now in anticipation of the eternal rewards that await them in glory. They can endure the difficulty of delayed gratification—they can *wait* to have their longings fulfilled—knowing that what (Who) lies ahead is far better than anything this "present age" has to offer.

The apostle Peter echoes this truth:

> Therefore, preparing your minds for action, and being sober-minded, set your hope fully on the grace that will be brought to you at the revelation of Jesus Christ. (1 Pet. 1:13)

Peter's concept of "preparing your minds for action," by the way, is what the King James Version describes as "gird[ing] up the loins of your mind." This refers to the ancient practice of gathering up the folds of one's robes when needing to take off in a hurry, tucking them inside a belt or gripping them with a fist. No one who needed to run from danger or dash into battle wanted to trip over his own hem while doing it.

Those who think eternally will live this way—mentally prepared, looking forward, ready to go. The more we keep our minds "straining forward to what lies ahead" rather than being encumbered by "earthly things" (Phil. 3:13, 19), the less likely we'll be to stumble in this area of self-control. Our thoughts and behavior will become more heavily influenced by the hope-filled promises of heaven than by the pressing issues of the moment, no matter how tempting or upsetting those issues may be.

Think of it this way. In a moment of weakness, you might be tempted to pull off the next exit and into the drive-through of a fast food joint to buy a burger that looked irresistibly big and juicy on the billboard you just passed. But then you remember you have reservations that night at Ruth's Chris Steak House. You think of that luscious steak you're going to sink your teeth into shortly. And all of a sudden, that fast-food burger seems cheap, mass-produced, and tasteless.

You can wait. You can say *no* to the drive-through because you're going to get to say *yes* to an amazing feast just ahead.

Later on in his first epistle, Peter again stresses the importance of being self-controlled in light of what is yet to come:

> The end of all things is at hand; therefore be self-controlled and sober-minded for the sake of your prayers. (1 Pet. 4:7)

If we don't have sober, sound, self-controlled minds and lives, we'll have difficulty praying (I get that!), and we won't be ready to face the Lord when He returns.

The solemn reality of giving account on That Day for every thought, word, and deed, and the joyous expectation of spending all eternity with our Savior—these are cause and motivation to cultivate a *sophron* lifestyle now.

We can wait! There's an amazing feast prepared for us just ahead.

In Christ Alone

When I think of having a "sound mind"—a *sophron* state of mind—I'm taken back to a tranquil scene from Jesus' ministry that is all the more remarkable in light of the intense turmoil that immediately preceded it.

Jesus had just disembarked from His disciples' boat, having miraculously calmed their "spirit of fear" by rebuking the winds and waves of a severe pop-up storm at sea. "Peace! Be still!" He'd commanded (Mark 4:39). And in so doing, by His confident, capable power, He had enabled His followers to regain their shattered self-control.

But no sooner had Jesus set foot on dry land than He encountered a man possessed by a multitude of demons. (The man identified himself as "Legion," the term for a large contingent of soldiers.)

The three Gospel accounts of this event (Matt. 8:28–34; Mark 5:1–20; Luke 8:26–39) paint a disturbing picture of a deranged lunatic whose strange, erratic behavior included running around naked and prowling among the dead bodies buried in the seaside ledges. Because of his violent nature, people had tried to restrain the poor man with chains, if only to keep him from slashing his bare skin with sharp rocks and other available implements of self-torture. Yet he'd always managed to snap the shackles people placed on him.

His condition was chronic ("a long time" . . . "night and day" . . . "always"). His behavior was dangerous to himself and others. As a result, he was isolated, lonely, cut off from relationships. Here was a man in deep mental and emotional anguish, extremely out of control. And to greater or lesser degrees, he bears a resemblance to many people today.

I think of women I've known who live with varying degrees of mental or emotional torment. Some of them (some of us!) act out in ways that endanger themselves and others. One woman poured out to me in an email her frustration with herself:

> I just had an outburst with my preschool daughter. I have lately found myself unable to control my communication with her or my other children.
>
> I grew up in a home where my mother was always raising her voice about her frustration with things I did. I am catching myself doing the very thing that I hated receiving from my mother. But for some reason I get really angry.
>
> I read about parents who have abused their children and wonder if I am also capable of that. I don't want my children to feel like they are always walking on eggshells . . . wondering when the volcano will erupt again.

And this man wrote to our ministry, asking us to pray for his wife:

> The ups and downs are mainly where she lives—constant panic attacks, anxiety, hurtful actions and attitudes toward herself, me, and the family. Throughout our marriage there have been short times of peace; but the majority of the years have been filled with spiritual turmoil and trouble, like living with the enemy—almost as if having to daily talk someone down off the ledge. It breaks my heart.

Undoubtedly this is how the family of the demonized man in Jesus' day felt. Heartbroken. Powerless. Fearful.

And just as no one was able to subdue or help the man, so many women (and men) today—Christians included—are being treated with a lot of different methods, but not really being helped. Not changing.

But the man Jesus encountered was changed. Dramatically changed.[6]

By the end of his dramatic confrontation with Jesus, we get a completely different picture of this man. Instead of thrashing and cutting himself and behaving in the wild manner that had scared people away, this former lunatic is sitting quietly with Jesus, "clothed and in his right mind" (Mark 5:15).

Unless we lean on Jesus for the power to put these truths into practice, we will not be able to find sustainable victory over our rogue thoughts and emotions.

In a *sound* mind. *Sophron.*

In both of these biblical instances—the disciples in the storm as well as the possessed man on the seashore—the common denominator in their recovery of self-control was a firsthand encounter with the living Christ.

He was their only hope.

Just as He is *our* only hope.

We can do everything conceivable to force mature behavior from ourselves. We can make promises and mean well. We can get eight hours' sleep a night and maintain a healthy blood pressure and pay attention to our hormone levels. We can even cram Scripture into our heads on a daily basis. But unless we lean on Jesus for the power to put these truths into practice, we will not be able to find sustainable victory over our rogue thoughts and emotions.

Spirit-produced self-control will elude us unless we're continually calling out to Him for the transformation He alone can bring about.

When the man once known as Legion—the one who'd lost every vestige of self-control—saw Jesus at a distance, "he ran and fell down before him" and cried out for help (Mark 5:6). A short time before, in their storm-tossed boat, Jesus' disciples had done the same, crying out, "Save us, Lord; we are perishing" (Matt. 8:25).

In both cases, Jesus heard their cry and stepped into their crisis. And when all was finished, order had been restored. Peace and quiet had replaced panic and chaos. Once there was bondage—to an unsound mind, to emotions out of control. Now there was *sophron*. And as you might imagine, it didn't take long for news about the transformation in the demonized man to spread throughout the region!

The enemy of our souls is doing a number on the minds of women today. And only the presence and power of Christ can restore us to our right minds. Only He can make us *sophron*. And to be *sophron* is to be adorned with the mind of Christ.

Not By Ourselves

Decadence, perversion, rampant substance abuse, and immorality—this was the prevailing culture of the Roman Empire in the first century, when Paul wrote to Titus. In the midst of that darkness, followers of Christ were called to be *sophron*—sober-minded, self-controlled. They stood out. They made a difference. They reflected the beauty, balance, and stability that the gospel brings to a mind, a life, a culture.

It's fair to say—judging from the frequent refrain of "self-control" found in Titus 2—that this particular trait is sort of a hub from which all the other pursuits and principles flow. And if so, few things should be of higher priority to us than the development of a clear-thinking, gospel-saturated, sound mind.

The change is not always as dramatic as the one that took place among the tombs in Jesus' day. It often occurs in the simple, everyday spaces and places of our lives. Such was the case with a woman who wrote to share with me how the Lord had exposed her non-*sophron* thinking and was in the process of replacing it with a *sophron* mind and heart:

> My husband was called into ministry about nine months ago and moved our family to another state. We took a pay cut of 50 percent, a space cut of 50 percent, and I took a joy cut of 50 percent or more.
>
> For the last nine months I have grumbled in my heart and often out loud about the things we no longer have or that I wish I had. I have coveted nearly every possession imaginable and been completely miserable.
>
> You have helped me realize that my ingratitude and grumbling spirit really is an attack on the life God has chosen for me—and that I have been detesting it. Thank you for bringing me to my senses and showing me once again the goodness of the God we serve.
>
> This little apartment will now be filled each day with joy as I thank the Lord for all He has chosen for me.

Don't you love that? What a great picture of the beauty of being *sophron*—our minds renewed by the truth, freed from the shackles of our peevish, demanding selves, living under the control of the Spirit of God. And joy filling the space invaded by His grace.

Making It Personal

Older women

1. What has been most helpful to you in learning habits of self-control and sound thinking? What has *not* helped?
2. What examples of not "thinking sensibly" can you think of from your own experience that you might share with a younger woman to help her with her own thought processes?

Younger women

1. Think of a recent time you weren't "thinking sensibly." What was the result? How might operating from a *sophron* mindset have changed that?
2. Identify an area in your life where you need to be more *sophron*. What practical steps could you take (including asking another woman for counsel) to acquire more self-control in this area?

Teach what accords with sound doctrine.

Older men are to be sober-minded, dignified, self-controlled,
sound in faith, in love, and in steadfastness.

Older women likewise are to be reverent in behavior,
not slanderers or slaves to much wine.

They are to teach what is good,
and so train the young women
to love their husbands and children,
to be self-controlled,
pure,
working at home,
kind,
and submissive to their own husbands,
that the word of God may not be reviled.

**. . . so that in everything they may adorn
the doctrine of God our Savior.**

TITUS 2:1–5, 10

CHAPTER 9

Passionate about Purity

Pursuing Holiness in an Unholy World

O Lord, keep our hearts,
keep our eyes,
keep our feet,
and keep our tongues.
WILLIAM TIPTAFT

THANKFULLY, SHE MADE ONE MORE PHONE CALL.

The first one had been to a cruise-ship captain, a dashing man she had met while working on a special ministry assignment, coordinating an evangelistic campaign in various port cities in the Caribbean. Though her husband of five years was also onboard, most of his time was tied up with the project. In the course of her own work, "Kaylee" had often found herself in close proximity to the captain. And increasingly—despite the red lights and warning signs flashing in her mind—she found herself looking for ways to "accidentally" be alone with him.

The captain respected Kaylee's husband and knew he needed to tread carefully. But he also enjoyed Kaylee's company. So when she just "dropped by" to talk or eagerly accepted his invitation to go scuba diving or pointed out how many interests they shared in common, he was more than willing to go along.

Nothing physical had happened between them. Not yet. But their discussions had grown more and more personal, less and less reserved. When Kaylee dared to hint at how she felt about him, his warm response had sparked a tingle that enlivened her waking hours with romantic daydreams. The scenarios kept playing in her head—the dashing sea captain, the adventurous lifestyle, the thrilling possibilities.

One afternoon about two months into this multistop journey, with the ministry project about to end, Kaylee phoned the captain from a remote location. She had been off the boat for several days attending to her responsibilities and found herself thinking of him during a stretch of unoccupied hours. So she called "just to talk"—and maybe to wonder. Was he as saddened as she by the prospect of their parting ways in a few more weeks? Somewhere in the course of that two-hour conversation, those seed thoughts took root and began budding into potential plans—plans to leave behind her married life in Colorado and set permanent sail on the Caribbean with this seafaring man.

Talk about your exotic romance.

But as soon as Kaylee ended the call, the dizzying emotions she had been fueling were suddenly invaded by the conviction of the Holy Spirit piercing her conscience, reminding her of her commitment to Christ and to her husband. When she got back to her room that night, she placed another call, this one to a longtime friend and mentor back in the States.

The two had developed a relationship over the years, sometimes meeting regularly, sometimes more sporadically. This older woman had always been a voice of reason, encouragement, and wisdom for Kaylee. And at this critical juncture, when Kaylee's once strong convictions had been eroded by deception and confusion, she felt herself being drawn toward a woman who was sure to tell her what she needed to hear, even if she wasn't so sure she wanted to hear it.

And that is why these cords of connection between us women are so important—because they're more than just standing appointments every other Tuesday. They're more than structured mentoring programs in our churches. As these relational ties are strengthened by time and life experiences, they provide spiritual protection and reinforcement. They become the personal touch that brings truth back into focus when it's been blurred into so many shades of gray.

And sometimes, at just the right time, a relationship like this may be the last available lifeline that pulls a disoriented swimmer back to shore, tugged to safety from the powerful undertow.

This is especially true, it seems, when it comes to issues of purity.

So much so that one of the core courses in the Titus 2 curriculum for women is "to be . . . pure." Along with the other courses Paul lays out, this is foundational if we want to adorn the doctrine of God. It is one of the "good" things older women must teach young women if the church is to be a beacon for the gospel in the world and the baton of faith is to be handed off from one generation to the next.

This call to purity touches every part and particle of our lives.

Of course, it's not just *young* women who need to be pure. *Be holy* is one of the great, recurring themes of Scripture—and a calling for every believer.

This call to purity touches every part and particle of our lives—what we do, what we say, how we think, our attitudes and motives. "Let us cleanse ourselves from *every* defilement of body and spirit," Paul urges in 2 Corinthians 7:1. No type of impurity is insignificant—hidden, "respectable" sins of the spirit are no less defiling than more obvious sins of the flesh.

Defiled and Unbelieving

Christian purity stands in stark contrast to what is characteristic of the unbelieving world. Paul describes the latter in Titus 1:

> To the defiled and unbelieving, nothing is pure; but both their minds and their consciences are defiled. They profess to know God, but they deny him by their works. They are detestable, disobedient, unfit for any good work. (vv. 15–16)

These unbelievers are, Paul says, "slaves to various passions and pleasures" (3:3). They are not free, but are bound to fulfill the lusts of their flesh. We see this everywhere we turn today. It's hard to overstate how mainstream impurity has become in our culture.

And I wonder: Have we lost our capacity to be shocked and grieved by sin? Are we so accustomed to raunchiness, filth, and viciousness on the public airwaves that we've become immune to its deadening effects in our own hearts? Have we become desensitized to unholy language and images that pass through our eye gate and ear gate into our mind and heart? Are our heroes the kind of people David called the "saints in the land," the "excellent ones" (Ps. 16:3), or are we more taken and enamored by the worldly and the provocative, the best dressed and most widely photographed?

After compiling an eighty-two-page document of research related to impurity in our culture, one of my colleagues wrote to me: "I feel like I need to take a mental bath. So much trash." Our world is awash in moral trash. And this is not something we can simply blame on "the culture." In one way or another, we are all contributors to the garbage, which flows out of contaminated hearts. We all need to take a mental and spiritual bath.

And that is exactly what Christianity offers. This is good news indeed.

Women Called to Purity

In the face of a culture where the most base, fleshly instincts were unrestrained and promiscuity was pervasive, Paul wrote,

> We ourselves were once foolish, disobedient, led astray, slaves to various passions and pleasures. . . . But when the goodness and loving kindness of God our Savior appeared, he saved us . . . by the washing of regeneration . . . (Titus 3:3–5)

Did you get that? We who belong to Christ have been saved—rescued—from our former life. We have been *washed* from sin—cleaned up, purified. We are different from unbelievers, and that difference should be obvious to everyone. It shouldn't be hard to identify whether we are really a Christian.

This thread runs through the book of Titus and, indeed, the entire New Testament. The unbelieving world is characterized by impurity, but followers of Christ are supposed to be pure. This is the reason He died a sacrificial death on our behalf:

> [Christ] gave himself for us to redeem us from all lawlessness and to purify for himself a people for his own possession who are zealous for good works. (2:14)

And in light of the price He paid to redeem us, believers are to be "above reproach" (1:6–7), "to renounce ungodliness and worldly passions, and to live self-controlled, upright, and godly lives" (2:12). Pure lives.

This applies to all Christians, of course. But Paul makes the particular point that Christian *women* are supposed to stand out by being "pure" (2:5)—or as some translations render it, "chaste" (KJV, NKJV). According to one Bible dictionary, the original Greek means "pure from every fault, pure from defilement, immaculate . . . not contaminated."[1] Another defines it as "without moral defect or blemish."[2] Warren Wiersbe describes it as "pure of mind and heart."[3]

This is no insignificant—or easy!—calling for women in a raunch culture that celebrates "girls gone wild" and sexual promiscuity.

Now the topic of purity is broader than sexual purity. But Scripture makes clear that sexual sin has particularly serious implications (1 Cor. 6:12–19). When God's good design for sex is thwarted and distorted, the damage can be devastating. That's why a discussion of purity has to include this vital issue.

The assumption used to be that immorality was mostly a men's problem. However, that notion is no longer valid (if it ever was). Take, for example, the fact that one in six women regularly views some type of online pornography and the vast majority of these women—something like 80 percent, a much larger ratio than men—will eventually follow up their virtual activity with actual, face-to-face relationships.[4] (I read of one marriage counselor with twenty years of professional practice who says that at one time, almost 90 percent of the infidelity she encountered was initiated by men. But these days, she says, it's closer to half and half.)

Regardless of the escapes and delights it promises, an impure life does not satisfy. In fact, it does the exact opposite.

As we explore this whole issue, I want to do so with both passion and compassion, because I realize the tender, sensitive places in a person's heart that my words can touch. They can stir up old regrets. They can expose hidden secrets. They can even be used by the devil to instigate waves of guilt and shame that can bury a woman in depression and despondency rather than lead her into the light of freedom.

But the pain and brokenness I've seen resulting from impure choices, particularly in the sexual realm, compels me to speak up.

Regardless of the escapes and delights it promises, an impure life does not satisfy. In fact, it does the exact opposite. Our communities—yes, even our churches—are littered with broken hearts that have been chewed up and spit out by the monster of impurity. They desperately need to see women whose lives show forth the beauty of God's purity and love, the difference His grace can make.

And, oh, the need for older women who have observed or experienced this fact and who will obey the Titus 2 appeal to speak into the lives of younger women, whether to help deal with the consequences of past choices or to help avert further fallout in one more life, one more marriage, one more family . . . one more time.

The apostle Peter—speaking specifically to wives in relation to their husbands, and yet establishing a principle that has broader application—said others can be won over to the truth "without a word" when they see "respectful and *pure* conduct" (1 Pet. 3:1–2).

According to one theological dictionary, the word translated "pure" both here in 1 Peter 3 and in Titus 2:5 suggests something that "awakens awe,"[5] the kind of life that inspires notice and creates an impact. Christian women who have pure hearts and lives become a walking advertisement for the truth and power of the gospel. Others can see that it really does change lives. In a dark, unholy world, those transformed lives will expose the darkness and draw sinners to the light of Christ.

"Teach what is good," Paul commanded the older women in Titus' city, "and so train the young women . . . to be pure."

The more pure we become, the more beautiful our Savior appears in the eyes of those who see His beauty reflected in us.

Yes, pure.

And contrary to what the world would have us believe, this is *good.* So older women, if we really believe that, why would we not want to do all within our power to help the young women in our lives to be pure?

The more pure we become, the more beautiful we become . . . and the more beautiful our Savior appears in the eyes of those who see His beauty reflected in us.

The Hard Work of Staying Pure

If we are in Christ, of course, we have been declared "positionally pure." His righteousness has been credited to our account. And He has promised that one day we will be clothed in white with Him in glory (Rev. 7:9).

This is the great hope and longing of every child of God. But what about right now? Is it really possible to be pure when we are surrounded by such muck and corruption?

My dad thought so.

Before he came to know Jesus, being pure was the furthest thing from his mind. But all that changed in his midtwenties when the Spirit captured his heart and he became a follower of Christ. From that point on, he was passionate about holiness.

And that is what he wanted for our family, as well. I can recall him telling my siblings and me that he desired for us to be "as pure as the driven snow"—not just in heaven someday, and not just when sitting in a church service, but even when just sitting at home or interacting with friends or choosing entertainment options or being alone with our thoughts at the end of the day.

Not just *positionally* pure, but *practically* pure.

The Bible says that's what God wants for us too. The Scripture urges us to pursue purity:

> The aim of our charge is love that issues from a pure heart and a good conscience and a sincere faith. (1 Tim. 1:5)

> Having purified your souls by your obedience to the truth for a sincere brotherly love, love one another earnestly from a pure heart . . . (1 Pet. 1:22)

And it repeatedly calls us to be sexually pure:

> Sexual immorality and all impurity or covetousness must not even be named among you . . . (Eph. 5:3)
>
> Let marriage be held in honor among all, and let the marriage bed be undefiled, for God will judge the sexually immoral and adulterous. (Heb. 13:4)
>
> For this is the will of God, your sanctification: that you abstain from sexual immorality. . . . For God has not called us for impurity, but in holiness. (1 Thess. 4:3, 7)

If we want to enjoy the freedom and joy of walking in purity, we do well not only to ponder these kinds of passages frequently, but to consider what it will take to follow their direction in our daily lives because, as we've seen, practical purity isn't easy. This part of our Christian walk requires focused, ongoing effort and training as well as the watchful encouragement of these crucial Titus 2 relationships.

We need women we can call on the phone who will go to their knees and call out to God on our behalf. We need friendships with those who understand that the most godly or well-intentioned woman is never immune to temptation or failure. We need intentional, mutually invasive relationships with truth-telling friends.

And yes, I meant *invasive*—in the sense that we allow these friends to step into our lives and we are willing to move into theirs. These kinds of relationships don't settle for staying on the surface where everything appears to be just fine. They don't stand on ceremony or hold back for fear of rejection. We don't refrain from asking tough questions and saying things that need to be said.

Of course we should do this "in a spirit of gentleness . . . [keeping] watch on [ourselves], lest [we] too be tempted" (Gal. 6:1). Of course we should act in true concern and humility, not jealousy or judgment. And this should generally take place in the context of established relationships, where genuine love and care are already a given.

We can look to Him to transform us by His grace—no matter what we've done, no matter where we've been—until our lives ultimately mirror the gleaming whiteness of His purity.

But we all need people in our lives who love us enough to probe our hearts, who will hold us accountable to walk in the light. And we need to be willing to be that kind of friend to others. There is a time when it's necessary to lean in, to say the hard things, to not be silent when one of our sisters is teetering toward compromise. This is how we "bear one another's burdens, and so fulfill the law of Christ" (v. 2). This is how we live out the beauty of the gospel—together.

In all of this, we must let God's Word reveal and determine what our hearts are meant to love, what our minds are meant to dwell on, what our relationships are meant to be like, and what our habits are meant to avoid. We can look to Him to transform us by His grace—no matter what we've done, no matter where we've been—until our lives ultimately mirror the gleaming whiteness of His purity.

Hints and Hedges

Ours is obviously not the first period in history to experience the intense battle involved in maintaining a pure heart and walk. Extended portions of the book of Proverbs, in fact, focus on this battle and warn about the damaging, deadly consequences of sexual sin (see chapters 5–7).

Or listen to Paul, in the first century, urging the believers in Thessalonica to take these matters to heart, to walk in God-pleasing, Spirit-empowered purity "more and more" for the health of their bodies and spirits, of their families and worship (1 Thess. 4:1). And in Ephesians 5:3 (NIV) he urges, "Among you there must not be even a hint of sexual immorality, or of any kind of impurity. . . ."

Not even a hint? Not "any kind of impurity"? To modern ears, that may sound antiquated, extreme—just not realistic in today's world. But consider the upside of pursuing a lifestyle of purity:

- the joy that comes from being fully surrendered to God, satisfied in Him alone
- the freedom that comes from living inside His loving borders of protection
- the depth of relationship with others that is possible when the barriers of impurity and impropriety are removed
- the unity that takes place within marriages when honesty and transparency replace secrets
- the impact in the lives of sons and daughters who witness their parents actually living what they claim to believe
- the opportunity to point others to Christ and the purity that is available through Him

Surely it's worth any price to obtain and maintain a life that is pure and above reproach. But is it really possible?

Purity can indeed feel like an unattainable standard. And in fact, it is—apart from the indwelling, enabling power of the Holy Spirit. But the very fact that Paul urges older women to *teach* younger women to be pure suggests that purity can be *learned*—by watching the example of these mentors and by listening to what they have learned in their pursuit of purity.

In that spirit, let me share with you several practical day-to-day strategies I have found to be helpful in my own life as well as the lives of others when it comes to sexual purity. Hopefully you'll find these ideas helpful and can use them as a springboard for discussion in your Titus 2 relationships with other women.

I think of these practices and commitments as "hedges." Picture the rows of manicured shrubbery a person might place around his or her property, establishing a ring of privacy, a barrier to unwanted intruders. Hedges help keep things out, and they help keep things in. That's what these habits can do in your life. And while these practices don't make us holy in themselves or render us less dependent on the Lord for the desire and the power to be pure, they can help us as we wage war against the lure of the world and the cravings of our flesh. They contribute to our sanctification as the Holy Spirit motivates and animates our practical purity.

Hedge #1: Choose discretion.

We don't hear much about discretion any more. This important quality has to do with being discerning and prudent in our interactions—our speech and our behavior—with others.

Discretion is what restrains a woman from confiding personal marriage problems to a male friend or colleague or from having deep, private, spiritual conversations with another woman's husband. It makes her careful about how she meets a man's gaze or responds to flirtation or inappropriate words or behavior on his part. It helps her avoid settings and situations where the natural thing would be to do something wrong.

Hedge #2: Value modesty.

We looked briefly at this topic in chapter 5 in regard to reverent behavior, but it certainly applies in terms of purity as well. I don't want to minimize a man's responsibility to maintain his own purity of thought and eye control. But the dress and demeanor of many women and teenage girls today leaves so little to the imagination, it can cause a man's temptation meter to spike.

Godly men who desire to have pure thoughts and behavior toward women have implored me to help women understand the power they wield and how much they need our support and assistance in their battle for purity.

As Christians, one of our chief commitments should be not only preserving our own purity, but also protecting and honoring the purity and morals of others. And when we behave or dress in a fashion that competes with a man's affections for his (present or future) wife, we work against the purity of his heart as well as our own.[6]

Hedge #3: Check your emotional attachments.

It never fails to undo me when I hear of another woman (married or single) whose heart and emotions have been drawn into relationship with a man who is another woman's husband. It happens in the workplace. It happens at the fitness center. It happens in the stands at their kids' ball games. Sometimes it even happens in the church and with men in spiritual leadership.

In many cases, the woman is as surprised as anyone. She didn't intend to go there. But she arrived at that point one careless step—one incremental compromise—at a time. One thought at a time that she nursed and gave free rein to rather than taking "every thought captive to obey Christ" (2 Cor. 10:5).

Before she knows it, she is in emotional and moral quicksand.

The fallout and unintended consequences of tasting forbidden fruit are always messy and painful. In the end, sin—alluring as it may be—never pays what it promises. Never.

You belong to a God who raises the dead.

So this needs to be zero-tolerance territory. When the first of these thoughts comes in, it needs to be the next one going out. No flirting with it, no toying with it, not even for a second.

Here's what you need to do, instead: If you're married, determine to put that emotional energy into lavishing your own husband with love and interest—even if you feel your marriage is dead. You belong to a God who raises the dead.

If you're not married, invest your mental and emotional focus into cultivating a more intimate relationship with the Lord. The moment you sense the smallest flickering desire drawing you into an intimate, imaginary circle with another man—desire that cannot be righteously fulfilled or acted on—redirect your attention and your affection toward an object you can rightly desire. Otherwise, you are setting yourself up for disaster—and the longer you give it to build up, the harder it will be to deal with it.

Hedge #4: Guard your electronic communications.

Texts, emails, and social media provide a fertile context for developing inappropriate relationships. Even though you may be miles apart and your interaction can feel completely harmless, it's amazing how quickly an "innocent" exchange on our electronic devices can pick up steam.

Carelessness on this front is a huge contributing factor to the breakup of marriages today. I heard it once again recently as a woman poured out her heart to me about how her husband is mired in an emotional (at least) affair with an old girlfriend he connected with on Facebook.

Secrets and clandestine communications have no business passing between married men and women (who are not married to each other) in electronic or any other form.

Scripture doesn't lay down specific ground rules for our digital communication, of course. But it does provide foundational principles we can apply to help us make wise choices and guard our hearts.

I want to honor the Lord and have a pure heart and walk. And I know I am no less vulnerable than anyone else to be deceived or led astray. So when it comes to electronic communications I have chosen to err on the side of caution.

For example, when it comes to personal text or email exchanges with a married man, I generally copy his wife or a mutual friend. And now, as a married woman, I am purposeful about not having exchanges with other men that I would not want my husband to see. I want to be vigilant to protect the marriages of my friends and colleagues as well as my own heart and marriage.

Hedge #5: Don't forget to lean on your trusted female relationships.

As we've seen, this is at the heart of the message of Titus 2. It's worth mentioning again here because it's such an important hedge against impurity. The power of sexual sin is often found in secrecy. When we get honest about our secret temptations and failures—whether sexual or in other areas—and bring them into the light, they lose their power. And when we get in the habit of sharing them with a caring older woman who has a track record of faithfulness and obedience, God can use her to steer us back in the direction of purity.

And here's another benefit of these woman-to-woman friendships. Many women, whether single or married, are drawn into inappropriate relationships because they are lonely and lack fulfilling, caring relationships. Healthy, caring relationships among women can be a means of grace to help meet those needs in legitimate ways.

If we aren't deliberate about pursuing purity, the natural bent of our hearts and the breakneck pace of life make it easy to cut corners, compromising for the sake of convenience.

And don't forget that mentoring can go both ways. As an older woman, I have found that developing these kinds of relationships with younger women can serve as a hedge in itself—providing reminders and an incentive to persevere in the pathway of purity.

Taking Purity Seriously

To some, these kinds of cautions may seem over the top, especially by modern standards. But if we aren't deliberate about pursuing purity, the natural bent of our hearts and the breakneck pace of life make it easy to cut corners, compromising for the sake of convenience.

It's a mistake to see these practical "hedges" as putting us in some sort of legalistic straitjacket. In reality, true freedom for ourselves and for others, exists only within purity's well-hedged borders.

Listen, if I'm driving on a narrow mountain road with hairpin turns, peering out my window at steep cliffs below, I sincerely hope that road has guardrails. I will not resent those barriers as inhibiting my freedom. Instead, I will be deeply grateful for the freedom they give me to navigate the road without driving over the edge and plummeting to my death.

It's the *absence* of guardrails ("hedges") that poses the real threat.

I can attest to this personally, having been single until my midfifties. As a woman with normal longings for intimacy and companionship, there were occasions and circumstances in which it was tempting (and would have been easy) to veer off the path of purity. How I thank the Lord for the protection and freedom these kinds of practical hedges afforded me in those years. And for how He satisfied my longings day after day, with His promises, His presence, and His precious love.

Now, as a married woman, it is even more apparent to me that God intends not to restrict or limit our happiness through His precepts, but to *bless* us—whether married or single—with the rich, sweet fruit of purity.

A woman who desires to be pure will not consider wise, practical hedges to be a hardship or a burden, but rather will see them as a means of grace to help her navigate life with freedom and joy.

I find that when women begin to take purity seriously, their consciences become sensitized to things they might once have dismissed. Off-color humor. Sexual innuendoes. Questionable entertainment. Flirtatious behavior. Indifference or resentment toward their husband's sexual needs. As they deal with these and other issues the Spirit brings to their attention, the thoughts and practices that once crowded out God's ways in their lives begin to be displaced, making room for pure thoughts, pure worship, and a purer freedom than the world's ways can possibly provide.

Pure desires.

Pure satisfaction.

In place of their short-term, misplaced emotions and attractions, they begin to see God's holiness, His covenant-keeping love. That's because for every hint of compromise we avoid, we experience greater freedom to draw near to God. Carefully maintained, Spirit-directed hedges do more than just keep out unauthorized intruders. They also provide a border within which a lovely garden can be planted.

God's desire—and it's important to keep this in mind as we interact with other women—is to give us so much more than our modest, careful interactions appear to take away.

Life played on the edges is a date with disaster.

Life spent pursuing the Lover of our soul and, for those who are married, pouring ourselves into the husband we can love without restraint is the path to life's purest pleasures.

The Scripture says of Jesus that He "loved righteousness and hated wickedness," as a result of which God "anointed [Him] with the oil of gladness beyond [His] companions" (Heb. 1:9). The same will be increasingly true of those who love and follow Jesus. And to the extent that we love purity and loathe sin (starting with that in our own hearts), our lives will point people to Him.

The Promise of Purity

Kaylee didn't go through with it.

When she hung up from the second phone call with her longtime friend "Rebecca," she knew what needed to happen next. She needed to wrap up her work responsibilities, get back on a plane, and apply the cleansing agent of confession to her resistant, runaway heart. Her husband had to be told. Healing had to begin. Purity had to become her new home.

Again.

"Do you remember the letter that's here in my files?" Rebecca asked her that day. She was referring to a commitment Kaylee had written out and signed and left in her friend's keeping years earlier.

Kaylee's past had included a moral failure during her college years. So more than five years earlier, at Rebecca's suggestion, she had written a letter expressing her commitment to pursue purity and inviting accountability.

Yet when Rebecca brought up that promise on the phone that day, Kaylee's first reaction was to resist it. This situation was different, she said. She had her reasons, she said. This relationship was not out of God's will for her. It was making her happy, she insisted.

But there's something about a promise—a solemn, sincere vow—that's able to block off a road that appears to head off into the sunset but actually leads off a cliff.

And there's something about that older woman we've allowed into our lives to "teach" us and to "train" us in purity. She holds us back. She holds us up. She holds us close when temptation is circling in the water, just as she holds us when condemnation is circling back to confront us over our failures.

You need a woman like that.

And you need to become a woman like that.

When she was in danger of making the biggest mistake of her life, when she was about to dishonor the Lord and perhaps throw away her marriage, there was a woman like that in Kaylee's life. A woman who pleaded with her to remember her vows and remember her God. By God's grace, Kaylee listened to the older woman's appeal. She came to her senses, realized what she was about to do, and repented. As a result, the course of her life was forever changed.

Today, nearly twenty-five years later, Kaylee is experiencing the blessings and the fruit of that watershed moment. She and her husband have a terrific marriage. They are serving the Lord together. And God is using her to speak into the lives of younger women, helping them avoid the same pitfalls Rebecca helped her avoid falling into decades ago.

Personal willpower simply isn't enough to sustain our vows to our holy God. If we are to mirror His purity to our generation in a way that truly makes a difference, we mustn't attempt to make it alone. We must do it together.

Together, in dependence on the power of the indwelling Holy Spirit, our struggle with temptation can yield to the joys of personal, practical purity.

The snow-white beauty of His purity.

Making It Personal

Older women

1. "Christian women who have pure hearts and lives become a walking advertisement for the truth and power of the gospel." Do you see yourself in this statement? Why or why not?

2. Do you have any "intentional, mutually invasive relationships"? Are you a "truth-telling friend," or do you hesitate to say the "hard things" to someone who is struggling in the area of purity? What holds you back? How can you speak truth effectively while remaining loving and gracious?

Younger women

1. Kaylee called Rebecca when she was battling moral temptation. Who would you call if you were in a similar situation? Do you have any "intentional, mutually invasive relationships with truth-telling friends"?

2. Personal, practical "hedges" can be a means of grace to help you navigate life with freedom and joy. What hedges do you have in place to help guard your heart and protect you from unwise, impure choices? Are there additional hedges that need to be put into place?

PART THREE

A Woman under Her Roof

Teach what accords with sound doctrine.

Older men are to be sober-minded, dignified, self-controlled,
sound in faith, in love, and in steadfastness.

Older women likewise are to be reverent in behavior,
not slanderers or slaves to much wine.

They are to teach what is good,
and so train the young women
to love their husbands and children,
to be self-controlled,
pure,
working at home,
kind,
and submissive to their own husbands,
that the word of God may not be reviled.

**. . . so that in everything they may adorn
the doctrine of God our Savior.**

TITUS 2:1–5, 10

CHAPTER 10

Taste of Heaven

Cultivating a Heart for Home

Love and labor, home and work—
these concepts need an eternal perspective.
CAROLYN McCULLEY

IT WASN'T ANYTHING FANCY—BUT WHAT A SWEET GIFT IT WAS.

My husband and I joined our sweet friends "Gretchen" and "Alex," along with their four children and another family member, for an evening in their home. We gathered around their dining-room table to feast on savory chicken-vegetable soup and fragrant bread. We talked, laughed, and played a spirited game of Toss Up. Then we closed the evening with an extended time of prayer around the circle. Surrounding us on the walls was beautiful original artwork that depicted biblical themes—just one way that Gretchen, who left a career in marriage and family counseling to minister to her own husband and children, uses her gifts to worship Christ and point her family and friends to Him.

This generous-hearted wife and mom is being pulled in many directions these days—juggling the needs of her husband, homeschooled children and teens, aging parents, a disabled sister who has come to live temporarily in her home, and a steady stream of college students who find a home away from home under her roof. And yet she intentionally makes her home a place of outreach and welcome.

She doesn't typically offer gourmet meals or Martha Stewart table settings. What she—along with her husband and children—does offer is extravagant love, warmth, acceptance, meaningful conversation, and smiles. Her home is not an idol or an end in itself. It is a tool, a means of putting the gospel and the grace of God on display.

My friend is giving those who come through the front (or garage) door a taste of heaven.

Because she—like all true Titus 2 women—has developed a heart for home.

A Home-Based Curriculum

Let's take a quick step back and pause here for a little refresher:

> Older women . . . are to . . . train the young women to love their husbands and children, to be self-controlled, pure, working at home, kind, and submissive to their own husbands . . . (Titus 2:3–5)

Paul truly said a mouthful when he outlined this curriculum for the "women's ministry" of the church in Crete roughly twenty centuries ago. Before we dive into these individual qualities, I'd like to make a few observations about this list as a whole.

For starters, I think you'd agree this list flies in the face of what a lot of people think these days. It was radically countercultural in Paul's day, and it is no less so in our day. But those who trust the wisdom of God and who are willing to swim upstream against the culture to embrace this timeless calling will find it a way of great beauty and joy.

Next, it's worth noting what is *not* on this list. Notice, for example, that Paul doesn't mention anything about the women's prayer life. There's nothing about their knowledge of Scripture or their evangelistic fervor.

That's not to say that these areas are unimportant. Every believer, man or woman alike, ought to pursue and embrace them, and Paul makes that point in other letters. But they aren't Paul's focus in this particular passage. Nor does he include instruction about a woman's vocational life or her personal ministry activities.

It's also interesting that Paul apparently assumes the qualities he highlights don't come naturally. He says younger women need to be *trained* in these important areas. They are skills to be taught and learned—one generation passing them on to the next.

And finally, Paul's list reminds us of the priority God places on the home. Four of these instructions for women in the church relate directly to the domestic sphere:

Our home life—far from being a separate compartment from our spiritual life and witness—is a foundational way we express the love of God and the beauty of the gospel.

- loving our husbands
- loving our children
- working at home
- being submissive to our husbands

And while the rest—purity, kindness, self-control—are broader topics, all are certainly vital within the context of home and family relationships.

So one important takeaway from this passage is that God cares about what happens inside the walls of our houses. Our home life—far from being a separate compartment from our spiritual life and witness—is a foundational way we express the love of God and the beauty of the gospel.

Home, as God designed it, is not a cultural convention or a matter of pragmatic convenience. It is intended to be a parable of the redemptive storyline in which He is intent on restoring Paradise, establishing His dwelling among men, and making beloved sons and daughters out of prodigals. Christian homes are meant to tell that story.

That is not to say that those who do not marry or bear children are excluded from this story—or that a discussion of the responsibilities and blessings of home leaves them stranded on the sideline.

No, at some level, Paul's home-based curriculum applies to all of us.

So if you're tempted to skip over these chapters because you're not in the "young wife and mom" demographic, I hope you'll hang in there with me as we explore how all of us can live out and adorn the gospel of Christ on the home front.

Not an Add-On

If you're anywhere close to my age, when you read Paul's prescription for young women, you may picture the *Ozzie and Harriet* generation of the 1950s. And you might consider that a good thing—*ah, those were the days!* Or you might recoil at the thought—*can you say "barefoot and pregnant"?* For sure, it would be a mistake to idealize that period or to try to return to another time.

It would also be a mistake to write off this portion of Scripture as being archaic and irrelevant.

All of God's Word is inspired and intended to be taken seriously. We must wrestle with how to apply its enduring truth to our own era and cultural context—including that little phrase in Titus 2:5, "working at home."

The phrase Paul uses here is rendered a bit differently in other Bible translations. Those of us who grew up with the King James Version remember it as "keepers at home." Still other translations read:

- "workers at home" (NASB)
- "busy at home" (NIV)

- "homemakers" (NKJV)

The main reason for the difference is a disagreement regarding the actual compound word that is used in the original Greek. Ready for a little language lesson? The oldest Greek manuscripts use the word *oikourgos,* a compound word that combines *oikos* ("home" or house") with *ergos* ("work")—literally, "one who works at home." This suggests a woman who is not idle, who is busy at home and active in caring for her household duties.

Other manuscripts, however, use a slightly different word: *oikouros,* from *oikos* ("house") and *ouros* ("keeper" or "guard").[1] This is where we get the rendering "keepers at home"—suggesting one who cares for the home, taking care of household affairs.

Some scholars favor the first as the more accurate reading, while others think it should be the latter. Thankfully, for those of us who are not Greek scholars, it doesn't matter a whole lot. In fact, both words shed helpful light on our mission and calling.

In either case, the general sense of the word is that of a woman who's devoted to her home, who has a heart for it. She's actively engaged and involved in its life on a high-priority basis.

Today it's common for homes to be little more than physical structures where people park their bodies at night, take their showers in the morning, and then disperse in a hundred different directions as they start their day. The clock ticks on the mantelpiece, the thermostat cycles off and on to regulate the temperature, the microwave dings as residents run in to grab a snack and then run out again, but there's little shared life.

And that's the *best*-case scenario. At *worst,* our homes are in utter disarray, characterized by active hostility and oblivious neglect. They may be decorated to the nines and obsessively up-to-date with seasonal front-door hangings, yet the relationships within the walls are seriously fractured—or at least emotionally distant and dishonest.

And this—or something like it—is what far too many women today have grown up with. It is their concept of "home."

Then here comes Titus 2 into this messy reality, reminding us that home is not an add-on to our "spiritual" life. It is part and parcel of our discipleship and our calling as children of God.

We can know the Bible backward and forward. We can have the whole neon rainbow of highlighter colors at our side, ready for study. But if we are not practicing *self-control* at home, if our children or husbands (or roommates or guests) wouldn't describe us as *loving* and *kind*, then something is off.

We can't separate our home life from our Christian life without missing something that is critical to our fellowship with God and our usefulness to His mission in the world. When we minimize the role of wife and mother or the importance of establishing and maintaining Christ-centered homes that put the gospel on display—or even when our main goal is just to keep everybody in line and on schedule—we shortchange the enormous kingdom impact our life at home is supposed to have.

Remember Paul's reference in Titus 1 to false teachers who were "upsetting whole families"? He didn't elaborate about what these people were saying, but he did indicate they were doing it for "shameful gain" (v. 11). That probably means their teaching was quite popular. It was selling well. So it's possible to imagine, from what we *are* told, that some of what these individuals were peddling was subverting God's design for families.

We see the same thing happening today. A young woman whose primary ambition is to be a godly wife and mother—as opposed to, say, a physical therapist or an architect—is treated as if she doesn't have a brain in her head or any ambition in her soul.

Several years ago, the announcement that a leading evangelical seminary planned to offer an undergraduate degree in humanities with a concentration in homemaking caused no small stir. One pastor, responding on his blog, characterized the degree program as "frivolous and foolish." He wrote, "A seminary degree in cookie-baking is about as useful as an M.Div. [master of divinity degree] in automotive repair."[2]

In light of such attitudes and assumptions, even among Christians, what are we to make of the fact that Scripture includes "working at home" in the core curriculum for the training of young women? A look back at the history of work and home can shed some light on the subject.

Ancient Realities and Modern Eyes

For longer than you or I have been alive, there has generally been a clear-cut division between what happens at work and what happens at home. Most people who "work" get up, leave their house, and go to another location (the public sphere) where they do the tasks they are paid to do before they return to their home (the private sphere), spend their paycheck, and start the process all over again.

But this now-familiar model is relatively recent. Prior to the Industrial Revolution, which spanned the eighteenth and nineteenth centuries, there was no such separation of work and home. The *home* was the economic engine of society, a place of productivity. Families—men, women, and children—all pitched in to produce goods that made it possible for their needs to be met and enabled them to care for others in need. Both the home itself and the work that took place in and around it were considered essential and highly valued.

By the twentieth century, however, all of that had changed. Rather than being a place of productivity—all hands on deck—the home had become a place of consumption. Today we decorate our homes to express our unique personality and style. We showcase them on Pinterest and Instagram so they can be admired by others. But for the most part, our "work" and our homes tend to run on separate tracks. And in general the public sphere—the marketplace where one is paid for one's labors—has become the more highly valued realm. The private sphere—homes that are outposts for nurturing loving marriages, discipling and training children, caring for disabled or elderly family members, and extending hospitality and care to friends and neighbors—has been devalued.

In the eyes of the world, as well as in their own eyes, women often derive their sense of identity and status from productive work done outside of the home, work for which they are financially compensated. Less status is conferred on daily labor that takes place in the home and is not rewarded monetarily. This division between the private and public sphere has given rise to heated debates (think "Mommy Wars") about the place of women and the meaning of home.

Far from demeaning women, Paul welcomed the participation and partnership of women in the ministry of the gospel.

However, when Paul exhorted older women to train young women to be "working/keepers at home," he was living in an entirely different setting than this post-Industrial-Revolution world of ours. It is important that we understand this in order to avoid interpreting passages such as Proverbs 31 and Titus 2 only through the lens of our modern cultural context.[3]

To our twenty-first century ears, it could seem that by urging women to be workers at home, Paul was diminishing their worth—implying that they were less important than men because, after all, unpaid "home work" is not as important as work done in the marketplace (the public sphere). We could conclude that Paul was discouraging women from contributing to their church, community, or culture. But to do that is to misunderstand the intent of this injunction.

Far from demeaning women, Paul was actually progressive for his time and culture. He called Christian women to be intentional about employing their heads, hearts, and hands for the sake of the gospel. The apostle worked with Priscilla and her husband in their tent-making business, remember, and his ministry in Philippi was supported by the business successes of Lydia. He welcomed the participation and partnership of these and other women in the ministry of the gospel (see Romans 16:1–16) and he never disparaged their work or their contributions. Rather, he encouraged them to utilize their skills and maximize their assets for the advance of the kingdom of God.

As I have meditated on and grappled with Titus 2 in the light of the whole of Scripture, I've come to believe that when Paul instructs women to be "keepers/working at home," there are some things he does *not* mean:

- He is not mandating that women are *only* to work at home or that the home is to be their only sphere of influence or investment. He is not saying that their domestic activities are to be their sole focus or that their home requires 24/7 attention at all times.
- He is not saying that women are singlehandedly responsible to do all the work that needs to be done in the home or that it is inappropriate for children, husbands, and others to help.
- He is not prohibiting women from performing tasks outside the home or from being compensated financially for such work.
- He is not implying that women have no place in the public arena or that they should not contribute to their church, community, or culture.

So what *does* Paul mean to say in this passage, and what do his words imply for Christian women?

For starters, the phrase *"working at home"* makes clear that women are to *work*. They are to be gainfully occupied. They are not to be like the young widows in Ephesus that Paul referred to in his letter to Timothy: "idlers, going about from house to house, and . . . also gossips and busybodies" (1 Tim. 5:13). Rather, they are to live honorably and to faithfully carry out whatever work God has given them to do.

As we have seen, the home in Paul's day (and in most eras prior to our own) was a place of employment and the small business unit of the local economy. And within this system, it was important for women to be productive and not idle. Although our twenty-first-century homes are not the center of productivity they once were, it should still be true of every woman who fears the Lord that

> She looks well to the ways of her household
> and does not eat the bread of idleness. (Prov. 31:27)

The alternate rendering, *"keepers at home,"* highlights the importance of preserving and prioritizing our homes. As we have seen, that doesn't necessarily mean it's the only or number one priority at all times. But he is saying to women, "Don't drop the ball!"

The apostle's instruction affirms that the work we do at home matters—not just to ourselves and our families, but to the wider community and to the cause of the gospel. Paul is not calling us just to feather our own nests and make ourselves comfy. As my friend Carolyn McCulley reminds us, our work at home is "a co-labor of love with our Creator *for the benefit of others.*"[4]

Even if our culture does not validate the significance of that work, God values it. And even though we may not be rewarded tangibly for it, God will reward our labors. The work we do in our homes has eternal value. So Paul is being strategic for the gospel when he says to women, "Don't fumble what matters in eternity."

This passage also implies that "young women"—that is, women in the child-bearing, child-rearing season of life—have a distinct responsibility to prioritize their homes and children. This is not to say that home and children do not matter in other seasons or that childless or unmarried women do not need to be concerned about their homes. But no woman (or man) has unlimited bandwidth; we all have to make choices. And younger women with children need to be particularly careful that other activities—even good ones—don't cause them to neglect their children and homes.

It seems to be the norm rather than the exception today for women to be chronically overwhelmed from overcrowded, margin-less schedules. Now, being busy isn't necessarily a bad thing—Jesus Himself worked hard and had some filled-to-the brim days. But in my personal experience, much of the stress and strain are the result of attempting to take on activities and responsibilities that compete with my core commitments and my priorities for that season (or that moment). Periodically we need to push the pause button and ask ourselves if some of those activities (jobs, hobbies, even ministry involvements) would be better postponed for another time when we can undertake them without violating other God-given responsibilities.

As the Scripture reminds us, "For everything there is a season, and a time for every matter under heaven" (Eccl. 3:1).

A Matter of Priority

So, does having a heart for home mean every woman needs to grind her own wheat and bake her own bread? Line her cellar with canned fruit and vegetables from her (organic) garden? Knit a quilt for her husband's easy chair? Put wall art decals on the walls of her children's bedrooms?

I've heard women mock and exaggerate such stereotypical "homemaking" activities as a way of dismissing—and thereby *missing*—the whole point.

What matters—particularly for married women and moms—is not what a woman's home looks like or what she does there, but whether she is giving it the appropriate *priority*. Is she fulfilling her God-given calling in her home and in the lives of her husband and children? Is she giving them more than just the leftovers of her time and attention? Is she investing her heart and best efforts in these priceless lives? Is she being diligent, productive, and intentional in the care and oversight of her home and in meeting her family's needs?

There is no one-size-fits-all, cookie-cutter approach to how this works. Having a heart for home will look different for different women, depending on the configuration and particular circumstances of their family and what best serves their needs at any given time.

I have friends and acquaintances who have chosen to be full-time "workers at home," at least while they are rearing children. This choice often requires significant sacrifice, but those who are willing and able to make it stand to gain many potential benefits and blessings.

Recently I had a spellbinding conversation with "Anna"—a bright, lovely twenty-two-year-old woman who reflected on her upbringing. Her mother, a gym teacher and basketball coach, returned home when God blessed her and her husband with children. "We didn't have cable TV and didn't go out to eat a lot," this daughter told me, "but we didn't suffer. I believe it was better for us this way." She shared how her mom had been involved in various types of activities, relationships, and ministries in the neighborhood and at church.

Now that the children are grown, Anna's mother considered going back to work outside the home. But as she prayed about this option, she realized it would limit her flexibility and availability. Now she is free to help her aging parents with unexpected medical needs that are beginning to arise. She leads Bible studies, helps neighbors with gardening, and is on call for blessing those around her in many practical ways.

I don't know this mom, but I see her reflection in her daughter—a deeply caring young woman who loves and serves the Lord and others, and hopes to follow in her mom's steps. And I see great value in Anna's mother's decision to dedicate her primary attention and effort to being a "keeper/worker at home." Such a choice should be supported and affirmed. Many women like her, while forgoing paid employment, engage in work that is nevertheless of great eternal value for the Kingdom—work such as caring for children, ministering to the poor, sick, and needy, extending hospitality, and volunteering in schools and at church.

Having said that, I could also introduce you to a number of other women whose hearts are no less at home, but who have chosen—for a variety of reasons—to work outside the home. Some hold down regular nine-to-five jobs. Others have found different ways to contribute to their family's financial well-being. I'm thinking of

- moms who run a small cleaning business in which they can involve their kids
- women who work from their home to give piano lessons, alter clothes, provide accounting services, or offer daycare
- a single mom who works tirelessly to support herself and her teen kids, but whose business allows her to set her own schedule so she can be with her kids as much as possible (From the time her husband left her, she has lived in an apartment in the home of close family members, providing an extra layer of "family" for her children.)
- a colleague whose husband was diagnosed with severe early-onset dementia while still in his forties and who juggles his care with freelance contract work to meet their financial needs
- women who have worked hard to provide for their family during their husbands' incarcerations while courageously striving to shepherd their kids' hearts in the absence of a dad in the home
- women who work alongside their husbands in family businesses, arranging their schedules to be able to tend to the needs of children, grandchildren, and elderly parents
- two nurses who work two or three shifts per week and swap childcare with each other

Is life a juggling act for these women? Absolutely. Do they sometimes lose their balance and feel their priorities are out of whack? No doubt. But each one has a heart for home. And each one is asking the Lord for wisdom to make the choices that would best honor Him in their current circumstances.

I realize there are many women who feel they don't have an option about whether to work outside their home or how to arrange that work. We live in a broken world, so the picture is not always ideal and the choices are not always easy. We are not called to determine or legislate specific life/family/work choices for others. But we cannot escape the fact that we are called to have a heart for our homes—to recognize the priceless value and the strategic importance of the eternal investments that are being made there.

We will diminish the impact of our ministry as believers if we allow home to become an afterthought.

Again, how this all plays out may change according to the different phases and changes of a woman's life. There may be seasons when a woman can have extensive pursuits outside her home without neglecting the priority of her home. Being a "keeper at home" looks different for me today than it did during my decades as a single woman. It will look different for a mom with preschoolers than it does for an empty nester or an older widow. Our responsibilities may change, our control over our time and schedule may be greater or less than what we've had in other seasons.

But no matter what our circumstances or season of life, home still matters for us women. And we will diminish the impact of our ministry as believers if we allow home to become an afterthought or resist God's call to be workers/keepers at home.

Resisting the Call of Home

I don't believe it's any coincidence that the adulterous woman in Proverbs 7 is described as "wayward; her feet do not stay at home" (v. 11). By neglecting the God-given priority of her marriage and home, she becomes more vulnerable to temptation and to dishonoring the Lord.

That was the case with a friend whose disdain for her home nearly cost her a marriage. In an email exchange, "Ellen" shared with me that her views on "homemaking" had been skewed from the time she was a child:

> The very mention of the word "domesticity" used to practically make me shiver. It spelled out a life of boredom, drudgery, thanklessness, and even slavery. It certainly wasn't anything I ever envisioned myself doing, much less desiring.
>
> Even though my mother and both grandmothers were "at home" mothers, I never witnessed the joy and freedom this calling can be for a woman. What I recall seeing was service done out of duty, not delighting in serving. My mother was a horrible housekeeper—cleaning only when the dirt was unbearable, washing the dirty dishes only when they outnumbered the clean ones, and doing the laundry only when we ran out of clean clothes. . . .
>
> When "Joe" and I married, I still had all of this damaged thinking inside me. . . . I didn't enjoy serving him or caring for our home. I do remember trying, but it was only out of a sense of duty, rather than with a heart that delighted to serve the Lord and bless my husband.

When her daughter was around seven, Ellen was asked if she'd be interested in helping out part time at a local ministry. Eager to escape the frustration she experienced at home and to find another outlet for her energies, she quickly accepted the opportunity. This was going to be great.

"I instantly fell in love with my job," she wrote. "I only worked while my daughter was in school, so the hours were perfect. But there were times when I actually resented having to stop work to go pick her up or having to stay home with her when she was sick."

As time went by and her daughter grew into young adulthood, "the ministry became my life," she wrote. "I stayed longer and longer hours, even came in on my days off. I gave no real thought to spending time with my husband, to helping out with meal preparation or laundry. He did all of that himself. And I thought I was doing exactly what I needed to be doing . . . what I *loved* doing."

Do you sense the seduction here? Have you felt it yourself? Can you see the justifications that led Ellen to overlook the needs of her husband and child, to ignore the warning signs that these relationships were deteriorating, while focusing the bulk of her attention onto other tasks and relationships she enjoyed more—and wrapping it all in the guise of Christian service?

The day would come when my friend's mild-mannered, go-with-the-flow husband would say he'd had enough. She wrote:

> Joe got tired of being used, abused, and neglected,
> and found someone who—at the time anyway—
> seemed to enjoy pleasing him and wanted to be with
> him, and he liked it.

And just like that, Joe was gone—into the arms of another woman. Of course, Ellen was devastated. She had thought she was doing what God wanted. And in the eyes of most outsiders, she was the "innocent party" in this broken marriage. But over the next several months, her eyes began to be opened to ways she had torn down her home, rather than building it up (Prov. 14:1). Without excusing her husband's sinful choices, she began to accept responsibility for how she had devalued and neglected her husband, daughter, and home.

Through a miraculous work of the Spirit in both their hearts, Joe and Ellen ultimately reconciled. God gave them both the gift of repentance and a whole new set of priorities. They began in their forties to rebuild the relationship and home God had intended for them to establish and enjoy years earlier.

But just think what they missed during all those years when both their hearts were far from home.

At the heart of the cross is the Lord Jesus opening His arms wide and saying, "I want you to come Home with me." When we cultivate homes where others can grow and be nurtured, we put the heart and character of God on display.

Don't miss the message here. The point of Ellen's story isn't the importance of cooking and washing clothes for the family. It's not a warning against ever being involved in work or ministry outside the home. It's just a reminder that in God's economy, something vital is lost when we neglect our calling at home.

Ellen's disdain for the practical aspects of homemaking was symptomatic of deeper heart issues. She needed to come home to God's heart and to let Him give her a vision for how she could serve Him and others through being a keeper at home.

As, in the end, do we all.

A Grand and Glorious Goal

Have you ever thought about the fact that God Himself is a homemaker? Psalm 68:5–6 calls Him the "Father of the fatherless and protector of widows," the One who "settles the solitary in a home." Psalm 113:9 expands on that theme, reminding us that God

> gives the barren woman a home,
>   making her the joyous mother of children.

Jesus, too, is a homemaker. "I go to prepare a place for you," He said to His disciples on the eve of His betrayal. "I will come again and receive you to Myself, that where I am, there you may be also" (John 14:2–3 NASB).

At the heart of the gospel, at the heart of the cross, is the Lord Jesus opening His arms wide and saying, "I want you to come Home with me."

And when we cultivate homes where others can grow and be nurtured, where they feel welcomed, loved, and cared for, we put the heart and character of God on display.

When we bring order from the chaos of scattered toys and pantry shelves, or when we brighten a drab corner of the room with a spray of flowers or a new color accent, we reflect the One who fashioned the world out of a formless void. We point others to the Creator, giving those who live with or visit us a tangible glimpse of His beauty.

When we prepare tasty, nutritious meals for our families, we point them to the One who feeds those who are hungry and satisfies weary and thirsty souls. We stimulate their appetite not only for their favorite dishes and desserts, but also for the One who provides all things for them to enjoy.

When we make sure that children's closets and dressers contain clothing that fits them well and accommodates their needs, we cast a vision of God's faithfulness—how He not only meets our physical needs, but also clothes us in His righteousness.

This connection may not be immediately obvious to our families. We might not be consciously aware of it either. But what God can do in the hearts of our husbands and children and even housemates, working through the orderly, graceful, creative, muscular labors of our homemaking, is far more significant than what appears on the surface.

The welcoming atmosphere we provide for our family and friends, the errands we run, the outings we plan, the care we provide in times of illness, and the efforts we take to promote wellness—each of these daily actions and a thousand others, reveals in miniature an aspect of God's nature. The often tedious and mundane tasks of homemaking become acts of worship, our ordinary movements works of art.

This is the goal of all our "working" and "keeping" at home—the previews of heaven we're able to provide to our husbands, our children, our neighbors and roommates and guests. With every act of planning and nurturing, we demonstrate realities that are supreme and ultimate. We create a taste for things above. Just as Jesus prefaced His promise of a heavenly home by advertising it as a way for our "hearts" not to "be troubled" (John 14:1), so our efforts in creating a pleasant home environment can bring peace to those who live or visit there, even as they anticipate their eternal home in heaven.

My friend Jani Ortlund captures this vision:

> Our homes, imperfect as they are, should be a reflection of our eternal home, where troubled souls find peace, weary hearts find rest, hungry bodies find refreshment, lonely pilgrims find communion, and wounded spirits find compassion.[5]

It's no insignificant calling, this ministry of homemaking.

And no, I'm not trying to glamorize the job of scrubbing tile grout with a toothbrush or wresting a twelve-pound roast from its bloody packaging or trying to select one of the half-dozen varieties of Drano in the plumbing aisle. I'm not sure *anything* could glamorize tasks like that! In my experience, just about any job, no matter how impressive its title, requires a measure of grunt work, and housework is no exception. Nevertheless, the tasks involved in being a "keeper at home" (grunt work included!) provide important opportunities to invite heaven's realities into the lives of those you care about most.

The "excellent wife" described in Proverbs 31 is perhaps the best known biblical example of a woman creating such a taste of heaven in her home. And she's pretty impressive—rising before dawn to provide food for her household, equipping her husband and children with what they need, modeling diligence and good planning, preparing her family for the inevitabilities of winter. In summary, "she looks well to the ways of her household and does not eat the bread of idleness" (v. 27).

This woman is servant-hearted and conscientiously cares for the practical needs of her family and home. It doesn't hurt—it *helps*—that she is also financially savvy and has a good business head on her shoulders. And when all is said and done, her life shines a spotlight on the God she fears and loves.

My own mother embodied this ideal in many ways. She and my dad were not only new parents when I arrived as their first child (nine months and four days after their wedding!); they were also relatively new believers. They had a lot of learning to do. But the Lord gave them wisdom and grace as they sought Him.

There would be seven of us children altogether—the first six born within their first five years of marriage. So the task of planning and managing and corralling the hubbub of life and ministry in the DeMoss house was not for the fainthearted. And yet my mother oversaw all this and more with remarkable grace. She served her family and her Savior through her devotion to our home. And countless people found Jesus in that home, having been extended the gracious hospitality and gospel witness my parents offered.

My mother worked hard to create an atmosphere in our home that reflected God's beauty, His order, and His merciful, welcoming heart. In so doing, she gave our hearts a taste for heaven.

That's what can happen when women devote themselves to their marriages and families and homes. That's the kind of impact we can generate when our lives reflect the importance and value of home.

Bring It Home

"But my mother didn't teach me these things," I've heard young women lament. "I don't know how to do a lot of that stuff." Yes, and much to our bewildered surprise, no training manual arrives in the mail as a twenty-first birthday present, suddenly granting us the domestic knowledge that women of this age group are somehow supposed to possess.

That's precisely why Paul wisely delegated this "working at home" instruction to older women with years of home experience. Such mentors can come alongside younger women and offer practical lessons for running a household and, more important, transforming a house into a haven of peace, contentment, and joy, and a base of operations for spiritual growth and fruitfulness.

In the hands of such a mentor, a young wife may learn that by working to keep her house orderly, she introduces an ease into the atmosphere of her home that blesses her and others who live there.

Through the gentle input of a veteran mom, a young mother who finds herself slipping downward from overwhelmed to discouraged to depressed to nearly nonfunctional can rebuild her shaky confidence. She discovers how to serve family without being swallowed up by chaos and unrealistic expectations.

Under the tutelage of an encouraging mentor, a college girl can begin seeing her apartment or dorm room as a place of potential beauty and Christian hospitality rather than simply a crash site or a glorified laundry hamper.

Surely this is what Paul was imagining when he instructed older women to take a personal interest in their younger sisters and daughters in the faith. He wanted to see the transfer of both life skills and spiritual perspective across the generations. He wanted to open new gateways of opportunity where the gospel could enter in and take hold. He wanted to see the church thrive and bear witness to the strength and unity that exist when God's people are running together in the challenging race of life. And in few (if any) places does this Titus 2 dynamic produce a more lasting impact than when applied to homes and family relationships.

Having been single for so many years, I want to add that within the context of the family of God, the borders of "home" include more (though not less) than biological family members. This means any and all of us can share in the responsibilities and rewards of making and keeping a home.

More times than I can count, I have experienced the joy of being invited into others' homes and finding there the gifts of friendship, grace, peace, encouragement, nourishment for my body and soul, and loads of laughter. I have found sweet consolation and prayer in the living room of a friend when I was disheartened or carrying a burden too great to bear alone. I have received wise counsel from godly mentors. I have found family.

I have also had the great joy of opening my heart and home to others—for most of my life, as a single woman:

- making pumpkin pies or decorating gingerbread houses in my kitchen with children whose parents were out on a date
- ordering pizza for a spontaneous gathering of a few close families
- sitting on a sofa listening to a woman pour out her heart about a secret sin she'd never shared with anyone else
- weeping and kneeling together with a couple whose marriage had been ravaged by infidelity
- hosting weekly Bible studies with coffee and dessert
- hosting wedding receptions in the backyard

- having a houseful (and I mean *full*) to ring in the New Year with fellowship, sharing, praise, and prayer
- opening my home for a season to a newlywed couple or a missionary family on furlough or an older couple whose A/C had gone out in the middle of July

Just thinking about what has amounted to hundreds of such occasions over the years brings a smile to my face.

Has it sometimes meant extra stress, weariness, and expense?

For sure.

Does all the activity and interaction sometimes feel overwhelming for this introvert?

No question.

Have I at times resented the messes made by others and the wear and tear on my "stuff"?

Truth be told, yes.

But has it been worth it?

A thousand times, yes!

This is where deep, rich friendships have been forged. This is where lives—both mine and my guests'—have been molded. This is where I have acquired "adopted" parents, siblings, children, and grandchildren. This is where we have grown, shared, wept, repented, given and received grace, and rejoiced as we celebrated Christ together.

At home.

Something sanctifying occurs when we're fulfilling the tasks God has given us for whatever season of life we're living. Our minds are protected from deception, our hearts from distraction, and our feet from wandering when we are focusing on the places and roles He has assigned to us.

When disorganized chaos is the norm, when too many irons are in too many fires, when we're constantly running on fumes, chronically frustrated and short-tempered, something's out of whack with our priorities. We've all been there. But we can't continue that way indefinitely and expect to stay sane and spiritually strong.

The apostle Paul could've told us that years ago.

In fact, he *did* tell us that!

So *older woman,* it's time to put to good use all that hard-earned wisdom and experience you've gained by walking through those challenging seasons. Take a younger woman by the hand; gently help her sort through the many competing demands she faces; help her see the value of cultivating a heart for home. And when she feels overwhelmed or like a failure, help her fix her eyes on Christ and encourage her to listen for His voice through the din. Be willing to roll up your sleeves and provide hands-on coaching for the practical skills she needs to build a home that honors the Lord. Remind her that her endless, tiresome labors in her home really do matter. And give her a vision for how what she is doing can give others a taste of heaven.

Rather than looking wistfully at how your life may look different in a different season, embrace your current season and calling as a gift from God.

And *younger woman*, thank God for that woman who has been further down the road than you have. Let God use her to encourage and support and train you—and learn well, because sooner than you think, it'll be your turn to take a younger woman under your wing and help her cultivate a heart for home. In the meantime, rather than looking wistfully at how your life may look different in a different season, embrace your current season and calling as a gift from God.

That's how we *all* come home to what matters.

Making It Personal

Older women

1. Being a keeper/worker at home looks different in different seasons of life. What does it look like for you in this season? What was it like for you in earlier years?
2. What insights and practical skills have you learned in managing your home that you could share with a younger woman to encourage her in making her home a place of fruitful labor and ministry?
3. Ask the Lord to put a younger woman on your heart who needs and desires encouragement, training, or practical help on the home front. Ask Him to make you alert and responsive to opportunities to serve in this way.

Younger women

1. What are some ways the gospel and the heart of Christ could be put on display through your heart for home?
2. Godly homemaking isn't about glamorizing mundane tasks, but rather taking advantage of every opportunity to "invite heaven's realities" into the lives of your loved ones. What do you see in Proverbs 31:10–31 that might help you carry out your own daily tasks to the glory of God?
3. In what area could you use some encouragement, training, or practical help from an older woman to be a more effective keeper/worker at home? Ask the Lord to direct you to an older woman who is willing and able to invest in this way.

Teach what accords with sound doctrine.

Older men are to be sober-minded, dignified, self-controlled,
sound in faith, in love, and in steadfastness.

Older women likewise are to be reverent in behavior,
not slanderers or slaves to much wine.

They are to teach what is good,
and so train the young women
to love their husbands and children,
to be self-controlled,
pure,
working at home,
kind,
and submissive to their own husbands,
that the word of God may not be reviled.

**. . . so that in everything they may adorn
the doctrine of God our Savior.**

TITUS 2:1–5, 10

CHAPTER 11

Need Help Lovin' That Man

Training Our Hearts for Relationship

Love through me, Love of God,
There is no love in me;
O Fire of love, light Thou the love
That burns perpetually.
AMY CARMICHAEL

WHAT IN THE WORLD HAVE I DONE?

Robert and I had been married for less than a month when that thought flooded forcefully into my mind. A series of circumstances and mishaps shortly following our wedding had taken their toll. I'll spare you a lot of the details. But to give you an idea . . . a water disaster in our home required replacing the wood floors on the first story and left us living and working virtually knee to knee in a tiny study for three weeks. (Did I mention I caused the flood?) That drama was compounded by misfiring relationally with some family members. And then there was the matter of serious sleep deprivation. (Let's just say sharing a bed after all those years of sleeping alone was a major adjustment for me.)

Anyway, in a panic-inducing moment, this man sleeping next to me in the bed—this amazing man who adored me and whom I adored—suddenly seemed like a total stranger. I found myself struggling to rein in my rogue emotions and wondering how we would ever build a loving, intimate marriage.

When I first led women through a study of Titus 2 many years ago, I was a single woman. Such thoughts and feelings—which I'm pretty sure most women who have ever been married have experienced at some point—were as yet unfamiliar to me.

Today, as I write this chapter, Robert and I have been married for just about ten months. We weathered that rough patch early on (thanks in large measure to my tender, humble, grace-filled husband) and came out the better for it. So I find myself looking at the subject of marriage with fresh eyes. For sure, I'm eager to learn more about what it means to love my husband well. (Robert says he loves living with a woman who is writing a chapter on how to love one's husband!)

And yes, loving husbands is right at the top of the list of what Titus 2 instructs older women to teach young women (v. 4). This is a vital way that married women and mothers live out their commitment to sound doctrine. This is how they adorn the gospel.

You and I may have vast knowledge of the Bible. We may have great gifts in teaching, leading, organizing, or serving. We may be star performers in our workplace and active in all kinds of church work and social concerns. But none of those things is worth much if we fail to love those in our own homes.

Radiant brides on their way to the altar can't imagine that the love they feel at that moment could ever fizzle out. So how is it that so many women who once gazed at their Prince Charming with stars in their eyes now look at him with eyes of hurt, hardness, and even hatred? What happens? Well, *life* happens. Problems and pressures and disappointments happen. Sin happens. No marriage is exempt.

And that's why young women need to be trained to "love their husbands."

But shouldn't love be a natural response? It should. But it isn't always—for a number of reasons. Sin kills love in marriages. Selfishness and pride kill love. And persisting in love beyond those other natural but deadly tendencies does *not* come naturally. By God's grace, however, and with the help and wisdom of spiritual mothers in the faith, it *can* be learned.

And keep in mind that this specific kind of training isn't just for married women. As one who was single for many years, I can testify to its value for *single women*. What a gift for those who contemplate future marriage to glean insight from women who've steered successfully through the marital rapids. And even those who never marry or don't expect to can learn how to develop appropriate relationships with men and how to bless and support the marriages of their friends and family.

Divorcees also need this kind of loving friendship as they seek to recover from the pain of dashed dreams and to be restored to a place of health and wholeness. Then, having been recipients of God's grace, they can become instruments of grace in others' lives. The presence of divorce in a woman's story need not disqualify her from training other women in loving their husbands. In fact, what the Lord has taught her as she hiked some of life's most treacherous paths can be invaluable in the lives of younger women who want a marriage that goes the distance and reflects the covenant-keeping love of Christ.

So though I speak directly in this chapter to married women, I hope those who don't have husbands will stay with me too. Because love is important to all of us—and all of us can use training in the dynamics of healing, encouraging, redemptive love.

Love That Feels Like Love

Markers on the graves of women from the New Testament era were occasionally known to bear the simple inscription *philandros* (husband lover) or *philoteknos* (child lover)—the same words Paul uses in Titus 2:4. The chief characteristic that marked these women's lives became the primary way of remembering them in death.[1]

They loved their husbands.

They loved their children.

And whether we're talking about then or now, it takes more than the heart palpitations of young love to enable a wife to love her husband for a lifetime. That kind of love requires intentional, woman-to-woman discipleship and mentoring.

"Train" them, Paul said, "to love."

This word—*philandros*—doesn't carry with it the physical, romantic, sexual aspect of love that is often so front and center in today's marital expectations. Romantic love is certainly an important aspect of the marriage bond, and the Bible does speak quite clearly, even quite graphically in spots (Song of Solomon, most notably), about the joys of sexual union. But that's not the emphasis Paul intended when he delivered his Titus 2 directive on love and marriage. His language instead conveys the idea of being a friend to our husbands, being fond of them, acting affectionately toward them, treating them with our utmost devotion.

Men long for respect and affection from their wives at least as much as they crave sexual expressions of love.

Enjoying them.

Finding pleasure in their company.

Liking them.

Loving them.

In many ways, this kind of love requires more effort and energy than other kinds of love. And it's important for wives to learn to love their husbands this way because of how men's hearts are fashioned by God. Here's something I've heard for years and am now learning first-hand to be true: Men long for respect and affection from their wives at least as much as they crave sexual expressions of love.

Wanting to test this premise, I once sent out an email to a few dozen male friends and coworkers, asking for their thoughts about how wives could bless and encourage their husbands. Some of these guys I knew to be soft-spoken individuals, men of few words. But not this time. This particular subject was one that drew each of them out.

Here are some of the common themes I heard from these men:

- They wanted their wives to express encouragement and belief in them and to compliment them for doing a good job, not just to consider it something that good husbands are supposed to do anyway.
- They wanted to be listened to long enough to get their full opinions out there before being critiqued.
- They wanted to be asked what they thought and to be noticed and thanked.
- When they messed something up or missed a relational cue, they wanted to know they would be met with grace instead of a lecture.

This last item seemed to be especially important to the men I surveyed. It wasn't that they wished to avoid responsibility for their actions or inactions. But a wife's forgiveness and mercy acted like rocket fuel, driving them to do differently the next time. Negative approaches like whining, rejecting, and pushing away just made it that much harder for husbands to keep trying to be the man they needed to be. The man they *wanted* to be.

The results of this informal poll reminded me that men flourish in an atmosphere of affirmation, encouragement, and respect. That's what motivates them to bless and serve their families. That's what feels like love to them.

Love for a Purpose

I've met many wives who are extremely responsible women. They serve their husbands faithfully and dutifully. But I wonder sometimes if these women really *like* the men they married. They don't seem to enjoy them. Their attitudes and their words don't indicate affection or fondness for them.

And I wonder what the church is missing by having so many marriages where this is the case. Because the most important objective behind befriending and thinking highly of one's husband is not simply to improve his self-esteem or free him from the fear of another rebuke. Rather, it's to move the marriage in the direction of its grander purpose. For loving our husbands well does more to honor Christ and make the gospel attractive than all our other words and actions combined, without that love.

Charles Spurgeon, the great British preacher of the nineteenth century, enjoyed a legendary love relationship with his wife, Susannah, or Susie, as he fondly called her. Both had major health issues—Charles suffering from chronic gout and seasons of deep depression, and Susannah unable to leave the house for fifteen years due to physical illness. Yet their love grew and remained strong even through intense trials and the challenges of a very public ministry. Their tender expressions of love and dedication, written to and about each other, are a joy to read. Spurgeon once wrote to Susie, for example:

> My Own Dear one—None know how grateful I am to God for you. In all I have ever done for Him, you have a large share. For in making me so happy you have

> fitted me for service. . . . I have served the Lord far more, and never less, for your sweet companionship. The Lord God Almighty bless you now and forever![2]

Susannah, in turn, wrote of her deep love for her husband when she compiled his diary and letters (published as *C. H. Spurgeon's Autobiography* after his death):

> I deemed it my joy and privilege to be ever at his side, accompanying him on many of his preaching journeys, nursing him in his occasional illnesses,—his delighted companion during his holiday trips, always watching over and tending him with the enthusiasm and sympathy which my great love for him inspired.[3]

Such beautiful, affectionate marriages—at least in real life—don't just *happen*. They grow as two people purpose, as Charles and Susannah Spurgeon did, to live for each other and to dedicate themselves together to a cause greater than themselves.

The greatest blessings of marriage, in other words, come as a by-product of seeking something else.

A Goal for Marriage

I've often found myself in a store searching in vain for a wedding or anniversary card that expresses what I really want to say. At times, I've been tempted to start a whole new line of cards for such occasions. It's not that the sentiments expressed are *wrong*. It's more a matter of what they leave out.

Almost invariably, you see, the focus seems to be on happiness, romance, and blessings for the couple. But when's the last time you saw a wedding or anniversary card that said anything about a mission or purpose in marriage bigger than the couple themselves?

A lifetime of happiness and smiles and holding hands and romantic moments is far too small a goal. Marriage is designed to display to the world in Technicolor the covenant-keeping character and faithfulness of God.

Now, don't get me wrong. I want to experience happiness, romance, and blessings in my marriage, and I desire the same for all my married friends. But a lifetime of happiness and smiles and holding hands and romantic moments is far too small a goal. What I most want for my married friends—and for Robert and me—is a life defined by God's vastly superior blessings and grand redemptive purposes.

Marriage, at its heart, is a sacred covenant between a man and a woman, designed to display to the world in Technicolor the covenant-keeping character and faithfulness of God Himself. Just as the Bible is the story of the heavenly Bridegroom faithfully seeking out and staying true to His chosen Bride, human marriage is a story intended to draw people toward the gospel, showing them the love of God through two imperfect individuals whose lives become one in Him and who are devoted to one another for better or for worse . . . for life.

What Your Marriage Can Be

Does that sound like too lofty a goal—if not for marriage in general, at least for your marriage in particular? As you look at the two people whose faces appear in your wedding photos—especially the way you look today, having dealt with your share of differences and difficulties—you may calculate your chances of approaching this marriage ideal as somewhere between slim and none.

And yet that's not the way Bible math operates—because things are different when God is part of the equation.

Regardless of its weaknesses and challenges, your marriage can be a beacon of gospel truth and hope to your children, your grandchildren, your neighbors, your extended family, and to all who know you.

And here's the most surprising part: *this noble outcome does not depend on your husband's getting his act together*.

You might want to pause and read that sentence one more time.

It's hard to believe, I know, but it's true.

As a wife, you have the ability to demonstrate covenant love in your daily interactions with your mate—regardless of what he does or doesn't do to meet your needs.

You can learn to love your husband no matter how he acts, what he says, what he does.

"But that's not fair!" you may respond. "Doesn't he need to do anything? Who could live with such a one-sided relationship?"

Sure, I understand that marriage requires cooperation and effort from both mates. I realize that one partner's failure or indifference leaves an inevitable residue on the other. In fact, we could spend a lot of time addressing the unloving ways some men treat their wives, how they fail in their commitment to their marriage, and how that can affect whole generations coming behind them. If you identify with that storyline, it may feel unfair and insensitive not to address men as well as women in a chapter on loving your spouse.

But it's just us women having this conversation. And the truth is, regardless of what our men *should* do, we cannot *make* them do it. It simply isn't helpful—and can actually be harmful to our own hearts—to focus on what we cannot control.

That doesn't mean there's not a respectful, loving, even direct way of stating our opinions and injecting our perspective into matters of disagreement, disappointment, or disobedience on our husband's part. In fact, we can often help our husbands by speaking the truth in a timely way with carefully chosen words. But helping our mate is not the same as trying to change him. That's God's job.

God is powerful enough to speak to your husband's heart, getting through to him in ways you can't, no matter how logical your arguments or how earnest your appeals.

What's your job, then? From a biblical standpoint, your job is to be the person who uniquely completes your husband. To support him. To encourage him. To be a friend to him. To like him.

To love him.

Loving your husband does not mean brushing sinful behavior under the carpet. In fact, that would be unloving.

To love him even when he's hard to love.

Because the truth is, *no* man is always easy to be married to. (No woman is, either!) Your husband is not all *he* wants to be, much less everything *you* may want him to be.

Ruth Bell Graham, the late wife of Billy Graham, understood this. After experiencing the up-close frailties and failings of her husband, Ruth concluded that "it was my job to love Billy, and God's job to change him." Every wife could say the same about her own marriage.

"But what if there's nothing about him to love?" I can hear someone protesting, and I hear the frustration and pain behind the protest. My prayer is that this chapter will encourage you to believe that even in such a case, God can put true love in your heart, enabling you to love as He loved you.

Let me make clear, however, that loving your husband does not mean brushing sinful behavior under the carpet or just holding everything inside when there are issues you and your husband are unable to resolve. In fact, that would be *unloving*. It is appropriate and at times vital for you to confide in a wise, godly older woman or a pastor or counselor who can give you biblical perspective, provide emotional and spiritual support, and help you determine the best course of action. The purpose is not to find someone to take your side against your husband, but to help you discern how to deal with his actions and evaluate your own heart and responses. And if your husband is breaking the law or you or your children are being physically threatened or harmed—hard as it may be, you should contact local civil authorities and ask for their help. According to Scripture, they are "God's servant[s] for your good" (Rom. 13:4).

Even such difficult cases are not beyond God's grace and redemption. They can become opportunities to learn to love the unlovable, as God has loved us. But the truth is, the majority of marriages don't fall into these categories. For most of us, learning to love our husbands is more a matter of addressing petty, everyday sin and selfishness that can drain the love and intimacy from a relationship. And amazing things can happen when we let God's love flow through us.

Your marriage really can be more than it is today. It can be far stronger and more vibrant than the sentimental poetry and soft pastels found on the stock wedding or anniversary card. It can be a living testimony of God's power and grace. That can happen. It can *still* happen. And your part in building what God desires your union to be is to love your man.

To love—and to help others love that way too.

Older woman, here's your chance to do something transformational with those hard-fought lessons you've learned as a wife of many years, to turn them into something other than longstanding grudges to pull out in case you're ever losing an argument. By passing along your firsthand observations and experience to a younger woman (married, soon to be married, or one day hoping to be married), God can use both your good days and your bad days to help create better days ahead for yourself and for someone you care about.

Younger woman, you should crave this kind of input, objectivity, and time-tested wisdom. You will be a better wife to your husband—and understand him better than you ever thought possible—by making use of another woman's experience. Just think of the roadblocks and hurdles you may be able to get past with the coaching and assistance of someone who has walked this path before you.

Practical Training

I enjoyed a memorable visit over lunch one day with three adult sisters and their mother. A number of times during our meal, one or the other's cellphone would buzz. Friends were calling, work was calling, kids were calling. With each call they'd glance down at the phone, note the name on the display, then turn off the sound without interrupting our conversation.

"You know, there's something Mom's always told us," one of the women said as we shared a laugh over how intrusive our phones can sometimes be. "If it's your husband calling, you always take the call."

Others can wait, but he's always first in line.

Now there's a good piece of practical advice from an older woman, a nugget that's easy to grasp and to begin putting into practice. One that's sure to send a message to any husband about his wife's love and respect for him.

And these are the kinds of pearls of wisdom that can be transferred and received as women sit down together, younger and older, asking questions and offering counsel, intent on training and being trained in the fine art of loving a husband.

Just imagine if women were to have these kinds of conversations rather than ones in which they tore their husbands down and commiserated with each others' marital woes. Think how many conflicts could be defused or avoided altogether and how much room women would find for love in their minds and hearts if gripe sessions were replaced with true support and woman-to-woman wisdom.

Such wisdom has been invaluable to me in my somewhat unusual position of being both an older woman and a fairly new wife. For years, I've been encouraging other women to love their husbands well.

Now I'm learning how to love *my* husband well. And I'm being encouraged in that journey by the example of many women I've watched and learned from over the years.

I'd like to pass on a sampling of practical insights I've gleaned from these women, much of which I'm finding to be applicable in my own marriage. If you're an older woman, there probably isn't anything here you haven't heard before. But these are things it's easy for all of us—even those of us who know better—to neglect as life gets busy.

1. Put your relationship with your husband ahead of your relationship with your children.

It's not coincidental that "loving husbands" precedes "loving children" in Titus 2:4. I've seen women get that reversed and end up with a lifeless marriage or no marriage at all.

Of course, children demand a lot of time, attention, and effort. If you're not careful, tending to them can commandeer the bulk of your focus and energy, allowing walls and distance to grow between you and your husband. So in the midst of those exhausting child-rearing seasons—and even as your children become adults—it's important to be intentional about prioritizing your marriage. That means things like

- initiating conversations with your husband about topics other than the kids
- springing for a sitter or trading child care so you and your man can have focused "you and me" time together. (Trust me, this is important to your husband, even if you don't think it's feasible.)
- letting your husband know you're on his side when the kids challenge his instructions or attempt to divide the two of you. (They probably will!)
- honoring your husband when there's a difference of opinion by talking privately with him and keeping a united front before the children.

- setting aside time to pray together and make sure you're on the same page about family issues.

Keeping your marriage strong and thriving is actually one of the best possible gifts you can give your kids—providing them with a secure, stable environment and a model of what healthy love looks like. And if you and your husband keep your hearts connected in those busy seasons, you'll be far more likely to have a solid, enjoyable relationship with him once the kids are out of the nest.

2. Look for ways to keep your relationship fresh and growing.

Daily life can be tedious and mundane. But you will do your marriage a big favor if you look for fresh, creative ways to love your husband, to enjoy him, to be his friend and his lover.

Remember the early days of your relationship?

- You were always looking for opportunities to bless or surprise him with simple acts of kindness.
- If he called at the last minute and said, "Can we go out for dinner tonight?" you probably didn't say, "Do we have to? I'm really tired." More likely you said, "I'd love to!" Then you dropped everything and got freshened up in record time.
- If he bought you something, you probably didn't protest, "We can't afford that!" or "I've already got two of those." Chances are you were delighted and thanked him for his thoughtfulness.
- If he threw his coat on a chair when he came in the house, you didn't huff and puff about his needing to grow up and be more responsible with his belongings. You were glad to hang it up for him without saying a word. So why do you make a big deal about it now?

That's not to say these kinds of issues should never be addressed. But rekindling some of the attitudes and practices you had when your relationship was young can help keep your marriage fresh. So can seeking out ways to enjoy being together, creating memories and staying connected. (Even after many years together, you might be surprised at what else there is to learn about each other.)

So in the midst of the routine and the endless tasks on each of your plates, take time to have fun together. To serve others together. To court one another and be romantic. To be spontaneous and also enjoy making plans for a special occasion. To develop new interests and shared experiences. Here are just a few ideas:

- Ask questions about your husband's day—and listen to the answers.
- Read a book together and share your thoughts.
- Drop your to-do list (and your honey-do list) long enough to snuggle up and watch some football or a movie with him.
- Invest in a pretty new nightie or evening outfit—something you know will please him.
- Text him a love note—or even a joke—in the middle of the day.
- Learn a new skill together (golf? a new language? guitar?).
- Stop what you are doing to wave good-bye or greet him at the door.
- Surprise him with tickets to a concert or event you'll both enjoy.

3. Be a student of your husband. Show interest in the things that interest him.

Robert is a lifelong Chicago Cubs fan. Becoming a Cubs fan myself (which first meant learning the basics of baseball!) has proven to be one practical way for me to love my husband. My interest in the "home team" has given us a new common interest.

Showing interest in Robert's DIY home-construction projects is another way I express my love for him. In fact, Robert is building a deck on our home this week, and I'm taking periodic time-outs from working on this book to ooh and aah over the progress, cheer him on, and replenish cold drinks and snacks. This says to him, *We're in this together. I'm thinking of you. I care about the things you enjoy.*

An important heart principle is at play here. Jesus taught that "where your treasure is, there your heart will be also" (Matt. 6:21). If you invest time, effort, and attention in your job or a hobby, your heart will be drawn in that direction. And when you invest "treasure" in your husband, your heart will be drawn to him. But if you choose to invest in someone else—a guy at work or an old boyfriend on Facebook, for instance—you may soon begin to feel things toward him that you've not felt for your husband in a long time.

It helps to remember that your husband's strengths and his weaknesses are exactly what you need to become the woman God wants you to be. And vice versa.

This is how an affair can begin or you and your husband can simply "drift apart"—because you've been investing your energy outside your marriage. But if you make the deliberate choice to focus your time, attention, and interest in your husband, you'll eventually find your love for him growing.

Choose loving actions toward him, and your heart will follow.

4. Remember that you are both sinners.

It may be tempting sometimes to mentally compare your husband to some other man who seems to be further along in his maturity or faith—or to some imagined, "ideal" husband. You convince yourself that your life would be so much easier if you were married to someone like that. But you're not. He's not married to a perfect woman either.

Both of you are flesh-and-blood humans with the capacity for love, hate, support, and betrayal. Both of you make mistakes, sometimes big ones. Both of you need daily doses of grace just to get through the day. And the more you can keep that in mind, the freer you will both be to grow in love for one another. The truth is, even the best marriage involves two sinners perpetually humbling themselves, getting to Christ, and receiving and dispensing grace.

Charles Spurgeon's words can be aptly applied to marriage:

> He who grows in grace remembers that he is but dust, and he therefore does not expect his fellow Christians to be anything more; he overlooks ten thousand of their faults, because he knows his God overlooks twenty thousand in his own case. He does not expect perfection in the creature, and, therefore, he is not disappointed when he does not find it.[4]

Growing in grace as husband and wife involves a lot of acceptance and a lot of "I'm sorry; I was wrong." It means assuming the best of each other and not judging motives, trying to understand, not insisting on perfection. It also means extending mercy and forgiveness when you let each other down or hurt each other in small ways or big ones. (I promise it will happen—then happen again.) But it helps to remember that your husband's strengths *and* his weaknesses are exactly what you need to become the woman God wants you to be. And vice versa.

And once again, maintaining this awareness is not dependent on how well your husband accepts and extends grace to you. It's a matter of relying on God to give grace to both of you as you persevere in learning more and more about love.

When you and I stand before the Lord in eternity, He will not ask us: What were your husband's failures and flaws? Did he love you well?

But in light of Titus 2, He may well ask: How well did you love your husband?

"Root, Root, Root for the Home Team!"

I don't want to leave the impression that I do any of this perfectly. Not by a long shot. In the short time Robert and I have been married, I have learned that my attitudes, words, and behavior have a profound effect on this man's heart. I have the ability to make him feel encouraged and cherished. But I also have the ability—more than any other person in his life—to deflate and discourage his spirit.

I am an editor by trade and by natural bent. That means I have spent most of my adult life noticing and trying to correct mistakes. Robert says I can spot an error on a billboard while speeding by at eighty-five miles per hour. My ability to open a three-hundred-page book and spot the solitary typo is legendary. But while that skill is useful when it comes to proofreading, it's not particularly helpful in relationships, least of all in marriage. If I'm not careful, I am prone to notice and point out the one thing that's wrong (in my view) and much slower to identify the ninety-nine things that are right.

On occasion, Robert has said, "I feel like you're editing me." Ouch. I know that in those moments he feels I'm not pulling for him. What he needs in those moments is an encourager, not an editor. So I've made it my prayer and aim to build Robert up and to be a means of grace in his life.

From what I hear from other women, I know I'm not alone in my "editing" tendencies. And I know that focusing on our husband's faults and failures can be highly toxic in a marriage relationship.

Does that mean you should never point out needs in each other's lives? By no means. We all need honest input from those who know us best and can help us see blind spots we may be oblivious to. But our ability to give humble, helpful critique and have it be well-received is in direct proportion to the effort we make to give the gift of encouragement.

Knowing how important (and neglected) this gift is in a marriage, I have often urged wives to take what I call the "30-Day Husband Encouragement Challenge."[5] The challenge has two parts.

First, *for the next thirty days, don't say anything negative about your husband—to him or to anyone else about him.* That doesn't mean he won't *do* anything negative. It doesn't mean there won't be anything you *could* say. It just means you're just not going to say it. You're going to choose not to think about or focus on those things.

Then comes the second part, the positive one, which is equally important:

Every day for the next thirty days, encourage your husband by expressing something you admire or appreciate about him. Say it to him and say it to someone else about him. Tell your children. Tell your mother. Tell *his* mother. Each day think of something good about your husband and tell him about it, then tell someone else.

Now you may be thinking, *I can't think of thirty things I appreciate about my husband!* Well, then, just think of *one* thing and repeat it every day for thirty days!

In the years that I've been offering this challenge, I've seen marriages change in a way that has been nothing short of amazing. Here's just one of thousands of responses I've received from women who have taken this challenge:

> I was at my wits' end with my husband. We have only been married a little over a year and have had some awful knock-down, drag-out verbal fights. It has been a serious struggle to keep from walking out the door and writing off this marriage.
>
> Begrudgingly, I began my campaign of encouragement toward my husband. I started leaving him notes in his truck, in his wallet, on his computer,

> taped to the mirror, but I did it with bitterness, anger, and hate in my heart. Right off the bat, my hard-hearted husband tried squashing my efforts, pouring out anger and frustration with me. I was hurt and about to quit what I'd started, but something made me keep going.
>
> Throughout the day, every time a thought would come to my mind about something we had been fighting about, I began to look for the positive things instead of the negative things and would send him a text or email or leave a note for him.
>
> This has been going on for over a week now. When I come home, the first thing I do is grab him and kiss him rather than just mumbling hello and going and changing my clothes.
>
> Last night my hard-hearted, closed-off, non-communicative husband broke down, opened up, listened instead of barking orders, and sat on the couch with me. He said, "This is the best week I've ever had! To just be here holding my wife in my arms is the best way to end a day!" In just one week, my marriage is on the path to being mended! My husband and I had an absolutely romantic evening together this week that we haven't had since our wedding!

On a scale of one to ten, your relationship with your husband may be at a negative two right now. And this little challenge is probably not going to give your marriage an overhaul overnight. But if you persist for the full thirty days, I believe it will change you. It will give you a different perspective. And in time, as you water the soil of your husband's heart with affirmation, appreciation, and admiration, you may see him change as well. Either way, you can't go wrong.

You and I know women who would give anything just to have a husband to encourage. My mother, widowed at the age of forty, is one of those women. Throughout her married life, she was a wonderful example of what it looks like to love your husband. She was just nineteen when she married my dad (he was thirty-two). And almost from that moment, their lives, hands, and days were filled to the brim—raising a large family, launching a successful business, and being actively involved in many different kinds of ministry. Mother could easily have resented the busyness and the intrusion on their relationship. But she and my dad were in this together. They were friends. They enjoyed each other's company and loved doing life as a team. And the difficult times (devastating business losses, a brain tumor that could have taken her life, a fire that destroyed our home) only drew them closer.

As does every human being, my dad had his share of preferences and habits some women might have allowed to become a source of irritation. But my mother adored him. She admired and affirmed him. She didn't make issues out of things that didn't matter in the big picture. Amazingly, to this day, I don't recall ever hearing my mom say a negative, critical word about my dad.

It's not that she mindlessly agreed with everything he said or did. She is a smart, capable woman with strong views, and my dad solicited and valued her input even when she disagreed with him. But in the course of giving that input, she still showed him honor and respect. And whenever she talked about him to outsiders, she could be counted on to uphold and enhance his reputation.

Just two weeks before my dad died unexpectedly of a heart attack at the age of fifty-three, my mother wrote in a letter to an assistant he had just hired: "After twenty-one years of living with this man, I truly believe I am the most uniquely blessed woman in the world." Her husband knew she felt that way.

I want my husband to know I feel that way about him too.

Building and Rebuilding Love

I'm convinced that a majority of marriages today have settled for far less than what God intends for their relationship. Some women—including those who've been married a long time—have forgotten how to love and respect their husbands. Some never knew how in the first place. Some have become discouraged and just quit trying.

If one of those is you, start by being honest. Don't make excuses, and don't give in to the temptation to deposit all the blame onto your husband. The truth is, even if your husband was wonderful in every respect, you still wouldn't be able to love him the way he needs to be loved apart from God's love flowing through you to him.

Only the grace of God can enable anyone to love another unselfishly over the long haul. We humans just don't have it in us. But the good news is, we *do* have God, and His very essence is love. In fact, as 1 John 4:8 reminds us, "God *is* love." And He is able to infuse His supernatural love into the most love-depleted heart.

A colleague confided in me about a time when her marriage was in crisis:

> I so clearly remember lying in bed next to my husband and praying desperately, "Lord, I've tried, but I just can't love him, at least not right now. I don't even *want* to love him. So you're going to have to do it for me and through me." He did. He gave me the strength and the resolve to act in love even when I didn't feel the least bit loving. And it took a while, but I gradually reached the point where I could back up those actions with loving intentions and, eventually, feelings. In the process, my ability to trust God took a huge jump.

That can be true for you as well—I'm sure of it. Even if the love in your marriage has dwindled into grudging obligation or deteriorated into full-scale resentment and contempt, it can be rekindled. You can *learn* to love again—at the cross. On your knees. With older women coming alongside you to encourage and show you how it's done, and with younger women reminding you of a time when your love for your husband was fresh and pure.

In talking with women who are struggling to persevere in loveless marriages, I have often shared this little-known stanza of a hymn written by Fanny Crosby:

> Down in the human heart, crushed by the tempter,
> Feelings lie buried that grace can restore;
> Touched by a loving heart, wakened by kindness,
> Chords that were broken will vibrate once more.[6]

You may have long ago given up hope of ever experiencing genuine love and affection in your marriage. But the Holy Spirit who lives in you can restore and waken feelings that have been crushed by the tempter. And as you persist in grace, love, and kindness, He can quicken feelings that have long been buried—or perhaps never existed—in your spouse's heart.

That's not to say that if you love your husband well, he will automatically or quickly (or ever) reciprocate. God does not guarantee that your commitment to love your husband will solve all the issues in your marriage. You may have to continue living with unfulfilled longings. (Remember that we will all have unfulfilled longings this side of heaven.) You may need to seek godly counsel from a third party. And in some cases, loving your husband will mean appealing for intervention from the spiritual leaders of your church and/or legal authorities. But regardless of how your husband does or doesn't respond, God will bless your obedience and your faith. By His grace, He can give you

Part of the mystery of marriage is that we and our husbands are one—not only in joys and victories, but also in loss and brokenness.

strength and comfort and even unexplainable joy in the midst of your circumstances.

Every woman possesses the power to tear down her house "with her own hands" (Prov. 14:1), especially if she persists in focusing only on what *her husband* needs to do instead of what *she* needs to do. Whatever your husband's sins or failures may be, your responding to him in harsh, critical, and unloving ways is no less a sin. And even if you don't routinely treat him to a running commentary of his shortcomings—making him feel as though he could never earn your acceptance and approval—your sighs of resigned indifference can be more than enough to erode your relationship.

But the "wisest of women," that same proverb states, "builds her house." And that wise woman can be you. You can learn to love your husband by overlooking minor faults and flaws or matters of personal preference. By refusing to keep score. By relinquishing the right to exact payment for wrongs. By giving him grace instead of giving him grief. By seeking God instead of seeking your own way.

By building—or rebuilding—your house on a foundation of God's unfailing love.

A Lifetime of Love

Part of the mystery of marriage is that we and our husbands are one—one flesh—not only in joys and victories, but also in loss and brokenness.

Even in *his* losses and brokenness.

By being willing to love our husbands within full view of his imperfections, we can become living demonstrations to them of the heart and spirit of Jesus. We can become conduits of grace to someone who can experience it from us as from no other.

This mission of loving our husbands is truly a high and holy calling. As we embrace and fulfill that calling, we not only extend blessing to the men to whom we've joined ourselves by covenant, but we also enter into greater intimacy and oneness with our Savior. By choosing the way of love, we invite the love of Christ to rule in our hearts as well as in our marriage. And in the process, our default responses can be transformed until we actually start enjoying our husbands again.

No one, including God Himself, expects us to be able to love our husbands in the way we've described without help or effort. But He has promised to provide the help we need. And the effort is so worth it. It can make the difference between a satisfying, thriving marriage and one that just barely hangs on.

Ultimately, marriage is about so much more than romance and passion and the discovery of a soul mate. It's about making a covenant commitment to love and then, with God's help and the help of mature women He has placed in our lives for this purpose, getting trained in how to do it. It's about representing the grace of God to our husbands as well as to others who watch our devotion in action.

It's about adorning the doctrine of Christ by giving the world a picture of love that never fails.

Making it Personal

Older women

1. As we get older, it's easy to lose track of why we married our husbands in the first place. If that is true of you, what are some specific things you could do to rekindle and deepen your friendship with the man you married and to enjoy him more?
2. What insights and resources could you offer to a younger woman when she begins to discover her marriage can't survive on just romantic love?
3. What younger woman has God placed in your life who could use some encouragement in loving her husband? Pray about how to reach out to her.

Younger women

1. Can you think of an older Christian couple who models strong loyalty, friendship, and love? As you observe them, what can you learn about how that kind of love is cultivated?
2. Would your husband say you are his encourager or his editor? What are some practical ways you could encourage and affirm him?
3. Is there an older woman who is encouraging and coaching you in your relationship with your husband? If not, ask the Lord to lead you to someone who could offer insight and prayer.

Teach what accords with sound doctrine.

Older men are to be sober-minded, dignified, self-controlled,
sound in faith, in love, and in steadfastness.

Older women likewise are to be reverent in behavior,
not slanderers or slaves to much wine.

They are to teach what is good,
and so train the young women
to love their husbands and children,
to be self-controlled,
pure,
working at home,
kind,
and **submissive to their own husbands,**
that the word of God may not be reviled.

**. . . so that in everything they may adorn
the doctrine of God our Savior.**

TITUS 2:1–5, 10

CHAPTER 12

An Unexpected Blessing

Discovering the Strength and Beauty of Submission

Both women and men get to "play the Jesus role" in marriage—
Jesus in his sacrificial authority,
Jesus in his sacrificial submission.
KATHY KELLER

"I *HATE* THIS BOOK!"

Next in line at the book table, she darted at me waving her copy of my book *Lies Women Believe*. I wasn't sure if she wanted me to sign it or if she wanted to throw it at me.

"Uh . . . okay, well," I stammered. "Tell me what you don't like about it."

"It's that thing about *submission*," she said, going on to declare that she'd never even *heard* of this notion before and that she certainly couldn't buy in to it. *Submission* . . . what in the world?

Our conversation didn't last long. Others were waiting. And believe it or not, standing in the same line was another woman who said essentially the same thing. Of course, they weren't the first (or last) readers to feel this way. But what surprised me about these exchanges was that they took place at an event for women's ministry leaders and Bible study teachers, hosted by a respected evangelical seminary.

Not long after I got back home, I was sitting at dinner with a handful of friends. I wanted to hear their thoughts on the subject, so I motioned to everyone around the table and said, "When you were a young wife, what was your concept of submission? Did you get it?"

These, too, were women I would have expected to be well acquainted with the idea, even as younger women. But they all responded in so many words, "No, I was clueless about submission—what it was, what it meant." One woman said, "My idea of submission was doing what my husband wanted as long as I agreed with it. [Ha-ha!] Otherwise . . ."

Such reactions—from basic misconceptions about what biblical submission means and what it should look like in a marriage, to vehement rejection of the whole concept—are not uncommon today.

And that's yet another reason why Titus 2 training is so needed today.

We focused in the last chapter on the first direct marriage exhortation in Paul's list: "Train the young women to love their husbands" (v. 4). And now we turn to the second: "Train the young women to . . . [be] submissive to their own husbands" (vv. 4–5).

At this point Paul could hardly be more out of sync with our fiercely independent, egalitarian Western world. Bring the subject up in most settings—even among some in the church—and you can expect to have people look at you as if you were an alien from another planet.

The tragic reality of domestic abuse makes the whole idea even more objectionable to many. In fact, it is often asserted that the church's teaching of submission in marriage actually promotes and fosters abuse of women. Those who take this biblical concept seriously are often ridiculed as unenlightened at best or misogynists (woman haters) at worst.

One column I read contends that "the sacred belief of male

headship, held by anyone in a position of authority or influence, poses a danger to human rights."[1] And a chapter I wrote on this subject some years ago elicited this strong reaction from a reader:

> How can you actually believe and print these things? Do you know that men, here in the US and in other nations, use things like this to dominate, beat, and kill their wives?

The whole idea of submission makes some women feel weak, worthless, and vulnerable to controlling or angry men. This is not surprising, when we consider how many women have experienced mistreatment at the hands of male authority figures.

From a human perspective, I get this reaction. To our finite, fallen minds, the whole idea sounds unfair, even preposterous.

The wisdom of God, however, is infinitely higher than human wisdom. He values and esteems many of the things we despise and reject. If we only could grasp His eternal purposes, we would be enthralled with the perfection and splendor of His ways. So when it comes to this (or any other) topic, we need to earnestly seek His wisdom rather than relying on our own limited, flawed perspectives.

And that's my goal in this chapter: to explore God's wisdom in relation to this question of submission in marriage. What does it mean? Why does it matter? How are our lives adorned as we submit to our husbands? How does our submission adorn the doctrine of God?

And by the way, if you're unmarried and perhaps starting to feel left out of these proceedings, please don't check out. As a relatively new wife, I'm so grateful for the opportunities I had as a single woman to cultivate a submissive heart. The principle of submission applies to all of us in one way or another, and understanding it will help you in many different relationships—with parents, children, employees and employers, and church leaders, not to mention a future spouse. It will also help equip you to the train younger women in your life in what it means to submit to their husbands.

Foundational Assumptions

So what are we to make of this *S*-word?

Let's start with two foundational assumptions:

1. Submission was God's idea.

It's not an idea some chauvinistic guys cooked up to suppress women. No, it's built into the original plan of our sovereign Creator, who wove relationships of authority and submission into the very fabric of the universe.

This is how He created everything to operate.

With structure. With order.

In the church. In the workplace. In the courtroom. In the White House.

And yes, in your house.

Not only are God's ways true and right; they are also beautiful and good.

There are those who do theological gymnastics to conclude that the Scripture doesn't actually call wives to submit to their husbands. But a plain reading of the text, both here in Titus 2 and elsewhere in the Scripture (see, for instance, 1 Cor. 11:3, Eph. 5:22–33, Col. 3:18, and 1 Pet. 3:1–6), clearly sets forth the principle of headship and submission in the marriage relationship.

The Bible is the pure, authoritative revelation of God and His will. It is the operator's manual for our lives. We don't get to pick and choose which parts we like. And this is *good news.* For who better knows how life should function than the Creator and Designer of life Himself?

2. God's ways are good.

Not only are God's ways true and right; they are also beautiful and good. He delights in the creatures whom He fashioned with His own hand, into whom He breathed the breath of life. And He wants them to delight in Him and to experience every blessing possible.

Our good, wise, loving God would never ask of us something that is not for our ultimate benefit. If we abandon or reject His good plan, we do so to our own harm, as well as to the harm of others and the gospel itself.

I'm not saying submission is easy. It can be excruciatingly hard.

I'm not saying it comes naturally. It doesn't.

We are all born with a rebel spirit (or, as I sometimes say, in a kickative mood). Apart from having a new spirit imparted by Christ, we all naturally resist yielding to the authority of another—whether divine or human.

But regardless of how we may feel about it at times, biblical submission is a gracious gift from the Lord. A good thing. A beautiful thing. It's a heart attitude and a way of life to be embraced not only for the glory of God, but also for our own blessing and the blessing of others.

In the Beginning

To find the roots of biblical submission, we need to travel back to the garden of Eden, where God first revealed His transcendent principles for the human experience. One of these is the relationship between husband and wife, which like the rest of creation was intended to exhibit God's glory and bring Him the worship and praise He deserves.

Genesis 1 describes the moment when God completed the pinnacle of His creation:

> God created man in His own image . . . *male and female* He created them. . . . And behold, it was very good. (Gen. 1:27, 31 NASB)

Genesis 2 unpacks this further, filling in details of how the woman was made from the man and for the man, then given to the man to complete him and to partner with him in fulfilling God's holy, eternal purposes.

That brings us to Genesis 3, where everything goes awry—including our understanding of submission.

Some theologians believe that submission in marriage is a direct outcome of the Fall, a consequence of the curse of sin that is reversed by the gospel. They base this view on God's prediction to Eve in Genesis 3:16 (NASB), following the forbidden-fruit episode:

> Your desire will be for your husband,
> and he will rule over you.

But by the time these prophetic words were spoken, the divine plan for ordering the universe and human interactions was already in place. God had established the divine arrangement of headship and submission as part of the original created order, *before* the Fall. In God's good, wise plan, the man and the woman were designed for different roles. And through their union they would depict distinct and complementary aspects of the redemption story that unfold throughout history.

Many centuries later, the apostle Paul and other New Testament authors would explicitly confirm this meaning. Some dismiss the New Testament teaching on submission in marriage in Titus 2 and elsewhere as being culturally bound and irrelevant for today's readers, simply an acknowledgment of the cultural norm of the day. These writers, they say, were simply giving women advice on how to live a righteous, holy life within that now-outdated cultural system.

But Paul himself, writing under the inspiration of the Spirit, specifically sets forth the divine order of headship and submission as being timeless and transcultural—the husband-wife relationship patterned after the God-Son relationship and the Christ-man relationship.

> I want you to understand that the head of every man is Christ, the head of a wife is her husband,[2] and the head of Christ is God. (1 Cor. 11:3)

For a wife, submission means accepting God's good order for her life, just as a husband submits himself to God in accepting God's order for his life. And it gives her the privilege of representing the mystery and the beauty of the Son's submission to the Father. For even within the Trinity, we see this paradoxical arrangement—seamless unity with separate roles and different identities, perfect equality with pure submission.

The Father and the Son, we know, are both equally God. And yet the Son chooses to submit Himself to the will of the Father:

> For I have come down from heaven, not to do my own will but the will of him who sent me. (John 6:38)

The submission of Christian wives to their husbands is a powerful and beautiful picture of the Son's submission to His Father and of the church's submission to Christ. These wives, together with husbands who love them selflessly and sacrificially, put the gospel story on vivid and compelling display.

What Submission Is Not

But let's get practical here. What does biblical submission mean in the context of our daily lives, as we wrestle with the inevitable rub of relationships?

I am convinced that much of the resistance to this idea comes from a faulty understanding of its meaning. It's especially important for those of us who are older women to be prepared to deal with the misconceptions that exist around this subject if we want to carry out our mandate to train younger women to be "submissive to their own husbands."

Here are some basics we all need to understand:

1. A wife's submission is not to men in general.

Every person—man or woman, young or old—has relationships that require submission, whether to parents, a boss, civil authorities, or spiritual leaders in the church. And all of us as believers are to have a humble, submissive attitude toward one another in the body of Christ (Eph. 5:21). However, when Scripture instructs wives to submit, it is specifically to "their own husbands," who have been established by God to serve as the head of their wives and to love them and lay down their lives for them.

2. Submission does not mean a wife is inferior to her husband.

Scripture affirms unequivocally that men and women are both created in the image of God and therefore have equal worth. They have equal access to the Father and are equally coheirs with Christ, sharing equally in the Holy Spirit, equally redeemed and baptized into Christ, equally partakers of His spiritual gifts, and equally loved and valued by God.

3. Submission doesn't subject a wife to a life of forced compliance.

The word used in the New Testament for "submission"—referring to the orderly fashion of following a leader—speaks of an act that is voluntary. In a proper understanding of marriage, no husband should ever force his wife to submit to him through coercion or manipulation. Submission is her willing decision not only to follow *him*, but ultimately and supremely to follow in obedience to her Lord.

4. Submission doesn't amount to slavish, groveling subservience.

A wife is not a hired maid. Not an employee. Not a child. Not a second-class citizen who bows at the feet of her superior. Submission is rather a joyful, glad-hearted, intelligent, loving responsiveness to your husband's God-ordained position as your spiritual head (see Eph. 5:22–23). And that headship doesn't mean your husband has absolute authority over you. Husbands are not the supreme authority over their wives. God is. Husbands have been *delegated* authority by God, and they will answer to God for exercising it in a humble, sacrificial, loving way.

5. Submission doesn't minimize a wife into mindlessness.

Being submitted to your husband doesn't doom you to a fate of blind, unquestioning obedience. You still possess valid opinions and the right to express them in a humble, godly way. As your husband's helper, in fact, you would be derelict in your duty not to bring things to his attention that he either doesn't see or doesn't seem to understand.

6. Submission doesn't mean husbands are always right.

Your husband is not God. (You already know that.) He is every inch the sinner you are. (You know that too.) So biblical submission cannot possibly be based on how wise or godly or capable your husband is, nor on whether his style or manner or personality is to your liking. Bottom line—he is not the one who makes this pattern work in marriage. God is. And God is the One to whom you and I are ultimately submitted in our marriages.

7. Submission never requires a wife to follow her husband into sin.

Your ultimate allegiance and loyalty are to Christ. If your husband abuses his God-given authority and requires of you something that is contrary to the Word and will of God, you must obey God rather than your husband.

Whenever women are instructed in Scripture to submit to their husbands, there is a corresponding command for husbands to love and cherish their wives.

However, my observation from listening to many wives in difficult marriages is that often their struggle is with being led in a way they don't prefer to go or just don't think is best, rather than in a way the Bible and conscience forbid. It's important to distinguish between the two in responding to a husband's direction.

8. Finally, a wife's submission never gives license to her husband to abuse her.

Never. Whenever women are instructed in Scripture to submit to their husbands, there is a corresponding command for husbands to love and cherish their wives. There is no possible justification for a husband to abuse his wife, whether in overtly physical or verbal ways or in more "respectable" types of manipulation and intimidation—what one pastor calls "polite abuses."[3]

If you are being abused (or suspect you are being abused), you must get help. There is nothing in the biblical teaching on submission that permits such treatment. If you (or your children) are being physically harmed or threatened, you should get to a safe place and contact both civil and spiritual authorities for protection.

Wherever people abuse the order God has established for any sphere, the problem does not stem from flaws in God's plan, but from humanity's sinful distortions of it. Therefore, the solution to problems that arise when this principle is applied in marriage is not to throw submission out with the bathwater, but rather to align our understanding and practice with what Scripture really says. Because when the system is working according to God's design, blessings flow to us from heaven, revealing to us, in us, and through us the beauty of His character and ways.

The Cost of Submission

That's not to say, however, that biblical submission—properly understood, faithfully followed, not twisted by abuse—comes easy. As we have already seen, it doesn't. Even those who agree with the principle of submission find its practice to be difficult at times.

For proof of its difficulty—if you need any proof—I take you to the epistle of 1 Peter. The prevailing theme of this New Testament letter is how to maintain hope and joyful endurance through suffering. The apostle Peter wrote it to the persecuted early church, urging them to remember Christ's example, to keep their eyes on their coming heavenly reward, and not to be ashamed of their faith even when it seemed they were standing alone amid fiery trials.

This theme of suffering runs through chapters 1 and 2 of 1 Peter. It is also prominent throughout chapter 4 and again in chapter 5. And I don't believe it's an accident that Peter brings up the subject of marriage (in chapter 3) right smack in the middle of these chapters.

Setting up the teaching on marriage, the last paragraph of chapter 2 (vv. 21–25) is a powerful testimony of how Christ submitted Himself to the will of His Father, even when it required suffering. All the while, rather than threatening or retaliating against sinners, Jesus "continued entrusting himself" to God, knowing His wise, loving Father would vindicate Him in the end. He did this all *for us*, leaving us an example, "so that you might follow in his steps." As a result of His obedience and His trust in God, He brought us spiritual healing and restored our wandering hearts to the Shepherd of our souls.

The very next paragraph, starting in chapter 3, verse 1, begins this way: "*Likewise* [in the same way], *wives*, be subject to your own husbands" and goes on to give some examples and reasons (vv. 2–6). Verse 7 continues, "*Likewise, husbands*, live with your wives in an understanding way, showing honor." And then the rest of the chapter centers on the theme of suffering for righteousness' sake, as Jesus did for our sake.

In tying the redemptive suffering of Christ to marriage, Peter wanted us to understand that both husbands and wives sometimes have to suffer in order to fulfill their God-given role and responsibility toward their mates. He reminds us that we can trust our situation and the outcome of our obedience to God, and that our willingness to follow in Jesus' steps (2:21), even when it is hard, can bring healing and restoration in the lives of others.

In his words to wives, Peter specifically addresses women whose husbands are not believers—a situation that was common in the early church. For a Christian wife whose husband does not share her faith—who perhaps resists her or ridicules the things that matter most to her—submission and showing respect can be a struggle. And yet for these women, as for those who persevere through *any* affliction with dignity and faith in God, the experience only serves to make their faith and character shine more brilliantly.

According to Peter, "respectful and pure conduct" and a "gentle and quiet spirit" are what give wives "imperishable beauty" (1 Peter 3:2, 4). This is how they adorn the doctrine they claim to believe. Far more effective than any tactics of manipulation, nagging, or angry tirades, a wife's submission to Christ—expressed in respectful submission to her husband—is the means most likely to reach her husband's heart and win him to become an obedient follower of Christ.

And this principle can be applied to any woman whose husband is not being obedient to the Word of God. When a woman denies the natural urge to resent her husband or retaliate against him, when she runs to the cross instead of running her mouth, when she maintains a gentle and quiet spirit and steadfastly hopes in God, regardless of her husband's behavior—that is no spineless, mousy, whimpering puddle of dominated femininity. *That is a woman of power.*

The hard-fought, God-honoring response of a submitted wife can be a means of drawing the most resistant husband to submit to God. This kind of submission is a mark not of groveling, but of greatness.

"But What if I Believe He's Wrong?"

"But," many women beg to know, "what do I do when I disagree with my husband's decisions or direction?"

Actually, this is the only time submission really becomes an issue in marriage—when the husband and wife don't agree on something. As long as everyone is on the same page, no one really needs to submit to anyone about anything. It's only when you look up and realize the two of you aren't on the same page—or even in the same chapter, book, or library—that submission is put to the test.

Such testing can involve minor disagreements that surface in the course of daily life. Or it can encompass bigger issues related to (for example) parenting decisions, financial matters, or sexual expectations and desires. Then there are the really thorny matters—such as the ones our ministry team sometimes hears about from women whose husbands are asking them to do something they believe is contrary to God's will:

- "My husband is not saved. I am supposed to be submissive to him. He does not want me to tithe. This is a big issue for him. What am I to do?"
- "What if he is an unbeliever and takes your young children to see R-rated movies when you plead with him to consider an alternative? Or what if he tells you to go to work and put your kids in daycare?"
- "My friend's husband has a large collection of evil music—sex, drugs, etc. He says he is a Christian, but he refuses to dispose of it. My friend does not like having it in her home (they have six children), but feels that to be submissive she cannot tell him to get rid of it."

The women asking these and other tough questions need more than a stock response from a remote counselor, author, or teacher who doesn't know them or their situation. They need someone who will walk with them, pray with them, weep with them, challenge them or advocate for them when needed, stick with them over the long haul, and help them discern step-by-step the best course of action.

That, of course, is exactly what Titus 2 provides for these women. And it is why ongoing, life-on-life relationships between younger women and seasoned, older women—in the context of the local church, where pastoral leaders can be brought in if necessary—are so important, and can be a great source of practical wisdom and encouragement.

That said, there are some general principles I have found useful when walking women through situations where they are being asked to submit to direction they believe is unwise or unbiblical.

1. Ask yourself: Am I generally submissive?

Biblical submission is first a heart attitude—an inclination or bent toward being leadable. The submitted wife has a general pattern of yielding to her husband's leadership rather than resisting his ideas and leadership. To be sure, a wife's submission involves actions and behavior. But what she *does* (submits) flows out of who she *is* (a gentle-spirited, responsive, amenable woman).

When biblical headship and submission work the way God ordained, the husband and wife are able to work together to accomplish a common goal rather than being pitted against each other. They are playing on the same team. And as with sports teams, when each position plays their part, the team wins games.

To change the metaphor, it's kind of like ballroom dancing. For the dance to work, someone has to lead and someone has to follow—but both partners can and should inspire the other to do better. When wives submit to their husband's leadership, it is easier for husbands to love and lead. And when men love and lead, it is easier for their wives to submit.

That's something to think about when you find yourself in a marital tug-of-war. Step back and evaluate the normal pattern in your responses to your husband. Is your response to your husband generally receptive and responsive? Or do you tend to reflexively push back and resist, making it tough for your husband to make suggestions or decisions without bracing for your inevitable objections?

Late one night, as I was writing this chapter, Robert shared with me a concern about my need to be a better steward of my time while under my looming book deadline. He gently challenged me to make some practical changes that he felt would make me more effective.

My knee-jerk reaction was to defend my way of getting things done, explaining that we are just wired differently (which is true). But the Spirit reminded me that this was an opportunity to humble myself and yield to my husband's counsel, realizing he has been given the responsibility to provide leadership in our marriage and trusting that God is using him to help make me more like Jesus.

So I swallowed my pride, thanked Robert for his input, and purposed to take it to heart. And over the next couple of days, I saw more clearly the wisdom of what he had said. I also began to experience a sweet infusion of God's grace in my life as I responded to his leadership.

This example may seem trivial compared to far bigger issues you are facing in your marriage at the moment. But our responses to these everyday exchanges really do impact our husband's responses to us. I've observed that men tend to choose one of two faulty alternatives when faced with their wife's resistance. They'll either become *overbearing*—just taking the ball and running with it—or they'll acquiesce into *passivity*. Neither one, of course, makes for good decision making or a healthy relationship. But the second—passivity—can actually be the most vexing for a wife. In fact, one of the most common frustrations I've heard expressed by Christian women is regarding their husband's slowness to step up to the plate and lead.

One friend said to me, "My husband doesn't like conflict or

confrontation, so he doesn't tend to give direction that he doesn't think I will want to comply with." Sometime later, when I asked this man for his perspective, he explained: "If a husband feels like his leadership is going to threaten the relationship, he will protect the relationship and not lead."

Another husband told me, "If everything is challenged and questioned, it's more difficult to lead than do nothing. So men may choose to do nothing instead of risking failure."

The point is, when a husband develops ingrained patterns of conflict avoidance, he'd rather just let his wife make the calls instead of risking damage to his pride or inviting further strife into the relationship.

And as a wife, that's not a good place for you to be. It leaves you exposed and unprotected, overloading your already full plate of responsibilities. It also makes you feel lonely and unsupported—because your partner has essentially opted out of engaging with important issues.

So it's helpful to consider . . . what's your bent?

To submit or to resist?

That's a good place to start.

2. Make sure you want God's will and glory more than you want your own way.

I realize that the command to submit to our husbands may feel like the height of unfairness. At times, the sense of vulnerability and loss of control can provoke fear. But it helps to remember that the ultimate issue is not our surrender to human leadership—to our husband—but rather to God. When you think about it, being asked to align ourselves under a God-ordained authority is really just asking us to be like Jesus.

"My food is to do the will of him who sent me," Jesus said (John 4:34), indicating that His greatest satisfaction came from doing what His Father asked Him to do. This decision was obviously costly to Him: "Being found in human form, he humbled himself by becoming obedient to the point of death, even death on a cross" (Phil. 2:8). But as a result of Jesus' chosen submission, the Father "highly exalted him" (v. 9), favoring Him with blessing that far outweighed the high price of His surrender.

The battles you face at home can sometimes put you in what feels like an impossible position. But if you could drill down to the heart of your struggle, you might be surprised by what you'd find. Could it be that you're simply afraid that what will honor God in this situation might be different from what you want?

I've discovered that once we've truly submitted ourselves to the will of God, it often becomes easier to submit to human authorities.

3. Share your concerns, but watch your attitude.

There's a way to say no, and there's a way to say no. You know what I mean? One of those ways can be accusatory and threatening, whiny and wearisome, demeaning and demanding. But the other way comes from a heart that is humble, loving, respectful, and aware that you likely hold in your hand the difference between a clash of wills or a calm, adult discussion.

Attitude is so important.

And attitude, obviously, begins in your heart. You may be able to control your tongue and facial expressions by force of will alone—sometimes. But you can only do it consistently when submission comes from within, not merely from outward compliance.

This is another reason why God's call to submission is a blessing—because it trains our hearts to resist what our runaway emotions would demand. And so the more deeply a wife yields—to God first, and therefore to her husband—the more likely it is that gentleness and well-spoken truth will bubble up from inside her instead of harshness and poorly worded arguments.

By making a difference in *you*, submission can make a difference in how issues in your marriage (or elsewhere—in the workplace or at church) work themselves out.

4. If you're still in disagreement, make your appeal—gently.

Share your heart—prayerfully, kindly, with carefully chosen words, and at an appropriate time. Sometimes this means waiting until your emotions have calmed down and your husband is in a better frame of mind to really hear your heart.

One helpful example of appealing to authority can be seen in Queen Esther, an orphaned Jewish girl who ended up married to the King of Persia. King Ahasuerus was an impatient, angry, volatile man, known in history for cruelty and horrible fits of rage. If you're familiar with this Old Testament account (in the book of Esther), you know that the king's chief official, Haman, manipulated Ahasuerus into declaring extermination on her people.

Esther's guardian, Mordecai, pleaded with Esther to ask her husband to halt these evil plans. And not surprisingly, Esther hesitated, fearing for her own safety. Finally she marshaled the courage to risk the king's possible rejection—or worse. But she prudently resisted the temptation just to blurt out her case all at once. To do so could have made Ahasuerus feel accosted or blindsided. Instead she invited both him and Haman—twice—to a sumptuous feast she had prepared. Only then, when the king was relaxed and in a favorable mood, did she make her request of him. And her approach proved to be a wise one. Haman's treachery was exposed, and Esther's people were saved.

I've often thought of this account when I have been tempted to dump my concern onto my husband or another person in authority rather than exercising restraint and considering the most judicious timing and approach. You might compare her tactics to a wife's saying, "Honey, there's something I really need to talk with you about. When would be a good time for us to sit down and let me share with you what's on my heart?"

Now, Esther had no guarantee the king would change his orders and call off the death squads, any more than a wife's gentle approach guarantees that her husband will come around to her way of thinking.

But the example of Esther's appeal to her evil husband illustrates that the timing and tact of a woman's appeal can make a man more open and inclined to listen and to consider her perspective.

This is not a matter of being coy or manipulative to get your way. We're talking about using gentleness and tact in making your case.

Granted, the line between the two can be a thin one. And Esther and Ahasuerus' marriage certainly cannot be held up as a model worthy of emulation. Nevertheless, I believe her example can be instructive when it comes to approaching a husband (or any other authority figure) with a difficult matter or a disagreement.

5. Once you've made your appeal, wait for God to intervene.

I had a boss once who wisely and kindly told me, "Nancy, it's fine to put your cards on the table, but once you put them there, take your hands off. Don't keep pushing."

My natural, firstborn temperament, I confess, is a lot more pit bull than golden lab. I can sink my teeth into something and not let go until whoever is on the other side of the issue finally says, "Okay, fine, you win."

Unfortunately, as I am learning, such pit-bull tendencies are seldom effective or productive in marriage—or in any other relationship. I've seen that when I approach Robert about a concern with a gentle spirit, then leave the matter with him, things go much better. When he knows I'm trusting God to work through his leadership, he's actually *more* inclined to listen to what I am saying. He feels a greater sense of responsibility and a heightened desire to seek the Lord and to love me well.

What a relief it is to know we are not responsible for wringing obedience out of our husbands. Only the Lord can do that.

What a relief it is to know we are not responsible for wringing obedience out of our husbands. Only the Lord can do that. What you and I need to do is *pray* for the men we married—and pray about our issues of disagreement as well. If there's wisdom in what we're asking our husbands to consider and they don't seem inclined to listen to us, then the best way to get through to him is go "over his head" to the One who can move his heart to do what is right.

This process requires patience. But it will show how big we really believe God is and whether we trust that He is powerful, sovereign, and good. In these seasons, the words of the psalmist are just what we need:

> Wait for the LORD;
> be strong, and let your heart take courage;
> wait for the LORD! (Ps. 27:14)

As the days go by, of course, we may find it's *our* hearts that God turns, not our husband's. Or perhaps we will find some sweet combination of the two. But however the Lord chooses to act, we will have chosen to walk in the place where His peace dwells and where He can do a deep, sanctifying work in our life and marriage.

Someone once told me about a time when she and her husband had come to an impasse over a particularly contentious issue. She felt strongly about what needed to be done and kept badgering him with her opinions. His opinions were just as strong, and he dug in his heels. Tensions escalated. Walls were going up. Her husband wasn't bending, and she sure wasn't going to be the first one to crack.

But one day, following yet another heated exchange, the Lord convicted my friend's heart about some of the things she had said and the attitude she was displaying. She went to her husband with a humble apology, explaining that God had caused her to see the harm she was doing and that she was fully prepared—even though she still disagreed with him—to submit to him and to his decision. "I'm praying for you, honey," she said, "and I'll keep praying over this matter. But I will back you on whatever you decide."

When this wife took her place under her husband's authority, he didn't take it as a thumbs-up victory. Instead, he began to feel the sheer weight of what was at stake and the need to listen to the Lord and follow His direction. All this husband wanted to do now—with his wife's trusting support—was to make sure he got this right, even if the right way was the one that had been her way all along.

This woman could've said, "I lost. I gave in. He won. I let him get away with it."

But no, she didn't lose.

She won, just as he won.

They won—because her trust in the Lord motivated her husband to a new level of discernment and obedience and a desire to do what was truly best for his marriage and family.

The Promise of Grace

What we need to remember—and what is so easy to overlook or minimize—is that our husband's role is a difficult one. No, not all husbands take it as seriously as they should, and many contribute to making their wife's obligations harder to fulfill than necessary, just as many wives make things difficult for their husbands. But do you know what? Whether your husband realizes it or not, God has placed on him the responsibility for the condition of his marriage and family. And he will be required to stand before the Lord to give an account for how he managed this stewardship.

God doesn't hold us responsible for fulfilling our husband's role. But He does hold us responsible for filling *our* role—not simply submitting to our husband, but pulling with him and upholding him in prayer. And yes, things can still go awry, even on the other side of our obedience. But even then, God promises (and never fails to deliver) grace sufficient for every challenge.

As we hope in God, as Jesus Himself did when suffering unjustly (1 Peter 2:23), we can experience freedom from fear. And our submission and trust in the Lord will showcase the beauty of the gospel:

> For this is how the holy women who hoped in God used to adorn themselves, by submitting to their own husbands, as Sarah obeyed Abraham, calling him lord. And you are her children, if you do good and do not fear anything that is frightening. (1 Pet. 3:5–6)

In the opening chapter of this book, I shared about a few private moments I spent with my lifelong friend Vonette Bright just before I walked down the aisle to become Mrs. Robert Wolgemuth. In true motherlike fashion, she wanted to be sure I was adequately prepared for this new life I was stepping into. Toward the end of our brief conversation, Vonette said something I've not forgotten—a bit of wisdom that has proved to be one of the sweetest wedding gifts I received.

"Submit to whatever brings him pleasure—in everything," she said with a smile, "and you'll be just fine!"

I've hesitated to share this advice, knowing it could easily be misconstrued. By no means was she encouraging me to satisfy any sinful desires my husband might have. And she was not implying that I would be my husband's slave, existing merely to fulfill his every whim. But this precious widow, who had enjoyed a deeply loving fifty-four-year marriage, knew firsthand the joys of having a disposition—an inclination—to follow and yield to her husband's leadership.

Vonette's words have come to mind many times since my wedding day. My natural bent is to push for what I want—what brings *me* pleasure. But in those moments when I have felt reluctant to be inconvenienced or to make a sacrifice to serve and bless my husband, this timely counsel from an older woman has helped recalibrate my thinking. And as I have tried to choose the pathway of submission, I have watched my kind, tender husband bend over backward to serve and please me.

I understand that not every husband will respond this same way and that some wives will not see the fruit of their obedience to God's Word in the short term.

I also understand that too often the concept of submission has been used as an excuse and cover for bullying or for a kind of spineless acquiescence. We should not turn a blind eye to such situations. Depending on the nature and severity of the circumstances, perpetrators need to be confronted and held accountable for their behavior, and those on the receiving end need to receive compassionate counsel and practical relief. But we cannot afford to let those distortions and perversions of submission cause us to miss out on the real thing.

We eagerly await the day when our great God will right all wrongs and will reward the faithfulness of those who have endured patiently under ungodly authorities—whether tyrannical rulers or selfish, domineering husbands.

In the meantime, He calls us to follow in the steps of our Savior, to hope in God, and to train each other in this biblical truth, trusting in His wisdom, goodness, and love, and experiencing the surprising beauty and power of humble submission.

Making It Personal

Older women

1. What are some of the ways you have struggled (or still struggle) with biblical submission in your own life and marriage? What have you learned? How could your experiences be a source of encouragement for a younger woman in your life?
2. How can you model and teach submission to younger women in a way that helps them see it as a blessing and not a burden?
3. What can you do to walk alongside a woman who is struggling with her husband's decisions? How can you offer support and encouragement while challenging her to think biblically?

Younger women

1. Would you consider yourself a biblically submissive woman? What does that look like for you? Is your general inclination to be responsive or resistant toward authority?
2. Do you often find yourself wanting your own way rather than seeking to honor the Lord and follow His direction through your husband or other authorities? How might a proper understanding of submission to the will of God help you? How does Christ's example inspire you?
3. Who is an older, mature woman or mentor you could ask for encouragement and counsel when you struggle to respond to authority in a biblical manner?

Teach what accords with sound doctrine.

Older men are to be sober-minded, dignified, self-controlled,
sound in faith, in love, and in steadfastness.

Older women likewise are to be reverent in behavior,
not slanderers or slaves to much wine.

They are to teach what is good,
and so train the young women
to love their husbands and **children,**
to be self-controlled,
pure,
working at home,
kind,
and submissive to their own husbands,
that the word of God may not be reviled.

. . . so that in everything they may adorn
the doctrine of God our Savior.

TITUS 2:1–5, 10

CHAPTER 13

Life-Givers in Training

Embracing the Gift of Motherhood

Mothering is at the essence of womanhood.
To live out a life as a nurturer in this self-centered,
godless culture will cost you. But the rewards . . . are rich indeed.
BARBARA HUGHES

YOU MAY HAVE SEEN A HUMOROUS PIECE ON THE INTERNET that proposes a series of "tests" for people who are thinking of having children. The activities the author describes are attempts to simulate what life with kids is like, giving people a taste of the real thing before they actually make the commitment. The tests include things like going to bed (again) at 2:45 a.m. and getting up when the alarm goes off at 3:00 a.m., spooning soggy cornflakes into a swinging melon suspended from the ceiling, inserting a coin into your car's CD player, and attempting to stuff a live octopus into a string bag so no arms hang out.[1]

We can all get a laugh (or more likely a knowing sigh) from these makeshift simulations of the high-wire acts and pyrotechnics that make up a typical day for a mother with little ones. But the jest is only effective up to a point. Taken too seriously, it can reveal a mindset I fear many young women bring with them into marriage—the idea that parenthood, for all its fanciful ideals and Facebook photo ops, is mostly just a hard grind of self-depletion.

As we seek to gain God's perspective on the calling and gift of motherhood, we need to ask what influences may have shaped our underlying beliefs on this topic (and others addressed in Titus 2):

- Are we just mimicking what we experienced growing up without stopping to evaluate whether those ways are true and good and wise?
- Do we mindlessly accept the philosophies promoted through popular culture—magazines, media outlets, or mom blogs?
- Or . . . are we looking to God's Word to determine His purposes for us in our various roles and callings as women, wives, friends, church members, workers, sisters, and, yes, mothers?

Kari was a mom in her midthirties when she attended one of the first True Woman conferences hosted by Revive Our Hearts. We had a booth set up where people could record a video testimony of how the Lord had met with them at the event. In her video, Kari told how she had received Christ shortly after the birth of her first child and how she and her husband had welcomed seven children into their home over the course of the next twelve years. She was a devoted mom who obviously valued children. And yet during that weekend, the Lord had exposed anger and frustration that had been building up in her heart for a long time. Without even realizing it, she had harbored a lingering sense that her husband, her children, life, God—all of them, really—had taken advantage of her, had stolen from her, had drained away opportunities and freedoms from her.

Kari's voice broke and tears started to flow as she haltingly testified to what had happened to her at the weekend event. Through the teaching of His Word, God had renewed her passion for motherhood.

Now the joy of what He had given her to do filled her heart. She was eager to get home to her little ones, to enjoy the privilege of being their mother and leading them to know and walk with Christ.

We posted Kari's video on our *True Woman* blog the following week, and the site was immediately flooded with responses from moms who related to her story. Many of them shared that they'd also come to resent God and their husbands for the burden of responsibility placed on them, that they'd often mourned the loss of desires and plans that had been laid aside to care for their families, that they'd chafed at not being able to go to Walmart when they wished or even to the bathroom by themselves. They bore witness to ways that unbiblical philosophies that circulate so freely in our culture had subtly (and sometimes *not* so subtly) invaded their thinking and left them feeling perpetually deprived and depleted. But they, too, revealed that God was recapturing their hearts and minds, rekindling their zeal for the high and holy calling of motherhood.

He can do the same for you.

No, the fresh winds of truth won't stop your toddler from throwing up on the morning you're leaving for vacation. They won't prevent your middle schooler from informing you in the car on the way to school that forty dollars and a signed permission slip for next month's band trip are due *today*. They're not likely to win over an angry stepchild or bring a prodigal son or daughter immediately to his or her senses after years of wandering.

Life goes on. Costs go up. Parenting is demanding, complex, and short on immediate rewards, no matter how passionate you are about motherhood.

But if you're a mother—a birth mom, a stepmom, an adoptive or foster mom, or anyone else actively involved in nurturing children—Titus 2 can help you remember that you've got a vital calling and ministry right there in the house with you, a ministry that isn't necessarily a drive to church or a Kenyan mission trip away. And it will assure you that your efforts in raising those little ones for His glory are not—and *will* not be—in vain.

I want to acknowledge at the outset that I'm not a mom—at least, not in the traditional sense. I now have the privilege of embracing Robert's two daughters and their husbands, and five teen and young adult grandchildren as "family"—an unexpected gift in this season of my life.

However, God, in His providence, has not chosen to give me children of my own. So what you will hear in this chapter is not so much the voice of my personal experience as it is the voice of my many mom friends. I have walked with these women and cheered for them through various seasons of motherhood. These moms have helped me better understand what it means to love children—little ones, adolescents, and adult kids; those who love and follow Christ and those who have walked away from Him; sons and daughters who embrace the values of their parents and others whose choices have broken their parents' hearts.

One thing I know for sure: God cares about children. Which is why He wants us to. All of us.

Delightfully Yours

But here's a news flash you don't have to be a mom to get: motherhood can be hard.

It's always been difficult, and today's supermom expectations—driven by media and the competitive spirit of today's culture—can make it even harder. No wonder so many young women today are postponing children or even deciding against having them at all. No wonder, if they do have children, they feel pressured to turn family into a contest, outdoing friends and neighbors, an extension of their own personal brand.

And all too often, they're feeling the strain. Mothers caught inside this constant buzz of activity may actually spend less time *with* their children than *around* their children. Even when they manage to keep the trains running on time (on most days, in most ways), they often forget which light they're supposed to be chasing at the end of the tunnel.

> *Most people will never see the sacrifices you make to parent your children, nor will you likely get a bonus at the end of the year to recognize and reward you for your efforts.*

Looking back at Titus 2, we're reminded that Paul instructed the older women to "train the young women to love their husbands *and children.*" And the kind of love he was talking about, you'll recall, was fondness and affection, friendship and enjoyment, taking delight in the objects of our love and finding pleasure in their company.

If you're in the parenting season at the moment, then you know that *delighting* in your children often takes a back seat to meeting the *demands* of your children. And that can turn the joy of loving children into nothing more than a series of repetitive, thankless duties to be fulfilled day after endless day.

You wouldn't be human not to wear down at times under the strain. And most people will never see the sacrifices you make to parent your children, nor will you likely get a performance review or a bonus at the end of the year to recognize and reward you for your efforts.

But if you're not careful, if you're not prayerful, if you let the days just pass by without being determined to use them for God's highest and best purposes—to remember the real reason you're doing all this—then the blessings He intends for you in this season may slip through your fingers. And your children may miss out on the vision of God's love you were intended to give them.

So how do you hold this impossible task in balance?

With help! And not only God's help, though of course that is

The Bible invariably describes children as gifts from God.

available to you. But God has chosen to work in your life through other women—Titus 2 women. Women who've been down this road, sharing life lessons they've learned along the way, providing support and encouragement to help guide you through the twenty-five-hour days of parenthood. Helping you remember to . . .

Enjoy children.

If you're a mom, you know better than I that the sometimes uncomfortable months of pregnancy and the hours of labor and delivery are just the beginning of many challenges ahead: sleep deprivation, colicky crying marathons, headstrong temperaments, anxious moments. And those who are watching their older children—even grown children—struggle and backtrack, stumble and fall could tell you stories that make the shoe-tying trials of toddlerhood seem tame by comparison.

Yes, mothering is hard. Initial enthusiasm for this season is often eclipsed by exhaustion, delight by drudgery.

But these children—as you know, yet perhaps need to be reminded—are *blessings*. The Bible invariably describes children as gifts from God. As a heritage. As a reward. As hope for the future. As something to be thankful for and enjoy.

"I will bless her," God said to Abraham, promising a son to Sarah. "I will bless her, and she shall become nations; kings of peoples shall come from her" (Gen. 17:16).

Isaac's blessing for Jacob included the prayer that God would "bless you and make you fruitful and multiply you" (Gen. 28:3).

When Esau met up with his brother years later in open country, amazed by the size of the approaching entourage, he asked, "Who are these with you?" Jacob answered, "The children whom God has graciously given your servant" (Gen. 33:5).

And the psalmist exclaimed,

> Like arrows in the hand of a warrior
> are the children of one's youth.
> Blessed is the man
> who fills his quiver with them! (Ps. 127:4–5)

Jesus recognized children as blessings and rebuked those of His followers who tried to shush them and shuttle them away as a bother and inconvenience. "Let the little children come to me and do not hinder them," He said (Matt. 19:14).

Jesus was expressing what most parents know but can easily forget amid the pressures of daily life. That little ones are blessings.

I once asked a woman who has a large number of children if she and her husband had always wanted a big family. "No, not at first we didn't," she said. "But as God began to bring children into our lives, I started noticing what He says about children in Scripture. His perspective is that they are a blessing and reward. And I thought, *Well, if God wanted to give me some other kind of blessing, like, oh . . . thousand dollar checks, I wouldn't say to Him, 'No more blessings! We don't have room for all those blessings you're trying to give us.'*"

As we open our hearts to children, we reflect the heart of our heavenly Father, whose love for His children never fails.

How true. And on days when you don't know if you can butter another piece of toast or settle another argument or read another story or sit through another soccer game in subfreezing temps, remember that these children are in your home for a relatively short period of time. And underneath all the dirt and diapers and doctor visits, even the hardships imply the presence of blessing that many would trade whole fortunes to possess.

So take a deep breath. In the midst of the hubbub, ask the Lord to slow your racing heart and to silence the voices of others' expectations that are ringing in your head. Look around to where life is happening for you right now.

And thank God for your children—whatever their age and size. Ask Him for a heart to enjoy them. Enjoy them when they're lovable and it comes naturally. And when they're difficult or demanding or disrespectful, don't lose sight of the fact that they are still a gift. A blessing. A sacred stewardship.

And if you don't have children of your own, enjoy others' children. Do it for Jesus' sake. Do it for the children's sake, and for the spread of God's kingdom to the next generation.

As we open our hearts to children, we reflect the heart of our heavenly Father, whose love for His children never fails.

Express affection.

A friend was cleaning out her purse one day and found a little piece of paper. (Who knows from how long ago; we women can sometimes span presidential terms between pocketbook purges.)

The note said simply, "Thanks, Mom, for coming to my game tonight."

Can you imagine the joy this mom felt when she read those words again? Amid a crinkly collection of store receipts, appointment reminders, and cough-drop wrappings, she had found treasure.

And if we adults are moved by such a tender expression of affection, imagine how your children need—and will one day remember—your verbal infusions of love and affection.

This brings to mind Jesus' baptism, when the Holy Spirit visibly descended in the form of a dove and the Father's voice echoed from heaven: "This is my beloved Son, with whom I am well pleased" (Matt. 3:17). It was an epic moment, with the three members of the Trinity all actively involved. But it was also an incredibly tender moment—

a Father declaring to a Son (and the world) that He loved Him and was pleased with Him.

Our heavenly Father set an example for all parents and for those who love and care for children of every age when He spoke those words of affection, affirmation, and approval.

I know it may sound elementary, but say the words often. Say them out loud. In writing. In texts. In private. In public.

- "I love you."
- "I thank God for giving you to our family."
- "I'm cheering for you!"
- "I'm so blessed to be your mom."
- "You're a blessing, a treasure!"

Whenever possible, underscore your words with loving physical touch. You can't do it enough. You can't do it too often. And though your kids may sometimes wipe off your kisses or wriggle to escape your hugs, those expressions of affection will not be lost on them. Each tender word, each kiss and hug, is an investment that will pay out across future years and generations as a rich inheritance of love.

When the apostle Paul wanted to express to his children in the faith how much he loved them, he likened his feelings to a mother's love for her children:

> We were gentle among you, like a nursing mother taking care of her own children. So, being affectionately desirous of you, we were ready to share with you not only the gospel of God but also our own selves, because you had become very dear to us. (1 Thess. 2:7–8)

Gentle. Nurturing. Caring. Affectionate. Desirous. Sharing. Self-sacrificing. Very dear. This is the kind of heart Paul calls for older women to help younger women cultivate toward their children. A heart that makes the gospel beautiful in the eyes of children and adults alike. A heart that needs to be expressed both in actions and in words.

What truly inspires us to love the children God has put in our lives is His calling, not the sweet expressions on their faces or the attention we gain from their adorable presence or their accomplishments.

We love them because *God* loves them, and we love them because He's *called* us to love them—even on those days when they are anything but sweet and adorable.

My dad died suddenly of a heart attack on the weekend of my twenty-first birthday. One of my brothers was killed in a car wreck at the age of twenty-two. In both cases, everything that was going to be said between us needed to be said before that day arrived so unexpectedly. So I'm acutely aware of how important it is to express our love now. Because even if everyone in a whole family lives to be a hundred, our opportunities for expressing love to one another are still limited.

So if you can, if there's a way—even with children who live far away or who are estranged—do it before it's too late.

Say it today: "I love you . . ."

Make children a priority.

You hear a lot today about "hover mothers" and "drama mamas," who wrap their own needs too tightly around their children, often failing to let them establish their personal identities and learn to take responsibility for their lives. But in my observation, another concern is that for some moms, their children's needs rank fifth or sixth on the priority list—behind work, friends, personal time, buying new stuff for the house, sometimes even church and ministry.

> *Your children need a mom who is attentive to the condition of their souls.*

My husband and I sat in a restaurant recently and watched as two women friends at the next table enjoyed a long, leisurely lunch and conversation. That whole time, the preschool son of one of them sat affixed to an iPad, isolated beneath a set of headphones, with absolutely no interaction with either of the grown-ups.

I'm not saying there is never a time for adults to converse and let children entertain themselves, and I don't believe children should always be the center of attention (an opposite and equally unwise extreme). But your children *need* you. They need a mom who is tuned, alert, attentive to their needs and the condition of their souls, who is intentional about engaging their little hearts now and for eternity.

Children live with their parents such a short time before they are grown and gone. So if your little ones are still at home, please make this time count. There will be time later for those other activities that you choose to put on hold until they are safely out of the nest.

And I would repeat this encouragement to women like me who do not have children of our own. We are part of the body of Christ, and we are all in this Titus 2 sisterhood together. That means children should be a priority for us too—as they were for Jesus when He was here on earth.

You may or may not particularly like kids. They may strike you as messy, disruptive, and unnecessary. But to love and welcome children is to be like Jesus (see Matt. 19:13–14). So let's be alert to ways we can reach out to them and bless them, as big sisters and spiritual mothers and grandmothers.

Seek them out and speak to them at church. Compliment them when you see evidences of grace in their attitude or behavior. Let them know you notice them and that you care about them. Come alongside their parents to support the raising of these children, whether by offering to babysit occasionally so Mom and Dad can go out by themselves or by engaging more directly in their lives.

One of the great joys of my life has been cultivating relationships with others' children:

- attending their sports events
- taking them out on lunch dates
- celebrating their special occasions
- staying connected through notes and texts and calls
- asking them questions and listening to their answers
- rooting for them through different seasons and transitions
- extending grace and staying engaged when they struggled in their faith journey

And some of the closest relationships I enjoy today are with the now-adult children I reached out to when I was in my twenties and thirties.

I have been blessed to participate in many of their weddings. And now they have children of their own, some of whom call me Yaya (Greek for grandmother). So my life as an older woman continues to be enriched and multiplied by nurturing relationships with children, teens, and young adults. Never anticipating that I would one day marry, I've said for years that I didn't fear growing old alone because all these kids who have been such a precious part of my life would care for me when I couldn't care for myself! Truly the Lord "gives the barren woman a home, making her the joyous mother of children" (Ps. 113:9).

Everyone benefits when we all join together to make "loving our children" a priority and to pass the baton of faith on to the next generation.

But don't put children first . . .

Now, this may sound contradictory to the whole idea of making children a priority. It is certainly a paradox. But embracing this paradox may be the key to loving your children well.

You've been uniquely tasked with transmitting the gospel—day by day, year by year, experience by experience—to the little ones you've been privileged to raise and nurture. It happens, Paul says, as you "love" your children—sharing with them the affection that God has for His children. So you must make the sharing of this love a priority—but *not* your first priority.

Here's what I mean.

Moms can be so overwhelmed by the mental, physical, and emotional outlay of parenting—in combination with other necessary responsibilities—that they forfeit time with the Lord in exchange for what feels like better ways of recharging. As a result, they simply don't have the capacity to give their children the love they need. Without meaning to, they have distanced themselves from the Source of true love for their children.

Certain seasons of parenting, of course, do make it difficult to consistently set aside chunks of time for prayer and Scripture reading. But even in such busy, stressful stretches, loving children well necessitates drinking from the fountain of God's grace and love.

I love the memory one of my friends shared of a morning when the phone started ringing. She was back in her bedroom trying to get some much-needed time alone with the Lord. One of her little ones, however, picked up the phone and, after a brief hello, told the caller, "I'm sorry, but my mommy is meeting with God right now. You'll have to call back later."

So sometimes, ironically, the best way to make your children a priority is to make time with God an even greater priority. That may mean weeding out other good but nonessential activities for a season. It may mean narrowing the number of activities your children are involved in. But at the end of the day, the time you carve out to spend in the Word and prayer—alone and with your children—will settle your heart, strengthen you, and enable you to love the little ones in your life better, and to see them for the blessings they are. In the process, you will be pointing them to Christ, training them to seek out His love as well.

The Privilege of Giving Life

So moms (and others), I hope you will delight in your children. Enjoy them. Let the priorities spelled out in Titus 2 shape your life so that the little ones as well as the bigger ones—all the ones who call you Mom (or Auntie or friend)—are able to legitimately describe you as "the joyous mother of children" (Ps. 113:9).

Motherhood is a privilege and responsibility like none other. What you're doing is vital, quite literally life-giving. I'd like to park on that term—life-giving—for a moment. It takes us back to the first mother. Have you ever realized it was only after their tragic fall into sin that the woman actually received a personal name like her husband, Adam?

It was Adam who named her: "The man called his wife's name Eve" (Gen. 3:20).

> *Eve's very name is a statement of faith in the promises and redeeming love of God.*

But . . . Eve. Why Eve?

Adam didn't just take Eve's name at random from a book of names—eyes closed, finger circling in midair, then pressed down at random to the page, going with whatever it landed on.

No, the name *Eve* held (and continues to hold) enormous significance, not only in God's plan for women and motherhood, but also in His grand design of redemption. For when Adam named his wife, the two of them had just made a fatal choice. In violating God's command not to eat from the only forbidden tree in the garden, they had called down upon themselves and future generations the justified curse of death.

And yet it was in that moment, when death was looming, that Adam named his wife *Eve*, which sounds like the Hebrew for "life-giver."

Eve's very name, in other words, is actually a statement of faith in the promises and redeeming love of God. The woman whose actions had brought death to the human race would now become, by the restorative action of a gracious God, the one whose body would produce physical *life* for the human race.

This legacy can be seen in the hands and hearts and physical capabilities given by God to generations of women who have carried on—and still carry on—the giving of life by bearing children and nurturing them. And we should marvel at this.

No, not all of us are given the privilege of bearing physical children. Some of us never have the opportunity to nurture children of our own, and some are called to raise children that other women gave birth to. And we are worth no less to the Lord than those with two, four, six, eight, ten biological children featured in the picture frames that line their hallways at home. But the tremendous value and responsibility invested in us as women by God, as those uniquely given the capacity to be bearers of life, means that we all share in His purpose for the ages. We all participate in Eve's life-giving legacy. And when we love children as He has instructed us to do—*our* children, *their* children, *your* children, *all* children—the gospel grows and brings forth the fruit of eternal life.

Motherhood is a privilege. But inherent within this precious privilege is also the potential for pain.

Privilege, Pain, Promise—and Perez

Motherhood is indeed a privilege. Having children in our lives is a privilege. It's all part of the life-giving blessing of being a woman. But inherent within this precious privilege—on this side of the Fall—is also the potential for pain, because anyone who accepts the call of motherhood risks having her heart broken as a result.

Mary of Nazareth experienced this pain more deeply than any mother who has ever lived. When she and Joseph took her infant Son to the temple forty days after His birth, the aged Simeon spoke divinely inspired words to prepare the young mother for what she would face:

> And Simeon blessed them and said to Mary . . . "Behold, this child is appointed for the fall and rising of many in Israel, and for a sign that is opposed (and *a sword will pierce through your own soul also*), so that thoughts from many hearts may be revealed." (Luke 2:34–35)

Yes, Mary was uniquely blessed to be the mother of the Son of God. And yes, this calling would bring exquisite joys. But with the privilege would come excruciating pain. Not the pain caused by her child's sin—something every other mother experiences—but the painful price her Child would pay for the sin of the world.

You are not Mary, of course. Her role in history—and in motherhood—is unique. But no mother escapes the pain of motherhood entirely—and neither will you.

Your children will disappoint you at times, just as you will disappoint yourself as a parent—something that happens most every day in small or large ways. You'll give in to their pleas and feed them junk food. You'll overreact. You'll lose your temper. Or you'll let yourself get distracted on a day when one of the kids wanders from your sight and inadvertently puts himself or herself in danger—a terrifying experience, even when everything turns out all right.

Even on the best days, a mother's job can be fraught with worry, fear, and guilt—which means moms must recognize their utter dependence on the grace of God, both for themselves and for their children. When mistakes and shortcomings rear their ugly heads, when yesterday's meltdown is seen more clearly in the light of a new morning, they can experience afresh the truth of the gospel that invites them to turn to Christ, receiving His mercy and forgiveness, and walking in renewed hope.

Motherhood is indeed a means of sanctification, meant to deepen your confidence in the One who can supply every grace to you through the indwelling Spirit of Jesus. That's true when the troubles you encounter are "ordinary" and relatively minor. But what about when your troubles with your children are major?

- When your marriage has failed or your husband has died and you're struggling as a single mom to reach past your pain to parent your children.
- When you suspect—or know—that a child is drinking or doing drugs.
- When your six-year-old is kicked out of school for fighting—again!— or your sixteen-year-old is failing classes left and right.
- When a child's special needs threaten to sabotage your marriage.
- When a son or daughter has embraced an immoral lifestyle.
- When a child rejects the truth of God's Word you've tried so hard to implant.
- Or when the phone rings with the news that there's been a terrible accident . . .

I can't tell you how many stories I've heard from mothers who have earnestly sought to love their children well and to lead them into a real relationship with Christ, and who still experience heartache over their troubled kids—sometimes for years. For so many, motherhood is a roller-coaster ride, with periods of crisis followed by brief glimpses of calm. No sooner do they dare to hope again than they are plunged back into a familiar place of anxiety, regret, guilt, heaviness, and too many fractured emotions to count.

If that's what loving your children has been requiring of you lately, I want to point you to a passage of Scripture that may give you fresh hope and courage.

The occasion was the improbable wedding of Ruth and Boaz, and the setting was the outpouring of blessing given to them by the people and elders gathered at the city gates.

> May the Lord make the woman, who is coming into your house, like Rachel and Leah, who together built up the house of Israel. May you act worthily in Ephrathah and be renowned in Bethlehem, and may your house be like the house of Perez, whom Tamar bore to Judah, because of the offspring that the Lord will give you by this young woman. (Ruth 4:11–12)

Perez. "Like the house of Perez."

Who's he?

Here's the story, which happened long before the days of Ruth and Boaz. Judah, one of Jacob's twelve sons, who would eventually be father to one of the twelve tribes of Israel—married a Canaanite woman (which was never a good thing) and had three sons. The older two were wicked and were put to death at the hand of the Lord. At some point thereafter, Judah's wife passed away as well. And some time after *that,* Judah took what amounted to a business trip, traveling to a certain city to shear his sheep. While there, he was intimate with a woman masquerading as a prostitute, who became pregnant from their casual union and gave birth to twin boys.

The woman in question, Tamar, was actually the widow of Judah's older deceased son. And the elder of the twin boys who were born to Judah and Tamar was . . .

Perez.

If you've gotten lost in this soap opera, don't feel the need to go back and unravel it. Suffice it to say the whole story was a convoluted, dysfunctional mess. Bad things happened and then got worse. But God's heart is always beating in the rhythm of redemption. And through this illegitimate, nearly incestuous birth, the line of Perez would extend to Boaz, the husband of Ruth . . . to David, the great-grandson of Boaz . . . and ultimately to Joseph, the husband of Mary, the mother of Jesus (see Matthew 1).

And that's the promise of the house of Perez.

We have a redeeming God who is continually in the process of making all things new and who is always working—even through our messy lives and stories—to write His story and to display His glory.

There is no situation, no matter how broken or bleak, into which our redeeming God cannot step, bringing supernatural help, healing, and hope.

Giving Life to One Another

Perhaps you identify with some of the details in Perez's family line. One or more of your children may have been born as the result of foolish or sinful choices, whether yours or others. One of your grown or teenage children may have brought an "out of wedlock" child into the world and into your family circle. Perhaps you're dealing with some other painful circumstance in the life of your child, and heartbreak is squeezing you like a vise, causing you to wonder whatever is to become of this one you love so deeply and intensely. Or perhaps the worst has happened, and you're wrestling with a grief that seems insurmountable.

But there is no situation, no matter how broken or bleak, into which our redeeming God cannot step, bringing supernatural help, healing, and hope. It might take time, and it might take you places you never expected to go. It probably won't look the way you would have scripted the story. But God is faithful, and He loves your kids more than you ever could. He *will* show up. When He does, I suspect, He will be fragrant with the incense of your prayers (Rev. 5:8) and carrying the container where He's captured every tear you've shed

(Ps. 56:8)—along with the prayers and tears of all the Titus 2 women you have turned to in your pain. And in time, no doubt, He'll have someone in mind who needs a mentor she can relate to, a woman who will need the encouragement of your testimony about God's faithfulness and grace even when your eyes were filled with tears.

Motherhood, like marriage and other callings in a woman's life, was never intended to be attempted alone, without counsel and comfort, without teaching and training.

Older woman, your hardest mothering days may be behind you. Your children may be launched, your direct influence on their lives diminished significantly. But your job is not done yet. Following in your steps are some tired young moms who need you. They need your voice of encouragement, calling them to press on in the race. They need your wisdom, gained in the trenches. They need your helping hands, reaching out to hold a crying baby. They need your time, perhaps to offer them an afternoon break or even an overnight getaway. They need your love for Jesus and your love for them, inspiring them to love Him and to love their husbands and children.

And *younger woman*, when you want to shriek, "My name's not *Mommy* any more—go call someone else!" and when you feel like a motherless child needing to be held yourself, remember that God has made provision for this very time. He has placed older women in the Body for just such moments, to be a means of grace in your life. Don't be afraid to let them know you need them. Don't be too proud to ask for practical help, insight, and prayer. You'll be giving them an opportunity to do what God has called them to do. These older women need you as much as you need them!

And, by the way, don't miss an older single woman who might be standing in the wings wondering if there is a place for her in this Titus 2, life-to-life arrangement. The opportunity to encourage young moms in a variety of ways during my years of singleness was a huge blessing to me, allowing me the joy of being a life-giver and forging many, lasting sweet friendships with families.

The writer to the Hebrews—seeking to bolster the faith of believers living in difficult days—emphasized the importance of avoiding isolation and maintaining such vital relationships:

> And let us consider how to stir up one another to love and good works, not neglecting to meet together, as is the habit of some, but encouraging one another, and all the more as you see the Day drawing near. (Heb. 10:24–25)

We women, we givers of life, are called to give life to one another as well as to the children He entrusts to our care. When the days are difficult, as they often will be—or even when they're just ordinary and entire days seem to be lived on autopilot—moms can find strength, courage, and wisdom by walking together with other like-hearted women.

As older women train and encourage younger women to love their children, the next generation will experience the beauty of Christ's love and their hearts be captivated by it—the Titus 2 way.

Making It Personal

Older women

1. Do you know a young mom in your church or community who is angry or frustrated about mothering? What can you do to encourage her and gain her ear so you can begin to gently pour God's wisdom about motherhood into her life?
2. Do you have a heart for nurturing children? How is that expressed? How can your life model biblical motherhood in positive, nurturing ways to the young women in your world?
3. Whether you're called "Mom," "Auntie," "Grandma," or "friend," your life can make a difference in younger women's lives. Examine your relationships today. How can you step up your teaching or mentoring influence in their lives? How can you love and encourage them or offer some practical relief?

Younger women

1. How has the way you were mothered shaped your perspective and feelings about motherhood? To what extent do those feelings and thoughts line up with God's perspective on motherhood?
2. God uses other women—Titus 2 women—in our lives to help equip us for our calling. Who are the women in your life you can call on for counsel and encouragement? How might one or more of them be able to help you deal with the "impossible task" of motherhood?
3. How might an older woman's insight, prayer, or practical help encourage you right now? How might your requests for help bless *them*?

Teach what accords with sound doctrine.

Older men are to be sober-minded, dignified, self-controlled,
sound in faith, in love, and in steadfastness.

Older women likewise are to be reverent in behavior,
not slanderers or slaves to much wine.

They are to teach what is good,
and so train the young women
to love their husbands and children,
to be self-controlled,
pure,
working at home,
kind,
and submissive to their own husbands,
that the word of God may not be reviled.

**. . . so that in everything they may adorn
the doctrine of God our Savior.**

TITUS 2:1–5, 10

CHAPTER 14

Instruments of Grace

Showing a Deeper Kind of Kindness

Pure kindness flows from God's saving grace and colors our lives with a joy that is winsomely contagious.

MARY BEEKE

FROM THE LOOK ON WOMEN'S FACES whenever the subject of Titus 2 womanhood comes up, it seems many of them are drawn to this ideal. They respect and desire the kind of character this passage calls them to, and they are intrigued by the possibilities of what God could accomplish *in* them and *through* them if they were to engage in the intergenerational friendships Paul describes in this passage.

I think that's why you and I are still here, digging into the Word to find out what the Titus 2 woman looks like, what sort of principles she embodies, and what she does to adorn the gospel—to see if she could actually look like us.

But God is not only interested in *what* we do. He is equally concerned with *how* we do what we do—with the heart behind our actions.

That's why I believe Paul included an admonition about being kind right in the middle of his core curriculum for women in the church (Titus 2:5). In fact, "kind" falls right on the heels of "working at home"—it's included in the context of our most intimate family relationships. I believe Paul is saying it's not enough to tend to the tasks and people assigned to us. God also cares about our motives and our disposition—how that service is carried out, how we treat and respond to our family, friends, and others.

Paul is the one, remember, who famously wrote, "If I speak in the tongues of men and of angels . . . if I have prophetic powers, and understand all mysteries and all knowledge . . . if I give away all I have, and if I deliver up my body to be burned, but have not love, I gain nothing" (1 Cor. 13:1–3).

Nothing.

He might similarly say, of women who serve their families and care for their homes, "If I have a house so spotless that people could eat off the kitchen floor . . . and if I can whip up incredibly scrumptious meals on a tight budget . . . and if I've transformed our home into a magazine-quality showcase . . . but I don't do it all with kindness, it's nothing."

Because, yes, Jesus can be seen and worshiped through such ordinary things as a crisply ironed dress shirt, a made bed, a ride to soccer practice, even a fresh batch of chocolate-chip cookies.

But not when they're performed without kindness.

Without that quality, those "good" things we do for others amount to noisy gongs and clanging cymbals. (Paul's words again.) And nobody can hear or feel our love for them over the tired, exasperated, frustrated racket we're making.

Like Jesus' friend Martha, we are sometimes "distracted with much serving" (Luke 10:40), "worried and bothered about so many things" (v. 41 NASB). We become stretched thin and stirred up, bothered and brittle.

And, all too often, unkind.

But I think there's often something more than just stress behind the sharp tone or impatient attitude that sometimes bubbles up and spills over as unkindness in our relationships. It's something we've already discussed in this book—the lack of a "sound mind."

A self-controlled—*sophron*—mind.

Because when we're not *sophron*, we're apt to see only what frustrates us, so we begin to resent the very people God has called us to serve.

When we're not *sophron*, we let ourselves get overwhelmed by our schedules and agendas rather than concentrating on the "one thing" Jesus said was "necessary" (Luke 10:42)— experiencing life in His presence.

When we're not *sophron*, we don't have any margin or heart for kindness.

So why don't we just pull over here for a while and drop in on Martha at her home in Bethany. And see what the lack of *sophron* did to one woman's mind in particular.

A Tale of Two Sisters

The occasion, you may recall, was a visit by Jesus and a band of His followers. (You can read the whole story in Luke 10.) We don't know for sure how many people were with Him, but it was probably a good-sized traveling party, perhaps two or three dozen people. And Martha, with her take-charge, firstborn temperament, was the de facto hostess for this impromptu gathering.[1]

At first, we assume, Martha was excited to see Jesus and the others in the doorway, thankful for the privilege of hosting her friend in the home she shared with her sister (Mary) and brother (Lazarus). But as Martha scrambled to clean and cook and make sure everyone was properly served and comfortably settled (while Mary chose to sit at Jesus' feet and listen to Him teach), a host of turbulent thoughts and attitudes began swirling in her head and heart.

I'm sure, like me, you'll recognize some of them:

- *Self-centeredness.* "Lord, do you not care that my sister has left me to serve alone? Tell her then to help me" (v. 40). Notice all the first-person language in these biting words, all the concern about "me"—what this responsibility is costing me, what people should be doing for me.
- *Insensitivity.* People had gathered around to listen to Jesus teach. But that didn't keep Martha from barging in, interrupting Him, disturbing everyone. She was more concerned about how she was being inconvenienced than about what others were needing or experiencing.
- *Accusation.* Asking if someone could give her a hand would have been an understandable request. But her words were accusatory—both toward Jesus ("do you not care?") and toward her sister ("my sister has left me to serve alone").
- *Resentment.* We can guess that Martha may have already been clattering the dishes in the kitchen a little more loudly than necessary. Her inner martyr had likely been muttering under her breath for quite a while. And when no one picked up on her "hint, hint" clues, she stopped even trying to squelch her rising anger. Out it came—loud and whiny and, yes, unkind.

Martha had grown irritated, impatient, demanding. There was an edge in her spirit, harshness in her voice. Serving was no longer a privilege—lovingly, gladly, graciously given—but a burden. The friends she had set out to serve had become to her a bother, a nuisance.

And beyond just being selfishly upset, Martha was willing to risk building a wall between herself and her sister. If not for Jesus' wise, gentle, corrective rebuke, we could easily imagine a few subsequent days of . . .

"Is something wrong, Martha?"

"Nothing's wrong."

"Well, *something's* wrong. I can tell."

"No, Mary. It's *not*!"

"Well, it sure seems like it."

"Would you please just stop?"

"Oh, Martha, don't tell me you're still—"

"I don't want to talk about it anymore, okay?"

"It was just that Jesus was here, and—"

"Exactly! And I would have been fine if you'd . . ."

The Scripture doesn't tell us what took place between the sisters after Jesus' visit. But when *sophron*—a sound mind, self-controlled thinking—goes missing, unkindness all-too-often shows up in its place, and relationships take a hit.

Older woman, many younger women in our lives are tired, frustrated, and feel alone in their efforts, as if no one cares about the sacrifices they are making. Their relationships at home and elsewhere are frayed. We are called to model kindness for them and to train these young women to develop a kind heart and walk.

Younger woman, this quality is essential to learn if you want to honor the Lord. It flows out of a *sophron* mind and a heart that is fixed on Christ, and it makes all the difference in the world—both in your personal well-being and in the atmosphere you create around you.

If we wish to progress together toward the Titus 2 model for women, if we want to adorn the doctrine and gospel of Christ and His beauty to the world, we need a different kind of heart.

A *kind* kind of heart.

Gifts in Kind

On the surface, a study on kindness could seem insignificant compared to the weightier subjects we've been addressing. It's easy to underestimate and overlook the importance of this quality. But I assure you that kindness is no trifling notion in the Christian vocabulary. I believe

Paul intended it to matter as much to us as all the other essentials of the Titus 2 curriculum for women.

That's because a woman's spirit and tone has the ability to determine the climate around her, whether at home, at work, at the gym, or at church. And this makes kindness indispensable—in our relationships with others and for our gospel witness in the world. When we submit to Christ's lordship and serve others with humility and kindness, our words and actions can have a greater impact on those around us than a hundred sermons and orchestrated church outreaches. But when we don't, when we give in to unsound thinking and unkind attitudes, everyone suffers.

Let's be intentional about pursuing kindness.

So with the same concern we feel for being pure and self-controlled, for avoiding slander and sins of the tongue, let's also be intentional about pursuing kindness—because it is every bit as important as the others.

Good and Kind

The Greek word translated "kind" in Titus 2:5—*agathos*—is rendered as "good" almost every other time it appears in the New Testament. Sometimes it is used as an adjective to describe another word, as in "good works" or "good deeds." Various Bible scholars and commentators define this word as meaning "good and benevolent, profitable, useful,"[2] "beneficial in its effect,"[3] and "kind, helpful, and charitable."[4]

What Paul is exhorting here, in other words, is more than simply a nice, friendly feeling. *Agathos* is kindness that goes somewhere. It's a benevolent disposition coming to life, turning into active goodness.

The kindness inside us, in other words, becomes the goodness that others receive from us. It's a process that starts inside and inevitably moves outward. It's not just *wanting* to be kind or having kind thoughts and feelings, but *being* kind.

Author Jerry Bridges reminds us that this kind of kindness and goodness is rooted in humility and others-centeredness—no small challenge, as our natural bent is just the opposite:

> Apart from God's grace, most of us naturally tend to be concerned about *our* responsibilities, *our* problems, *our* plans. But the person who has grown in the grace of kindness has expanded his thinking outside of himself and his interests and has developed a genuine interest in the happiness and well-being of those around him.[5]

Am I a kind woman? In heart attitudes as well as outward actions? This is a question that pierces us when God's Word holds up a mirror in our family rooms and kitchens and hallways, our cars and minivans and workplaces. At times, instead of kindness and goodness, what we see reflected back is harshness and criticism. Barking and berating. Touchiness and irritability.

We may try to justify ourselves. After all, aren't we the ones who make sure everybody gets their meals and has their clothes washed?

Yes.

Will we leave the office early tonight and leave everyone to do our work for us?

No.

Will we fail to show up when we're scheduled to help out at church?

Of course not.

Will we come around later, if necessary, to apologize if we reacted sharply toward someone earlier in the day?

Maybe—although we may be tempted to point out the circumstances that provoked us.

The people in our lives know they can count on us to be there when they need us. And if our spirit isn't always kind while we do our serving, is that really such a big deal? Shouldn't they just be thankful for all we do for them?

So we go through our days, checking off items from our to-do lists. We perform the duties others demand or expect of us. But are we doing it with a kind heart?

And if not, then what good are we really doing, and how are our relationships being affected?

Channels of Blessing

I love the New Testament account of a follower of Christ most commonly known as Dorcas (the Greek equivalent of her Hebrew name Tabitha). The book of Acts tells us that she "was full of good [*agathos*] works and acts of charity" (9:36).

Here was a woman whose relationship with Christ moved her to pour out her life in practical acts of kindness toward those in need. Her life was a picture of true kindness in action. And the phrase "full of" ["abounding with"—NASB] implies that her charitable acts were not performed as begrudging service or out of a mere sense of duty. That became even more clear when tragedy struck, and the life of this generous-hearted woman was snuffed out:

> In those days she became ill and died, and when they had washed her, they laid her in an upper room. Since Lydda was near Joppa, the disciples, hearing that Peter was there, sent two men to him, urging him, "Please come to us without delay." So Peter rose and went with them. And when he arrived, they took him to the upper room. All the widows stood beside him weeping and showing tunics and other garments that Dorcas made while she was with them. (vv. 37–39)

This poignant description of the widows she had blessed, grieving next to her lifeless body, suggests that Dorcas genuinely cared for the people she served with her acts of kindness. They didn't just miss what she had done for them. They missed *her*.

Who will weep at your funeral as they think about your kind heart and the ways you have served and blessed them and demonstrated the kindness of Christ to them?

And how will you be remembered by your family, your closest friends, and others who knew you? Will they remember only what you did for them, or will there be a lingering fragrance because of how you did it?

Will they remember both the sacrifices you made *and* the smile they could always count on to warm their day?

Will they remember the extra time you took *and* the way you put your arms around them at the end of the day and told them how much you loved them?

Will they just remember the chugging sound of the washing machine running while they were drifting off to sleep, or will they also recall the soft sound of your voice humming a tune while waiting for the last load to dry?

Will they remember you as both a hard worker *and* an instrument of grace and goodness?

It's not clear what Dorcas' friends expected Peter to do when they called for him to come after the beloved benefactress died. But what happened next quickly got the attention of the whole town:

> Peter put them all outside, and knelt down and prayed; and turning to the body he said, "Tabitha, arise." And she opened her eyes, and when she saw Peter she sat up. And he gave her his hand and raised her up. Then calling the saints and widows, he presented her alive. And it became known throughout all Joppa, and many believed in the Lord. (vv. 40–42)

All that time and effort spent making clothing for widows who had no other means of support had spelled L-O-V-E. And such kindness stood in stark contrast to the unbelieving world, where widows were often left to fend for themselves and faced probable destitution. Dorcas' life shone a spotlight on the love of Christ. It endeared her to those who had witnessed and been touched by her kindness. The power and beauty of her life moved them to call for the apostle when she died. And as a result of her being raised back to life, "many" put their faith in Him.

And that's the ripple effect of Christian kindness and the impact it can have on our witness in the world.

Kindness—true goodness—sometimes shows itself in tireless effort and sleepless nights. It can translate into grocery shopping for the family instead of shoe shopping for ourselves. It can mean relinquishing our plans for the afternoon when a daughter really needs to talk or hosting neighbors on a Friday night instead of enjoying a quiet evening to ourselves.

When we serve people, we serve Christ.

But the goal of it all is to show others the goodness of Christ—on a practical, personal, you-matter-to-me basis. And to do that consistently and well, we all need the training, accountability, and support Titus 2 relationships can provide. Older women need to model *agathos* for younger women and teach them the value of kindness. And younger women need to learn from older women that *people* matter more than any other *tasks* you might accomplish.

And, yes, people can be perturbing. Marriage and family life would be a lot less stressful if husbands and children didn't sometimes act irresponsibly or disregard our feelings or instructions. Ministry would go more smoothly and be less demanding if people weren't so needy or would just get their act together. Many of the issues we face in our jobs would go away if it weren't for inexperienced coworkers, demanding clients, or impatient customers.

Yes, people may cause the lion's share of our headaches. But when we serve people, we serve Christ. And when we treat people with kindness rather than indifference or impatience, we become channels of blessing, dispensing gracious words and actions that can't help but adorn the gospel of Christ.

Kindness Begins at Home

The woman whose description we know so well from Proverbs 31 is another lovely, biblical model of kindness in action. Wherever this strong, gifted, diligent woman goes, she leaves a trail of goodness, and she ministers grace to everyone around her:

> She opens her mouth with wisdom,
> and the teaching of kindness is on her tongue. (v. 26)

Nowhere am I more tempted to be selfish and lazy than in my home and my closest relationships. Too often, we show more concern and kindness for complete strangers than for those who live under the same roof with us.

But note who benefits first from this woman's industry and goodwill. For her, kindness begins at home. With her family. With her inner circle. With those who share her daily life. Her kindness toward her husband, for example, is displayed in a daily commitment that remains undiminished with the passing of time or when their relationship may be in a hard place:

> She does him good, and not harm,
> *all the days of her life*. (v. 12)

Not a day is wasted by lashing out in frustration and anger or being passive-aggressive. Every day is seen as an opportunity to do her husband good with her attitude, words, and actions. This is a huge gift she gives to him—and to herself, as her husband responds with the highest of praise for his wife.

The Proverbs 31 woman's selfless, thoughtful deeds also bless her entire family as she labors tirelessly and faithfully to ensure their needs are met.

> She is not afraid of snow for her household,
> for all her household are clothed in scarlet. . . .
> She looks well to the ways of her household
> and does not eat the bread of idleness.
> Her children rise up and call her blessed . . . (vv. 21, 27–28)

The fact is, nowhere am I more tempted to be selfish and lazy than in my home and my closest relationships. And I fear this is true for most of us—wives and moms, as well as those who live with other family members or friends. Too often, I'm afraid, we show more concern and kindness for neighbors, colleagues, store clerks, or complete strangers than for those who live under the same roof with us or who are related to us by blood or marriage.

If a couple were staying at our house for the weekend, we'd be sure clean towels were in the bathroom, their linens were freshly washed, dinner was flexible to their schedule, and a fresh pot of coffee was brewing in the morning. But when our own kids and husband need something—well, they know where the refrigerator is and how to turn on the oven.

Right?

Managing a busy household, dealing with the daily tasks related to serving husbands and kids—or whatever other responsibilities you may have—requires diligence and discipline day in and day out. It requires hard work, sometimes exhausting work. But it also requires kindness—or as one commentator put it: "a lack of irritability in light of the nagging demands of mundane and routine household duties."[6]

And that's where things can get challenging. It's so easy for us to be like the woman who once lamented to me with refreshing candor, "I'm only good enough to look good to the world." At home, it's often another story.

When I'm out speaking at a conference, I can be exceedingly gracious, kind, and patient with long lines of women who want to share their burdens and their (at times long, detailed) stories, looking them in the eyes, never complaining about my tired, aching back and feet. But when those closest to me—in my home, my family, or our ministry—need a listening ear, an attentive heart, or a thoughtful act, I can be preoccupied, unfeeling, or just too busy.

Who among us hasn't had the experience of being in the middle of a tense, unkind exchange at home, only to instantly change our tone and talk warmly with an outsider who calls or stops by? What does that say to our loved ones about how we value them and about the authenticity of our "kindness" to others?

Yes, kindness at home takes extra effort. Home is where we experience most acutely those daily annoyances and disappointments that tempt us to develop an attitude. So kindness at home also requires extra helpings of grace, which in turn requires daily dependence on God and the support of our Titus 2 sisters.

Already, in the short time I've been a wife, I've witnessed at moments the distance-creating, intimacy-killing impact of a lack of kindness on my part toward my husband. Unkind words spoken thoughtlessly, kind words left unspoken, inconsiderate actions; being too self-absorbed to notice and celebrate an accomplishment in my husband's business; wounding him in sensitive areas with insensitive teasing; being too busy with my own stuff to carry out small acts of kindness that would serve and bless him.

But I've also experienced the incredible importance and power of kindness in a marriage. I have seen it modeled in the marriages of some of my closest friends and of my Titus 2 mentors. And Robert's tender heart and his consistent kindness—always looking for ways to serve and bless me—have inspired me to be more tuned in to how I can do good to him. Being the recipient of his kindness has increased my desire to outdo him in this area.

Often, I've found, it's the little things—the simple expressions of gratitude and kindness—that express love to my husband and set the tone in our relationship. Leaving encouraging sticky notes in his *One-Year Bible* when he is headed out on a trip. Turning down the sheet on his side of the bed at night. Delivering a sandwich and cold root beer on a hot day when he's outside working on a project. Stopping in the middle of a busy work day to head downstairs to his study and find out how his day is going. Honoring his preferences over mine. Assuming the best when he forgets to tell me a piece of news. Choosing to overlook some perceived (or real) slight rather than grinding his nose in it. A kind heart expressed in kind words and kind deeds oils our relationship and softens and draws our hearts toward each other.

Your call to kindness at home will probably take different forms from mine. It may involve curbing a sharp reaction to a childish accident, replenishing the fridge with snacks for a teen, helping a roommate with a project, repeating yourself gently to an elderly parent. But if we were all to demonstrate true kindness toward the people who know us best and see us at our worst, our more public displays of affection would likely ring more true. And I suspect that if we showed more kindness at home, we'd also find ourselves growing genuinely kinder toward everyone else.

From Home and Beyond

Kindness needs to start at home and in our closest relationships. But it doesn't need to *stay* there. As we train each other and let ourselves be trained in kindness, here are some of the other places where our goodness could—and should—be evident.

The family of God

"As we have opportunity," the Bible says, "let us do good to everyone, and especially to those who are of the household of faith" (Gal. 6:10).

Especially to those.

Many people view "church" as primarily a place to show up once a week and invest an hour of time into their spiritual savings account. But that's not what church is supposed to be! Jesus intended His church to be a family—a "household." Not a place, but a people who live out the gospel daily; redeemed men and women who gather together regularly for worship, encouragement, instruction, and service. And the many opportunities for kindness that exist within these relationships—woman to woman, friend to friend, older to younger, younger to older, family to family—can provide a rich source of blessing that builds each other up and keeps each other going.

The roots of this kind of mutual care and consideration among God's people can be traced back to the Old Testament, where the law prescribed, for example, that if you saw an ox or a sheep wandering astray, you weren't allowed to just ignore it. If you knew the person it belonged to, you were to walk it back to its owner. If you weren't sure whose it was or if the journey was more than you could manage, you were to take the animal home with you and keep it safe until the owner came looking for it (see Deut. 22:1–4).

That's the kind of loyalty and kindness that is meant to mark our relationships with fellow members of Christ's body. For as 1 John 4:20 tells us, "he who does not love his brother whom he has seen cannot love God whom he has not seen." And when we open our hearts in generous love and a spirit of kindness toward our fellow believers, we testify to the kindness we've received from God.

So as you encounter fellow believers at church, at Bible study, as they come to mind through the week, or even as you interact online, consider how you might be able to extend kindness that goes deeper than shallow "Hi, how's it going?" hallway conversations. Because most people *aren't* doing "fine, thanks." And your gift of timely kindness—asking sincere questions, expressing interest in the happenings in their life, offering practical assistance for a need they're facing, or stopping to pray together—may be the means by which God ministers grace to them that day.

The poor and needy

Throughout the Scripture we see God's heart for the underserved and the overlooked, the weak and the disenfranchised. The noble woman of Proverbs 31 expresses that heart as she

> opens her hand to the poor
> and reaches out her hands to the needy. (v. 20)

No, it's not our responsibility to solve everyone's problems, to feel as if the weight of people's suffering is ours alone to bear. But God does call each of us to be sensitive toward the plight of those He brings to our attention. And He calls us to demonstrate His kindness to them in practical, need-meeting ways.

And who better than those who have been on the receiving end of God's amazing kindness to be on the lookout for people who are in need of His grace—especially those who may not be expecting anyone's help.

Reaching out in kindness can be as simple as choosing to "see" a person panhandling on the street instead of looking the other way—looking that person in the eye and offering a little something without judging how they will spend it. It can involve asking a widow to sit with us at church, helping out at a food pantry, offering to take a senior in the neighborhood to doctor appointments. But as God leads and as we follow, the borders of our kindness may eventually reach far beyond our natural comfort zone or our normal circle of relationships.

I've watched in awe, for instance, as many of my friends have opened their hearts and homes to care for "the least of these"—orphans, abused or neglected children, special needs children—through foster care, providing "safe homes," and adoption. What a beautiful way to put on display the heart of our heavenly Father who opened His heart and home to bring us into His family when we had nothing to offer Him except our poverty, dysfunction, sin, and need.

If it weren't for Christ showing kindness to us, not one of us would have a single blessing to our name.

In recent years, I have received much joy through occasional involvement at a women's prison where God is at work in an unusual way. The opportunity to offer the kindness of Christ to damaged, broken women who are incarcerated on drug charges or as sex offenders, even some who are serving life sentences for first-degree murder, has reminded me that grace grows best in hard places. It has opened my heart to experience deeper streams of His kindness and blessing, often through the very women I am reaching out to.

Our enemies

And now for the most radical sphere of all—showing kindness to enemies. Responding with gentleness and goodness to those who dislike or even hate us. Doing good for those who would do us harm. Actively seeking the good of those we have reason to fear. That's a prospect that can tie our stomach in knots.

But if it weren't for Christ Himself showing kindness to *us*, not one of us would have a single blessing to our name. We would simply be God's sworn, forever enemies, with no hope on our part of anything except His righteous wrath and just judgment.

Paul says as much in the third chapter of Titus:

> For we ourselves were once foolish, disobedient, led astray, slaves to various passions and pleasures, passing our days in malice and envy, hated by others and hating one another. (v. 3)

That's a description of *you and me* before Jesus saved us. Even for those of us who came to know Him as young children, at our core, we were disobedient, malicious, and hateful. So how did God treat us? Here's how:

> But when the goodness and loving kindness of God our Savior appeared, he saved us, not because of works done by us in righteousness, but according to his own mercy . . . (vv. 4–5)

His goodness and kindness toward us were not based on how we treated Him or on any worthiness in us. Likewise, the kindness we are to show to others is not conditional on their behavior or acceptability. Rather, it's an expression of the kindness we have received from Christ, flowing through us to others.

Even to our enemies.

"I don't have any enemies," you may say. But think again. We're not necessarily talking about supervillains here. Your enemies could simply be people with whom you seem to be at odds. Think about who annoys you or resents you, who often hurts or angers you, who you tend to approach warily if at all. They may be among your family or within your church or from your past. They may live near you, necessitating all-too-frequent contact. Or you may be distanced from them, preferring never to see them again if you can help it.

But consider: what might the kindness of God be leading you to do if your heart was like His heart? And what might it look like if your response toward these people reflected the blessing Christ poured out on you when you were still His enemy?

To be kind is to be like God. And when we are kind to those who are undeserving and unkind to us, we show them the amazing, undeserved kindness of God.

Christ-Centered Kindness

"Be kind to one another," writes Paul in Ephesians 4:32.

"Teach what is good, and so train the young women . . . to be . . . kind," he adds in Titus 2:3.

Our kindness may be the window through which those around us are enabled to see His beauty.

Agathos—kindness of heart, kindness in action—is an indispensable part of the Titus 2 curriculum for both older and younger women.

Such kindness can be costly—costly to our time, our plans, our comfort, our privacy. But when we exercise it in Jesus' name, kindness can provide us with some of our best opportunities to do what we've been put on this earth to do—to bring glory to God and make known the life-giving, transforming gospel of Christ.

Our kindness may be the window through which those around us are enabled to see His beauty. Because kind women—younger and older together—paint an exquisite picture of the gospel. Our lives put on display "the riches of [God's] kindness"—the kindness that "is meant to lead [us] to repentance" (Rom. 2:4). The kindness that can bring about true transformation in those who experience it through us.

The kindness that adorns both us and the gospel we proclaim.

Making It Personal

Older women

1. Dorcas showed the kindness of Christ by helping the poor and needy around her. How might you use your skills to show kindness? How might you mentor or encourage a younger woman in the process?
2. Many younger women feel tired and overwhelmed and can become frustrated when their service and sacrifices appear to go unnoticed. What did you learn in that season that could be helpful to share with a younger woman who is struggling?
3. How could you reach out in kindness to a younger woman in a way that would encourage her and help lift her load?

Younger women

1. Who comes to mind when you think of a Dorcas—a woman who loves Jesus and is a model of kindness and ministering to people's practical needs? What can you learn from her example?
2. Would the people who live in your home and work with you consider you a kind woman? Why or why not?
3. When we get stretched and overly busy with tasks, it's easier to be cranky than kind (think of Martha). How could meditating on the kindness of Christ be an encouragement and motivation to show kindness when you're in that place?

Teach what accords with sound doctrine. . . .

Older women likewise are to be reverent in behavior,
not slanderers or slaves to much wine.

They are to teach what is good,
and so train the young women
to love their husbands and children,
to be self-controlled, pure, working at home,
kind, and submissive to their own husbands,
that the word of God may not be reviled.

Show yourself in all respects to be a model of good works,
and in your teaching show integrity, dignity,
and sound speech that cannot be condemned,
**so that an opponent may be put to shame,
having nothing evil to say about us.**

**. . . so that in everything they may adorn
the doctrine of God our Savior.**

TITUS 2:1–10

EPILOGUE

A Woman Overjoyed

Tying It All Together . . . Beautifully

This city shall be to me a name of joy,
a praise and a glory before all the nations of the earth
who shall hear of all the good that I do for them.
JEREMIAH 33:9

WE BEGAN THIS BOOK WITH A WEDDING. MY WEDDING. God's wonderful surprise gift to me long after I assumed it would never happen.

Now, as I sit here putting the final touches on this book, Robert and I are approaching our first anniversary. And a lot has changed since that never-to-be-forgotten wedding scene. My lovely white wedding dress is packed up in a box, sitting in storage. There's no make-up artist or hair stylist anywhere in sight. In fact, I haven't done a thing to my hair since yesterday and don't have a drop of make-up on. Robert is out of town, and I'm dressed in work-at-home-no-plans-to-see-anyone attire. (I do plan to change before he gets home later this evening!)

Our home is generally quiet these days, and our lives have settled into a "normal" routine that includes conversation (lots of it), simple meals, church, friends, relaxation, sleep, prayer, and meaningful but

We are not the picture-perfect couple that smiles back at us from the wedding photos displayed in various places around our home. We believe it's worth the price for our marriage to be able to point others to the loveliness of Christ.

strenuous and time-consuming work. Like most people we know, we live a pretty unremarkable, unglamorous life—quite unlike the glorious three-day celebration we experienced on our wedding weekend and the sweet days that followed at a friend's home in the Caribbean.

Robert and I love each other even more than we did the day we said "I do," and we've experienced many happy times in our first year of marriage. But as I've already mentioned, we've also had our share of misunderstandings, missteps, mistakes, and stressful moments—figuring out how to blend our different lifestyles and patterns into our new life as one. Some tears have been shed along the way. The days always seem too short to do everything we had hoped to get done. And at times we fight the temptation to become isolated from one another and independent in spirit—to forget that we need each other.

For sure, we are not the picture-perfect couple that smiles back at us from the wedding photos displayed in various places around our home. We know better than anyone else how weak and frail and sinful we are.

Yet even in our more difficult moments we press on—together—because we believe we are called to this. We remember that we can't do this alone. We realize that the dailyness and even the struggles we face are forging for us a deeper oneness and joy than would otherwise be possible. We believe it's worth the price for our marriage to be able to point others to the loveliness of Christ. And we know that unfettered, unsullied joy will ultimately be ours at the end of the journey.

It seems to me that Robert's and my experience of the last year has some similarities to your experience and mine as we seek to live out the calling of Titus 2.

You and I know that Christ and His gospel are exceedingly lovely. We know it is an extraordinary privilege to belong to Him. We aspire to be the women He made us to be and to fulfill His calling for our lives. And we are exceedingly grateful for those moments when we sense His nearness and revel in His presence, when we are enthralled with His beauty, when we know the joy of being and doing what He has put us here on this earth to be and to do.

But then there are the days—perhaps most days—when we feel more like earthbound plodders than heaven-bound pilgrims. When we lament our selfishness, sinfulness, stubbornness, and slowness to grow in these qualities we know to be pleasing to Him.

Yet we press on in our mission. We keep pursuing our calling to magnify Christ, and we persevere by faith, with the grace we receive from Him each day. We know the challenges and hardships are deepening our oneness with the Savior and conforming us to His likeness. We believe it's worth any price to put His beauty on display during our sojourn in this world. And we trust we will experience unending, unclouded joy when we see His face at the end of the race.

Growing Pains

As we've traveled through these verses from Titus 2, at times you may have felt—as have I—woefully inadequate, convicted by how far short you fall. I would remind you that the point of exposing our sin and insufficiency is not to burden us down with our failure. Rather, the goal is to get us to Christ, whose mercy and grace are our only hope, and to make us realize our utter dependence on Him for anything resembling Christian character in our lives.

If you're a believer in Christ, He has already imputed to you His righteousness. You couldn't possibly be any more pleasing to the Lord,

There are days when we feel more like earthbound plodders than heaven-bound pilgrims. Yet we press on in our mission.

even if you tried—because not an iota of your personal standing with Him is based on your personal effort. His covenant love is based on *His* performance, not yours. And it is His love and faithfulness that motivate and enable you to walk in a way that honors Him.

The conviction you feel, therefore, is not meant to induce you to try harder, as if you could somehow work yourself into better favor with God. No, it's intended to let true repentance lead you back to the true Source of all this love, kindness, and self-control—the only One who's able to make you a beautiful, adorned Titus 2 woman.

Yet even if you've taken God's grace to heart, I suspect that some of what we've talked about in this book still feels a little—or a lot—overwhelming. No book can change our lives into totally manageable, easily handled, pieces. As long as we live here as fallen people on a fallen planet, the puzzle pieces will never quite look like the picture on the box. There will be days—many days—when everything seems like an incomplete jumble, and only the Spirit of Christ, at work in us and empowering our obedience, can keep moving us in the right direction.

But that's part of the beauty of Titus 2! It brings to these messy realities the promise of reinforcements for the struggle, and recovery of our divine calling and purpose.

Younger woman, it comes in the form of practical and spiritual mothering that meets you at your points of inexperience and your need for training. This gift of intergenerational connection and community helps to settle your heart and to set you on a sound path for the future—not to mention providing another set of hands to help you get there. And even when your questions seem to have no answers, at least now you have a caring prayer partner and confidante to walk with you and encourage you during the waiting times.

And *older woman,* you have the opportunity to see fruit growing again on seasoned, perhaps long-dormant limbs—not just by writing another check or promising to pray (important and valuable as those are), but also by investing one-on-one, face-to-face in the lives of younger women who, perhaps to your surprise, are eager for what you have to offer. The vacuum of an empty nest or semiretirement is filled by a sense of mission that makes you eager to get out of bed in the morning.

And so, even with life a complicated maze of obligations, disappointments, longings, and uncertainties—new health scares, financial strain, painful losses, and bone-tired weariness—God settles and stabilizes our hearts, even as He broadens us beyond ourselves and our own personal concerns. He places us in close-knit, Christ-centered relationships, through which we can experience and express more of His love. He makes us at home in others' homes—and others at home in ours—to unite us across generations and protect us against our tendencies toward insecurity and isolation.

To give us friendship.

To give us growth.

To give us hope.

To give us . . .

Joy.

Yes, we will feel overwhelmed at times. Choosing to invest in other women or to receive another's counsel and care involves cost and sacrifice. But none of that can compare with the refreshment, connectedness, and joy we receive from these relationships, not to mention the greater joy of glorifying God through fruitful lives.

What's at Stake

Throughout his short letter to Titus, Paul gives instructions to believers in various seasons and stations in life. He shows us what it looks like when all believers live in a way that "accords with sound doctrine" (2:1).

In this book we've focused intently on three verses in chapter 2 that address specifically how the beauty of the gospel is put on display as women—older and younger—live it out together.

We've grappled with what it means when Paul says we should be reverent in behavior, not slanderers or slaves to much wine. We've examined his curriculum for what older women are meant to model and convey to their younger daughters and sisters in the faith—to love their husbands and children, to be pure and self-controlled, to be working at home, kind, and submissive in their marriages.

And we've seen that what Paul has drawn for us in this description is really a portrait of the heart of Christ—His love, His purity, His self-control, His kindness, His submission to the will of His Father. We are to make it our aim to look and act and talk and think like Jesus!

In the rest of Titus 2, Paul goes on to remind us (vv. 11–12) that it is the grace of God (undeserved as it is) that not only saves us, but enables us to live that kind of life "in the present age."

He also encourages us (v. 13) with the promise and blessed hope of seeing Jesus when He returns—a joyous prospect that helps us stay the course and press on when we are tempted to give up or when our efforts seem fruitless.

But there's one more thing I want you to see in Titus 2, something that helps us understand *why* it matters so much that we learn and practice these qualities. This understanding puts a frame around the picture we've been admiring and reminds us what is at stake here.

Paul didn't just toss around these concepts as being good ideas, you see, nor did he intend that these truths were solely for the purpose of our personal spiritual growth, or even for the benefit of other believers with whom we learn and live them out. In Titus 2, he lays out three "purpose clauses" that give us an even grander, greater motivation for taking this message seriously. These three clauses, which are three different ways of making essentially the same point, remind us that our lives as believers have a major impact on how those around us view and respond to our message.

In other words, the *reason* we are called to live as Titus 2 women (and men) is so . . .

1. "That the word of God may not be reviled" (Titus 2:5)

A comparison of other translations gives us a fuller sense of Paul wants us to understand:

- "that the word of God will not be dishonored" (NASB)
- "that God's message will not be slandered" (HCSB)
- "that no one will malign the word of God" (NIV)
- "that the word of God may not be blasphemed" (NKJV)

This last rendering is actually a transliteration of the Greek word used in this verse. It's the word *blasphemeo.* It means just that: "to blaspheme, revile . . . to hurt the reputation of."[1] One commentator offers this paraphrase: "so that God's Word may suffer no scandal."[2]

Paul's point is simple and sobering. When we call ourselves Christians and claim to believe God's Word but do not live according to it, the Scriptures will be dishonored in the eyes of those who are watching us. Any disconnect between what His Word says and the way we live will give them ammunition to speak evil of God and His ways.

Instead, the example of our lives should earn the respect of onlookers, making the Word of God more attractive and compelling to them, not more repulsive.

2. "That an opponent may be put to shame, having nothing evil to say about us" (Titus 2:8)

Paul was not afraid to speak out against the hypocrisy of those who taught one thing to others but whose lives contradicted their message. To such people he would say, horrified, "The name of God is blasphemed among the Gentiles because of you" (Rom. 2:24).

In Titus 2:8, he warns against that same hypocrisy, cautioning us not to give others reasons for rejecting Christ by allowing there to be a gap between what we profess and what we practice. The consistency of our Christian character should keep people from being able to accuse us of pretending to be something we're not.

3. *"That in everything [we] may adorn the doctrine of God our Savior" (Titus 2:10)*

Or as the NIV puts it, "so that in every way they will make the teaching about God our Savior attractive." Just as our lives can cause people to revile the truth, they can also cause people to admire it.

Just think. We have been given the opportunity—and the responsibility—to live in such a way that people who have no respect or love for the gospel will be compelled to ooh and aah over its beauty.

These three purpose clauses all address the quality of our witness. They call us to conduct ourselves in such a way that our lives reveal the inherent beauty of the message of the gospel. Although only one uses the actual word, they are all about *adorning* the doctrine of God.

Life to Life

History has preserved for us a letter written by Clement of Rome, one of the early church fathers, to the believers in Corinth, just across the Mediterranean waters from the island of Crete. This epistle, dated around AD 96, was written to express concern over the backslidden, divided condition of the church—a situation he reminded them was "highly incompatible with God's chosen people" and had brought their good name "into serious disrepute." But Clement also reminded these believers of an earlier season, when their behavior had beautifully adorned the gospel they professed. He observed the profound impact the gospel had made on people's lives, making specific mention of the women:

> Nobody could spend even a short while among you without noticing the excellence and constancy of your faith. . . . Your womenfolk were bidden to go about their duties in irreproachable devotion and purity of conscience, showing all proper affection to their husbands; they were taught to make obedience the rule of their lives, to manage their households decorously, and to be patterns of discretion in every way.[3]

Clement clearly recalled seeing the gospel on visible, enthralling display in the lifestyles of everyday Christian women in Corinth, and he was eager for this to be the case once again. As I read this description of the gospel at work in and through women's lives, I can't help but believe that if it could happen in a profane, debauched culture such as that of the first-century Roman Empire, then surely it could happen today.

And I think it does happen. In fact, I've witnessed and participated in this dynamic—women living out the beauty of the gospel together—over and over again.

I've watched it transform resistant, reclusive teenage girls into shining models of Christian faith and beauty.

I've seen it redirect young wives and mothers from giving up on their marriages and walking away from the whole stressful mess.

I've observed older women dare to return from the sidelines and get back into the race, discovering that what young women really want and need from them is not an impressive personality and résumé, but simply a heart that truly desires Christ and is seeking to obey Him.

My own life has been molded and changed in precious ways—both as a younger woman, and now as an older woman—by this gift of intentional, life-to-life friendship, community, and discipleship.

I'll admit I came to a point, somewhere around age fifty, where my heart and body just wanted to start coasting. I was tired. And I was tempted to believe I'd already done enough, that I could afford to take it easy from here.

But here's what my heart knows to be *really* true, even when my feet and back are screaming otherwise. I can't live for Christ and live for me at the same time. If I choose myself, I'm choosing to miss out on something a lot more valuable than my self-centered desires and comfort. And I can attest that as I have chosen Him, He has continually amazed me with His persistent faithfulness and joy.

He has let me stand close enough to the action when He captures a younger woman's heart that the abundance He pours out into her overflows to refresh my own spirit.

And whenever my heart has grown weary, He has kept me close to older women who continue to inspire me out of the overflow of their walk with God.

Throughout this book, I've told you about the influence of older women like Vonette Bright, Leta Fischer, and my own mother. I want you to meet one more Titus 2 woman—a dear friend who touched my life in a beautiful way.

Joyce Johnson—known to many of us whose lives were blessed by her influence simply as Mom J—exemplified the joy older women can experience as they pour themselves into younger women.

Joyce died less than three months after the passing of her husband, to whom she'd been married for almost sixty-five years. She had known significant loss along the way—including the tragic death of her seventeen-year-old daughter, the oldest of their five children, less than a month before high school graduation. Yet Mom J's resiliency and trust in God's sovereignty only deepened and grew through such experiences, guarding her heart from self-pity and resentment.

I first got to know Joyce when she and her husband, friends of my parents, invited me to live with them in Southern California while I finished my last two years of college. She was in her early sixties at the time, and the mark she left on my life was indelible. I wasn't the first young person she and Dad J had received into their home, nor would I be the last. Her ministry of mentoring would continue all the way to the finish line of her race.

One of the last times I spoke with her, in fact, she told me excitedly about the twenty-year-old single girl she was regularly discipling and meeting with. At age ninety-two! And loving every minute of it.

Mom J never stopped blessing me with her interest and love. As I said half-seriously when I spoke at her funeral, I didn't know if I'd be able to write any more books after she was gone—not without knowing that Mom J was out there marinating them in her faithful prayers. I recall the passion God gave her for holiness while she prayed me through the writing of a book on that topic.[4] She eagerly began marking in her Bible every reference to holiness she could find. For the better part of a year she wrote to me often, exuberant and convicted over what God was showing her along those lines.

She never stopped growing and learning. And whatever God taught *her*, she transferred to others—life to life.

I want to be a Mom J.

And I want to see a whole generation of Mom Js raised up.

Every glimpse I see of that taking place causes my heart to rejoice. As I was in the final stages of writing this book, a dear friend—an empty-nest mom and grandmom—wrote to me:

> When I was a young adult, I saw no one in my church or sphere of influence who taught or modeled these things. *Taking Titus 2 to heart changed the entire course of my life.* I take legacy and living a life of mentorship seriously. My heart's desire is to be one of those older women.

How might our homes and churches be different if they were filled with such women?

What kind of impact might these women make among unbelievers in our families and our communities?

And what might it look like to see a genuine, God-ignited revival, spreading like wildfire through the linked arms and hearts of women (and men) who are passionate about adorning the gospel of Christ? This is the vision Paul had for that band of believers on the isle of Crete in Titus' day. And this is the vision the Lord has put in my heart for our day.

The women around you, overwhelmed by the undertow of life, need more than a book to read or a class to attend. They need you.

Our *goal* for what we're talking about here is as grand as the glory and majesty of God. But the *method* He has prescribed for us is as simple as women sitting down together, opening up their lives and the Word, receiving and passing on to others the baton of faith and Christlike character.

The women around you, overwhelmed by the undertow of life but longing to be beautiful—adorned—need more than a book to read or a class to attend or more worship music to play.

They need you.

They need your presence, your concern, your prayers.

As we live out the beauty of the gospel—younger and older women together—we will be beautified and blessed and, yes, overjoyed. That beauty will spill over into our homes, our churches, our workplaces and communities, and ultimately into our world.

And in the end, Christ will be "glorified in his saints, and . . . marveled at among all who have believed" (2 Thess. 1:10).

Such pure beauty. Such eternal joy.

Let's pursue it—let's pursue Him—together.

Notes

Chapter 1: A Woman Adorned and Adorning

1. Nikolaus Ludwig von Zinzendorf, "Jesus, Thy Blood and Righteousness," 1739, tr. John Wesley, 1740.

Chapter 2: Doctrine, You, and Titus 2

Epigraph: John Piper, "The Ultimate Meaning of True Womanhood," message delivered at the 2008 True Woman Conference, Desiring God, http://www.desiringGod.org/resource-library/conference-messages/the-ultimate-meaning-of-true-womanhood.

1. Blue Letter Bible Lexicon, s.v. "anatrepō" (Strong's G396), Blue Letter Bible website, version 3, https://www.blueletterbible.org/lang/lexicon/lexicon.cfm?Strongs=G396&t=ESV.
2. Charles R. Swindoll, *Insights on 1 and 2 Timothy, Titus*: Swindoll's New Testament Insights (Grand Rapids: Zondervan, 2010), 256.
3. Paul uses this term not only for non-Christians, but also for those who claimed to be in the faith but whose doctrine and lifestyles gave no such evidence.
4. John MacArthur, Jr., The MacArthur New Testament Commentary: *Titus* (Chicago: Moody, 1996), 88.

Chapter 3: Don't Give Up on That Modeling Career

Epigraph: John MacArthur, "God's Plan for Older Men and Older Women," sermon delivered February 7, 1993, Grace to You, http://www.gty.org/resources/sermons/56-13/gods-plan-for-older-men-and-older-women.

1. Helen Roseveare, "A Call for the Perseverance of the Saints," address delivered at the Desiring God National Conference, September 29, 2007, http://www.desiringGod.org/messages/a-call-for-the-perseverance-of-the-saints.
2. Warren Doud, *The Epistle to Titus: A Grace Notes Bible Study,* online study downloaded as pdf from Grace Notes: Online Training in Bible Teaching, http://www.gracenotes.info/TITUS/Titus004.pdf, 30.

Chapter 4: Grow Up and Step Up

Epigraph: Cathe Laurie, "How to Bake a Pie," Cathe's Notes, Virtue, October 24, 2014, http://www.harvest.org/virtue/sections/cathes-notes.html/?p=11050.

1. Tom Nelson, "The Priesthood of the Believer," sermon preached at Denton Bible Church, Denton, TX, September 23, 2007, https://www.dbcmedia.org/?s_cs=1&s=1269.
2. Daniel C. Arichea and Howard A. Hatton, eds., *A Handbook on Paul's Letters to Timothy and Titus,* UBS Handbook Series (New York: United Bible Societies, 1995), 284.

Chapter 5: Revival of Reverence

Epigraph: Rochelle Fleming, "Titus 2 Women—Reverent Behavior," pdf downloaded from Light-Work blog, http://lightwork.typepad.com/lightwork/files/Reverent.pdf, 2.

1. William Barclay, *The New Daily Study Bible: The Letters to Timothy, Titus, and Philemon,* 3rd ed., rev. (Louisville: Westminister John Knox, 2003, orig. pub. 1956), 279.
2. "Titus 2:3-4 Commentary," s.v. "hieroprepes," Precept Austin, http://www.preceptaustin.org/titus_23-4.htm.
3. Thomas C. Oden, *First and Second Timothy and Titus,* Interpretation: A Bible Commentary for Teaching and Preaching (Louisville: John Knox Press, 1989), 115.
4. Frederic William Farrar, in *Streams in the Desert,* vol. 1, comp. Mrs. Charles E. Cowman (Cowman, 1925; Grand Rapids: Zondervan, 1965–66), September 13.

Chapter 6: You Don't Say

Epigraph: Jon Bloom, "Lay Aside the Weight of Slander," Desiring God, December 19, 2015, http://www.desiringGod.org/articles/lay-aside-the-weight-of-slander.

1. Martin Luther, *Luther's Works, Vol. 21: The Sermon on the Mount and the Magnificat,* 41, quoted in Jason Garoncy, "Luther and Calvin on Slander (and Women)," January 14, 2010, http://jasongoroncy.com/2010/01/14/luther-and-calvin-on-slander-and-women/.
2. Spiros Zodhiates, *The Complete Word Study New Testament*, reissue ed. (Chattanooga: AMG, 1991), 913.
3. William Barclay, *The New Daily Study Bible: The Letters to Timothy, Titus, and Philemon,* 3rd ed., rev. (Louisville: Westminster John Knox, 2003, orig. pub. 1956), 280.
4. Jonathan Edwards, *Memoirs of Jonathan Edwards,* vol. 1 in *The Works of Jonathan Edwards* (Carlisle, PA: Banner of Truth, 1976), xlvi.

Chapter 7: At Liberty

Epigraph: Renee Johnson, "I Found Life," quoted in "Finding Liberty from Addiction," Revive Our Hearts Radio, October 10, 2008, https://www.reviveourhearts.com/radio/revive-our-hearts/finding-liberty-from-addiction. Used by permission of the author.

1. John MacArthur, Jr., *The MacArthur New Testament Commentary: Titus* (Chicago: Moody Press, 1996), 78.
2. Elizabeth Cohen, "Line between Overeating and Binge Disorder Is a Thin One," CNN.com, February 24, 2007, http://www.cnn.com/2007/HEALTH/

conditions/02/22/VS.binge.eating/index.html.

3. Study published in *Alcohol Health and Research World,* quoted in Sharon Hersh, "Even Good Women Get Hooked," *Today's Christian Woman,* July 1988, http://www.todayschristianwoman.com/articles/1998/july/8w4082.html.
4. Joan Caplin, "Confessions of a Compulsive Shopper," CNN Money, November 4, 2005, http://money.cnn.com/2005/07/20/pf/shopper_0508/index.htm.
5. John McDuling, "This Chart Suggests America's Addiction to Television Is Not Normal," Quartz, http://qz.com/178161/this-chart-suggests-americas-addiction-to-television-is-not-normal/.
6. Shannon Ethridge, "What Women Must Know about Lust," *Charisma,* June 22, 2011, http://www.charismamag.com/site-archives/610-spiritled-woman/spiritled-woman/13881-what-women-must-know-about-lust.
7. Lindsay Roberts, "I Was Addicted to Romance," *Today's Christian Woman,* September 2008, http://www.christianitytoday.com/mp/2002/004/1.34.html.
8. Jon Bloom, "Lay Aside the Weight of Self-Indulgence," Desiring God, August 29, 2014, http://www.desiringgod.org/articles/lay-aside-the-weight-of-self-indulgence.
9. Gabrielle Glaser, *Her Best-Kept Secret: Why Women Drink—And How They Can Regain Control* (New York: Simon & Schuster, 2013), 17–18.
10. This is apart from what the law considers to be legal intoxication alcohol levels for operating motor vehicles.
11. National Institute on Alcohol Abuse and Alcoholism, "Alcohol's Effects on the Body," https://www.niaaa.nih.gov/alcohol-health/alcohols-effects-body, accessed June 29, 2016.

Chapter 8: A "Sophron" *State of Mind*

Epigraph: J. Hampton Keathley III, "Marks of Maturity: Biblical Characteristics of a Christian Leader," https://bible.org/seriespage/mark-10-self-control.

1. W. E. Vine, *The Expanded Vine's Expository Dictionary of New Testament Words: A Special Edition* (Minneapolis: Bethany, 1984), 1057.
2. Ibid.
3. Spiros Zodhiates, *The Complete Word Study New Testament* (Chattanooga: AMG Publishers, 1991), 947.
4. William Barclay, *The New Daily Study Bible: The Letters to Timothy, Titus, and Philemon* (Louisville: Westminster John Knox Press, 2003), 278.
5. A pdf of this chart is available at www.ReviveOurHearts.com/sophron. Permission is granted to reproduce the full pdf for yourself or others.
6. This is not to suggest that treatment for people with severe mental illness may not be necessary or helpful or that an encounter with Christ will automatically and immediately free them from their infirmity. However, no treatment will solve problems that originate in the heart, apart from cooperating with the Spirit of Christ in dealing with those issues.

Chapter 9: Passionate about Purity

Epigraph: Quoted in "25 Quotes about Purity," Christian Quotes, http://www.christianquotes.info/quotes-by-topic/quotes-about-purity/#ixzz42zs1XjC2.

1. W. E. Vine, *The Expanded Vine's Expository Dictionary of New Testament Words: A Special Edition* (Minneapolis: Bethany, 1984), 175, 903.
2. J. P. Louw and Eugene Albert Nida, eds., *Greek-English Dictionary of the New Testament: Based on Semantic Domains*, quoted in William E. Wenstrom, Jr., "1 Timothy 5:21–22," pdf downloaded from Wenstrom Bible Ministries website, www.wenstrom.org/downloads/written/exposition/1tim/1tim_5_21-22.pdf, 58.
3. Warren W. Wiersbe, *Be Faithful: It's Always Too Soon to Quit!*, New Testament Commentary, 1 & 2 Timothy, Titus, Philemon (Colorado Springs: David C. Cook, 2009), 124.
4. Patrick F. Fagan, "The Effects of Pornography on Individuals, Marriage, Family and Community," Research Synthesis, December 2009, pdf downloaded from MARRI (Marriage and Religion Research Institute) Research, http://downloads.frc.org/EF/EF12D43.pdf. Read a summary of the full report at http://marriagegems.com/2010/04/02/porn-use-increases-infidelity-divorce/.
5. Gerhard Kittel and Gerhard Friedrich, eds., *Theological Dictionary of the New Testament,* tr. Geoffrey W. Bromiley (Grand Rapids: Wm. B. Eerdmans, 1964), 1:122–24.
6. My booklet *The Look: Does God Really Care What I Wear?* (Niles, MI: Revive Our Hearts, 2003) offers a fuller treatment of this subject. Available at www.ReviveOurHearts.com/look.

Chapter 10: Taste of Heaven

Epigraph: Carolyn McCulley with Nora Shank, *The Measure of Success: Uncovering the Biblical Perspective on Women, Work, and the Home* (Nashville: B&H Books, 2014), 22.

1. "Titus 2:5 Commentary (Titus 2 Resources)," Precept Austin, updated February 21, 2015, http://www.preceptaustin.org/titus_25.htm.
2. "Criticism of Southwestern Homemaking Course Angers Professor, Radio Host," Baptist News Global, July 10, 2007, https://baptist news.com/2007/07/10/criticism-of-southwestern-homemaking-courses-angers-professor-radio-host/.
3. I am indebted to my friend Carolyn McCulley for helping me better understand the history of the home and for her input on this chapter. She expands on these ideas in her excellent book (with Nora Shank), *The Measure of Success: Uncovering the Biblical Perspective on Women, Work, and the Home* (Nashville: B&H Books, 2014).
4. McCulley with Shank, *The Measure of Success,* 57. Emphasis is the author's.
5. Jani Ortlund, *Fearlessly Feminine: Boldly Living God's Plan for Womanhood* (Colorado Springs: Multnomah Books, 2000), 147.

Chapter 11: Need Help Lovin' That Man

Epigraph: "Love Through Me," poem in *Edges of His Ways* by Amy Carmichael, ©1955 The Dohnavur Fellowship. Used by permission of CLC Publications. May not be further reproduced. All rights reserved.

1. J. H. Moulton and G. Milligan, *Vocabulary of the Greek Testament* (Peabody, MA: Hendrickson, 1997), 668.

2. "The Love of Charles and Susannah Spurgeon," Christianity.com, http://www.christianity.com/church/church-history-timeline/2001-now/the-love-of-charles-and-susannah-spurgeon-11633045.html.
3. Charles Haddon Spurgeon, *C. H. Spurgeon's Autobiography: Compiled from His Diary, Letters, and Records, by His Wife and His Private Secretary*, vol. 2, 1854–1860 (London: Passmore & Alabaster, 1899), 291–92.
4. Charles Haddon Spurgeon, "Ripe Fruit," sermon no. 945, delivered August 14, 1870, at The Metropolitan Tabernacle: Sermons Preached and Revised by C. H. Spurgeon During the Year 1870 (London: Passmore & Alabaster, 1871), 448.
5. For daily ideas and support in this exercise, visit the "30-Day Husband Encouragement Challenge" at www.ReviveOurHeart.com/challenge.
6. Fanny J. Crosby, "Rescue the Perishing," 1869.

Chapter 12: An Unexpected Blessing

Epigraph: Kathy Keller, "Embracing the Other," ch. 6 in Timothy Keller with Kathy Keller, *The Meaning of Marriage: Facing the Complexities of Commitment with the Wisdom of God* (New York: Riverhead Books, 2011), 201.

1. Jocelyn Anderson, "Submissive Question: We Have a Right to Know Sacred Beliefs," *Orlando Sentinel,* August 23, 2011, http://articles.orlandosentinel.com/2011-08-23/news/os-ed-michele-bachmann-theology 0823120110822_1_michele-bachmann-male-headship-beliefs.
2. Some translations of this phrase use the words *woman* and *man* instead of *wife* and *husband*. The original Greek words can have both meanings, so the translation must be based on the context. The context of this verse is clarified in the ongoing discussion of 1 Corinthians 11:7–9, which refers to the original man as head of the original woman, the man being the husband and the woman being his wife. In this way, 1 Corinthians 11:3 parallels Paul's teaching in Ephesians 5:22–33, which sets forth the headship of a husband and the submission of a wife.
3. Dave Dunham, "A Word About Polite Abusers," Pastor Dave Online, June 30, 2016, https://pastordaveonline.org/2016/06/30/a-word-about-polite-abusers.

Chapter 13: Life-Givers in Training

Epigraph: Barbara Hughes, *Disciplines of a Godly Woman* (Wheaton, IL: Crossway Books, 2001), 167.

1. Colin Falconer, "Are You Ready to Have Babies? Take the Test," *The Huffington Post,* February 11, 2014, http://www.huffingtonpost.com/colin-falconer/are-you-ready-to-have-babies_b_4377307.html.

Chapter 14: Instruments of Grace

Epigraph: Mary Beeke, *The Law of Kindness: Serving with Heart and Hands* (Grand Rapids: Reformation Heritage, 2007), 31. Quote adapted with permission from the author.

1. Scripture does not explicitly state that Martha was the eldest sibling in her family. But many commentators believe the text suggests that this was the case—also that the home belonged to her and that she was responsible for managing the household.

2. Spiros Zodhiates, ed., *The Complete Word Study Dictionary: New Testament,* rev. reissue ed. (Chattanooga: AMG, 1993), 62.
3. W. E. Vine, *The Expanded Vine's Expository Dictionary of New Testament Words: A Special Edition* (Minneapolis: Bethany, 1984), 493.
4. Matthew Henry, *Commentary on the Whole Bible,* ed. Leslie F. Church (Grand Rapids: Zondervan, 1961), 1902.
5. Jerry Bridges, *The Practice of Godliness: Godliness Has Value for All Things,* rev. ed. (Colorado Springs: NavPress, 2008), 189.
6. Thomas D. Lea and Hayne P. Griffin, *1, 2 Timothy, Titus*, vol. 34 of *The New American Commentary* (Nashville: B&H, 1992), 301.

Epilogue: A Woman Overjoyed

1. Spiros Zodhiates, *The Complete Word Study New Testament*, reissue ed. (Chattanooga: AMG, 1991), 884.
2. William Kelly, cited in John MacArthur, Jr., *The MacArthur New Testament Commentary: Titus* (Chicago: Moody, 1996), 88.
3. Clement of Rome, "The First Epistle of Clement to the Corinthians," in Andrew Louth, ed., *Early Christian Writings: The Apostolic Fathers,* tr. Maxwell Staniforth, rev. ed. (London: Penguin Classics, 1987), 23.
4. Nancy Leigh DeMoss, *Holiness: The Heart God Purifies* (Chicago: Moody, 2005).

Heartfelt Thanks

I HAVE QUIPPED THAT THIS BOOK about younger and older women growing together has taken so long to write that in the process I have transitioned from the young woman category to the older woman one—not to mention transitioning from being a single woman to being a married one.

For sure, there have been lots of twists and turns along the way—a lot of life lived and lessons learned—and more sweet providences than I can count. Not the least of these are the many humble, gifted, servant-hearted friends who believe in this message and have partnered with me to see it take shape in the form of this book. Among them . . .

- *Greg Thornton, Paul Santhouse, Randall Payleitner, Judy Dunagan, Erik Peterson, Ashley Torres, Connor Sterchi, and the entire Moody Publishers team*—whose faithful, diligent efforts, along with their patience, prayers, and encouragement have been a great gift
- *Lawrence Kimbrough*—who took 144 pages of my notes and hours of my audio teaching on Titus 2 and organized, framed, and fashioned it all into an excellent working draft
- *Anne Christian Buchanan*—editor extraordinaire, who stuck with me through at least four complete, painstaking rounds of substantive edits on a 350-page manuscript
- *Mike Neises*—Director of Publishing and Events for Revive Our Hearts, who has played an invaluable, mostly unseen, role in the development of each book I've written
- *Erik Wolgemuth and the rest of the Wolgemuth & Associates team*—who dove in headfirst midway through this project and have been a great help in getting it to the finish line

- *Tim Challies*—for his thoughtful theological review and his help in sharpening specific points to make them more clear, helpful, and biblical
- *Tom and Roz Sullivan*—who lovingly assisted with grocery shopping and delicious meals, so my husband (who was also working on a book) and I could stay at it
- *Martin Jones, Sandy Bixel, Hannah Kurtz, and Leanna Shepard*—who graciously provided administrative support and kept countless plates spinning to enable me to write with a minimum of distraction
- *Dawn Wilson*—who tirelessly assisted with research, dug up quotes, and suggested Making It Personal questions
- *Paula Marsteller*—who kindly read through the manuscript twice with her great eye for details, made many helpful edits and suggestions, and collaborated on the Making It Personal questions
- *Jennifer Lyell, Carolyn McCulley, Mary Kassian, and Kimberly Wagner*—who gave feedback on certain chapters and helped me grapple with how to communicate effectively and biblically on specific issues
- *"The sisterhood"*—whose friendship, wisdom, prayers, encouragement, and love are one of the greatest blessings of my life
- *My dear "Praying Friends"*—who faithfully carry me through every significant undertaking with their earnest prayers on my behalf
- *Robert Wolgemuth*—my precious husband and cheerleader, whose prayers, encouragement, and input have been wind beneath my wings as I worked on this book over the past year

These women and men are "my fellow workers . . . beloved in the

Lord" (Rom. 16:3, 8). They each deserve far more credit than they will get this side of heaven, and they adorn the gospel with their lives, their love, and their labors. My life is more fruitful and this book is more effective as a result of their partnership. To them and to the Lord Jesus I offer my deepest gratitude.

Also by Nancy

A 30-Day Walk With God in the Psalms

A Place of Quiet Rest: Cultivating Intimacy with God through a Daily Devotional Life

Becoming God's True Woman, ed.

Brokenness: The Heart God Revives

Holiness: The Heart God Purifies

Surrender: The Heart God Controls

Brokenness, Surrender, Holiness: A Revive Our Hearts Trilogy

Choosing Forgiveness: Your Journey to Freedom

Choosing Gratitude: Your Journey to Joy

Lies Women Believe: And the Truth That Sets Them Free

The Companion Guide for Lies Women Believe

Lies Young Women Believe: And the Truth That Sets Them Free (coauthored with Dannah Gresh)

Lies Young Women Believe Companion Guide

Seeking Him: Experiencing the Joy of Personal Revival (coauthored with Tim Grissom)

The Quiet Place: Daily Devotional Readings

The Wonder of His Name: 32 Life-Changing Names of Jesus

True Woman 101: Divine Design: An Eight-Week Study on Biblical Womanhood (coauthored with Mary A. Kassian)

True Woman 201: Interior Design: Ten Elements of Biblical Womanhood (coauthored with Mary A. Kassian)

Voices of the True Woman Movement: A Call to the Counter-Revolution, ed.

The Time of Her Life

Tracy started writing when her cruel, heartless husband ripped her away from her dream job – shopping for rollercoasters for the UK's leading theme parks – to live in America with a brand-new baby and no mates. In a cunning plan to avoid domestic duties and people who didn't understand her Derbyshire accent, she wrote *No-one Ever Has Sex on a Tuesday*. It went on to become a No. 1 bestseller and publishing phenomenon. Since then, Tracy has written many more novels and been published successfully around the world. She now lives back home in Derbyshire with her husband and children.

To keep in touch with Tracy, visit her website and follow her on social media.

www.tracybloom.com
@TracyBBloom
/tracybloomwrites

Also by Tracy Bloom

Single Woman Seeks Revenge
I Will Marry George Clooney (By Christmas)
Strictly My Husband
The Last Laugh
Dinner Party
The Wife Who Got a Life
The Weekend Before the Wedding

No-one Ever Has Sex series
No-one Ever Has Sex on a Tuesday
No-one Ever Has Sex in the Suburbs
No-one Ever Has Sex on Christmas Day
No-one Ever Has Sex at a Wedding
No-one Ever Has Sex on Holiday

TRACY BLOOM

The Time of Her Life

HarperCollins*Publishers*

HarperCollins*Publishers* Ltd
1 London Bridge Street,
London SE1 9GF

www.harpercollins.co.uk

HarperCollins*Publishers*
Macken House, 39/40 Mayor Street Upper
Dublin 1, D01 C9W8

First published by HarperCollins*Publishers* 2024
1

A catalogue record for this book is available from the British Library

ISBN: 978-0-00-861911-4

Typeset in Sabon LT Std by Palimpsest Book Production Ltd,
Falkirk, Stirlingshire

Printed and bound in the UK using 100% Renewable
Electricity by CPI Group (UK) Ltd

This one's for all you mothers out there. It's the hardest and the best role anyone could ever have. You are all heroes – keep up the good work

Chapter 1

Kim loved the anticipation of a party. The opportunity to create memories that lasted a lifetime literally gave her goosebumps. She was sure that tonight's party would be no exception, especially as she was throwing it and the guest of honour, her husband, was totally in the dark. She couldn't wait to see his face when he walked in on his special surprise which was surely going to win her the award for wife of the century.

Looking down at the pile of napkins and cutlery in front of her, she began to count. So there were fifty-three people coming as long as Uncle George's knee wasn't playing up, and Alison and Neil from next door got back from their holiday in time. She had one unopened pack of forty cream napkins with 'fifty' written on them and one already opened pack. They'd used some of the napkins on Tuesday when it was Richard's actual birthday and his parents had come round for dinner and cake. She decided she should just wrap them around the knives and forks then she would know she definitely had enough. She drew up a bar stool at the kitchen island, asked Alexa to play some party music and began to wrap.

She looked up as she did so to check that everything was ready. She'd already laid out the buffet, courtesy of Costco, and it sat waiting under acres of clingfilm on the dining table, pushed up against the wall of their open-plan kitchen-diner. Helium-filled fiftieth birthday balloons jiggled in a line in front of the bifold door that overlooked the garden. Such a shame a glimmer of sharp autumnal weather had suddenly arrived. It would have been great to be able to throw the doors wide open and dance on the patio late into the night. A makeshift bar had been set up on the central kitchen island. Bottles of Richard's favourite red wine were lined up along with a selection of spirits. She'd got some lager in for her dad and her older nephews, whilst an abundance of prosecco was stocked up in the wine fridge.

Pride of place over the bifolds hung a banner. Primary colours on flimsy foil shouted out HAPPY 50th BIRTHDAY in case anyone forgot which of her husband's birthdays they were there to celebrate. She'd been tempted to get another one reading GOOD LUCK to mark the departure of her son off to university the following day but she thought Harry might just murder her.

Yes, they were ready. She could relax. Not that she suffered with pre-party anxiety. Unlike her husband who tended to get agitated and pace the room, asking annoying questions like, have we got enough toilet rolls? It was one of the reasons why she had decided to make this a surprise party. So he could just arrive and enjoy it without any of the anxiety he seemed to suffer with before a big social occasion. Fortunately, Richard had been running some kind of lab experiment at the university where he worked for the past few months on Saturday afternoons so she could rely on him being out of the way until 6 p.m. guaranteed. Apparently, they were on the brink of some kind of amazing discovery in the chemistry world. Richard often tried to explain to Kim the research he did alongside his lecturing at Lancaster City University. She'd perfected the understated nod over the years because she knew it was important to him but she really didn't understand much of what he was saying. She suspected the same was true of Richard when she tried to explain the intricacies of hairdressing. She could see the glazed look settle as he tried to ask intelligent questions about feather cuts and extensions. The fact that they still both made an effort to understand each other's contrasting careers after twenty years, Kim felt was probably an important factor in them still being married.

She wondered if she should just check on Harry as she wrapped the last set of cutlery. He was supposed to be finishing his packing ready for the drive to Nottingham the following day. She'd been itching to get involved but Harry had kept her firmly at arm's length. She'd offered to take him clothes shopping, hoping that it would be an opportunity to revamp his 'never going to get a girlfriend' wardrobe of gaming T-shirts and tracky bottoms, but he'd refused, reluctantly agreeing to a grumpy trip to Ikea instead to get essential kitchen equipment. Still, at least it was happening. He was going to university. It hadn't been an easy ride. The nerves had got the better of him during his exams – he'd come home white in the face after his maths A level, convinced he'd flunked it, refusing to even have a conversation for days. He'd thrown up the morning the results came out, declining to let his mum accompany him to school to discover his fate. He'd not flunked it but he'd not got what he'd needed to get into his preferred choice so had embarked on the nerve-wracking process of going through clearing. After a nail-biting couple of days he received an offer from Nottingham Barton University to study chemistry, following in his dad's footsteps, albeit not quite in the illustrious surroundings of Durham where Richard had excelled.

Kim, however, had been overjoyed. Her son going to university! The first of her family line ever to proceed to higher education. It was a proud, proud day. Though watching her son nearly screw up the opportunity had brought back memories of her own teenage years. She'd stayed on to do A levels but then had fallen under the spell of a bad boy – Eddie – and partied too hard with him to achieve what she needed to get into higher education. Not particularly caring at the time because she was 'in love', she grasped hold of an apprenticeship at the hairdressers where she was a Saturday girl and never looked back. When Harry started considering his choices post-school, however, she couldn't help but wonder what might have been if she hadn't met Eddie. Would she have made it to university? Would her life have been entirely different? But she'd dismissed the thought because if she hadn't become a hairdresser then she never would have met Richard when he burst into the salon that day and they never would have got married and Harry wouldn't exist. So, for that reason she was delighted with the path fate had led her down. In any case, now her son was going to university, she hoped that she could at least enjoy a small part of the experience through him.

She looked up as she heard heavy footsteps down the hall and hoped it was Harry showing signs of completing his packing.

'Are you nearly done yet?' she asked him. 'Can I do anything to help?'

'I'll do it later, Mum, stop fretting,' he replied, helping himself to a can of Coke Zero lined up on the breakfast bar ready for the party. She sighed. She knew that she needed to let him do it – he was about to leave home – she wasn't going to be there to do anything for him after tomorrow. Her tall, skinny, scruffy Harry was going to have to work out the practicalities of life all by himself. She wondered if she dared ask him to just give the downstairs loo a quick clean before the guests arrived – probably not. He'd make a right mess of it.

Harry was staring down at his phone. 'One of the other guys in my house has already arrived in Nottingham,' he said. 'He's put on the group WhatsApp that the house is really grim. Reckons there are no en suites.'

'No en suites?' asked Kim. 'Does he think he's moved to the Ritz or something?'

'I think he's pretty posh actually. His name's Angus

and he went to a private school somewhere up in Scotland. Reckons he'd never heard of Nottingham before he got a place through clearing. He's going to be a total nightmare to live with.'

Kim looked at her son. He didn't seem overly enthusiastic about his departure to Nottingham tomorrow. Then again she knew he was still worrying that he'd let his father down by not getting better grades.

'It's meant to be,' said Kim firmly, a great believer in fate. 'You were meant to go to Nottingham all along. Amazing things are going to happen there. It's like your dad coming into the salon the day before he started as a mature student up at the uni.'

Harry shook his head. 'Please, not this story again,' he said.

'All right, I'll save it for my speech later at the party. My point is that this is all meant to be. Nottingham was always where you were meant to end up.'

'With Angus,' said Harry, raising his eyebrow.

'He sounds fun. Posh and Scottish. What's not to love? Who else is on this WhatsApp group then?'

'Someone called Sonny who has messaged so many times with so many questions that I'm just ignoring him. The last message I saw he was asking about loo roll holders. Then apparently the fourth room is empty. Some girl has changed her mind and isn't coming, so no idea what might happen there. The joy of going through clearing, hey?'

'At least you've got *somewhere* to live. What with all the halls being full. It could be a lot worse. In any case it's all meant to be, Harry. One of your new housemates could turn out to be your lifelong buddy, or partner or even husband.'

Harry looked sideways at his mum. 'I keep telling you, I'm not gay, Mum.'

'I know. I'm just trying to show you it's okay if you are.'

'I'm not.'

'Shame there are no girls moving in then. You could have been meeting your future wife tomorrow.'

'Muuum! Enough. More than likely we are all going to hate each other and at least one of them will be a mass murderer.'

'Can I just say again how proud I am that you are going to university?'

'Thanks, Mum,' replied Harry, glumly looking down and kicking the side of the kitchen unit.

There was a sharp knock at the back door, causing them both to jump. The door opened and Vicky, Kim's best friend, poked her head in.

'Can I come in?' she askcd.

'Of course, come on in,' said Kim. 'We are just about ready.'

'Oh hello, Harry,' said Vicky, putting a large white box on the kitchen island. 'You all ready for the big day tomorrow?'

'Is he hell,' said Kim, grinning at her son.

'And what am I going to do with this heartbroken woman once you are gone?' Vicky asked Harry, putting her arm round her friend.

'I'm sure you'll find something to keep you amused,' said Harry.

Harry was right. Best friends since primary school, Kim and Vicky mostly saw the funny side of life and could often be found still giggling like schoolgirls at something pretty stupid. The last time had been when Kim had got her leg stuck in the cat flap because she was trying to prove how much more flexible she was since she started doing Pilates. Harry had come home from school with them both lying on the floor at the back door in fits of laughter trying to get Kim's leg out using a bottle of olive oil. For days afterwards the cat looked like he was having an extremely bad hair day! Which made Kim and Vicky laugh even harder.

'Vicky's threatening to start taking me to bingo,' Kim told her son. 'As if my son leaving home isn't traumatic enough.'

'Aah, get on with you,' said Vicky, punching her friend. 'You know you'd love it if you came. Just come and give it a go. Leave all your prejudices at the bingo door. Now do you want to see this cake then? I've done exactly what you asked for. Hopefully I've got it right.'

Vicky carefully lifted the lid off the box to reveal a large oblong cake decorated in white fondant icing. Sitting on top of a pile of books in the middle of the cake sat a moulded figurine in a black gown that looked remarkably like Richard, albeit his heavy rimmed glasses and bald head were a gift to any caricaturist. At his feet were the beautifully iced words, 'Happy Birthday Richard'. Underneath was the number five written large with a small three to the top right of it.

'Why five cubed?' asked Harry, peering in.

'Because that equals fifty,' said Kim, beaming. 'Thought I'd try and be a bit different to signify your father's profession.'

'But it doesn't equal fifty,' said Harry.

Kim felt her face drain. 'Yes, it does. I worked it out on the calculator.'

'Five cubed is five times five which is twenty-five then times another five which is one hundred and twenty-five.'

Kim stared at her son. 'Are you sure?'

'I have just sat my maths A level,' he replied.

Kim turned to face her best friend. 'I did say that you needed to leave that stuff to Richard,' Vicky said. 'A normal fifty would have done the job.' She smiled then broke into a laugh. 'Can't believe you got it wrong. I told you to double check, didn't I?' She started to snigger.

Kim felt her heart start to race. She'd never been any good at maths. She reckoned she was numbers dyslexic. The minute she looked at them her brain went pear-shaped.

'You wouldn't let Richard cut your hair, would you, so why do you suddenly think you're Stephen flipping Hawking?' said Vicky, starting to openly laugh at her friend.

'What do we do?' asked Kim, biting her lip, trying not to panic.

Vicky reached her hands inside the box and lifted the cake out. 'Knife,' she demanded, holding her hand out. Kim withdrew a sharp knife out of the block next to her and handed it over. Vicky hovered over the iced numbers.

‘Oh, I can’t look,’ said Kim, covering her eyes. There was silence as Vicky set about eradicating Kim’s miscalculation. No one dared breathe.

‘There you go,’ she said after a moment. ‘No one will ever know.’

Kim withdrew her hands and looked down. The numbers had disappeared, the remnants smudged on the end of the knife.

‘I won’t tell anyone,’ said Vicky, staring down at the cake. ‘I think I’ve got a five and a zero candle at home. I’ll bring them with me later. We’ll stick to a number we are certain of, shall we?’

‘Good job you spotted it,’ said Kim to Harry. ‘What would your father have said?’

‘Stick to the hairdressing,’ they both chimed.

Chapter 2

Richard arrived at the front door at 6 p.m. like he always did on a Saturday. Kim was grateful for a moment that he was a man of habit, allowing her to install all the guests in the house by 5.40 p.m., being careful to leave any cars parked a couple of streets away. Her family had been the first to arrive, all bringing bags of crisps and trays of tinnies despite her telling them there was a full buffet and enough drink to sink a battleship. Her mother had also brought a half-drunk bottle of sherry and two bottles of her dad's favourite Newcastle Brown, as if Kim hadn't worked out what her parents' favourite beverages were after all these years.

'Well I didn't want to put you out,' her mother, Janice, had said when Kim had protested at the bring-your-owns. 'And I wasn't sure you'd bother with sherry, seeing as Richard doesn't like sherry and it's his party.'

'You don't have to drink what Richard drinks just because it's his birthday, Mum,' said Kim, exasperated. However much she tried to get her mother to treat Richard as just an ordinary person, her mum just couldn't get past the fact that he was a university lecturer which made her just a bit in awe of him. She was overly cautious of what she said or did in his presence for fear of showing her working-class roots. As for her dad, Graham, a machinist in a factory all his life, he'd long since decided that him and Richard worked on two different planes and with neither of them being men of many words, they exchanged pleasantries whenever there were family gatherings and then left well alone.

Her dad quickly installed himself in front of Sky Sports in the front room whilst Janice hovered nervously wondering what to do with herself. Kim's brother then arrived with his wife and nineteen-year-old twin sons and soon the air was filled with the hiss of ring pulls being released and the glug of lager being consumed at speed. Before long Kim's mates started to pour in too, shooting the noise level way up. They were mainly her friends from way back who also grew up in this small Lancashire city dominated by the university on the outskirts. They had of course become Richard's friends in time, welcoming him in with the usual warmth laced with slight suspicion that natives of the north of England reserved especially for southerners. They all greeted her mum and dad warmly and soon got stuck into opening bottles of wine and discussing the day's sporting events or frantic transportation of children to various activities. Kim had given Richard's colleagues from the university the latest time to arrive, thinking she wouldn't quite know how to entertain them in the absence of her husband. Whenever they socialised she always felt just a tad self-conscious, worried she might say something stupid in the presence of their massive intellect. They were always perfectly nice to her and asked her about her job and admired her skill, but she wasn't sure if it was politeness of the well-educated or genuine interest. She'd invited a couple of fellow lecturers and their spouses as well as Richard's boss and his wife. Kim always knew that a hazard of this party was going to be the mixing of her working-class family, her mates from way back and the eggheads from the university as she jokingly called them. She'd tried to coax Richard's parents into staying for the party, having arrived for his actual birthday in the week. However, they were keen to get back to Cornwall and their commitments to a bridge club. His two brothers did terribly difficult to understand jobs somewhere abroad, making it impossible for them to be there. Similarly, all Richard's friends from his past lived in all corners of the UK, resulting in his fiftieth birthday party looking suspiciously more like a party for Kim with the addition of his work colleagues. But to be fair, Richard wasn't the most sociable of people. She was the one who made sure he had a social life. When they first started dating, she took him on a pub crawl around Lancaster and he couldn't believe how many people she knew and chatted to.

'I guess I just like talking to people,' she told him. 'Part of the job really, being a hairdresser and all that. The best part probably.'

'It's the worst part of my job,' he told her. 'If I could just do my research and not have to talk to anyone that would be just perfect.'

'You don't like talking?' she asked him, totally amazed.

He blinked back at her. 'Well, I like talking to you,' he said, taking her hand. 'I really like talking to you.'

She'd blushed and their eyes had locked. It felt like such a compliment from him. Plus, she wasn't used to men saying they liked talking to her. They were usually only after one thing and it wasn't a good chat! She'd suffered a long line of Jack-the-lads only interested in talking cars or talking dirty and who spent all their money on wheel trims and bucket seats. They thought a good night out with their girlfriend was taking them to darts night so they could make eyes at the fit barmaid serving drinks. On their second date Richard had taken her to a posh Indian restaurant with stiff white napkins and tablecloths and whose peak time was 7.30 p.m. and not 11.30 p.m. She'd realised then that she was actually dating a grown-up who treated her like a human being and not just a sex object.

Kim felt her heartbeat go through the roof when her husband walked through the door expecting to come in, say hello and then head upstairs to shower away the smell of chemicals from the lab, as he always did. She knew that the shy intellectual who had stumbled into her salon over twenty years ago for a haircut would definitely not have enjoyed a surprise birthday in his honour, but she hoped that after all this time being married to her, he had learned the art of enjoying himself without it having to involve some intellectual endeavour.

'Surprise!' they all shouted as he walked in before immediately launching into a chorus of 'Happy Birthday' directed by Kim.

Kim watched the look of total astonishment cover his

face as he tried to process what was happening. He looked around him taking in the faces that had joined forces to surprise him. As they came to the end of the singsong the partygoers gathered round, slapped him on the back and shook his hand. Kim watched, grinning, until the cluster had died down then walked towards him, arms outstretched. 'Happy Birthday,' she said, embracing him. 'Hope it's not too much of a shock.'

He blinked at her. 'I don't know what to say,' he said, 'I . . . I had no idea.'

She laughed. 'It's been so hard keeping it a secret from you. I thought you were going to guess the other day when I left a canister of helium in the hallway. You walked right past it. I thought you were bound to rumble me.'

'No,' he said. He actually looked a bit pale. 'I promise you, I had absolutely no idea.'

She put her arms around his waist and kissed his neck. 'I could get anything past you, couldn't I? You want to watch that. If I can keep a party a secret then what else could I get away with? Perhaps I will have that affair with Ryan Reynolds I've been promising myself.'

'Who? What?!' he said, looking flustered.

'Ryan Reynolds. He keeps calling me, begging me to go out with him but I keep saying my husband's too smart not to spot his wife having an affair.'

'Who's Ryan Reynolds?' asked Richard. 'What are you talking about?' All the colour had drained from his face.

'Ryan Reynolds is a very hot Hollywood actor,' she told him. 'I can't believe you don't know who he is.'

'And he's been calling you?'

'Of course he hasn't. Please will you start reading more *OK* magazines. He's not calling me! I'm just saying you need to be careful because if I can keep this shindig a secret from you, then who knows what else I could be hiding.'

Richard looked bewildered which was pretty common whenever she threw any popular culture references at him. Whereas she found reality TV and celebrity gossip websites relaxing, he was more likely to read the periodic table for fun.

'Look,' she said. 'This is all for you. A party to celebrate you. Everyone is here because they love you and they want to say happy birthday in style. So why don't you go upstairs and have a shower and come down and have some fun?'

Richard nodded. 'Thank you,' he said finally. 'I really didn't expect this.'

'I know,' said Kim, clapping her hands in glee. 'I'm so happy I managed to surprise you. No pressure for my fiftieth in two years' time, whatsoever.'

He nodded and started to back out of the room. 'Right, I'll go and get changed,' he said. 'Be back soon.' He turned to leave.

'Don't forget to put your "I AM 50" badge on,' she shouted after him as he disappeared upstairs.

In Kim's opinion the rest of the party went swimmingly. The buffet was a triumph. Since she'd discovered Costco platters, her whole outlook on entertaining had changed enormously. Any excuse for a party and a Costco rolled sandwich platter, quite frankly. Her mother, however, was not so sure and she had turned her nose up at the sushi plate. Harry had dared his nana to try the raw fish at which point she had demanded it be put in the microwave before eating it.

Her and Vicky had of course got the dancing going after a few glasses of prosecco, putting on the tunes of their youth and encouraging others to join them as they bopped to the likes of Wham!, Duran Duran and Abba as well as their joint personal favourite, the irreplaceable Whitney Houston. Their version of 'I Will Always Love You' was something to behold wherever it occurred. Whether it be in the bars of Spain in their youth or right here in the middle of the kitchen-diner at 10.30 at night.

'Do you think it's time for the cake, Mum?' said Harry, sidling up to her after the rendition, perhaps keen to get her away from the singing.

'Yes, you're right,' she gasped. She had been waiting for the neighbours to arrive. Alison and Neil. They were due back from a few days in the Lake District and said they would try and come. She hadn't told them why as she didn't trust Neil not to let the cat out of the bag to Richard. He was such a gossip and a blabbermouth. They were their closest friends as a couple and were their only friends who didn't start out originally as Kim's friends. When Kim and Richard had moved onto the new estate to much excitement – Kim couldn't quite believe she got to live in a house with a utility room and an en suite – Alison had been their first visitor from next door, bottle of wine in hand. They had hit it off straight away. Alison did some very important job in admissions at the university so she could keep Richard up to date on the inner workings of the establishment, whilst Neil worked in sales for a pharmaceutical company and entertained them with tales of his travels all over the country.

Kim looked round to see if they had arrived yet. She spotted Alison deep in conversation with the birthday boy so they must have slunk in without her noticing. Time for cake then and some obligatory toasts. They had an occasion to celebrate.

'Can I have your attention please,' she shouted, tapping a spoon on a glass after she had made sure everyone had some bubbles in hand. 'I want to thank you all so much for coming and managing to keep it all a secret from my husband. As you all know, he is a very clever man but somehow we all managed to get this past him, so well done you all.'

She gave everyone a small round of applause.

'So we couldn't let this occasion go by without a celebration. What I want to say to you, Richard, is that you need to see turning fifty as an opportunity. Take it as a new lease of life and a chance to try new things. Fifty is the beginning and not the end, and please, please replay this speech to me when I turn fifty at the surprise birthday party that you are now no doubt planning in your head for me.'

A wave of laughter rippled through the room.

'What you may not realise is that not only is it Richard's birthday, it is also the anniversary of the day we met.'

An 'aaah' floated around the room.

Harry rolled his eyes.

'I will never forget this man literally falling into the salon, and gasping that he desperately needed a haircut before he met his supervisor for his PhD. Of course I had no idea what he was talking about. The only supervisors I had ever met were the lunch supervisors at school.'

Kim's old school friends giggled.

'But I didn't question him as he looked desperate,' continued Kim. 'So I delayed my lunch, sat him in a chair and started to cut his hair. He had much more then, of course.'

Another titter floated round the room.

'I asked him about his supervisor and his PhD and when I had finished cutting his hair, he still hadn't finished telling me about his PhD.'

Richard's fellow lecturers burst out laughing.

'So I told him he had to let me go or else I would never get any lunch. Then he offered to buy my lunch as a thank you for cutting his hair at such short notice and at the end of lunch he *still* hadn't finished telling me about his PhD and so he invited me out to dinner. I'd already fallen for him but never in a million years did I think he would fall for me. I thought he was just after cheap haircuts.'

Kim turned to face her husband. The tears in her eyes made them sparkle. He still looked in shock. For a split second she wondered if it had all been too much for him but she firmly pushed the thought out of her mind. Who wouldn't love all this love and attention showered on them?

'I'm so happy that I get to throw you a surprise fiftieth birthday party and I'm so happy that you chose our salon to walk into all those years ago,' she continued. 'I dread to think what my life would have been like if you hadn't needed a haircut that day. And I know you don't need me to cut your hair anymore, but I love you and I would like to wish you many happy returns on this great day, and I can't wait to spend many more birthdays with you in the future.'

She raised her glass and watched as all her nearest and dearest raised their own and wished her husband a very happy birthday. This had been such a good idea, she thought. Who ever regretted a party?

There were, however, some slight feelings of regret starting to emerge as she hobbled round the kitchen just before midnight trying to clear up. Her strappy sparkly shoes had been uncomfortable but they were so pretty that there was no way that she wasn't going to wear them. She'd kicked them off the minute the last guest had disappeared and now she looked like she had some kind of disease as she limped her way around and around the island, stacking the dishwasher with dirty plates and scraping remnants of food into the bin. She had, of course, put the essential clearing up soundtrack on. Queen at full blast. Singing 'We Are the Champions' at the top of your lungs somehow seemed to make clearing up go so much quicker.

Richard brought a pile of plates in from the lounge where the teenagers had decamped to play video games fairly early on in the night. She playfully bumped her hip against his in time to the music. He walked off back into the lounge, no doubt to retrieve more debris.

She carried on her singalong clearathon, feeling smug that the night had gone so well. She'd even had a decent conversation with Richard's boss's wife who it turned out was also a *Love Island* fan. Who would have thought it?

Maybe the next time they all went out the conversation wouldn't need to solely revolve around university life.

She sensed Richard walk in again behind her. She turned to see him putting clingfilm over some leftover sausage rolls. She walked up behind him and put her arms around his waist.

'I hope you had a good time,' she said into his back. 'I know you're not mad keen on surprises but I knew if I told you, you would have said no, and I couldn't bear not to celebrate your birthday. And I wanted you to see how much everyone cares.'

He didn't say anything. He didn't turn around.

'Tell you what,' she continued, allowing her hands to wander up his chest. 'What say we ditch the clearing up and go upstairs and really celebrate your birthday?' She slipped her fingers between two of his shirt buttons to feel the skin of his chest. Richard clamped his hand over hers.

'Stop,' he said.

'What?'

'I said stop.'

'What's wrong?'

He didn't answer, just stood absolutely still, his head bent low. She tried to pull away but he held her hand firm against his chest, preventing her from doing so.

'Richard?'

'I can't do this anymore,' he said slowly.

'What do you mean?'

'I . . . I can't do this. Us. I can't do us anymore.'

Kim couldn't grasp what he was saying. She was clearly having a stupid moment. 'What are you saying, Richard? I don't understand.'

He paused.

'It might help if you looked at me,' she said.

She saw his head shake. He didn't move.

'I didn't know you were going to throw me a party, or else I would have stopped you,' he said.

'I know,' she laughed. 'That's exactly why I didn't tell you.'

He shook his head again, then covered his eyes with his hand. 'I'm leaving you,' he said. 'I'm so sorry, but I'm leaving you.'

'No,' she said stepping back, pulling away from him, confused. 'No way. No. We just had a party.'

He slowly turned round to face her. He still looked like the man she married and yet he also suddenly looked like a complete stranger.

'What's happening?' she cried. 'What's going on?'

He breathed deeply and looked up. 'It's over, Kim. Our marriage is over.'

She felt the walls cave in. 'No,' she said. 'No. No, this isn't happening.'

He nodded his head. 'It is. Why did you have to throw this silly party? I was going to tell you tomorrow. After we got back from taking Harry. On a walk or something. Nice and calm. Not like this.'

'So this is all my fault?' she cried. 'Because I threw you a party?'

'I didn't mean it like that. I just meant that, well, telling you after you've done all this makes me seem like a total bastard.'

'And you telling me my marriage is over in a field is so much better, is it?!'

'No, no, you're overreacting.'

'Overreacting! You have just told me my marriage is over after I threw you a surprise party.'

'Oh God,' he said, putting his head in his hands. 'Why are we even talking about the party? The party should never have happened. Why didn't I wait until tomorrow?'

Kim tried to slow her breathing down. Her head was still jumbling, trying desperately to grab hold of strands of information. She was at a loss for words, something that never happened. It occurred to her that there was something she needed to ask. What was it? Oh yes, of course, 'Is there someone else?' she demanded.

The look on his face told her everything.

'Who?' she gasped. 'How? When?'

She was shaking her head rapidly now as if the more she shook it the more chance there was that the whole conversation would disappear. Richard was staring at her but saying nothing. He was completely white.

'Who?' she demanded, wanting to strike him, wanting to thump this terrible deed out of him.

'Alison,' he muttered.

The Alison who immediately sprang to mind seemed implausible. No, it was ridiculous to think that he could possibly mean their neighbour, Alison. Not her.

'Alison who?' she asked.

He gave her the look he sometimes gave her when he had to explain something he didn't think needed explaining. 'Next-door Alison,' he added.

For the second time that evening she felt the world collapse around her. It didn't make any sense. None at all.

It was completely ridiculous. Not next-door Alison. Alison who regularly popped in with her husband for a drink. Who she'd shared her prized family Lancashire hotpot recipe with, who went with her every year on the train to Manchester, Christmas shopping. Not that Alison. Alison who came round to her house once a month to get her hair done, at mates rates!

'I don't understand,' she said. 'I only coloured her hair last week.'

'She feels really bad about that,' he replied.

'She feels bad about letting me colour her hair and not about sleeping with my husband behind my back?!' Kim yelled.

'She feels really bad about that too,' he said quickly. 'She said to make sure you knew she feels absolutely dreadful about it all.'

Too much information. 'She knew before I did that my marriage was over?' she gasped.

'Well, I suppose yes, unfortunately yes, unavoidable that she would know first, but I didn't plan it. You need to know that. None of this was intentional. It just sort of happened. I didn't mean for it to happen.'

'Oh, your dick just fell into her by accident, did it?'

'No, you know what I mean.'

'No, I don't know what you mean. How did this happen exactly? How did this monumental fuck-up happen?'

He swallowed and looked down.

'Look at me when you are telling me how you started an affair behind my back,' she demanded.

He looked up, breathing heavily. 'It was the graduation ball last summer.'

'This has been going on since then?' She felt herself sink to her knees. She buried her head in her hands.

'Kim,' she heard him say and felt his hand on her shoulder.

'Don't touch me,' she shouted, shoving his hand away. 'Just tell me how it happened.'

She felt him lower himself next to her and sigh heavily. 'Remember I got roped in at the last minute to attend. Mike Phillips was supposed to be representing the chemistry department then he broke his leg so he couldn't go and somehow I drew the short straw. I didn't want to go. But Alison had also got roped in and, well, she was all upset because she'd been forced to call the police because she'd found a couple of students taking drugs in the science block stairwell and it had really rattled her and so I took her back to my office to calm her down with some wine and well . . . '

Too much information. Kim could picture everything so clearly in her head. She hadn't needed to know the exact build-up to the moment it all began. She could even picture what Alison was wearing. She had a fuchsia knee-length cocktail dress that they'd bought together one day in Preston. The one that Kim had told her made her look sexy. She bet she had worn that. She could picture Richard taking it off her, over his desk in his office. She wanted to cut out her eyes, the picture was so clear.

She looked over to him. 'But it didn't stop there,' said Kim. 'You didn't say, "Oh, that was a massive mistake. Let's not do that again."'

He shook his head. 'There is no research project at the uni on Saturday afternoons,' he said.

'What? You've been shagging in the lab every Saturday?'

'No,' he said. 'Sometimes we just go for a walk.'

'Oh, that's fine then,' she said bitterly.

'Like I said, we never meant for this to happen. We didn't plan it.'

'No, it's all Mike Phillips's fault, isn't it? Is that what you are saying? If it hadn't have been for Mike's broken leg then this never would have happened?'

'That's not what I mean. We just . . . it just . . . what can I say, neither of us could help ourselves and we tried to stop, honestly we tried, and we found that we couldn't and well now here we are.'

Great. Kim now had a picture in her head of Richard and Alison in a shagging marathon.

'We really are both so sorry. Alison told Neil this morning before they left the Lakes. He's gone to stay with his parents.'

'So, I'm the last to know. Even Neil knew before me.'

'Alison made him promise to let me tell you.'

'She's so unbelievably fucking considerate. How kind of her to think of my feelings.'

'She really is as devastated as me. We never meant for this to happen.'

'Don't say we,' she said as she lashed out at him, hitting him on the arm and struggling to get to her feet. 'You are not a *we*. You do not get to say that. We are a *we*. We are married. Did you hear that? We are married. Whereas your other *we* is just shagging behind their partners' backs. That's not a *we*. You do not get to call her and you a *we*.' Tears of frustration were now pouring down her face.

Richard pulled himself up onto his feet. 'Sorry,' he said. 'Sorry. I can't tell you how sorry we are.' He moved towards her to try and embrace her. She lashed out, flailing her arms at him. 'Get out,' she shouted. 'Just get out. I don't want to see you. Just get out now.'

'But I can't . . . '

'I couldn't give a shit what you can't, just get out. Leave me alone. Just go, NOW!'

'Shh,' said Richard, raising his eyes to the ceiling. 'Let's not wake Harry.'

'Why not?' she screamed at him. 'So, you don't have to tell him that you've decided to take a sledgehammer to the family?' She landed a blow on his left arm. He winced and backed away, startled. She had never wanted to hurt someone so much in all her life. She picked up the nearest thing to her on the kitchen island to throw at him. The fondant figure off the top of his birthday cake bounced pleasingly off his forehead, leaving a scar of white icing.

'Just GO!' she screamed again. He turned and strode quickly out the kitchen. She was breathing heavily, tears running down her cheeks. She watched as he closed the front door behind him. She tried to calm her breathing down so she could listen. Sure enough, a few moments later she heard muffled voices coming from next door's front doorstep before a bang as the door closed behind her husband seeking refuge in Alison's house.

Chapter 3

Kim had been up since six. But she had been awake since at least four. After Richard had left, she had slumped back down on the floor for a long time, trying desperately to anchor her thoughts somewhere. But her thoughts kept flinging themselves all over the place. From crawling over every single detail of what Richard had said, to her hatred of Alison, to all the times she must have done her hair for her since she started sleeping with her husband, to last New Year's Eve when they had had them over to toast new beginnings, to raking over every moment of the party including Richard's face when he walked through the door, to seeing him whispering in the corner with Alison, to her speech, her damn speech where she praised her husband to high heaven and gave her precious thanks for the day she met him and her wonderful life she had with him and how she was looking forward to her wonderful life in the future.

All brought to an abrupt end just a few hours later.

She felt sick to the stomach. Sick to the stomach over her gushing about her oh so perfect husband and her oh so perfect life in front of everyone. And now it was all gone. Everything.

She couldn't wait for those texts to come flooding in, congratulating her on an excellent party and thanking her for her superb hospitality. How could she face them all, telling them it was all a lie? She had been living a lie and she didn't even know it. And the lie was being played out right next door. She couldn't even look in the direction of Alison's house. Couldn't even bear to see it.

How was she going to function? How was she going to bear being next door to that? How was she going to bear facing everyone? How? How? How could he do this? The man she had married partly because she was convinced he would never do this.

It struck her at some point during the early hours of the morning that today was the day that they were meant to be taking Harry to university together. Today was a big family day. A landmark. One which she had envisaged she would need to hold her husband's hand throughout, just to get her through it.

Was that what they had planned, then? That they would take Harry to university, get back and then Richard would announce he was leaving? It was so shocking she couldn't even begin to get her head around it. Richard was her rock. Always had been. It was his steady, reliable, trustworthy nature that had attracted her to him in the first place. Richard solved her problems. Not created them. But he had been secretly planning the biggest problem of all for a married couple. That after their only son had left home he was leaving too. And not only that, he was going to move next door? Expect her to put up with him living literally on her doorstep?

She couldn't do it. She couldn't face that. She couldn't face watching the two of them begin a life together just as hers had ended. She had to get away from here.

She wracked her brains for where to go. All her friends and relations were in Lancaster. Usually, she loved that fact. Loved that her roots were so deep. But not now. Now she longed for that special friend who lived in London or Manchester. If she'd gone to uni, she'd have friends in far flung places, but not her. Hairdressers' friends tended to stay close.

She started to panic – she had to get away. There must be somewhere she could escape to just while she made an attempt to make sense of what had just happened to her life. She picked up her phone off the bedside table and began to scroll through Facebook, praying to find someone who might be able to offer her refuge. But no one came to light. She found herself straying onto her messages, already finding several from people who had attended the party. She ignored them apart from Vicky's, half wondering if she might be awake and available to offload to.

> Great party, mate – smashed it. Hope Richard liked the cake. Told you he wouldn't spot the deletion! Will be thinking of you tomorrow. Hope all goes well with dropping off Harry in Nottingham and his flat is not too much of a dump! Will be here with tissues and wine when you are ready. V xxx

She must have drifted off into a fitful sleep as she woke up sometime later, confused and disorientated, until the events of the previous evening came crashing down on her again. She froze for a moment until she remembered the conclusion she had come to before she fell asleep.

Her overnight bag was in the hall by the time Harry stumbled downstairs sometime after nine. She'd been tempted to go and wake him but decided she needed him to be in the best possible mood so best leave him to wake up under his own steam. She had also been tempted to finish off clearing up from the party after her efforts had been cut short so dramatically. But then she had decided she didn't need to. Let Richard discover the congealed dip and hardened birthday cake that had been left out all night. She did, however, take some joy in picking up the fondant icing figurine of her husband, left lying on the floor after it bounced off his head, and crushing it to a pulp in her hand, letting the broken pieces drop to the ground where she crushed it into the rug with her shoe.

Harry stopped short in the hall. 'Did you want me to use that bag?' he asked, pointing to her overnight bag next to the door. 'I thought you wanted me to take the silver one?'

'No, that's mine,' she replied. 'Come on,' she said, striding over to it and picking it up. 'I want to get going. Get on the road as soon as we can.'

'But I thought we were leaving at around eleven?'

'Change of plan,' she said, opening the door and walking out. 'We're going as soon as you're ready.'

She clicked open the boot of her Vauxhall Corsa, trying very hard not to look up at the bedroom window in her neighbour's house. Harry appeared at her side in his pyjamas and without anything on his feet.

'What are you doing?' he said.

She bit her lip to try and stop the tears that were already threatening to ambush her eyes.

'Slight change of plan,' she said. Turning round and striding back towards the house. 'I'm taking you to university. Your dad's not coming. Now can you get dressed and let's get going.'

'What do you mean, Dad isn't coming?' said Harry, catching up with her back in the hallway.

'He can't come,' she said.

'Why not?'

She sniffed hard, wondering briefly if she should make up some lie until she could gather herself enough to explain the truth to her son. But she had no capacity for storytelling, no brain power for creativity, so she would just have to tell him how it was. She closed her eyes, trying to control her breathing.

'Your dad,' she started. 'Your dad announced last night that he's leaving me. That he's been having an affair with Alison next door and our marriage is over. So that's why he isn't coming. Because he's next door shagging Alison.'

'What?' said Harry, shaking his head, looking utterly bewildered. 'That can't be true. Not Dad?'

'Yes, Dad. Your dad, my husband.' She still couldn't quite believe it herself even though the words were coming out of her mouth. 'If you want to be sure then I suggest you knock on next door and ask him yourself.'

'Not Dad!' said Harry, sinking to sit down on the stairs.

'Yes, your dad,' confirmed Kim. 'Your father. The man himself.'

Harry was staring into space with a gormless expression on his face, shaking his head.

She sat down next to him and put her arm around his shoulders.

She took a deep breath. 'I know it's a lot to take in. Believe me, I'm still taking it in, well trying to. But one thing I have taken in is that I can't sit in a car with him all day. Not today. So, I'll be taking you to uni. I thought that would be the best.'

Harry gulped, still staring into space, and nodded. 'Okay,' he said.

'And I thought I might just find a hotel for a couple of days. I can't be here, you see. I need to get away.'

'What! But, why?'

'I can't stay here, Harry. I just can't,' she said, pulling a tissue out of her sleeve. 'I can't stay here next door to that,' she said, pointing through the wall vaguely in the direction of Alison's house. 'It's fine, really. I'll just find a Travelodge or something in Nottingham. I just need to get some space. I'll drop you off and work it out. You don't need to worry about it. You just worry about settling yourself in.'

Harry looked at his mother. She wondered what he saw. She always prided herself on being fun Mum, lively Mum, always there to put a smile on his face. And here she was with tears dripping off her nose.

'Okay,' he said slowly, still looking totally bewildered.

She wished she had time to let him process what was going on. She wished they had time to talk things through, but they didn't. She wanted to be well out of here before Richard came knocking on the door. The thought of seeing him sent shivers along her spine.

'Do you think you can go and finish packing?' she said as gently as possible.

He blinked at her and nodded. He stood up and walked up the stairs.

Kim buried her head in her hands. Her son had looked so confused. He'd had such a shock. He clearly didn't know what he was supposed to do. But neither did she. She just knew they needed to get away as soon as possible.

It was an hour before Harry was finally ready to go, giving Kim massive anxiety. She was desperate to leave way before the allotted time they had discussed with Richard. She couldn't bear the thought of even seeing his face this morning. She kept offering to help her son which of course he refused. She watched, feeling her blood pressure going through the roof, as he brought out bag after bag and piled it next to her car for her to cram into her tiny Vauxhall. She started to wonder if they would have no choice but to take Richard's Volvo estate. She went to look for the keys in the chest of drawers in the hall and realised he must have them with him. So she was faced with a choice of going to get the keys from Richard or asking her son if he would take less stuff to uni.

'Is there anything we can come back and collect another time?' she asked him hopefully as he dumped a box containing his PlayStation 5 next to the car. 'Maybe this?'

Harry stared at her. 'The PlayStation is going,' he said.

'Okay, okay, anything else, do you think? It's not all going to fit in.'

Harry sighed, peering in the boot. 'What about that stuff?' he said. He pointed at a blue bag containing a full set of pans and kitchen implements painstakingly purchased from Ikea the week before in the hope that Harry would somehow cook rather than live on takeaways and toast.

'But you'll need that, surely?' she said.

He raised his eyebrows. He'd said at the time that perhaps one pan to cook beans in would be sufficient.

'No,' he said. 'Believe me, the PlayStation will get much more use.'

'Come on, Harry. You need something to cook with,' she pleaded.

She literally jumped out of her skin as she heard a door open behind thcm. It was the sound she had been dreading all morning.

'Dad!' said Harry, looking over his shoulder.

'What are you doing?' said Richard, approaching fast. Kim reached over and picked up the Ikea bag.

'Put the PlayStation in,' she told Harry firmly, heading back towards the house. It was time they left. Even if they did have to leave behind the frying pan.

'I thought we were leaving at eleven?' said Richard.

Kim stopped in her tracks on her way back into the house. She swivelled round.

'There is no *we* leaving at eleven,' she said. 'You made

it very clear last night you are now a different *we*. And so *we*,' she said pointing at her and Harry, 'are leaving as soon as we can.'

'But . . . but you can't go in your car. There's not enough room.'

'There is. We are all packed up now, aren't we, Harry? We were just about to go.'

'So where are you taking that?' asked Richard, pointing at the blue Ikea bag in her hand. She looked down as though she had forgotten it was there.

'Absolutely none of your business,' she declared. 'None of this is any of your business anymore. You said so last night. We are done, so keep your nose out.'

'But . . . but . . . ' said Richard, floundering. 'I want to take you to Nottingham,' he said, turning to his son. 'We can manage that, can't we? I'd like to explain. Well, try to. Let's just unpack Mum's car, put it in mine and then we'll all go together. We can do that, can't we?'

'No we can't,' said Kim. 'You made that simple family occasion impossible. You have ruined it. You, Richard, so go back inside to your new home and let me and Harry get on the road,' she said, waving her free arm at Alison's house. A movement at the front door caught her eye and to her horror Alison appeared at the door in her dressing gown.

'Kim, please let me explain,' she said, stepping towards her. 'Please, I never . . . '

'No, get away from me,' shouted Kim. She thought she might throw up. 'Get right away from me.'

'Please can we just sit down and talk and . . . '

'No,' said Kim. 'No – go away. I have nothing to say to you.' She put the Ikea bag down and reached in for the nearest culinary weapon. She pulled out a frying pan and brandished it in Alison's direction. She was vaguely aware that Audrey Watson who lived opposite was now on her doorstep in her dressing gown, brazenly having a gawp.

'Kim, please,' said Alison. 'Please listen to me. You need to let me explain.'

'I don't need to let you do anything,' declared Kim. 'You let yourself sleep with my husband. I think that's quite enough, don't you?'

'Mum?' said Harry, edging towards her. 'Give me the frying pan.' He was holding his hand out towards her.

'Please put the pan down,' she heard Richard say.

What the fuck? she thought, as she hurled it at him and made a dash for the car.

'Get in,' she shouted at Harry as she ran past him. 'We are going now.' She jumped into the driver's seat, slammed the door and turned the ignition key. Where was Harry? They were making their escape. Why hadn't he leapt in the car after her?

Richard loomed in her window. 'He's just getting his inhaler stuff,' he shouted at her.

She bit her lip, praying for him to disappear. She stared straight ahead, trying not to catch the eye of Audrey opposite who had now been joined by her husband to watch the spectacle.

'This is silly,' she heard Richard shout through the window. 'I'll come in the house and let's talk. You don't need to leave like this. Let's talk and we'll take Harry later.'

She turned sharply to face him. 'I never want to talk to you ever again,' she shouted back at him. 'Ever.'

'You'll have to. There are things we need to discuss. You can't just walk away.'

Harry finally climbed in beside her.

'Ready?' she asked him.

'Ready,' he said, sinking down in his seat as though he wanted to disappear.

She crunched the car into gear and immediately stalled it. Of course she did. The tears were stinging her eyes but she was determined to get away before Richard could see that. She started the car again and reversed out of the drive at speed. Clipping the kerb as she did so.

'Jesus, Mum,' muttered Harry.

She made it all the way to the edge of the estate they lived on when she stalled the car again as she attempted to pull away from a T-junction, tears streaming down her face.

'Stop, Mum, you are going to kill us both. Get out the car and let me drive,' said Harry.

Kim looked at her son in bewilderment. She had no idea what she was doing.

'We are still in the middle of the junction, Mum. Do you think you can pull in over there? There's a car right behind us.'

The car behind beeped loudly. Fumbling with the keys, she somehow managed to restart the car and pulled into the bus stop a bit further along. She slumped back in her seat, breathing heavily.

Someone's phone started to ring. It was Harry's. He pulled it out of his pocket.

'It's Dad,' he said.

She didn't reply.

Harry put the phone to his ear. 'Hello,' he said.

For some reason it crossed her mind that he would be calling to tell Harry it was all a mistake. That it hadn't happened. That he was joking when he said he'd had an affair with their neighbour and that their marriage was a failure and they should go back immediately so they could travel to Nottingham together.

'Okay,' she heard her son say. 'I'll tell her.' He put his phone back in his pocket.

'He said to tell you that there are roadworks on the A52 through Derby so you should take the A50 down to junction twenty-four of the M1.'

Kim turned to stare at him.

'He's worried because you don't have satnav in this car, he says,' her son continued.

'He's worried because I don't have satnav,' she repeated. God, she wished she'd had better aim with that frying pan.

'I think I should drive, don't you?' said Harry.

She nodded and tried to get out of the car without taking her seatbelt off. Harry released her and she got out and slumped in the passenger seat and closed her eyes hoping that everything would disappear.

Harry put the radio on but soon switched it off again as Steve Wright announced his 'Sunday Love Songs'. They drove in silence as Kim stared out the window at the cars whizzing by on the motorway. All getting on with their normal lives. All except her, who no longer had a normal life.

They didn't speak until they were approaching Keele services on the M6.

'I'm hungry,' Harry announced. 'Let's pull in here.'

Kim merely nodded.

They pulled into a parking spot facing the entrance to the services. 'Are you coming?' asked Harry.

Kim didn't reply. She was watching an elderly couple walk across the front of their car. They weren't even holding hands or anything. They were just together and it made her want to howl.

'You might want to go and wash your face,' said Harry.

Kim looked at him sharply then pulled down the visor to look in the mirror. Last night's mascara was all over her face. She looked like a freak.

'Why didn't you tell me?' she wailed.

'Because . . . because . . . there was other stuff going on,' replied Harry.

'You've let me walk around like this all morning?' She couldn't believe it.

'I've just told you, haven't I?' he replied. 'I'm going to eat,' he said, getting out of the car and slamming the door.

She watched him walk across the car park, feeling the tears spring to her eyes yet again. What was she doing taking this out on Harry? None of this was his fault. But she had no way of managing her feelings right now and she was so tired, so desperately tired.

She kept her head well down as she walked through the busy service station, praying there was somewhere she could buy face wipes. Turns out it's hard to find something when you have to look at the floor. She somehow managed to find some in the healthcare section of the newsagents and was, for once, grateful for self-checkout rather than having to face a real sales person in a shop.

She scanned the face wipes through but suddenly felt her legs buckle when she glanced over at the treats section tempting her at the till. There were the familiar yellow bags of jelly babies. She'd had it all planned. When the three of them stopped at a service station for lunch en route she was going to buy a bag of jelly babies for old times' sake. It was the Jacobs family's sweet of choice for any long journey. Always had been ever since Harry was probably five years old. They'd fight over the orange ones, agreeing that you had to eat the orange ones from the feet up. That was the kindest thing to do. However, they would take great joy in ripping the heads off the green ones, the least favourites. Richard would make Harry break down in fits of giggles by popping a green jelly baby in his mouth and then allowing its bottom half to protrude out of his lips before thrashing around pretending the green jelly baby was fighting to get out.

The vision of the three of them giggling stupidly over the great green jelly baby gobbler was so vivid it was like a scene out of a nightmare, just before the killer strikes and obliterates everyone. She turned and walked as fast as she could towards the ladies' bathroom, head down.

It was worse than she'd thought as she dragged the face wipes over her cheeks and under her eyes. She looked like a different person. Usually, she didn't have a hair out of place, and she never went out without her makeup done. She'd always taken pride in her appearance and that had only increased when she met Richard. Given his professional status and her lack of it, she felt like she shouldn't ever let him down by looking scruffy or unkempt. In her view most people would wonder why someone as smart as Richard had married a hairdresser and so she really needed to keep up appearances. However, as she looked in the mirror now she saw a dowdy middle-aged woman with scraped back hair, naked eyes and lips, dressed in a crumpled hoody.

Who was that woman staring back at her blankly?

She had absolutely no idea. She had never seen her before. She didn't recognise herself. And the look in her eyes. It was like all the life had been taken out of them. They looked dead. Normally her whole face, her whole body danced with life. People remarked on her energy. Often. She didn't know who this person was. Who her cheating husband had turned her into.

She walked back through the service station in a daze, avoiding everyone's gaze. Normally she would be the first to catch a stranger's eye and smile. She loved people. She loved to engage. But not now. She really wanted to crawl into a hole and die.

Harry was back at the car by the time she got back. She climbed in and went to put on her seatbelt.

'You didn't lock the car,' he said. 'You left the keys in the ignition.'

'Sorry,' she muttered, staring straight ahead.

'Someone could have nicked everything. The PlayStation was in plain view.'

'Sorry,' she said again, leaning her elbow on the window and resting her chin on her hand.

'Did you get something to eat?' he asked.

'Not hungry,' she replied.

'Have some of these,' he said, dropping something in her lap. 'You need to eat something.'

She looked down. There in her lap was a yellow packet of jelly babies.

'Don't worry,' he said. 'I'll eat the green ones.'

Kim immediately felt herself implode. She screwed her eyes as tight as she could to stop the avalanche of tears but it was no good. The Hoover Dam wouldn't have stopped those tornadoes coming.

As Kim sobbed, she felt her son take her hand which made her sob even more.

She had no idea how long they sat like that but it felt like forever until she could get any words out at all.

'I just didn't see it coming,' she said, shaking her head. 'I had absolutely no idea.'

Harry gave a big sigh and leaned back in his seat, staring at the roof of the car. 'I did,' he muttered.

'What?!' said Kim, turning to him sharply. 'What do you mean?'

'I came home one lunchtime during my exams and his car was parked outside but he wasn't in the house,' he said, still staring at the roof of the car. 'I thought it was a bit weird but then about half an hour later he came in with Alison. I could hear them laughing in the hallway, then they came in the kitchen and they were well shocked to see me. Didn't know what to say, then Dad reckoned they'd had to pop back to pick up some papers from Alison's.'

He turned to look at his mother. 'I'm sorry. I should have said something. But . . . but I guess I didn't want to believe they were up to anything. But then Alison started being overly nice to me, asking me how I was all the time when she hadn't taken any notice of me before. She gave me twenty quid to go out and celebrate when I got my place at Nottingham.'

'Did you take it?' asked Kim.

Harry nodded. 'I'm sorry,' he said. 'I'm so sorry.'

Kim couldn't believe what she was hearing. It was all too much. Alison and Richard popping back at lunch-times to no doubt have sex! Harry having suspicions but saying nothing about it. Alison sliming round her son in a lurid future stepmum-type fashion. Why had she not picked up on any of this? Why? Had she been sleep-walking for the past year?

She shook her head. All she wanted to do was sleep but thoughts were bombarding her weary brain.

She sighed and leaned back in her seat. 'Let's just go, shall we?' she said, closing her eyes.

Chapter 4

They didn't speak for the rest of the journey. Kim drifted in and out of fitful sleep and disturbing thoughts. Eventually they passed a sign saying, 'You are now entering Nottinghamshire'. She sat up in her seat and rubbed her eyes. Harry had managed to balance his phone on the dashboard and was using a map app to find his way to the house. She glanced over at him to see his face was set in a deep frown. She needed to pull herself together somehow. This was not how Harry should be entering student life. He should be feeling pure anticipation and excitement. She somehow needed to get into proud-mother-dropping-her-son-off-for-his-new-life-at-uni mode rather than woman-who-has-just-found-out-her-life-is-in-tatters mode.

The kind-sounding lady on the app said, 'Turn left at the next junction and you will be at your destination.' Kim literally felt her stomach flip over. She looked out of the window as they passed a line of rundown looking shops. There was a general store of the low budget chain variety, a chippy, a pizza delivery place, a betting shop, a hairdresser and a charity shop. She looked into the hairdresser's which looked similar to the one she had served her apprenticeship in in the nineties, except it clearly hadn't changed since the nineties with its dated posters of dated haircuts and a grim-looking brown leather sofa in the window. She briefly thought about her clients back in Lancaster. Thank goodness she'd decided to take next week off so didn't have the prospect of having to call and cancel a load of appointments. She knew there was no way she could face cutting hair at the moment. When Harry was born she left the salon and became a mobile hairdresser so she could have the flexibility to look after him. It had worked really well, but the plan had always been to open her own salon once Harry started secondary school and didn't need her so much. Richard had said it was a great idea until he got offered a sabbatical at Edinburgh University for a year when Harry turned eleven, taking him out of the home for four nights a week. Kim essentially became a single mother, leaving no time for her ambitions to be realised. Then long summer holidays abroad visiting Richard's brothers made the prospect of running a salon back in Lancaster impossible. Kim had been fine with it. Family first and all that.

She felt the car come to a halt and Harry start to reverse into a parking spot. She glanced over to her left and looked up at her son's new home. Number fifty-one Leopold Street. Harry hadn't seen it before today as he'd gone through clearing so there had been no luxury of previewing and selecting his accommodation. He'd had to take what he could get. Halls were full and so here he was in a random house round the corner from a chippy and a hairdresser's stuck in the nineties.

The faded red door had a rusting number fifty-one nailed to it above a rusting letterbox. The door was straight off the street, no drive, no front yard, no protection from passers-by. It was very similar to the house she had grown up in in Lancaster. Mid terrace, Victorian probably. Built for the workers. How ironic that the very houses built for the physical grafters all those decades ago were now appropriated for the study of books. Somehow it calmed Kim. This is what she had grown up with. It was like going back in time. She glanced over at Harry to see his reaction. He'd grown up in a brand-new detached, four-bedroom house with a drive and double garage, en suites, a utility room and grass in the backyard. Kim knew without having to look there would be no grass on this property. Harry gave a deep sigh and opened the car door.

They met behind the car and Harry opened the boot. Kim was itching to say perhaps they should go look round first – see the place and then unload – but she kept quiet. Best let him take the lead. He was in charge now.

He plucked the box with the PlayStation in off the top and strode up to the door. He turned the handle but it didn't budge. It was locked. He put the box down and tried again. Nothing.

'How do we get in?' he asked, turning to his mother.

This was the time when Richard would have taken control. Worked it out. Been logical. Been smart. Asked Harry to look at his emails and find forgotten instructions as to the location of a key perhaps. But Kim and Harry just looked at each other, clueless.

'Try the doorbell?' said Kim with a shrug.

Harry turned to the door, then back to his mother. 'No doorbell,' he said, a look of panic starting to appear in his eyes.

Kim studied the door.

'Door knocker,' she said, pointing.

'Oh yeah,' said Harry, blushing slightly. He knocked loudly and firmly and stood back. They stood side by side in silence.

No one came to the door.

'What shall we do?' asked Harry.

Kim didn't know. She didn't know anything anymore. She shrugged.

Harry stared at her, clearly thinking she had the answer, but he was mistaken. She had no answers anymore.

She looked down, avoiding Harry's gaze, and noticed a lockbox fixed to the wall next to the front window.

'Lockbox?' she said, pointing.

'What?'

'Lockbox. There, look.'

Harry stared at it then slapped his own forehead. 'Oh yeah,' he said. 'Angus said something on the WhatsApp group about that.' He reached in his back pocket and started scrolling. '1234,' he muttered before bending down and reaching for the box. Kim wondered at what point she should suggest they didn't use that number to protect the security of the house.

The box popped open and Harry opened the door into a narrow hallway. Kim could already picture the layout before she went in. Narrow hallway with stairs in front leading to the next floor. Door on the left at the bottom of the stairs leading into a lounge that in turn led to a kitchen at the back. The lounge décor was familiar from her childhood. Painted woodchip and brown leather furniture on a practical mottled brown carpet. Dominating the room were two alcoves either side of a blocked-in chimney breast which sported a tired-looking gas fire. The two alcoves were fitted with low cupboards and shelves to the ceiling which were already crammed with lines of cans of beer and bottles of wine. One shelf in particular stood out. Clearly someone had ransacked their parents' drinks cupboard and half-empty bottles of spirits jostled for room alongside a silver cocktail shaker. Kim thought about the six pack of lager she'd packed in a box for Harry to bring, thinking perhaps he could share them on his first night. The parents of this particular student were in a different league.

She wandered after Harry into the kitchen. It was long and narrow with a small table at the end in front of a French window out to the yard. It appeared to be fairly well equipped. Well, appeared to be if you could see past the carnage on the worktop. White bread was spilling out of an open packet. A tub of butter and a packet of cheese had been left out; crumbs were strewn everywhere including the floor. Kim felt her hands itch to at least put the butter and cheese back in the fridge but she stopped herself. She absolutely mustn't start that game.

Harry grunted his approval and squeezed past her, walking through the lounge to head upstairs. Kim stared round her once again and fought the instinct to clear up after someone else's mess in the kitchen. It so wasn't her job. They had to work it out for themselves.

Now what should she do? Follow Harry? She trudged up the stairs and stuck her head round the door of the bathroom at the top of the stairs. It smelt of boy/man already. The faint hint of poo mixed with competing deodorant and aftershave. She felt herself heave, trying not to think of her en suite at home and her vanity unit with full light-up mirror. She realised she hadn't seen a downstairs toilet. One bathroom for three men. That was going to take some serious shit, that bathroom. She could hear Vicky giggle at her own joke. Kim might have laughed if the thought hadn't been so grim.

Turning onto the landing there was an empty single room on her right and a door facing her. She thought she could hear Harry shuffling round inside. She knocked tentatively on the door. 'Is that you, Harry?' she asked.

'Yeah,' came the answer.

She pushed the door open to find Harry lying on the floor messing with wires and plugs under a desk and with monitors and consoles strewn around him.

'Nice room,' she said even before she had looked round. It wasn't too bad. More woodchip, but painted fairly recently to be fair. A double bed in the corner, a decent sized desk and a classic house clearance wardrobe. Small and made of peeling orangey wood. Harry was not big on clothes so it probably made no odds to him. A large window on the far wall overlooked the street and into the house opposite where Kim could see a teddy bear hung from a noose-like piece of rope. No doubt another student house, or the home of a psychotic child.

Kim and Harry were just getting the last of the items that had been rammed in the boot of her car when a red van pulled up next to them. A boy got out of the passenger seat. He had a big round face and a riot of thick, wavy hair cut in an unfashionable nineties style, very short on the sides and too long on the top. His unremarkable face was lit up by a beaming smile and his eyes blinked rapidly behind silver-rimmed, NHS-looking glasses. His unbranded hoody was zipped right up to the top as though his mother had told him to be careful not to catch a cold. He was wearing bright red jeans.

'This is Harry,' he said to his mum, pointing at Harry. 'This is Harry. I told you about Harry, Mum, do you remember? We are on the same floor. Hi Harry. It's me, Sonny. From WhatsApp. Do you recognise me?'

'Hi Sonny,' said Harry, straightening up, looking bemused by the effervescent boy.

'Are you sure that's him?' said Sonny's mum, striding forward and peering at Harry. 'He doesn't look much like a student.'

Kim was aghast. Sonny looked like he'd only just had his bar mitzvah. At least Harry was sporting some five o'clock shadow.

'What are you studying then?' the woman demanded.

'Chemistry,' replied Harry.

The woman nodded. 'Sonny's doing geography,' she said. 'He wanted to do criminology but you don't get much crime down in Devon, well not where we live anyway, but there's plenty of geography. So, we said to him he could come to university but he had to do something useful. He can come back to Devon when he's finished and do geography. Right, Sonny. Let's unpack this van, shall we? It won't unpack itself, will it?'

Sonny grinned then stepped forward and flung his arms around Harry. 'This is going to be amazing,' he said before shouting, 'Coming Mum,' in a singsong voice before he disappeared round the back of the van out of sight. Harry looked at his mother with a bewildered look on his face. Kim couldn't remember the last time she'd seen her son physically touch someone apart from her. He certainly didn't welcome hugs from his grandparents anymore. And to her knowledge he'd never had a girlfriend. She'd long suspected that he avoided human contact because that would require showering more. Keeping clean was not high on her son's list of priorities and he seemed like the type of bloke who was quite happy to forsake a relationship if it meant he could keep his showering regime to a minimum.

'That's everything,' said Harry, slamming the boot down.

She followed him in and up the stairs to dump his bedding on his bed. All his stuff was piled in the middle of the room. Shoes and trainers tumbled out of bags for life, video games were already scattered all over the floor, his suitcase was open and half the contents ransacked to find the hoody he was now wearing. It was already chaos. She watched as Harry sat on the chair at his desk, picked up a gaming controller and started to play. No sign whatsoever of putting his long-awaited university room into any kind of order. She was glad she'd decided against the couple of pot plants she was going to hand to him to make his room look nice. No doubt they would have got chucked on the floor spilling soil and goodness knows what onto the carpet which would have stayed there until the end of time.

What would she be doing now, she thought, if this day had gone to plan? She and Richard had discussed taking Harry out for a meal, once they'd dropped his stuff off in the house. Fill him up before they headed back up to Lancaster. She certainly hadn't intended to settle him into his room. Put his bedsheets on for him, file his underwear away. No, she was certain she wouldn't have done that. She would have to take a deep breath and walk away. Leave him to it. She decided she would just wander down to the kitchen and perhaps unpack Harry's limited kitchen stuff. She'd packed him some tea bags so she might make herself a cup of tea, then she should really start looking on her phone for a hotel to stay in.

She was just wiping the kitchen table with a wet cloth so she could sit down and have a cup of tea without getting crumbs all over her when there was a loud tap on the kitchen door and the next thing she heard was a female voice saying, 'Cooee – can I come in?'

Sonny's mum's head appeared round the corner of the door.

'I'm Valerie,' she said, walking towards Kim and holding out her hand. 'So sorry not to introduce myself properly earlier.' Kim offered her hand back before realising she was still holding the dishcloth. She threw it in the sink and then offered Sonny's mum her wet hand. She watched as Valerie shook her hand and then wiped it on her denim skirt.

'I hear you are staying over,' she said.

'Yes, well . . . ' Kim started to say.

'Good for you,' she said. 'If I'd have known that room up there was for mothers I'd have been in like Flynn. Of course I would. No idea they had that kind of option available.'

'No, actually it's not . . . '

'I don't blame you for getting in first and keeping quiet about it. I'd have done exactly the same if I'd have known. Exactly the same. Mind you, not that our Geoff would have been able to cope without me for more than a couple of nights, but still, if I'd known, perhaps us mums could have done a rota between us or something. You know. Me stay a few days, do a shift as it were and then you take a turn, then the other mums. Still, the rest of us didn't know so here we are. But we have you here so that's great. Brilliant. You can keep an eye on everyone. Let us know how they are all doing. And seeing as you're here, well, Sonny, bless him, I love him to bits but I am worried he can't look after himself, you know. First time away from home and all that. Maybe I've mollycoddled him.

Some might say that, but you do, don't you? You do with sons. It's just a mother's instinct, that's all. I wasn't like this with my two daughters. No way. They were cooking and cleaning from a very young age. Very independent, they were, but Sonny, well, boys just aren't made like that, are they? They are not meant to be domestic animals. They are hunter gatherers. That's how they were made. They weren't meant to know how to look after themselves. I blame those cavemen. They started it. If the cavemen had been taught how to wash up rather than spear an ox then we might be in a very different state now. Still, here we are and I'm so glad you're here.' Valerie reached over and grabbed Kim's wrist, giving it an almost painful squeeze, then she bent down and picked a bag up off the floor.

'So,' she said. 'I'm going to give you Sonny's medication. Good news is he doesn't need his inhaler very often now and don't panic, he has one with him, but he is prone to losing them, so if you could keep the spares then he'll always know where to find one.'

'I don't think you understand . . . ' began Kim, horrified.

'It's okay, you don't have to keep this stuff in any special conditions or anything. Just on that shelf up there would be fine. I'll tell him before I leave. Now also in here is his spare EpiPen . . . '

'No . . . ' started Kim. 'No, really . . . '

'I know what you are going to say,' said Valerie, clutching her arm in a vice-like grip once again. 'You are going to say you would be too scared to use it even if you saw my son on the verge of death from anaphylactic shock. I can assure you that once you do see someone on the verge of suffocation then all instincts kick in and you will be able to use it. I can guarantee. I've done it many times. You'll find the first time a bit intimidating but after two or three you'll soon get the hang of it, but if you are worried then I'd advise you to remind him that satay contains peanuts if he makes any hint of having a takeaway. Oh, and if you could remind him every morning when he goes, to take his EpiPen, that would be great. He is prone to forgetting it. I've informed the university of his condition but I'm not convinced that they have communicated it widely enough and so I am feeling very nervous about him being at risk every time he walks through the door.'

Kim was speechless. Why did this woman think she was moving in to become her son's surrogate parent? Some serious miscommunication had gone on somewhere.

'Now last thing,' said Valerie, delving into her bag again. She pulled out a packet of condoms.

Kim's jaw dropped open.

'I was going to give these to Sonny, you know, to keep him safe and all that, but seeing as you're here then perhaps you could keep them for him. He'll put them somewhere and forget and then . . . well goodness knows . . . I dread to think . . . and I don't want any young lady trapping him or anything, you know, by getting pregnant. He's way too good for that so I've told him he must always take precautions. Don't worry, we've had "the chat", he knows all about it, I'm not asking you to do that or anything, but if you could keep these for him. You know, for when the time comes. He'll feel okay coming to ask you, I'm sure. Not as embarrassing as asking the other lads, I would have thought. And in case you're wondering, there is one missing. Newquay last year. Geoff got a bit fruity. You know what it's like on holiday. A bit of sunshine and some beer and it sends some men loopy, doesn't it? Thank goodness they sell them in toilets now. Not what it was like in our day, hey?' she said going into peals of laughter.

Valerie looked at her watch and gasped. 'I promised Geoff I'd leave before it got busy on the roads. Better go. Now can I ask one last favour? I've made up lots of meals for Sonny and put them in the freezer and I've told him how to defrost them and that different ones need different times but I'm sure he wasn't listening. Can I show you where they are and what you have to do and then he can always come and ask you, can't he? Might stop him getting food poisoning.'

Kim watched, speechless, as Valerie walked out of the kitchen towards the hallway. The next thing she heard was Valerie shouting, 'Sonny' at the top of her voice. A few seconds later, Valerie and Sonny arrived back in the kitchen.

'Now Sonny, I'm going to show you how to use the microwave in front of this nice lady here so if you have any questions, you can just ask her.' Valerie pointed at the microwave and Sonny opened the door and peered into it like he'd just discovered the door into Narnia.

'You must remember to shut the door before you set the timer. The door cannot be open. Do you hear, Sonny?' She was talking very slowly.

'Yeah, yeah,' said Sonny, waving one hand at her whilst spinning the glass plate on the bottom of the oven with his other hand. 'Look, it spins,' he said, grinning. 'How cool is that? Is that to make it more interesting to watch whilst it cooks?'

'No. Listen, Sonny, Harry's mum, what was your name again? Harry's mum is going to look after you so there's no need to worry.'

Sonny looked up at her and beamed. He really was the most smiley person she had ever met.

'It's Kim but . . . ' she began.

'Like Kim Kardashian?' said Sonny in excitement. 'Are you named after her?'

'Err no, she's about half my age. No, look, I don't know what's been said but I'm not staying here at all. I don't know why you think that. I mean, I'm staying over, but I'm going to find a hotel, I'm not staying *here*. In this house. So, I can't help you. Sorry.' She walked forward, holding the bag of Sonny's life essentials in front of her.

Valerie stared at her but did not take the bag.

'Her husband is having an affair with the neighbour,' Sonny stage-whispered to his mum. 'That's what Harry said. He said she was staying over so I assumed he meant here. Sorry, Mum. My bad!'

Kim looked at Sonny, horrified.

Valerie stared at Kim before stepping forward and encasing her in her arms.

'You poor, poor woman,' she said, nearly suffocating her. 'Exactly the same thing happened to my sister. Except it was our cousin he went off with. Can you imagine?' She stepped back, shaking her head.

Sonny stepped forward and hugged her himself.

'I'm so sorry for your loss,' he said, taking a step back again. 'Any time you want to talk, you can get in touch on WhatsApp, Snapchat, Insta – whatever is your media of choice.'

Valerie gave him a proud look before turning back to Kim.

'Still, whilst you are in Nottingham then it will be no trouble, will it, to just keep an eye on this one,' she continued, nodding at her still beaming son. 'He's a lovely lad and no trouble but he just needs a bit of help settling in. Would calm my mind no end knowing he had someone like you popping in over the next few days. I mean, he might just about grasp the microwave, but I can tell you that gas hob frightens the living daylights out of me. He'll have no idea.'

'It's all right, Mum,' said Sonny, putting his hand on his mum's shoulder. 'I've got this. Gas hob, no problem.'

He walked over to the hob, studied the dials for a couple of seconds and then twisted one. He turned back to face them, beaming again. 'Look, I can switch it on and I even know which one is on. It's that one at the back. I can tell by the diagram.'

He said all that to the accompaniment of unignited gas hissing in the background.

Valerie was the first to get to the dials. 'You are going to blow the whole house up doing that,' she shouted as she turned the dial back to off. She turned to face Kim. 'I really think it should be a house rule that Sonny is not allowed to touch the gas cooker, don't you?'

'House rules are nothing to do with me,' protested Kim. 'And this is nothing to do with me either.' She stepped forward with the bag, pushing it into Sonny's arms. 'You need to work this out for yourself.'

'Well, thanks a bunch,' said Valerie with a huff. 'I thought you would understand as a mother. Thought it wouldn't be too much trouble just to keep an eye out. He doesn't even know how to do his own washing.'

Kim stared at her aghast. 'Well perhaps you need to take responsibility for making sure he knew the basics before he got here. That's not my problem, it's yours.'

Kim turned to leave the kitchen.

'Not surprised her husband left her,' she heard Valerie mutter behind her.

Kim walked up the stairs to find Harry, thinking that this was probably her cue to leave. Not that she really wanted to. The thought of walking out the door and going to some faceless hotel room was not appealing whatsoever; however, the thought of going back home was even less attractive, so she really had little choice. She knocked on Harry's door and peered into the room. He was nowhere to be seen. Where had he gone? She heard a sound coming from the upper floor. Maybe he had gone to meet whoever was living upstairs. She backed out of Harry's room and walked up the stairs to the top floor.

As she turned the corner onto the landing, she could see an open door in front of her. The room was dark, clearly curtains hadn't been drawn, but the light was still on. A damp towel sat in the doorway and clothes littered the floor. She stood stock still. She couldn't hear any voices at all. It didn't sound like there was anyone up here. She listened for at least thirty seconds. She couldn't hear a soul.

But then she had to do it. She couldn't leave an unnecessary light on, could she? Just a waste of money. Who did this child think he was, leaving electric lights on in broad daylight? She inched her hand round the door, turning her face away so as not to look in the room. She felt up and down the door post until she felt the switch and turned it off.

'What the fuck?' was the next thing she heard come from inside the room. She thought her heart would stop. She dashed into the other room leading off the small landing and hid behind the door, her heart beating loudly. She hardly dared breathe.

'Fucking lights,' she heard someone growl as they clearly flicked the switch back on.

She stood in the empty room, trembling, until there was no sound coming from next door. Perhaps he had been asleep? With the lights on? She took in her surroundings. To her right was a large window overlooking the backyard and the back of the houses in the next road. In the corner stood another classic house clearance wardrobe. This one was of more recent extraction, however. Perhaps more of an MFI vintage in black veneered chipboard. She was sure her brother had had the exact same model in the eighties. The black finish of the wardrobe contrasted heavily with the white veneered desk on the opposite wall which was so small she suspected it was actually a child's desk. Tucked underneath was an old crusty dining chair which one might find in a pub that had never been refurbed and never would be. She pitied the poor student who was destined for this space.

The single bed stretched along the entire back wall. The sight of the bed reminded her how exhausted she was. Perhaps she should just lie down for a little while. Recharge her batteries. She lowered herself onto it, hearing the strain of steel springs in the single mattress. She froze, half expecting the guy in the room next door to come striding in to see who was there. The mattress was bare and bore the stains of an active life. She dreaded to think. She'd just lie down for a minute or two though, she thought. She really was very tired. Just whilst Harry got himself sorted. Then she'd go down and say goodbye and leave. Yes, that's what she would do.

A very loud fart reverberated through from next door. That was the last thing she heard before she fell asleep.

Chapter 5

Kim couldn't work out where she was when she woke up later in the pitch black. In fact she didn't really know what day of the week it was. Was it still today, or was it tomorrow? And where was she? The room felt funny and it was a bit cold. And she wasn't really very comfortable. Something was covering her but she wasn't quite sure what it was. She reached her hand down and pulled at it, rubbing it between her fingers. Maybe it was a sheet or possibly a duvet cover without a duvet. She pulled herself up on the bed and groaned at the thumping pain in her head. She ran her hands along the wall, her heart beating fast, suddenly panicking that she might be trapped in the room forever. Her hand hit something and she heaved a sigh of relief as she found the switch and clicked it on. The bare bulb fizzed into life, causing her to blink rapidly and clutch her head to try and deaden the thumping pain. Eventually her eyes got used to the harsh light and she took in her surroundings under the cold brightness of a halogen bulb. The worst student room in the history of the planet, she thought. How on earth had she fallen asleep here?

She scrabbled round on the bed searching for her phone. She needed to know how long she had been passed out for and then she really needed a drink and something to eat. Then perhaps she would feel better.

She screwed her eyes up looking at the screen. No, that couldn't be right, could it? The time appeared to start with an eleven. She couldn't have slept for that long. And why hadn't anyone woken her up? Then she spotted that she had a notification of a message from Richard.

> Dear Kim. I realise you are upset and I deserve everything you want to throw at me. But please come home. Wherever you are just get in the car and come back and let's talk. Richard.

'Wanker,' muttered Kim, sinking back down onto the bed. She put her head in her hands. Aaaaargh! She wanted to scream. She felt empty and lost. She stared into space for a good half-hour before her stomach rumbled and she realised she had to eat something and she desperately needed water. She had no choice but to venture downstairs. She prayed that the rest of the household had gone out. She could slip downstairs without anyone noticing. Surely the first night here would involve going out and partying. She picked up her phone again to check on the time. The time had a zero in front of it now. It was tomorrow. No wonder she was hungry. The only thing she had eaten in the last twenty-four hours was a few jelly babies.

She pushed her hair out of her eyes, coughed, straightened her hoody and opened the door. She could hear music faintly in the distance. She crept downstairs just in case people were already asleep in their beds, but the further she got the louder the music became. There was somebody up. They were in the kitchen playing music very loudly and she could smell . . . pizza. If it hadn't been for the smell of pizza she may have turned round and gone straight back up to the room and hidden until the morning.

As she walked through the lounge she could hear voices, definitely more than one. A voice she didn't recognise. Deep and gravelly and Scottish.

She poked her head round the door of the kitchen.

Harry, Sonny and what must be Angus were sat around the small table which was covered in open pizza boxes at the far end of the kitchen. So jammed was the space that tins of lager resided on the floor next to the chairs.

'Well, here she is,' said the one who must be Angus. 'The phantom snorer in the room next door.'

'I'm so sorry,' she said, entering the room, actually feeling herself go red. 'I've no idea what happened there. I never meant to fall asleep.'

'I was looking for you everywhere,' said Harry, with his mouth full. 'Then Angus said there was someone snoring in the room next to him and there you were. Out cold.'

'I wouldn't let them wake you, Kim,' said Sonny, shaking his head. 'I told them that you needed your sleep. You know, given what you've gone through.'

‘How are you feeling now, Mum?’ asked Harry.

‘Better, sort of, well I’ve got a headache but I think that’s because I’ve not really eaten today,’ said Kim as she hovered by the table not knowing what to do with herself. ‘I’m so sorry. I meant to go to a hotel. I didn’t mean to get in your way.’

‘You’re not in the way at all,’ said Angus before gulping at his lager. ‘Especially when she clears up this mess, hey lads.’ He collapsed into peals of laughter.

Harry had the decency to look at his mum apologetically.

She took in Angus. Harry had mentioned he’d gone to private school in Scotland. She could see that he had already installed himself as man of the household, taking the prime seat at the head of the table so he could hold court. He was stocky and tall with light auburn hair and a ruddy complexion. He could have been your classic rugger bugger if it wasn’t for the well-cut hair and the designer jumper. Angus didn’t rock up at a barber on a Saturday morning when he was desperate, she could tell. Angus had been brought up having expensive haircuts. He wore a green jumper with a zip at the neckline with the subtlest hint of a polo player on the right-hand side indicating its not so subtle expense. Angus didn’t get dragged to the shops kicking and screaming like Harry did, refusing to try anything on and refusing anything that wasn’t black or grey. Angus had taste and an open wallet. If not Angus, then his mother clearly did.

‘Have some pizza, Kim,’ said Sonny suddenly, holding his box up to her. ‘It’s got green stuff on it.

I thought it was like courgette or something, but it's super-hot.'

Angus peered over at Sonny's pizza.

'They're green chillies.'

'Oh,' said Sonny. 'Right. Wow, green chillies. Wow, they are hot.' He waved his hand in front of his mouth. 'Try some, Kim, really. You get used to it after a bit.'

'I err, I don't want to get in your way,' she said, looking nervously at her son.

Harry shrugged and carried on eating, which she took as a sign it was okay to have some pizza.

'Come on, sit down,' said Angus, holding out a tin of lager. It came across as an instruction rather than a request.

She took a seat and reached over and took a slice of Sonny's pizza. Pepperoni and hot chillies, her favourite. She would have liked a plate but didn't want to draw attention to herself by asking for one and she had no idea where one would be found. No one had yet put anything away; unopened boxes were scattered across the floor.

'We've had *the* best night,' said Sonny to Kim. 'Just like dream first night at uni. I can't believe it.'

'Great, where did you go? Did you go onto campus, find all the other freshers?'

'Nah,' said Angus, swigging at his beer. 'Pub at the end of the road. Been there every night since I arrived.'

'The landlord knows his name,' said Sonny, wide-eyed. 'How cool is that?'

Angus shrugged as though that was perfectly normal.

'It's brilliant,' continued Sonny. 'Two-for-one all night.

All night! I couldn't believe it. Never seen anything like it.'

'It won't last,' said Angus. 'They're just trying to entice the students in at the beginning of term, get them used to going there then they'll up the prices. Mike told me he does it every year. Works every time, he says,' Angus chuckled to himself.

Wow, the chillies on the pizza were really hot. She needed a drink, fast. She balanced her half-eaten slice on Harry's box lid and then opened her can of lager, taking a hefty gulp to quench her thirst.

When she came up for air, Angus was nodding at her appreciatively. 'Good effort,' he said. He picked his own can up and took a long gulp, shortly followed by Sonny. Harry kept his head down, concentrating on devouring his second fast food meal of the day. She felt like the worst parent ever.

'Pub does good food too,' said Angus. 'I've eaten there every night. Basic but good. I had a great pie and chips in there earlier.'

Kim goggled at the enormous pizza that Angus was now devouring. Perhaps she wasn't such a bad parent after all.

'I'll probably end up eating there most nights,' he continued. 'Mum's organised some meal box delivery thing. You know, when they send you all the stuff but then you have to cook it yourself. I mean, what's the point in that? Why would I want to do that when there is a perfectly good pub down the road?'

Kim had to stuff pizza in her mouth to stop herself from saying anything. She felt her eyes water as the chillies hit her taste buds. Who was this kid?

'Mum tried to make me bring everything but the kitchen sink, thinking I'd be cooking gourmet meals every night,' said Harry, giving her a look. 'Fortunately, there wasn't room in the car so I'll be sticking to my bacon butty diet, I reckon.'

Kim thought she'd better not comment as she'd been the reason why the bag had to stay behind since she'd been the one to use the frying pan as a weapon.

'You going to be making that girl who lives opposite bacon butties, then, Harry?' Angus asked.

Kim's head flew up. Angus was looking at her. He winked. Yes, winked.

'No,' said Harry, shaking his head, a shade of red creeping up his neck.

'I reckon she'd like you to,' said Angus. 'She's definitely into you. I can tell. Never looked back at me once I introduced her to you.' He winked at Kim again. 'Suki liked him, I swear,' he stage-whispered to Kim.

'No, she didn't,' repeated Harry. He glanced at his mother and looked as though he wanted the ground to swallow him up.

'Didn't she invite you over to play computer games?' said Sonny. 'Wow, a date on your first day at uni. You are a legend, Harry.'

'It's not a date,' said Harry directly to his mother. 'So don't get your hopes up. She's just stuck on a level, that's all. Said I'd go and show her how to do it.'

Kim shook her head. 'Of course,' she said. 'Nice of you to help her.'

‘Show her how to go up a level, is that what it’s called around here?’ said Angus, shaking with laughter and slapping Harry on the back.

‘It’s not a date,’ said Harry to Angus firmly. ‘We both just like computer games.’

‘I’ve never had a girlfriend,’ sighed Sonny.

‘Bloody hell,’ said Angus. ‘Where have you been?’

‘Crowshot in Devon mainly,’ he replied. ‘It’s really quiet and I’m related to half the girls and the other half seem to be my mates. They don’t fancy me. I clearly send off the wrong signals.’

Kim stole a look at Sonny. He wasn’t wrong. He looked like he got dressed in the dark and now he had tomato sauce smeared up his cheek. He had no chance really.

‘Traffic light party tomorrow night,’ said Angus, pointing at Sonny. ‘We are going to get you a girlfriend.’

‘No way,’ said Sonny, his eyes lighting up. ‘I saw that on the schedule. What is a traffic light party anyway? I assumed it was just for town planning undergrads or something?’

‘No, stupid,’ replied Angus. ‘It’s where you pick up a girlfriend. You wear red if you are unavailable, amber if you might be available and green if you are all systems go. Green means gagging for sex, basically.’

Kim tried hard not to show Harry up by looking shocked at the way he was talking.

‘Wow,’ said Sonny, his eyes on stalks. ‘Seriously, that is how it works? Wow. You make it sound so easy.’

‘It is. Piece of cake. By the end of tomorrow night, you could be losing your virginity.’ Angus winked at Kim yet again. She really wished he wouldn’t do that.

It was making her feel quite uncomfortable. She daren't look at Harry at all.

'I can already feel that this is going to be the best week of my life,' grinned Sonny, appearing to not give a toss about Angus's assumption about his sexual status. 'Are we all going to go? What colour will you wear, Harry, what with Suki opposite?'

'It's *not* a date,' he said again firmly, his mouth stuffed with pizza.

'Do you think she'll be going?' asked Sonny. 'You have to wear green if she's there. But what if she's wearing red? What will you do then? But she might wear red because she's interested in you and then if she sees you in green then she'll think you are not interested in her because you've gone to a traffic light party basically declaring you are open to offers from anyone.'

'I probably won't go,' said Harry. 'Not sure it's my type of thing.'

Kim was about to remind him that he had promised that he would make an effort to join in everything and make friends and not stay on his computer all day. But she thought better of it as she had no business being here to make any such comment. What she really wanted to tell him, of course, was that he should go to the party wearing green and chat up Suki. That would make her feel so much happier about leaving him here. Knowing he had found a girlfriend would really reassure her that he was settling in.

'You have to come,' declared Sonny. 'Please. Just wear amber. But please come. You're going, Angus, aren't you?'

'Of course. Hoping this accent is going to go down a treat.' He winked again.

'But you said you had a girlfriend earlier,' said Sonny. 'You'll be going in red, surely?'

Angus shrugged. 'Poppy just started medicine in Edinburgh last week and by all accounts, medics are crazy students. Like they go mental shagging each other. I've got mates who are medics and I know what they are like.'

'So did you split up then?' asked Sonny. 'Before you came here?'

'No . . . no . . . I just don't expect that she'll be waiting for me with a Christmas present at the end of this term, so why should I wait for her?' He paused. 'Don't you think, Harry's mum?' he asked.

'Please call me Kim,' she replied.

'Okay, Kim,' said Angus. 'She's not going to wait for me, is she? You're a woman, you should know.'

Kim looked back at him wide-eyed. She was in no position to give advice on relationships at this present time. 'I don't know,' she replied. 'Whoever knows.' She bit her lip. She could not cry. Not here. Not now. Oh yes, she could. The tears fled her eyes down her cheeks like someone had turned on the tap.

'Jesus, Mother,' said Harry reaching under his pizza box for some paper napkins and stuffing them in her hand. 'Sorry guys,' he said to Angus and Sonny. 'It's been a really long day.'

'I'm so sorry,' Kim added, hastily scraping the scratchy napkins across her face. No one said anything. She reached up and grabbed her tin of lager and gulped some down.

‘I’m so sorry for your loss,’ said Sonny, putting his hand on her shoulder.

‘He’s not dead,’ sniffed Kim. ‘He’s just . . . he’s just . . . ’

‘Shagging the neighbour,’ added Angus.

She looked up sharply.

‘I told him what happened,’ explained Harry. ‘Seemed the easiest way to explain why my mother was asleep in the spare room from the middle of the afternoon.’

‘I mean on your own doorstep,’ said Angus. ‘That’s way harsh.’

Kim swallowed, the tears cascading down her cheeks. She sighed. ‘May I?’ she asked, reaching over to take another slice of Sonny’s pizza.

‘Please, please, take it all. Whatever you need. Please eat my pizza. It’s the least I can do.’

She stuffed a huge bite of pizza into her mouth and stared at the floor, tears dripping off her nose.

Angus belched.

Sonny giggled.

Harry carried on munching.

‘I’m so sorry,’ she gulped when she had finished chewing. ‘You shouldn’t be having to deal with this. It’s just . . . it’s just . . . so hard. It only happened yesterday and . . . and . . . I really don’t know what to do.’ She gulped again and looked at Harry. She couldn’t believe she was making such a show of herself, today of all days and here, in his new student house share with his new housemates. What on earth must they be thinking?

‘It’s all right, Mum,’ said Harry. He gave her a half

smile and she felt a wave of relief come over her. She'd needed to hear that.

She wiped her lips with the back of her hand. Sonny handed her a piece of kitchen roll and she blew her nose and wiped her eyes.

'I'll get out of your way now,' she said, standing up.

'Where are you going to go?' asked Sonny.

'I'll just find a hotel,' she said, shaking her head. 'It's fine.'

'What, now!' said Sonny horrified. 'No way. You can't go out and find a hotel now. It's after midnight. Stay here. No one is using that room. Sammy Thwaites decided last minute that she would rather work in an Amazon warehouse than move in with us so the room is empty until she can find someone to take it on. Her parents have guaranteed her rent for the whole year. Can you imagine? They must be fuming. So, you can stay for a bit. I can't imagine they will find a replacement this quickly.'

Kim couldn't believe what she was hearing. Neither could Harry and Angus by the looks of it.

'No, honestly, I couldn't do that, really. It's not fair,' she said.

'Of course it is,' said Sonny. He looked over at his housemates. 'It's all right, isn't it? I mean, we can't send your mum out onto the streets, can we? Look at her!'

Kim realised she must look a total wreck as both Angus and Harry took in her dishevelled appearance and still dripping nose.

Kim squirmed. She watched as Harry's eyes darted between the three of them trying to work out what to do. How could she have put in him this situation, on today of all days? His first day, starting his new life at university.

'I'll go,' she said to Harry. 'I'm cramping your style. You don't need to be worrying about me right now.'

She automatically started clearing up dirty napkins as though she had already become mother to them all and therefore was designated clearer upper.

Harry put his hand out to stop her. 'You don't need to do that, Mum,' he said.

She nodded just as another tear dripped off her nose. She couldn't even lift her head to look at them.

'Make her stay, Harry,' said Sonny, his voice cracking.

'Is it all right with you, Angus?' she heard Harry tentatively ask. 'If it's just for a few days?'

'Sure,' she heard Angus say. 'You can let her tidy up though. I mean, don't stop her doing that, whatever you do.'

Kim looked at her son. He gave her a tight smile. She mouthed a 'thank you' to him. In one moment she had become the child and Harry was the parent. She was so grateful she felt a fresh wave of tears try to overwhelm her but she fought to hold them back.

'Brilliant, cool,' said Sonny, clapping his hands in glee. 'I'll let my mum know that I've found a responsible adult to give my spare EpiPen to for at least a few days.'

Chapter 6

This time Kim knew exactly where she was when she woke up as the sun shone through the thin curtains straight into her eyes. She blinked then groaned, attempting to turn over in her bed but just getting ravelled up in the empty duvet cover, causing the bed springs to groan back. She lay stock-still listening. Were the others up? Had they already left the building? What time was it?

Unbelievably the hands on her watch seemed to want to tell her it was past midday. It couldn't be, surely? She rolled over to grab her phone off the floor. Yep – after midday was confirmed as the waking hour. She lay back, confused. What had happened to time since Saturday night? Everything had got cockeyed. But still – after midday – she hadn't slept in until after midday since she was, well, a teenager. She wondered if her fellow teenagers had also slept in this long. Surely not. No one sleeps in this long under normal circumstances. There had to be some extreme event such as one's husband shacking up with the next door neighbour, surely?

She extracted herself from the tangled mess of the duvet cover and put her feet on the floor. She had brought her bag in from the car before she'd gone back to bed in the early hours of the morning. She rifled around in it until she found a towel. She was so grateful that the boys were willing to let her stay but right now she needed to go to the bathroom and she could do with a shower, and the enormity of the task in this strange house felt quite overwhelming. Should she go to the bathroom in her pyjamas? The bathroom being on the floor below meant that she risked meeting a strange man on the landing, bra-less. God had been kind to Kim on the breast front and she could fill a D cup very well, but what happened when she was not safely encased by a D cup was not a pretty sight. Lopsided and droopy was not how she wished to be caught racing across the landing. This was why en suites were invented. So no one had to see your boobs flapping around under flimsy fabric apart from your partner.

She'd just hold her towel in front of her. That would have to do. Block all observation of the lopsided and droopy. But she needed a shower. So should she put her pyjamas back on for her return journey from the bathroom to the bedroom? But that always seemed so wrong. Putting slept-in clothes back on after a cleansing shower. She'd have to take her clothes in with her. Get dressed in the bathroom and then she could walk out head held high, nothing to hide, fully bra'd up. It was her only choice. There was absolutely no way she was streaking up the stairs with just a towel wrapped round her. That was a fool's game.

She gathered up her washbag and towel and, holding them firmly in front of her chest, she ventured out of the room.

All was silent. Perhaps they had all gone out and she had nothing to worry about. She glanced to her right to see Angus's door wide open, curtains drawn and lights on. She didn't dare switch his light off again. Perhaps later when she was sure he had gone out.

For some reason she felt it necessary to tiptoe down the stairs. Past Harry's room whose door was firmly shut, then past Sonny's whose open door revealed a peek at a desk already laid out with relevant stationery next to open curtains. That was a vacated room, she was sure. Perhaps they *were* all out.

She pushed open the door to the bathroom and quickly locked it behind her. Warm damp air filled the room from a fairly recent shower and there was that smell again. Male scented deodorant or aftershave with a back note of poo. She reached over to open the window behind the sink to let some fresh air in and to allow herself to breathe. This was not good. She looked down to see a sink already awash with toothpaste not sluiced away. On the windowsill two washbags spilt an assortment of toiletries. A blue canvas washbag had Sonny written on it in gold. Of course it did. An industrial sized two-in-one shampoo and conditioner for hair with dandruff stood next to it. No wonder his hair was a frizzy mess; she'd have to get him off the two-in-one stuff – it really was no good for some hair. An industrial sized bottle of shower gel stood next to it. It was enormous. The whole house could use it and it would still last them until Christmas. Either Sonny liked to wash a lot or his mum was keen on wholesale shopping. In contrast Angus's toiletries were very different. His washbag was black leather with many compartments. This was a man who travelled a lot and so was used to packing his washbag for every eventuality. She spotted high-end brand shampoo and conditioner as well as other hair products including wax and gel. There was also pore cleanser and spot clearer and moisturising shower gel. Someone had taught him the tricks of the trade. Angus's mother had evidently never stepped foot in a Costco; she clearly did however cruise the cosmetics aisles of department stores. No sign of Harry's washbag. Of course there wasn't. She wondered if he had washed at all since he arrived. Oh dear. What did that say about her? That she had taught him nothing about self-hygiene?

Hopefully she had taught him not to leave wet towels on the floor though as she turned around to pick up two damp towels thrown in the direction of a rail rather than draped over it.

The shower, of course, was a whole other experience. She pushed the shower curtain aside to step into the bath. At least the shower curtain was new even if its geometric purple and orange colour was quite jarring. She suspected it was an attempt to distract from the mouldy grouting around the cracked tiles. She struggled to turn on the limescale encrusted tap let alone adjust the temperature, scalding her hand which caused her to jump back in surprise. The smell of her own shower gel soothed her somewhat but it also reminded her of her en suite back at home, possibly her favourite room in the house. Her mother had been in awe when she'd shown her round. No one in the family had ever had an en suite before. It had two sinks. Two sinks! Janice could not believe it. Who had a sink to themselves? She'd never heard of such a thing. Kim used to have her own sink in an en suite in a brand-new four-bedroom detached house. And now here she was, sharing a bathroom with three men, nervous about walking along the landing to get to the bathroom. She felt the tears start to threaten. She couldn't cry again. She was sick of crying.

Post-shower she put her now slightly damp clothes on in the cramped bathroom, trying hard to not get her feet wet from the soggy carpet as she balanced precariously to poke them through the leg holes in her knickers. Pulling her hair back into a ponytail, she gathered up her washbag, her towel and her pyjamas into a bundle and took them back to her room. Time to brave the kitchen and seek out some breakfast.

The state of the kitchen was worse than the bathroom. Boxes of kitchen equipment no doubt packed by caring parents still lay around causing trip hazards and an awkward bending over manoeuvre to fill the kettle. There was a jar of coffee next to a used spoon. It was nice instant with Gold in the title. She hoped whoever it belonged to wouldn't mind if she took just a little before she ventured out to the shops to get some supplies for herself. Pizza boxes still littered the table. She walked over and flicked open one of the lids. One piece of pizza left, congealed and stone cold. She was about to throw it away when she decided that since no one was going to eat it then she might as well. She hated to see food go to waste.

She wandered through to the living room and found the remote control. The TV stood in one of the alcoves. She flicked to find Holly Willoughby interviewing someone about which are the best crystals to improve the aura in your home. Not a subject she thought she'd find useful anytime soon. All the other channels seemed to either have house buying or house renovating programmes on. Was that all the daytime audience were interested in, their bloody home? She switched off the TV in frustration and fished her phone out of her pocket and took it off silent mode. She'd put it onto silent the previous night. She never normally did that because she needed to know Harry could contact her if needed. But she figured as he was only on the floor below he'd come and wake her if there was some kind of emergency. And she'd got sick of hearing her phone ring only to see it was Richard trying to call her.

Five missed calls that morning from him. And on a Monday too. She was sure he had lectures on a Monday morning. Or perhaps he didn't. She had previously thought he was running some important tests every Saturday and yet he wasn't. He was shagging Alison. Or maybe sometimes going for a walk!

Her phone started to light up in her hand before she had a chance to switch the silent mode off. 'Go away,' she shouted until she saw it wasn't Richard. It was actually her friend, Vicky.

'Hi,' she said, putting the phone to her ear. 'I've been meaning to phone you.'

'Where the hell are you?' Vicky screeched down the line. 'What's happening? Richard's just been here looking for you. He wouldn't tell me why, just gave that dopey surprised look he has when he doesn't know what is going on.'

Kim nearly laughed. Richard did always have a shocked expression when he didn't understand something. Like he expected to understand everything. Even the very existence of *Love Island*. Like someone like him could ever understand the joy many people got from watching young, attractive people show they are just as insecure as the next person.

'Are you all right?' asked Vicky urgently.

'I'm fine, don't worry,' said Kim. 'Well, I'm alive at least. Put it that way. Did Richard tell you what happened?'

'No! He just banged on my door at 8.30 this morning. I mean, 8.30! And asked if you were here. I tried to explain that no, you don't live with me last time I looked, that you live with him in case he hadn't noticed, but he got all uppity, told me I wasn't helping with my sarcasm and walked off. He looked like shit as well, Kim. Two days of stubble and he was still wearing the clothes he wore for the party.'

Kim gasped. Had he not been home? Perhaps he hadn't taken his house keys with him next door. Perhaps he was locked out of his own house. She felt herself smile. That news might just make her day.

'What's going on, Kim?' asked Vicky. 'You been

having an affair you haven't told me about, you swine? Because that is what it looks like.'

'No!' said Kim. 'Not me, him, Vicky. Richard's been having an affair.'

'No way!' gasped Vicky. She paused. 'He's not the type. He's not got it in him.'

'He most certainly has,' replied Kim. 'And he's got it in Alison next door, that's who he's got it in.'

'No way. Anal Alison. Not her? No.'

'Anal Alison?'

'Yeah, Anal Alison. Always takes her shoes off at your door. Takes you on those cosy-wozy shopping trips to Manchester like she's your best friend or something.'

'You were jealous! You never said.'

'Well, not now obviously if she's ended up doing the dirty with your husband. But Richard and Alison? I can't believe it. It just doesn't make any sense. She looks like the type to iron her underwear with starch, that's all I'm saying. Do you remember when she wanted me to do her a birthday cake for her mum's seventieth birthday? Her words were and I quote, "I want it fairly plain; you know, subtle. No fondant figures or sparklers or feathers. Just quietly sophisticated." Quietly fucking sophisticated! Has she seen my cakes? Quietly sophisticated would be an insult to one of my cakes, I can tell you. What a bitch. Can't believe you were friends with her.'

'Well, not anymore,' replied Kim flatly.

'Shit, Kim, I'm sorry. I'm bleating on about how she insulted my cakes and she stole your husband.'

Kim didn't reply.

'I have to ask how? I mean. She's nothing on you. Seriously. How?'

'Richard said it was at the graduation ball last year. Some crisis happened, she got upset, he got her drunk and the rest is history.'

'It's been going on since last year?'

'Apparently. He told me he was running experiments in the lab at uni every Saturday but he wasn't, he was with her.'

'Oh my God, your speech the other night,' gasped Vicky. 'You were so . . . so . . . '

'Stupid,' finished Kim.

'Geoff asked me why I didn't do a speech like that for him when he turned fifty and I told him if he'd bothered to even buy me a card for my last five birthdays then he may have stood a chance.'

'It makes me want to weep just thinking about it,' said Kim. 'It's why I had to get away. Imagine facing everyone to tell them that your husband has been having an affair after doing that speech.'

'Yeah, see what you are saying. Total bastard though for ditching you straight after you said all that. He must really have a thing for her.'

'Thanks.'

'Sorry, mate. So where are you?'

'I'm in Nottingham with Harry. I was going to stay in a hotel but there's a spare room in his house so they've said I can have it for a few days, just to give me some space.'

'You are in a student house?'

'Yes.'
'Miss Houseproud of the Century.'
'Yes.'
'What's it like?'
Kim looked around at the bottles lined up on the shelves and through the door at the chaotic kitchen.
'Pretty much how you would imagine.'
'A shit-hole.'
'Nicely put. But yes.'
'Oh my, Kim. And the other housemates?'
'Angus is a posh Scottish rugby boy who thinks he's going to eat out for every meal and Sonny is clueless, utterly clueless. His mother gave me his medication to look after, including condoms.'
'You are sharing with three men?'
'Yes.'
'How many bathrooms?'
Kim paused. 'One.'
'Oh my God!' exclaimed Vicky. 'That's just cruelty. After all you've been through. I can smell that bathroom from here.'
'You probably can,' agreed Kim.
'You, in a student house,' said Vicky. 'Didn't see that coming.'
'So far it seems to be draughty, disorganised and smelly. I'm sleeping under a duvet cover on the creakiest old spring bed you can imagine.'
'Duvet cover?'
'I only brought an overnight bag. Sonny has lent me his spare duvet cover. At least it's better than being on my own in a hotel.' Kim felt her shoulders sag

and she felt like bursting into tears. How had her life come to this?

'Do you want to come and stay here?' said Vicky. 'I mean, you'd have to share with Ellie but I'm sure she wouldn't mind. Mind you, she does have her boyfriend staying most weekends which is pissing me off, so you'd be doing me a favour to be honest.'

'No, it's okay,' replied Kim. 'I couldn't foist myself on poor Ellie. Or get in the middle of one of your family fallouts.'

'Fair enough. But you need to let me help you. Can I bring you some stuff down?' asked Vicky. 'I could drive down at the weekend. Put a load of stuff in the back of the cake van.'

'No, you can't do that. In any case I'm not staying long, I don't think. Not that I know where I'm going to go but I can't stay here long at all.'

'Stay until Friday and I'll come down and we'll work it out. We'll make a plan,' said Vicky. 'I am your best friend in case you had forgotten.'

'Alison was never my best friend, you know that, don't you?' said Kim.

'I know. I'm just winding you up. Now send me your address and I'll make sure I get all my deliveries done early.'

'You really would do that?'

'Of course. Miss the chance to see you in student digs? I don't think so. We could make a night of it. Go out on the town.'

'I'm not sure I'll be up for that. And I have no clothes.'

'Rubbish. It will cheer you up. I'll bring you something to wear.'

Kim sighed. A night out with Vicky did seem like just what the doctor ordered. But she hadn't anticipated staying here until after Friday. She'd have to check if that was all right with the others.

'I'll have to check if it's okay to stay until then. Do you still have a key? It sounds like Richard can't get in if he's still wearing his clothes from Saturday.'

'Looks like it. Yes, I do have a key. You don't want me to give it to him, do you?'

'Goodness no,' replied Kim. 'Let him figure out how to get into his own home.'

'I'll go when I'm sure he's not there,' replied Vicky. 'But I'll be sure to make it obvious someone has been. Leave a light on, close the curtains or something like that. Really freak him out. Want me to post one of Bailey's turds through Alison's letterbox whilst I'm at it?'

'Tempting,' agreed Kim, 'but not really my style. If Richard hasn't been in though, he won't have seen your amazing cake that I smashed onto the kitchen floor. I'm sorry you will have to see that. You put so much effort in.'

'It's okay,' said Vicky. 'I'll even clean it up for you.'

'You shouldn't have to do that.'

'What are real friends for? I'll clean it up and then I'll post it piece by piece through Alison's letterbox. Including the fondant figurine of Richard.'

'I threw that at him.'

'Nice one,' replied Vicky. 'Look, I've got to go. So sorry

– I'm out delivering cakes. Are you going to be okay? Shall we talk later?'

'Yeah, thanks. I'm just in shock really, I guess. I never saw it coming, Vicky. I had absolutely no idea. I feel like such an idiot.'

'The last thing you are is an idiot, Kim,' said Vicky.

'He's taken me for an idiot though, hasn't he?' replied Kim mournfully.

'He's the stupid one, Kim. Just you remember that. Falling for old frosty knickers next door over you. Now that's stupid.'

Vicky swallowed. She felt like a prize idiot and no one else would ever convince her otherwise.

Nothing was capable of distracting her on the television so she wandered back into the kitchen. She had thought of going out to buy food, but even that felt like a daunting task. But she needed to do something. She couldn't sit and mope all afternoon. She would normally have done at least five haircuts by now and would be sat having her packed lunch with one of her clients who would be asking her all about Richard's party that she had been excitedly telling them all about for weeks. She should have been saying what a great time everyone had and how Richard had no idea and he really thought it was the best surprise ever and she was the best wife ever. Only she wasn't sat crowing about the surprise party she'd thrown for her husband. She was surrounded by unopened boxes worrying about whether it would be the right thing to unpack them all. Get stuck in. Sort the kitchen out.

In the end she decided that she really had no choice. If she didn't do something to occupy her spiralling out-of-control head she would actually scream. They'd all be grateful, wouldn't they? Glad they didn't have to do it? They'd be pleased, surely? And if she didn't do something she thought the hands on the clock might actually grind to a halt.

And sure enough the time did go faster, not quite fast enough but definitely faster. Applying herself to the conundrum of what to put where gave her some relief from her inner turmoil. She put what she assumed were Angus's pristine saucepans in the cupboard next to the oven, adding what she assumed were Sonny's well-used overspill collection from his mother. She did consider that Angus's complete dinner service from John Lewis was unlikely to be used in a student household and would have been more suited as a wedding present, but she washed every plate and every bowl before putting it in an overhead cupboard along with Sonny's slightly chipped offcuts. She must remember to tell Vicky to bring up the Ikea bag and maybe include some additions to it for Harry. She had already noted there were no mixing bowls and a lack of wooden spoons. She began a list on her phone to send to Vicky.

She stacked all the empty boxes in a corner when she had finished before clearing up last night's pizza party and wiping down all the surfaces. She surveyed her work. Much better. They could do with a kitchen roll holder and a decent set of knives and it would actually start to look like someone might cook in here. She made herself a cup of coffee then sat down at the table to complete her list of what Vicky should bring up with her on Friday.

Harry was first back.

He walked into the kitchen, dumped his bag on the floor and reached for the kettle.

She was itching to ask him if he'd had a good day. Ask him where he'd been, what he'd been up to. Had he been to campus? Had he got his timetable? Had he met anyone? So many questions but none that didn't sound like the overbearing mother who had gatecrashed his freshers' week.

'All right?' she eventually said when he was not forthcoming with conversation.

'Fine,' he grunted. He turned round and walked out.

What did that mean? Was he fine or was that a not really fine but I'm going to say fine because I don't want to talk about why I'm not fine? She knew those kind of 'fines'. She'd often used them. What now? Call him on the mobile and ask him how his day had been? That is what she would have done had she been at home. She'd have waited until after dinner for sure but she would have been on that phone firing out the questions and getting to the bottom of what 'fine' means. Did this 'fine' mean he's found his first day at uni totally overwhelming and scary and he had no idea what he was doing? Or did this 'fine' mean that the day had gone well but coming home to his mother in his student house share had put a dampener on it? She sighed, realising she'd already used up her question-asking token for the day so picked up her cold coffee and dragged herself upstairs past Harry's firmly closed door and shut herself in her room out of harm's way.

She must have gone to sleep again because the next thing she heard was shouting outside her door. It was dark. She really needed to stop this falling asleep during the day thing, it was so confusing.

'I'm not going with you dressed like that,' she heard Angus say. 'And you're not going dressed like that. You look stupid.'

'But you said to dress in green,' Sonny protested. 'You said last night that at a traffic light party you dressed in green to show that you are available, and that's what I am. I am very, *very* available.'

'I know I said green but I didn't mean *that* green. Most people put a sticker on their shirt, that's it. They're subtle about it.'

'But I don't want to be subtle. What if the sticker falls off, what then? I could get missed by someone. Or what if they are colour-blind? People are, you know. Many people mistake red for brown. At least this way you can pretty much guess I'm in green even if you are colour-blind.'

'I think someone in space would be able to see you were dressed in green.'

She had to go and take a look. What on earth was Sonny wearing?

She opened the door to her room hoping to make it look as though she was popping out to the bathroom rather than coming to find out what the hell was going on. However, she never made it to the bathroom. She was stopped in her tracks by the sight of Sonny, dressed head to toe in a bright green leprechaun costume that consisted of a lurid green nylon suit and a lurid green top hat with a shamrock painted on it.

'Oh,' was all she could say, stepping back in surprise.

'What do you think?' said Sonny, turning towards her to display the full throttle of his green-ness. 'I found a fancy dress shop and asked them for their most green outfit and this is what they came up with. No one is going to miss me at the traffic light party, are they?'

'Err well no, definitely not. No doubt about that,' agreed Kim. She noticed Harry at the bottom of the stairwell looking up nervously. He was dressed in jeans and a polo shirt which had a mustard-coloured collar which could have been interpreted as amber. She could tell he was self-conscious about that level of commitment to the traffic light theme and was probably horrified by Sonny's all-in approach.

'We can't rock up with you dressed like that,' said Angus. Angus was sporting a designer racing green shirt and dark jeans. To be fair, Sonny didn't stand much of a chance next to him, so literally playing the joker card was maybe his only shot.

'The Uber will be here in five minutes,' said Harry, looking at his watch. He was jiggling his leg like he always did when he was nervous.

'You need to change,' Angus told Sonny.

'But I've worn it now,' said Sonny, looking crestfallen. 'I won't be able to take it back. And . . . and I just wanted to be clear, you know. That I'm most definitely available.'

'Perhaps just wear the hat and then normal clothes?' said Kim tentatively. 'No one will miss that and you can always take it off if you get too many offers.'

Sonny stared at her and then at Angus.

'Yes,' said Angus. 'Just go. Come on, hurry up, or else the cab won't hang around.'

Sonny ran down the stairs, pushing past Harry.

Harry looked up at his mum and nodded. She read it as some kind of maybe approval of her intervention. He turned and headed downstairs. She might dare ask him tomorrow night how his day has been. Angus brushed past her. She fought the urge to shout after him that he had forgotten to turn his light off . . . again.

She waited outside her door until she heard the front door slam and they were gone. She walked downstairs to the kitchen. Not a cupboard or a door had been opened. No cutlery or crockery used. Screwed up chip papers cluttered the kitchen table.

Chapter 7

The next morning Kim's eyes popped wide open. She was wide awake. She had no idea why. She had lain awake half the night listening to Angus woo a girl next door. He wooed her for so long with his Scottish lilt that she thought perhaps he had bored her to death. But he hadn't. There was silence for a few minutes and then the sounds of low moans coming from the room next door filled her disbelieving ears. Really? So these so-called traffic light parties actually worked? Angus had gone out dressed in a green shirt and returned, woman in hand, and now he was having sex! Kim lay there in despair. She grabbed her hoody off the floor and wrapped it round her head, turban-like. She didn't think she had ever been in a more awkward situation. Scratch that. Trying to leave home whilst watched by your errant husband, his bit on the side and the next door neighbour. That was right up there too.

She lay in her bed for the second morning as the sunlight streamed in, straining to hear the whereabouts of her fellow housemates. The wind blew against the window but that was all she could hear. What she really wanted to do was go and get herself a cup of coffee, in her pyjamas, and perhaps watch some mind-numbing telly whilst she avoided thinking about how to handle the rest of her life. As she'd lain in bed the night before with her hoody wrapped around her head her future seemed to open out before her like a vast gaping black hole. She realised she had spent the last twenty years moulding her life around her husband and her son. Her own life had taken a backseat. So who was she if she wasn't busy being Richard's wife and Harry's mum? She realised she had absolutely no idea.

She tiptoed down the stairs, listening carefully for signs of life as she did so. Harry's door was shut as usual, Sonny's was open. She could see his leprechaun hat discarded on the floor. She hoped he'd had some luck at the traffic light party, albeit maybe not as much as Angus clearly had had.

Downstairs she made her way across the living room. Still no signs of life. Not a peep coming from the kitchen when she paused at the door, just to check. She pushed it open only to find that actually she wasn't alone in the house. Not at all. Sat at the kitchen table, tapping intently at a phone, was a girl. Very attractive and with long, wavy dark hair. She barely batted a fake eyelash when Kim entered the room.

'Hi,' she said, glancing up from her phone.

'Hi,' replied Kim. 'Err, mind if I make myself a cup of coffee?'

She shrugged. 'Course I don't.' Her fake fingernails tap-tap-tapped across the screen.

Kim flicked on the kettle and put a teaspoon of coffee in a mug.

'Sorry, I won't be long,' the girl said, not looking up.

'No problem,' replied Kim, leaning against the worktop. 'Take your time.' She suddenly felt very aware of the level of her drooping breasts. The girl wore a green velvet bodycon top displaying an impressive and fully supported amount of cleavage. She looked away.

'There, done,' she said, looking up and smiling whilst putting her phone face down on the table. 'Just texting my housemates to tell them where I am. I'm Isla by the way.' Kim detected a soft Scottish accent. Was this Angus's squeeze from last night? Perhaps he knew her from home. Perhaps it wasn't a one-night stand. Perhaps she should adjust her opinion of Angus and of Isla for that matter.

'I'm Kim,' she said, offering her hand to shake but quickly withdrawing it when she thought about where Isla's hand may have been.

'Angus said he had a live-in housekeeper but I didn't believe him,' said Isla, chuckling. 'I thought he was bullshitting me. Bloody hell, he really is loaded, isn't he?'

'No, goodness no,' said Kim. 'No, I'm not the housekeeper. He was bullsh— lying to you. No, I'm . . . well I'm . . . one of his housemate's mothers, actually.'

'Riiight,' said Isla looking more wary of this explanation than of the one where she had been employed by a student as a housekeeper.

'I err, I'm staying for a few nights. Trouble at home. You know. Needed somewhere to go in a hurry. Not stopping long though. I'll be gone in a few days.'

Isla nodded thoughtfully. 'Abusive husband, right?' she said, putting her hand on Kim's arm. 'I'm so sorry to hear that. My mum's a therapist up in Edinburgh. She deals with that type of thing all the time. I can send you her details.' She picked up her phone and the tapping started again. 'Let me AirDrop you.'

'No, no,' said Kim. 'He wasn't abusive. I mean not in the violent sense. No, nothing like that. No, he just slept with my neighbour, that's all.'

'Oh,' said Isla, looking almost disappointed and putting her phone back down. 'Right. Do you want to talk about it? I mean I don't want to pry or anything, only I'm doing a psychology degree and intend to become a child therapist so this is my kind of thing, you know. Why don't you sit down?' She motioned to the seat opposite her.

Kim shook her head. Sharing intimate details about the breakdown of her marriage with a stranger who she'd overheard shagging her housemate was definitely not her type of thing.

'It's okay,' she smiled. 'You know I have to . . . erm . . .' the sad fact was she didn't have to do anything.

'Honestly, I have time,' urged Isla. 'Seriously, take a seat.' She pulled the chair out for her. 'I know these things can be painful. Heartbreaking. Tell me, is your neighbour male? Is that why you don't want to talk about it? If that was the case then I promise you it's more common than you think. My mum is getting many more cases where couples are splitting up later in life like you, due to suppressed sexuality.'

Kim shook her head again. 'No,' she said. 'My neighbour was called Alison, very much female.' Kim felt like she had disappointed for the second time.

'Really,' said Isla. Like that was a surprise fact. For a split-second Kim wished her break-up was more dramatic, more contemporary. Her husband going off with the next door neighbour suddenly sounded so old-fashioned!

'I'd better go get dressed,' said Kim, pouring boiled water into her mug. 'It's been great meeting you.'

'Yeah, sure. I'll probably see you later on when Angus gets back,' replied Isla. 'We really connected. Maybe it's the Scottish thing. Us Scots need to stick together, you know.'

'Did you meet at the traffic light party then?'

'Oh no,' said Isla. 'Outside the chip shop up the road. I was with someone Angus has on Snapchat and they spotted each other on Snap Maps and we got chatting whilst he waited for his southern fried chicken and, well, you know. When you know, you know, right? I think he could be a keeper. His auntie knows my godmother. What are the odds? Meant to be, I reckon. Do you have his number? He forgot to leave it for me.'

And this woman was trying to give her advice on her relationship? Even Kim could tell that Angus was totally not a keeper. She stared at Isla – what to do? Did she stick up for this poor, deluded girl and stop her making a total fool of herself or did she stick up for Angus who was kindly allowing her to stay in the house?

'No, I don't have his number,' said Kim.

'Oh,' said Isla in an accusing manner as though Kim was deliberately trying to withhold it from her. 'Does he have a girlfriend?' she asked suddenly.

Now that really confused Kim. Surely Isla wouldn't have slept with him if she thought he had a girlfriend. Then again there were plenty of people out there happy to sleep with other people's husbands and wives . . . Alison!

'Erm . . . I'm not sure. I think he was seeing someone back home. But I'm not sure it was serious. I mean, I don't know. You should ask him.'

Isla stared back at her, blinking, then said, 'He said he didn't have a girlfriend back home.'

Kim felt instantly sick. She didn't want to be in this conversation. 'Well, you know, he just mentioned someone in passing. They may not have been in a relationship. I really don't know. I mean I probably know even less about him than you do.'

She continued to blink her heavily mascaraed eyelashes then suddenly got up. 'I have a lecture,' she said. 'Forgot, it's Tuesday, thought it was Wednesday. Need to go. Bye.'

'Isn't it freshers' week?' Kim muttered after her. 'So, no lectures?' The door slammed behind her. She hoped she'd not landed Angus in it, but then again if she were in Isla's position she would so want to know exactly what Angus's relationship status was. Kim suspected that Angus actually was holding a massive flame for his girlfriend in Edinburgh. She could tell by the way he talked about her. And men who messed women around weren't exactly top of her list at the moment.

It took about half an hour for Kim to start missing Isla as a day empty of any activity or purpose stretched before her. God she was bored. If only she had said yes when Isla had offered to listen to her story of the breakdown of her marriage. That would have killed at least an hour. Who cared if she knew that Isla had nothing of value to contribute to her predicament? Isla had no life experience. She may think studying for a psychology degree qualified her to unscramble people's problems but Kim knew only too well that there was a lot more to it than that. Isla would no doubt have tried to tell her of theories and studies all designed to help people tackle how they live. Kim had always believed that the most valuable thing you can do for someone who is going through a difficult time is to listen. That's what most people wanted. Just to have someone hear them. She'd learnt that through her hairdressing. The number of times one of her clients had sat in the chair and downloaded whilst she added the odd remark here and there. Nothing much, just the odd murmur of agreement or maybe even a suggestion of a different viewpoint. She prided herself on the fact that often her clients got up from their chair not only lighter of hair but also lighter in demeanour having shed their concerns and worries as she calmly went about her work.

She doubted very much if Isla had the capacity to just listen. She was far too sure of herself and eager to offer an opinion. Still, it would have been nice to talk to someone – anyone. Rather than sat scrolling through TV channels hoping that something would grab her attention and whisk her thoughts somewhere far away.

She was so bored that when her phone rang, she was grateful. Despite the fact it was Richard. Maybe it was time to talk. She certainly had the time.

'Hello,' she said.

'Oh, hi, you picked up, thank goodness. Why didn't you pick up before?'

'Because I didn't want to.'

'I've been worried about you.'

Kim was already weary of this.

'That's not my fault, is it? It's yours.'

'Where are you?'

'I'm at Harry's.'

'Staying at Harry's?'

'Yes.'

'In his room?'

'No! Of course not. There is a spare room.'

'How is Harry?'

'Why don't you ask him yourself?'

'He won't pick up his phone.'

Kim felt a small surge of triumph. She didn't want Harry to take sides but knowing he wasn't having clandestine talks with his father made her feel really good.

'Like I said. That's your fault, isn't it?'

Richard said nothing. She could hear him breathing heavily. She realised that she was the one who drove most of their conversations. Richard not being the most sociable of people, he relied heavily on Kim to do most of the heavy lifting when they were out and about. Well, she felt no need to drive the small talk anymore. She remained silent.

'We need to talk,' he said eventually.

'Fire away,' she replied.

She knew he would hate that. Richard reacted to the conversation; he didn't make it. She couldn't wait to hear his starter for ten.

'I need a key to get into the house,' he said. 'Mine are inside.'

She sighed. Riveting. So they were going to talk about his access issues to the house rather than his massive indiscretion with the next door neighbour.

'Mum has a set,' she replied.

'I can't go and ask your mum for a set.'

'Why?'

'Because she'll want to know why. Have you told her yet?'

'No.' To be honest she was putting it off. She needed to get her head in the right space first. She was pretty sure she knew how her mother would react. Kim was certain that her mother always thought she was unworthy of Richard. That their dramatically different backgrounds were always going to be a barrier to future happiness. She realised that she would eventually have to tell her that Richard had had an affair with the next door neighbour at which point her mother would ask her what the neighbour did for a living and then would give an 'I told you so' look when she told her Alison worked at the university.

Richard had fallen silent again as they faced this impasse.

Kim was determined not to fill the silence for him.

'When are you coming back?' he asked.

'When I'm ready.'

'I need to get my contacts prescription so I need to get into the house.'

'So?'

'Is there anyone else with a key apart from your mum?'

'Don't think so,' Kim lied. Why wasn't he asking how she was? Why was this blasted key to the house the only thing he cared about? Why was he showing absolutely zero concern for his wife of nearly twenty years? Her wedding day flashed through her mind. She could still picture the look on his face when she appeared at the top of the aisle in her local church. The church she had been to countless times for christenings and funerals and carol concerts and other people's weddings. She stood there in the familiar surroundings gazing at this man who had come from afar and taken her heart. She remembered she thought he looked like he'd come home, so utterly contented was his smile. She'd asked him later and he'd said it felt exactly like that. That marrying her felt exactly like coming home.

The memory made tears swell in her eyes. She felt herself let out a sob. She didn't want to cry on the phone to him but she couldn't hold it back.

'So will you post me your keys then?' he asked, as she tried to control her emotions.

'Oh fuck off,' she cried, flinging her phone across the room. 'Fuck off, fuck off, fuck off,' she screamed, thumping her fists against the worn sofa before thrusting them into her eyes to try and stop the flow of tears. Twenty years of marriage and he couldn't even ask how she was. If she needed anything. If she was coping okay. No concern whatsoever over the devastation he had wreaked.

She shouldn't have done it. But she felt so unbelievably alone and so unbelievably sad. She looked up at the vast array of bottles lined up in the alcove. She reached up and grabbed one, drained the last of the tea dregs out of her mug and sloshed red wine into it. It was the only way she thought she could get through the day.

Chapter 8

Kim had spent half an hour pacing the living room waiting for Vicky to arrive. The last three days had been the longest of her entire life. Devoid of anything other than keeping out of the way of her housemates and trying to free her mind of all the dark clouds that her new situation had engulfed her in. To her utter shame she had taken to stealing shots from the array of bottles that lined the shelves in the lounge. She took good care to distribute evenly which bottles she drank from so as to go unnoticed, which resulted in the mother of all daily hangovers, but she had to do something to blot out the pain and at present this felt like her only option.

She'd also snuck another one of the delicious bottles of wine that lined the top shelves. She promised herself that she would replace them as soon as she could face going into the city. She wasn't stealing them. She was just borrowing them, she told herself. For medicinal purposes.

Her extremely low profile in the house meant that no one had asked her when she was leaving but she knew her days were numbered. She couldn't possibly stay here much longer. She'd have a night out with Vicky and they would come up with a plan, and then she would get out of there. All would become clear after talking to Vicky, she prayed.

When Friday did finally arrive she was slightly concerned however that Vicky was most excited about living the 'student lifestyle' for the night, whatever she thought that was, rather than actually seeing her friend. Vicky had called twice during the day to ask what one wore for a night out in Nottingham. Kim was bewildered.

'What you would wear for a night out in Lancaster,' she replied.

'I know, but, you know, we'll be mixing with the student crowd. I don't want my middle-aged dowdiness to stand out like a sore thumb.'

'We won't be mixing with the student crowd, I imagine,' replied Kim. 'I was thinking we would just go to Pizza Express.'

'Right, right,' muttered Vicky. 'You're right. Just because you are staying in a student house doesn't mean you are a student. I guess I just thought, you know, we might pretend for the night we are students, just because we can and well it's exciting, a new city, where no one knows you. We can do what we like without the local jungle drums beating out our bad behaviour.'

'I've booked Pizza Express,' said Kim firmly.

'Okay, okay,' said Vicky with a sigh. 'Dough balls it is.'

* * *

The doorbell finally rang just after seven at night. Vicky hadn't been able to get away any earlier because she'd had to deliver a twenty-first birthday cake in the shape of the Incredible Hulk to a party.

Kim ran to the door and flung it open. It had been less than a week since she had seen her friend but it felt like forever. So much had happened.

They embraced.

Vicky took a step back and said, 'What in the name of the god that is Ryan Reynolds is this hellhole?'

'Thanks,' replied Kim. 'I'm trying to ignore the rotting door and the windows that need painting. In fact, I've been quite successful. Turns out not going out at all is very effective for ignoring the fact that you're living in the most neglected looking house on a street of neglected looking houses.'

Vicky looked up and down the road. 'It's not Bowland Crescent, is it?' she said.

'No,' replied Kim.

'However, Anal Alison does not live on this street.'

'Exactly,' replied Kim. 'Exactly.' She glanced at Vicky's van parked behind her. Was that her enormous cheese plant from her kitchen sat on the front seat?

'You brought Bjorn,' said Kim, feeling tears inexplicably spring to her eyes. 'Why on earth?'

'I couldn't leave Bjorn to fend for himself, could I?' said Vicky, opening the van door. 'That would be wrong. And a night out with you is not complete until we have danced around the kitchen with Bjorn to "The Winner Takes It All". Besides, I thought it would really screw with Richard to see that he was missing.' She lifted the plant off the seat and handed it to Kim.

It made Kim very happy. She had spent many a drunken night dancing with Vicky in her kitchen to Abba, Richard refusing to join them. So much so that Kim often picked up the plant to be her partner which had been called Bjorn after the member of the greatest pop band of all time.

'I don't know where we will put him, mind,' said Kim, wiping a tear from her eye. 'There's hardly room to swing a cat never mind dance with a cheese plant.'

'Shall we get unloaded?' said Vicky, looking at her watch. 'I sort of did a smash and grab. I so didn't want Richard to spot me and demand the keys. So I've no idea if I've got what you said you wanted for the kitchen for Harry.'

She flung open the door to the back of the van which was crammed with what looked like everything but the kitchen sink.

'You bought the mop bucket?' questioned Kim, still clutching Bjorn.

'Well,' shrugged Vicky. 'I thought maybe three blokes might be in need of a mop.'

'I guess so,' said Kim, pulling a face. 'Right, let's get unloaded.'

By the time they had finished there was kitchen paraphernalia all over the table and you couldn't see Kim's bed for the three-foot high pile of clothes.

'Why on earth have you brought all these clothes?' she asked.

'I thought you'd want a choice of what to wear tonight,' Vicky said. She turned to look at the wardrobe.

'I have never seen such a small wardrobe,' she said. 'It's like they bought it from a doll's house or something.'

'Why have you brought my Christmas party dresses?' asked Kim, holding up a short red sequinned number.

Vicky turned to look. 'I guess I thought that you'd need, you know, a pulling outfit.'

Kim shook her head as she picked up another short, backless cocktail dress.

'I brought that one because you look as sexy as hell in that. I mean, even my Geoff noticed and you know he's not normally tuned into these things. Pamela Anderson could walk by him walking the dog and he'd bend over and pat the dog.'

'I wore this one to Richard's Christmas drinks party last year,' said Kim. 'He must have already been sleeping with Alison. What a waste. Bet he didn't even notice what I was wearing.'

'Of course he bloody did,' said Vicky. 'He was besotted with you; anyone could see that. It's just Anal Alison . . . I don't know . . . Anal Alison perhaps does anal and he fell for it. Dozy twat.'

Kim shook her head, ignoring Vicky. 'It's obvious, isn't it? Why he left me. He can talk to her, she's smarter than me. I was always punching above my weight. Always. This was bound to happen. He was always going to find someone cleverer than me.'

'Bullshit,' replied Vicky. 'You are the smartest cookie I know. So, you may not have gone to university but who gives a damn about that? That doesn't prove anything. You are as smart as anyone I have ever met.'

'So are you saying he's gone to Alison for the sex?' asked Kim.

'Course he has. It's always about the sex with blokes. Such dickheads.'

'Not sure that makes me feel any better,' replied Kim.

Vicky got up and put her arms around her. 'You are an amazing human being. You are not to blame here. You did nothing wrong; do you hear? It's Richard who is the dickhead and not you. Now are you going to put some glad rags on and are we going to hit this town or are we going to stand here talking about Richard?'

'We need to put all the kitchen stuff away first,' said Kim, looking mournfully down at the heap on the bed. 'The boys can't come home to find a slow cooker and a breadmaker in the middle of the floor. They'll think . . . they'll think aliens have infiltrated the building and left strange telepathic equipment in their house share. We'll get back and they'll be trying to tune it in to an alien frequency. Do you want to break it to them that actually all it can do is make a healthy soup?'

'Sod that,' said Vicky. 'We'll be back before them, won't we? We'll clear the decks then. I've been looking forward to a night out all week. Come on, chop, chop, get that dress on.' She nodded at the short black backless dress in her hands.

'Are you kidding me? We're going to Pizza Express not . . . not . . . somewhere posh or anything.'

'Aaah, but who knows where we might end up in this brave new world of Nottingham? Who knows who we might meet? Come on, no one knows us, let's go for it. You need to let loose, young lady, and I think that is exactly the right dress to do it in.'

Kim looked at it dubiously. She knew she needed excessive shapewear to fit into that dress, which sounded like the opposite of letting loose. But then she remembered how she felt when she last wore it. She felt amazing. And she could do with a bit of that if she was honest. It had been a while.

'Okay,' she said. 'But only if you dress up too. There is no way I'm going out in that and you in jeans.'

'Well,' said Vicky. 'Funny you should say that. I just so happen to have that frock I wore to Cassie's evening do last year. You remember the black lace number.'

'Oh yes. I know the one you mean. And you packed that? Just in case you managed to persuade me that we were going out, out?'

'Whatever happened, missy, I knew that tonight we would be going out, out!'

'We cannot go in there dressed like this!' declared Kim, as they peered into the window of the well-known pizza restaurant.

Vicky didn't answer. She was looking up and down the street, anywhere but inside the pizza place. Kim peered inside again, desperately searching for some reassurance that a backless cocktail dress would blend in with the families with young children colouring in the menu and the spattering of couples staring awkwardly around, clearly on first dates.

'There's a man over there wearing socks and sandals,' pointed out Kim. 'Six-inch heels and socks with sandals do not go into the same room together. I think we should go home and change.'

'No,' declared Vicky. 'We can't go all the way back now. Why don't we go in there instead?' She pointed at what looked like a wine bar on the opposite side of the street.

'But I've booked a table,' said Kim.

'So, unbook it.'

'But we are already late for it. What with you insisting on me doing your hair.'

'This dress needed an updo,' replied Vicky.

'This night did not need that dress or that hair,' replied Kim. 'I don't quite know how this has happened. All I wanted was an American Hot; no one eats an American Hot with an updo.'

Vicky reached out and grabbed her friend's hand and frogmarched her over the road, towards the wine bar. Kim halted outside the door.

'I've booked Pizza Express,' she cried.

'Pizza Express will survive and you'll survive without an American Hot. We'll get a drink and then we'll cancel the booking online. Now come on. We've wasted enough time.'

They tottered into the bar to be met by a very smiley waitress dressed all in black.

'Welcome to One More Wine Bar,' she said. 'Have you been before?'

'No,' replied Vicky. 'We haven't been anywhere before.'

'Great, no problem. So, this is a self-service wine bar. It's really easy. I give you this card and you put it into any of the five vending machines located around the bar and you pick your wine. When you are ready to leave just go to the till and you can settle your bill. Can I find you a table, ladies? There's one just come free over there.'

The very smiley girl indicated a table for two in the window as she handed over two plastic cards. Kim and Vicky were sitting down somewhat bewildered before they knew it.

'Self-service wine,' hissed Vicky. 'Tell me I have died and gone to heaven. I LOVE Nottingham already.'

Kim looked over at her friend. She was getting far more enjoyment out of the consequences of the collapse of her marriage than was strictly decent. Still, trust Vicky to find an opportunity for a good time out of any circumstance!

'So, what do you think we do?' whispered Vicky. 'Go up individually, or together, or do we just leave our bags on our seats? This is just like buffet breakfast at the Premier Inn. The dilemma of quite how to navigate a veritable wine buffet and not miss out on anything.'

'There's a board there, look,' said Kim, pointing to a chalkboard on the wall listing all the wines. 'I'll have the South African Chardonnay,' she said. 'You go and get them. I know you are dying to play with the wine vending machine.'

'You see, those three words sound so right together,' said Vicky. 'It's like it should be a well-known phrase or saying, "wine vending machine". It's almost poetry.' She stood up and strode over to the nearest machine, grabbing two glasses from the rack above and studying the instructions.

Kim surveyed her surroundings. She felt totally like a fish out of water. Maybe that was because she was wearing the stupid dress that Vicky had told her to wear, or the fact that rather than being in good old familiar Pizza Express munching on dough balls they were in some concept bar where you served yourself £8 per glass wine. Or was it that just a week ago she would have just finished a full day at work and would be most likely sat in the kitchen-diner drinking wine with her husband, talking through their days? Her chat would be mostly about people, the lovely ones, the tricky ones, their individual trials and tribulations. Then Richard would tell her all his people stuff, never teaching stuff, she didn't understand that of course, but she did understand people. It made her feel actually quite smart when he poured out his issues and she could offer advice. Like the time she told him to just ask his colleague why she always refused to work with him on research papers rather than fester about it. She even told him how and when to ask so she wouldn't feel threatened. It turned out that she disagreed about one of the principles of his paper so Kim told him to take her for a coffee and ask her why. He came back delighted with her advice saying he'd had the best, most stimulating discussion he had ever had with another lecturer and they had ended up agreeing to start a research project the following year.

It was one of her favourite times with her husband. Friday nights, just chatting and drinking wine. But she wasn't at home talking to her husband now. She was here, surrounded by happy couples, waiting for her friend to calm down from the excitement of being out in a new city, dressed like she was going on to some fancy celebration somewhere. Except she wasn't. She was already lost on this night out. She had no idea who she was or where she was or why she was here.

Vicky plonked a large glass of wine in front of her.

'How cool is that? Why has no one done this before?' she demanded, sitting herself down. 'No queue, you pick what size glass you want and it's proper wine. You can see the bottles inside the machine. It's not coming out of some big vat out of the cellar or anything. Or a wine box. Real bottles of wine, Kim! God, this might be the best night of my life. So glad I came. Cheers.'

She held her glass up and Kim reciprocated. 'Makes splitting up with my husband so worthwhile, hey?' she said.

'Oh Kim. No! That's not what I meant. I mean, I wish I was anywhere but here with you six days after you discovered your husband was having an affair with the next door neighbour. Anywhere. But if I had to pick a place to be six days after you discovered your husband having an affair with your next door neighbour then it would be at a wine buffet. This is perfect.'

Normally Kim loved Vicky's ability to look on the bright side of absolutely everything and normally she was pretty good at it herself, but somehow even wine vending machines were not putting a positive spin on her day.

'Do you want me to ask you how you are feeling?' asked Vicky, putting a sympathetic look on.

Kim nodded. But was fearful of her answer.

'How are you feeling?' asked Vicky.

Kim swallowed. 'I can't describe it,' she muttered. 'It's like an out of body experience. I can't actually believe this is happening to me. It's like I'm watching someone else go through all this. Like a TV show or something and at some point, it's going to end, and I'll switch it off and it will all be back to normal.'

For the first time since she arrived, Kim saw the excitement die in Vicky's eyes to be replaced by concern. 'I can't imagine what it must feel like, mate. I mean, I know I moan about Geoff and all that but one thing I do know is that he's solid. We're solid. Neither of us are perfect by any means but I just know that we wouldn't let each other down. Sorry, not sure that's helpful.'

'I thought that about me and Richard,' sighed Kim. 'Thought that the last thing we would ever do would be to betray one another.' She looked up at Vicky. 'Sorry. Perhaps I shouldn't have said that.'

Vicky shrugged. 'You say whatever you need to say, Kim.'

'I keep going over and over it in my head. What happened? Where did I go wrong? What didn't I see? Why didn't I spot that he was up to something? I'm normally really good at that type of thing. You know, I can tell if one of my clients is going through it, or that something is wrong, often in the way they sit or a look on their face. And then I start cutting their hair and I'm normally right. I only have to ask how they are and it all comes pouring out. Why didn't I see it with Richard, Vicky? I just can't work it out.'

'Perhaps because you didn't want to see it. You had too much to lose. You probably saw it and chose to ignore it; the thought of something being off was too scary to face up to.'

'Maybe,' nodded Kim. 'I mean, I do remember thinking this non-existent research project was preoccupying him. It was making him a bit distant. Stressing him out.'

'There you go. You saw the signs. Totally logical to think it was the research project. That's not your fault.'

'I never said anything because, well, I was afraid he'd come up with some scientific jargon and I wouldn't understand and then I wouldn't be being very helpful. I'm pretty good when he's got a problem with colleagues or students but I've learnt to steer clear if it seems like it's anything to do with his actual subject.'

'So, you didn't ask what was bothering him?'

'No. I never asked.'

'Because you were scared you wouldn't understand the problem?'

'Correct,' replied Kim. 'Wish I'd have said something now. I should take my own advice sometimes, shouldn't I?'

Vicky smiled at her. 'The one where you always say, "It's good to talk."'

Kim blew her cheeks out. She felt tears threaten yet again. It was something she always told her clients when they apologised for offloading their woes. She didn't mind, she told them. 'It's good to talk,' she always said. Her clients who were over forty smiled in recognition at the famous slogan from the telephone ads of the mid-nineties. Those under forty just nodded, oblivious to the fact that it was possibly Oscar-nominated Bob Hoskins' most famous line. She looked at her friend and realised that it really was good to talk. She was so used to listening to other people share their problems with her that she had forgotten that it was perfectly acceptable to share her own worries with others. Maybe she should have said to Richard that she was worried about how preoccupied he was. That she felt something was wrong.

After all, it was good to talk.

'I feel like such an idiot,' she told Vicky. 'I feel an idiot for not spotting it. For not seeing something. I mean, he must have been unhappy to go off with Alison in the first place, mustn't he? If he was happy then it wouldn't have happened, would it? Why didn't I spot that he wasn't happy in the first place?'

'You can't blame yourself for that. He should have said something if he wasn't happy. Talked to you rather than dick about with someone else.'

'I suppose,' said Kim reluctantly. 'But I feel such a fool for thinking it was all great. His party. Oh my God, I can't even think about what a fool I made of myself there. In front of everyone saying basically how flipping amazing our marriage was.'

'You didn't make a fool of yourself,' said Vicky, reaching over and putting a hand on her wrist. 'He made a fool of you.'

Kim paused and stared at her friend. Okay, so maybe it was good to talk but perhaps not so good to talk to Vicky. She did have a habit of being just a bit too blunt.

'It's no better, is it?' she pointed out. 'Whether I made a fool out of me or he did, I'm still a fool at the end of the day. The biggest fool that there could ever be. And with Alison. Our neighbour. I can't imagine what everyone will say.' She hid her face in her hands. 'I don't think I can ever go back,' she said through her fingers. I just can't.' Kim let her shoulders slump and felt the tears start to show their face. 'What am I going to do?' she said, taking her hands away. 'I'm homeless. I've lost everything.'

Vicky looked at her, bewildered. 'Christ, I'm so shit at this,' she said. 'I'm sorry. You know me. I'm there for you come rain or shine, whatever, but the only therapy I'm any good at is of the laughter variety. You put me in a serious situation and I screw it up. I say the wrong thing. Not like you. You are genius at it. You always say the right thing when I need picking up. You need a "you" right at this very moment and not a "me". "Me" is rubbish at this.'

Kim couldn't help but smile. And she couldn't argue. Vicky was her good time girl. She had only one mode of lifting the spirits and that was through having fun, not talking it out. Kim would have to seek someone else to offload to. She took a tissue out of her bag and blew her nose. 'Tell you what,' she said. 'You're better at advice and sympathy when you are drunk . . . '

'You are so right,' said Vicky, slapping her forehead. 'I never thought of that. I once told Mr Adler, the grumpy old git from down our street, that he should stick his clapped-out wreck of an old banger where the sun don't shine when I was hammered. Do you know, the very next day he put it away in his garage. Even my insults get passed as advice when I'm pissed.'

'I wouldn't bank on it,' said Kim. 'But I'll tell you what, let's try this talking thing again later after a few more of these. We might be able to work out how I avoid going home ever again by then.'

'Most definitely,' said Vicky. 'Cross my heart and hope to die,' she said solemnly. 'Now what do you want to try next?' she asked, getting up.

'Oh no,' said Kim, indicating for her to sit down. 'I think you'll find it's my turn to experience the wonders of vending machine wine. Step away from the machine. I'm going in.'

Vending machine wine proved to be a disaster to two women out on the town, one trying to drown her sorrows and one trying to have the time of her life. After five large glasses in under an hour there were some severe impediments to speech and mobility.

'I cannot drink any more,' said Kim. 'Things are moving in ways they shouldn't including my stomach and that wine glass. I think we had better head back soon.'

'Good idea,' said Vicky, clapping her hands together. 'I cannot wait to meet your housemates.'

'No,' replied Kim, shaking her head. 'I've been keeping a very low profile in the house. Trying to stay out of their way. I've not even told them that you are coming or staying over. I'm assuming we'll get back before them tonight so we'll sneak in, go to bed and you can go in the morning and they will be none the wiser. Okay?'

'Right you are,' said Vicky, saluting. 'I shall be totally incognito. They will never know that I'm there.'

Kim and Vicky's arrival back at the house had not gone to plan. They'd left the wine bar when they realised that they were spending more time going to the toilet than drinking wine. A sure sign that they were drunk. They got to their feet and hobbled on their high heels over to pay the very smiley waitress who now was not so smiley with them, which might be something to do with the fact that within the last half hour Vicky had burst into song and done a passable rendition of Ed Sheeran's 'Lego House'. She'd been trying to cheer Kim up with its relevant lyrics of picking up the pieces and Kim had thought it funny but clearly the very smiley waitress did not. She took the charge cards for the wine off them and delivered the cost of their evening with an icy smile.

'Blimey,' mumbled Vicky, staggering back slightly. 'Turns out serving your own wine is mighty expensive. Good job we don't have to pay ourselves a tip!' She roared with laughter at her own joke. The now very unsmiley waitress clearly did not find it funny at all.

Having settled their hefty bill and staggered outside, they paused to consider their next move.

'I could murder a pizza now,' said Vicky.

‘We can’t go into Pizza Express dressed like this *and* drunk,’ said Kim, taking her turn to stagger back on her heels. ‘Wrong on so many levels. In any case it’s shut, look.’

‘What I would do for a dough ball, right now,’ said Vicky, pressing her nose against the window like some poor starving orphan. ‘Please sir, can I have some more dough balls?’

‘Taxi,’ shouted Kim, raising her arm as she saw a cab approaching.

‘I can’t leave without doughballs,’ moaned Vicky.

‘There’s a chippy at the end of my road. We’ll get some food there and take it back.’

‘A chippy?’ asked Vicky. ‘Do they do gravy or are we too far south?’

‘I’ve no idea,’ said Kim. ‘The boys have been but I never have. This is the Midlands; I think they’ll have gravy in a chippy.’

Vicky eased herself into the cab. ‘I hope you are aware this is a very high-risk strategy,’ announced Vicky as Kim got in the other side. ‘We are heading to an unknown chippy with unknown gravy facilities.’

‘Come on,’ said Kim. ‘Let’s live a little; you said you wanted to try something new whilst you were here. Well chips without gravy could be it.’

‘I love you,’ Vicky told the man behind the chip counter when he confirmed that they did indeed do chips and gravy. ‘I’ve never met you before, but I can tell you that right at this very moment, you are the love of my life.’

‘She’s drunk,’ Kim confirmed to the man.

'We're drunk,' said Vicky. 'Don't you go pinning it all on me. We got caught out by a dodgy bar, Max,' she informed the man behind the counter after she had scrutinised his name tag. 'One where you could serve yourself. It's a total hazard. It really should not be allowed.'

The man said nothing, just shovelled hot steaming chips into two trays and poured rich dark gravy on them.

'It's the most beautiful thing I have ever seen in my life,' announced Vicky when he handed them over.

'She's easily pleased,' said Max with a smile. 'I'm the love of her life and my chips are the most beautiful thing she has ever seen.'

'I hate to burst your bubble but she says that to all the chippies,' said Kim.

Max nodded. 'Story of my life,' he said, handing over a tray of chips to Kim who promptly staggered back on her heels and dropped all her chips and gravy on the floor.

'Oh my God,' she gasped. 'Oh, I'm so sorry.' She couldn't believe it. She glanced back up at Max. His smile had vanished to be replaced by a resigned look as though he'd seen this scene a hundred times already. He disappeared towards the back of the shop and returned quickly with a long-handled dustpan and brush.

'Let me do it,' said Kim, totally mortified.

'No, really. It's okay,' said Max. He shook his head. 'It's normally the students chucking food all over the floor, not women . . . '

'Of a certain age?' asked Vicky.

‘I wasn’t going to say that,’ said Max. ‘I was going to say women dressed up like you.’

Kim watched in horror, the gravy oozing all over the floor.

‘We’ve been out celebrating the end of Kim’s marriage,’ announced Vicky.

Max looked up, surprised. ‘Well always a great thing to celebrate, the end of a marriage,’ he said sharply. He leaned the dustpan and brush against the window and returned to his spot behind the counter. ‘That’s £4.80, please,’ he said holding out his hand and not making eye contact. Clearly chucking food all over the floor hadn’t been the thing to upset him, but celebrating the end of a marriage was.

‘I’ll pay for another tray of chips,’ Kim said. She was starving and she needed something to soak up the alcohol.

Max stared at her before reluctantly serving her some more chips. ‘You’ll keep hold of them this time, will you?’ he asked, handing them over.

‘Promise,’ she agreed. *What a grumpy git*, she thought.

They stumbled home, munching on hot chips until they got to the front door. Kim reiterated her early warning that they were to be incognito and should be quiet even though she was sure that the rest of her housemates wouldn’t be in.

They giggled their way down the hall and pushed open the living room door.

There was Angus, Sonny, Harry, and another girl sitting in the room, a couple of bottles of wine were open on the coffee table and it looked like they were playing computer games on the TV.

'Oh, shit,' said Vicky, taken totally by surprise. 'I'm not supposed to be here.' She stumbled, grabbing hold of the door frame, and dropped her chips in Angus's lap who was sitting right next to the door.

'What the hell?' he said, leaping up. Unfortunately, he was wearing light coloured chinos and the gravy instantly made unseemly marks on his groin. 'Who the hell are you?'

'Vicky!' said Harry, also getting up and looking flustered. 'What are you doing here? Mum, what's going on?'

'You look amazing, Kim,' said Sonny from his seat on the floor. 'Killer dress or what?'

'See, I told you it was the right dress to go out in,' said Vicky, trying to brush chips off Angus's groin.

'Leave me alone, woman,' said Angus, leaping back.

'Oh my God,' said Kim. 'I'm so sorry. I err, we err . . .'

'We thought you'd be out?' said Vicky. 'It's before midnight. What kind of students are you?'

'Shush, Vicky,' said Kim. 'Everyone, this is Vicky, my friend, she's just popped down to see me. We only meant to go to Pizza Express,' she turned to tell Harry. 'Honest, but then we got dressed up and it seemed a shame to waste it so we ended up in this wine bar and . . .'

'It wasn't our fault,' said Vicky. 'You could serve yourself. How unbelievably brilliant is that?'

'Really?' said Sonny to Vicky, his eyes wide.

'Really,' said Vicky. 'Is this Sonny?' she asked Kim. Kim nodded. 'I can tell from your description. Sonny, you would love it,' she told him. 'You just walk up to a machine and put a card in and it gives you *wine*.'

'That sounds amazing,' declared Sonny. 'When can we go there?' he said, looking round at his housemates.

'I'll take you,' said Vicky.

'Would you?' asked Sonny, his eyes even wider. 'You look cracking too, I have to say. I'm Sonny by the way. Let's be friends,' he said sticking his hand out.

'No, no, no,' said Kim, reaching out to grab Vicky's arm. 'There's nothing to see guys, honestly. We'll be out of your way in no time. We'll just get a cup of tea. Slide back through here as quiet as mice, you won't even know we've been here. Come on, Vicky.'

'Coming,' said Vicky. 'Mustn't forget to bring Bjorn in from the yard. Do you remember, you told me to remind you. He must have dried out by now.'

'Who's Bjorn?' asked Sonny, looking around bewildered. 'You've left someone in the yard all night?'

Vicky laughed. 'No, he's a plant. Well, he's more than a plant. He's our late-night dance partner actually. Thought he could keep Kim company whilst she's here. Don't worry, he takes no looking after, he just got a bit of a dirty bottom in my van and so we thought we'd leave him outside to dry out.'

'Enough of Bjorn,' said Kim, shaking her head at Vicky. She needed to shut her friend up and fast, she was making them look like complete lunatics. She started to pull her towards the kitchen.

'Mum, what are you wearing?' exclaimed Harry as she brushed past him.

She turned back and stared. 'What do you mean?'

'It's . . . it's . . . got a bit missing.'

'It's backless,' said Sonny, hunching his shoulders

as though Harry was an idiot. 'Do you not watch the awards shows? Standard issue. If I ever won an Oscar and I was married then I would like my wife to wear a backless dress. You know, if she wanted to. I wouldn't make her or anything. But backless is the way to go. Especially if you have won an award.'

Everyone in the room stared at Sonny.

'You think about these things?' asked Angus.

'Yes,' nodded Sonny enthusiastically. 'Don't you?'

'Is this your mum?' said the girl, getting up and standing behind Harry.

Kim watched with horror as her son went bright red.

'Yes,' he muttered. 'Suki, Mum, Mum, Suki.'

Kim tried to stand up straight and not wobble on her heels. What she would do to kick them off and just collapse. But she needed to focus despite the fact that things were swimming around her again. This was possibly her son's first girlfriend she was being introduced to. This could be her future daughter-in-law for all she knew. She pulled down the hem of her dress then straightened up. Kim towered over Suki who was petite with dark hair streaked through with a deep red. If she had coloured it herself, she had done a decent job, Kim thought. She wore ripped black jeans and heavy boots and a hoody with a Japanese style print on the front. She had four earrings in each ear. She was clearly a smart, intelligent woman, who had a very clear idea of her own androgynous style. Kim immediately felt uncomfortable in her short, backless dress which conformed to every stereotype of an ancient view of femininity. She couldn't imagine Suki wearing anything that so blatantly sexualised women. Suki would think she was a tart who deserved to lose her husband. That's what this young, intelligent, enlightened woman would think. She would take one look at her in her sad, middle-aged uniform of mantrap clothing and write her off immediately.

'Hello,' she said, holding her hand out to Suki. 'I'm so sorry you are not meeting me at my best. I don't normally go out dressed like this, well I do, but not for just a casual Friday night out, but you see, well Vicky, this is Vicky by the way, my friend. Well, she drove all the way from Lancaster and she told me to wear this dress because she said I looked hot in it. And well, I'm just a bit vulnerable at the moment. I don't know if Harry explained but me and his father are going through a difficult time and so it seemed kind of a good idea at the time to wear something that made me feel good . . . but I'm sorry about that. I'll wear jeans next time. I have some just like yours. And I have a hoody. I'll go out like that next time. I promise. Sorry, Harry,' she said finally looking at him as she watched Suki grow more and more uncomfortable as Kim came out with incomprehensible drivel. She had no idea what she was apologising for. Actually, she did. She was apologising for everything. Especially for standing here at this very moment in the front room of his student house share, very drunk, in a short backless dress, making a total fool of herself in front of his possible girlfriend. Really life could not be any worse.

And then it was.

She felt it begin but unfortunately, she didn't have

enough warning. She felt saliva fill her mouth and her stomach felt strange but she was too drunk to connect the dots. What was this a sign of? Oh yes, of course. She was about to throw up. She had an inexplicable flash back to the chip shop and the gravy oozing all over the floor and that was all it took to cause her stomach to spasm and for her to throw up all over Angus's shoes.

Chapter 9

'I'm so sorry,' said Kim twelve hours later. 'I really am. I'm just such a mess at the moment.'

She was sat at the kitchen table with Harry, Angus and Sonny opposite her, the evidence laid out between them.

A carrier bag filled with scrunched up newspaper which she could only assume from the smell was her cleaned up sick from the night before.

Two empty bottles of wine.

Two empty pizza boxes.

One half drunk cup of coffee.

An empty carton of milk.

Several bottles of nearly finished spirits.

'Shall we start with the empty wine bottles found in the recycling?' asked Angus.

'At least she put them in the recycling,' said Sonny. 'That was the right thing to do, wasn't it?'

'They were not hers to dispose of either down her neck or in the recycling,' said Angus.

'I can explain,' said Kim. 'Well, I can try. It's just that Richard, I mean your dad, I mean Harry's dad, my husband . . . '

'The one shagging the next door neighbour?' pointed out Sonny.

'Yes, that's him, well, he rang a few days ago and I was bored so I answered and then it transpired that he hadn't rung to see how I was, he rang because he can't get in the house and the bastard, sorry Harry, but he wanted me to post my keys and that tipped me over the edge and so I couldn't help myself and I reached for the alcohol . . . '

'Couldn't you have reached for the alcohol from the shop on the corner rather than taking it from my stash?' demanded Angus.

'I couldn't face going out. I'll replace it, I promise I will. I always meant to. I'm so sorry, Angus.'

'You're going to drive to the Dordogne, are you, to my dad's mate's vineyard?' asked Angus.

'You know someone who owns a vineyard?' asked Sonny in awe.

'My godfather actually,' replied Angus.

'Wow,' said Sonny, looking at Angus as though he'd just found out he was related to Prince William.

'But that's irrelevant,' said Angus, brushing Sonny's admiring glances to one side. 'The fact remains that you have, in the last few days, stolen my wine, my coffee and my cold pizza which I fully intended to have as a mid-afternoon snack.'

'She had mine as well,' added Harry, miserably looking at the floor.

'You even stole your son's food,' confirmed Angus. 'What do you have to say for yourself?'

'You had just left it here. It wasn't in the fridge

or anything. I assumed it would have been chucked away,' pleaded Kim.

'Well, you assumed wrong,' replied Angus.

'You had to eat, didn't you, Kim?' said Sonny. 'Especially after all that wine you drank. It's totally understandable really.'

'Thank you,' she muttered, gratefully. 'I put all the kitchen stuff away the other day,' she pointed out hopefully. 'In case you hadn't noticed.'

'Did you?' the three of them said, looking around. Clearly none of them had spotted it at all. Clearly none of them had needed any cooking utensils either, which was frightening, but perhaps it wasn't the time to point out that they should be considering their nutritional needs better since recently she only seemed to have consumed alcohol, pizza and chips and gravy.

'I'm sorry your husband was mean to you on the phone,' said Sonny, putting his hand on his shoulder.

Kim nodded her thanks.

'But I think it's time you went now,' cut in Angus, leaning back in his chair and folding his arms. 'I mean, stealing our food and drink is one thing. I expected to maybe have to label my own milk perhaps when I moved into a student house but I never expected to need to lock up my wine store so my housemate's mum can't steal it.'

'Oh God, I'm so sorry,' said Harry, putting his head in his hands.

'It's not your fault, mate,' said Angus to Harry. 'None of us can help the parents we have. Believe me, I know.'

'I've screwed up,' said Kim. 'I can see that. All I can say is how sorry I am.'

'And,' continued Angus. 'What the hell did you say to . . . to . . . that girl who was here the other morning?'

Kim wracked her brains. 'What girl?'

'Scottish girl. Can't remember her name,' said Angus.

'Do you mean Isla?' she asked fearfully.

'Yes, that's it. She collared me on campus and informed me never to contact her again because she knew all about the fact that I had a serious girlfriend. Not that I was ever intending to contact her again but still, clearly someone had been shit stirring.'

'You brought Isla back here from the traffic light party?' asked Sonny agog.

'Yep. Well actually from outside the chip shop,' said Angus.

'Do you . . . did you . . . ' asked Sonny.

Angus nodded.

Kim found herself nodding too.

'What!' said Angus. 'You weren't listening, were you?'

'I . . . I . . . could hear you talking . . . you know before . . . ' she trailed off.

'Aren't you supposed to talk before sex?' asked Sonny, looking very confused. 'Isn't talking like foreplay?'

No one answered. Kim felt like she needed to enlighten him.

'Depends on who's talking,' she said. 'Ryan Reynolds only has to open his mouth and it's foreplay but other men, not so much. Sometimes you are better off just keeping quiet.'

'Right, right,' said Sonny. 'Got it.'

'Unbelievable,' said Angus, shaking his head. 'And

then you thought, did you, that you should make sure she was aware of my status before she left?'

'No!' said Kim. 'It wasn't like that. I came down to find some coffee . . . '

'My coffee?'

'Err yes, and Isla was sat here and actually the first thing she told me was that you had said I was your live-in housekeeper.'

'How else am I supposed to explain an old woman living in the house?'

'I'm not old,' said Kim.

'Okay, older.'

'Over sixty is officially old, my mum says, so technically Kim isn't old,' pointed out Sonny.

'She's clearly not student age though, is she? And so it was just easier to tell her that she was our housekeeper rather than someone's mum whose husband is having an affair.'

'Yeah, because a lot of students have housekeepers, right?' said Kim.

'Look, it's your fault I'm having to explain you at all so don't have a go at me.'

Kim bit her lip and glanced at Harry. He was sat staring straight ahead looking mortified. What was she doing?

'Look, I'm sorry Angus, really I am. We got talking and she asked me point blank if you had a girlfriend and so I was on the spot so I mentioned you might have one back in Scotland, but I told her to ask you. That I wasn't sure. And well, I guess I was looking out for her. I just didn't want her to get hurt. That's all.'

'Why would she have got hurt?'

'You just said you were never going to contact her again. And you sort of have a girlfriend.'

'That's because I wasn't into her, not because of my girlfriend, I mean Poppy. I don't know what is happening with Poppy.'

Kim bit her lip again. What to say? Kim thought Angus actually really cared about Poppy, he just didn't know what to do about it. All his bravado and apparent desire to sleep around was driven by a fear of rejection by her. Perhaps not the right time to point it out to him though. Not whilst they were in an altercation about stealing his property.

'Should I send my keys to Dad?' asked Harry, clearly wanting to move the conversation along and be free from this awkward standoff.

'No,' said Sonny, looking horrified. 'Can't you see it's the keys that tipped your mum over the edge in the first place? She doesn't want him to have the keys. She doesn't want him to be able to get in the house.'

'That's very nice of you to offer to send him your keys,' said Kim to her son, 'but to be honest I really don't see why we should make it easy for him.'

'So instead, when he rings, you're going to get drunk, steal other people's food and ward off any girls Angus brings back to the house?' replied Harry.

'No,' said Kim. 'Of course not. I'm . . . I'm mortified that I've behaved this way.'

'I might bring a girl back to the house?' said Sonny. 'One day?'

'When that happens, Sonny, we'll hire a marching band and put bunting up,' muttered Angus.

‘Will you?’ asked Sonny, looking excited.

‘Totally,’ agreed Angus, rolling his eyes.

Kim was looking at her son. What had she been thinking? She had only made a bad situation worse.

‘I’m so sorry about last night, too,’ she said, reaching out to touch his arm. ‘You know what Vicky’s like. She led me astray. And the stress of everything, but it was unforgivable. Coming home drunk and then throwing up all over the carpet in front of your girlfriend . . . ’

‘She’s not my girlfriend,’ he replied, slamming his hand on the table. ‘We just . . . we just like the same computer games, that’s all.’

‘Okay, okay,’ said Kim. ‘I’m sorry. Whatever she is she seems like a really lovely girl and I’m so sorry if I . . . ’

‘Just stop, Mum, please. Just stop.’ He turned to look at Angus and Sonny. ‘I’m so sorry about this, guys. I never thought I’d be apologising for my mother’s behaviour my first week in university but here we are. Strange times. Really strange times. I should have given her a talking to right from the start but you don’t expect to have to do that, do you? All I can say is that this is not my real mother sitting here . . . ’

‘What?’ gasped Sonny. ‘I didn’t see that coming! Who is your real mother then?’

‘No, no, I mean she is my real mother, I just mean she’s not behaving how she normally does, because of what’s happened. I mean if you met my dad you’d perhaps understand. It’s been such a shock. He really is the last person you would ever expect to do this.’

No one said anything until Angus muttered, 'Not like my dad then.'

Everyone turned to look at Angus.

'What do you mean?' Harry asked him.

Angus shrugged. 'Oh, my dad is an expert at it.'

'Expert at what?' asked Harry.

'Affairs.'

A silence fell over the room.

'Wow,' said Sonny.

'I'm really sorry to hear that,' ventured Kim.

'Not your fault,' replied Angus. 'It's just how it is in my family. He has a fling. Mum finds out. He promises never to do it again. That promise generally has a shelf life of say a couple of years, I'd say.'

'Your poor mum,' said Sonny.

Angus shrugged again. 'First time it happened she chucked him out. She was a total mess. Crying all the time.' He glanced at Kim as if to say that his mother had behaved exactly like she was behaving. 'I was only about eight, I reckon. But he would come over every night and plead with her. Tell her he had made a huge mistake. Eventually I got up one morning and there he was at the breakfast table. He never left again.'

'What happened the next time?' asked Kim.

'Oh she was upset, really upset, but a bit less than when it first happened. She gets angry every time, throws stuff around, makes threats and then there he is still sat at the breakfast table the next morning. Normally, of course, not long after my mum suddenly has a new car or a new piece of jewellery.'

No one knew what to say.

'So I do get it,' said Angus to Harry. 'Dealing with dysfunctional parents – not fun, not fun at all.'

'Thanks, mate,' said Harry.

'I once caught my mum shaving my dad's backside,' said Sonny. 'I think that screwed me up pretty bad for a while.'

'I would have thought that you come from a pretty dysfunctional family,' said Angus.

'Thanks,' nodded Sonny. 'I appreciate that.'

Kim bit her lip. This was a nightmare.

'I'll go,' she said, getting up. 'I'll go and pack my stuff now and get out of your hair. I really shouldn't be here.'

'No,' said Sonny, grabbing her arm, looking genuinely stricken. 'You can't go. You can't go and live next door to your husband and his fancy woman. You just can't. It'll kill you.'

'I'll just have to deal with it,' she said. 'It's not your problem. I'll pay for the wine and the coffee and the milk,' she said to Angus. 'It was unforgivable. And I'll scrub the living room carpet and leave you money to buy pizzas for everyone tonight. Why don't you have a party or something, invite some people round. Pizzas on me.'

She swallowed as they all stared back at her. 'I'm sorry,' she said again. 'You've all been brilliant and I've been shit. I've been the worst possible guest and the worst possible mother,' she continued, glancing at Harry. 'I'm just grateful that you put up with me for a little while, when I needed it. It really was very kind of you. I should have acted more like a grown-up but instead I was a mess. So, thank you and if ever in the future any of you are in a mess then I owe you. Okay? I mean that. I owe every single one of you and you can turn up on my doorstep anytime you like and I'll take you in. I really mean that.'

Sonny's lip started wobbling.

Harry was staring at his mother shaking his head slightly like he had no idea what he was supposed to do. 'I'm sorry, Mum,' he said. Kim thought her heart would break. He had absolutely nothing to be sorry about.

Angus was glancing between the three of them. 'Look, maybe if we set some house rules,' he said, leaning back in his chair.

'House rules?' said Sonny, turning to him. 'I've always wanted to live in a house with house rules.'

'I meant for Kim,' said Angus. '*We* don't need house rules, *we* should be able to do what the hell we like, but clearly if we are going to continue in this situation then boundaries need setting. Agreed?'

Kim stared at him in disbelief. What was happening?

'Okay then,' said Angus, leaning forward and pointing at Kim with his index finger. 'Rule one is that you are not to treat this place like a hotel. You need to buy your own food and drink.'

Kim had her mouth open; she couldn't speak.

'Next rule is that you wear earplugs at night,' continued Angus. 'I don't want an oldie next door putting me off my stride because I think she's listening.'

'I'm . . . I'm s-s-s-sorry,' she stuttered.

Sonny was staring at Angus aghast, as was Harry. They all looked as confused as Kim.

'Talking is still good before sex though, right?' asked Sonny. 'Just so I know. And does this mean Kim is staying?'

'Next rule,' said Angus, ignoring Sonny. 'Is that under no circumstances do you talk to any girls who enter this house, do you understand?'

'What about if I bring a girl home?' interrupted Sonny. 'I mean I'd like to introduce her to Kim. I think she would feel more comfortable if she thought there was another woman in the house to make friends with.'

'We will cross that bridge whenever in the next millennium we come to it,' said Angus. 'Anything else apart from the obvious?' he asked, looking at Sonny and Harry. 'And by that, I mean she should feel free to clean up and sort the kitchen out and generally keep the place tidy. I mean it's the least she can do if she's going to stay, right?'

Kim had no idea if he was joking or not so she said nothing. She looked at Harry who was staring at Angus.

'It would be strictly on a temporary basis, of course. Just until Kim gets herself together,' continued Angus. 'I mean, I really couldn't imagine anything worse than starting university life with someone's mother in the next room, but . . . well . . . as long as she abides by the house rules then I think I can cope for a short time.'

Harry was clearly contemplating Angus's words. She held her breath. It would solve her immediate problem of not wanting to go home. Anything would be better than that.

Harry turned to look at her and after what seemed like an age, he opened his mouth.

'There's one more rule,' he said to her. 'If you are going to stay, you need to get out, Mum,' he said. 'You can't stare at a screen all day. It's not good for you. You need to get out every day. Be around people or else you are going to go mad and drink too much and do stupid stuff.'

Kim stared back at her child. The boy who she had told countless times over the course of his life to switch off the screen and get out. Perhaps he had listened. Perhaps she wasn't as bad a mother as she thought.

'I promise,' she whispered, trying very hard to stop herself from reaching over and taking his hand. This all had to be so difficult for him. And he was right, she did need to get out more, if not for her sake, for her son's.

'I promise I'll be better, really, I will. I'll find something to do to keep me busy, I promise.'

'Temporarily busy,' pointed out Angus. 'Shall we set a limit until the end of this term? How about that? One term and then you are gone, vamoose, this house then returns to its rightful bachelor pad status.'

'Of course,' gushed Kim. 'I can't believe you are giving me this chance.'

'We'll need to check it's okay with the girl who'd originally rented the room, of course,' continued Angus. 'But I would think she'll be grateful to get some of her rent back,' he said. 'I'm assuming you'll stump up for her rent if you want to stay?'

'Yeah. Of course,' spluttered Kim. 'Absolutely. Yep – no problem. Thank you. Thank you so much.'

'I'll message her,' said Angus. 'Let her know we've found someone to have her room until Christmas.'

'This really is amazing of you,' said Kim. 'I've no idea how to thank you.'

'Yeah, well,' said Angus getting up to leave. 'Last warning. Pull yourself together or else.'

Chapter 10

'What do you mean you haven't posted the keys?' demanded Richard when he called her the following day. 'Are you driving back today then? When can I expect you?'

'No, I'm not driving back today.'

'Tomorrow?'

'No. I'm not coming back for a while.'

'You can't stay with Harry, Kim. It's not fair. And you'll never cope living like a student.'

'I will. I'm staying. We've just agreed some house rules. They've said it's okay.'

'No, they haven't.'

'Yes, they have. I'm going to pay rent and everything.'

There was silence on the end of the line. Then Richard said, 'And how do you expect to do that?'

'Out of the joint account, I guess,' she said after a moment's thought.

A heavy silence hung again.

'You want me to pay your rent in a student house share when there is a perfectly good house here that

I'm paying the mortgage on, that currently neither of us are living in?'

'That's not my fault.'

'It is, because you won't send me the keys.'

'I won't send you the keys because of what you did.'

'So this is revenge? I thought you were better than that, Kim.'

'Well, you thought wrong then.'

Richard paused for a moment.

'Send me the keys and I'll pay your rent,' he said. 'But don't say I didn't warn you that living with three boys in a student house is not going to suit you in the slightest. You'll be back here before you know it.'

She knew it was petty but she didn't want to send Richard the keys – why should she? Why should she do anything to make his life easier? She could, of course, point out that he could get a locksmith in but that was up to him. Knowing Richard, he would have thought of that but would have considered it desperate measures and a waste of money given she had a perfectly usable set of keys.

However, that left her with needing money in order to pay her rent. She had her own account, of course, but nowhere near enough in it to pay substantial bills. And she didn't want to have to go cap in hand to Richard. Not really. That would only prove what he was saying, that there was no way she could survive living down here. No, she had to think of something else.

It came to her in the middle of the night. What to do. She realised what an appalling example she was setting her housemates. She was doing exactly what she had lectured Harry about not doing. Sitting around, wallowing, getting bored, getting drunk, not standing on her own two feet. And Harry himself had told her it was a condition of her staying that she got out more and found something to do. She needed a job, is what she needed, and she knew where she was going to get one. There was a hairdresser's at the end of the road who was clearly in dire need of someone with all her skills to get the punters in. She'd go down there the very next day and ask them if they had any work available.

By the time she got up she had it all planned. The first thing she had to do of course was message all her existing clients in Lancaster. She decided to tell them that she was taking a break from hairdressing until after Christmas due to unforeseen circumstances. Typing the text, she gave her unreserved apologies and said she would be in touch in the New Year. She of course had no idea where she would be in the New Year, which was a frightening thought, but she hoped that at the very least she would be in a better place than she was now.

With that done she set to work on her own hair, creating an elaborate updo to showcase her talents to her new prospective employer. She held back somewhat on the makeup; she didn't want to look too bridal after all so she went natural and was pleased with the final effect. How could anyone turn that blow dry down for a job, she thought as she looked in the mirror.

She had to admit that she did have butterflies in her stomach when she stepped outside the door. What would they think of her Lancashire accent? Would she have to explain that she was here because her husband was sleeping with her next door neighbour? Would they guess she was doing the insanely terrible thing of staying in her son's student house share? Would they judge her?

She wouldn't tell them. She'd lie. She couldn't deal with the judgemental looks. She'd make something up and all would be fine.

She checked her appearance in the shop window before she pushed the door open and walked in.

'No walk-ins today, love,' said the lady without looking up, stood behind a Perspex glass counter. There were products on display that Kim hadn't seen in ten years. She also hadn't been in a hairdresser's in a long time that had a twirly stand of dangly earrings on the countertop that looked like they had been there since the nineties. 'Brenda's gone in for a knee op so it's just me and I'm fully booked.'

Kim looked around. The salon was completely empty apart from the lady behind the counter who was studying what looked to be an old-style appointments book. 'I haven't come in for a haircut,' announced Kim.

The woman finally looked up. She was maybe in her sixties. She had a stout figure and was wearing a blue nylon tabard. Her glasses were attached to a chain around her neck and she wore her hair in a big, jet-black dyed bun on the top of her head. Kim's immediate thought was that she needed a decent colourist round her. The black was too harsh. Her hair needed taking back to her natural colour which she guessed was possibly brunette and then she would look great with some honey and blonde tones to blend more with the inevitable grey that was lurking at the roots.

'Oh,' said the woman taking off her glasses and peering at her. Kim wondered if she might have gone over the top with her elaborate updo.

'We don't do ear piercing,' stated the woman. 'I know it says on the sign outside, but we haven't done that for a good ten years.'

Kim waited for an explanation as to why it was still on the sign but none was forthcoming.

'Actually, I've come in to ask if you have any jobs going?'

The lady blinked back her. 'No,' she said, looking back down at her bookings ledger.

Kim stood stock still. She hadn't factored that answer in. She really needed this.

'Erm, I've all the qualifications,' she continued. 'I've recently done the Gold Triple Star course on colouring and I can do extensions and weaves. Wedding hair, that's my speciality, I've done a huge amount of wedding hair.'

The woman looked up at her again and gave her a withering look. 'We don't do wedding hair here. Not the demand, see. It's all pensioners and students.'

'Okay, well what about prom hair or Christmas ball hair? There's always an occasion for a great hairdo. And I'm a whizz with a blow dry for your pensioners. Honestly, I can make the thinnest strands look like a lion's mane if you just give me five minutes with a dryer and some mousse.'

The woman gave a big sigh. 'Me and Brenda cater for our ladies perfectly well, thank you. Now as you can see, I'm very busy so if you wouldn't mind.' She raised a hand to indicate the location of the door.

'Didn't you say Brenda was having a knee op? Don't you need someone to cover for her? I could do that. Temporary would be great, perfect in fact. Did I mention that I also do eyelash and eyebrow tints? Cheap as chips to do. You could put a sign in the window, start with a special offer or something. Eyelash tints are amazing, once you've had them you cannot understand why you never had them before. Look,' she said, striding forward to show the lady her own tints. She fluttered her eyelashes in her face whilst explaining they were blue/black and had been done a month ago and still looked great.

The lady leaned back as Kim leaned in closer. She had a curled lip that would indicate that she was not impressed by Kim's tinted eyelashes. Aaah well, in for a penny.

'I could sort those grey roots out for you no problem too,' she said. 'When's your next appointment? We could do it now and I could show you my skills. I am a whizz at grey hair, you ask my mother. She's as grey as a badger but you would never know. Everyone compliments her on her hair. What do you say?'

The woman thought for a moment and then said, 'I think you'll find that I don't have grey roots. I am perfectly capable of sorting out my own hair, thank you very much.' She walked out from behind the desk in slippers which was possibly the most shocking thing Kim had ever seen in a hairdresser's. The lady walked to the door and held it open for her.

Kim had no choice but to leave. That had gone

really badly. She'd never had to apply for a job in her life. She'd started as a Saturday girl when she was fifteen and worked her way up until she got poached by Sharon to go and work in a new salon in the city centre. Then when she'd had Harry, she'd set herself up as a mobile hairdresser accumulating clients through word of mouth and recommendation. Her excellent skills were all she'd needed. She'd never had to ask for a job before. Clearly it wasn't her forte.

She stood outside the hairdresser's feeling totally and utterly dejected, not quite knowing what to do. By the time her housemates came home tonight, she needed a job. Fact. She needed to show them that she was moving forward, that she wasn't going to be under their feet. And she needed money.

Perhaps she should head towards the city centre, try her luck in some other hairdressers. But she wasn't sure where to go and really couldn't face the idea of rejection again. She trudged along the row of shops thinking she should really go to the corner shop and get some replacement coffee for Angus. But then she stopped in her tracks. There in the corner of the window of the chip shop was a sign.

HELP WANTED – MOST NIGHTS
– THAT MEANS UNSOCIABLE HOURS –
NO TIME WASTERS!

Kim gulped. Not the most welcoming of job adverts. And really, did she want to work in a chip shop? Perhaps she did. Working nights could actually take away the loneliness of the endless evenings in alone. And she wouldn't have to think, would she? Wouldn't have to talk like she did when she cut hair. Come to think of it, that could be good. Inevitably you ended up becoming a bit of an agony aunt when you were a hairdresser. When people sat down to have their hair done some of them treated it like being with a priest in a confessional. Everything came out with the implicit knowledge that it would go no further. Hairdressers never told, right? Just listened and added the odd word of encouragement here and there. Agreed with the bride-to-be she had been totally right not to invite her stepmother to the wedding. Nodded when Mr Brown mulled over having a word with his son about the company he was keeping. Shook your head in horror at the way Shelia had been treated by her boss over sick pay.

That's what you were as a hairdresser. You didn't just cut people's hair. You listened to their lives. Normally she loved that. Loved talking to people. But maybe not at the moment. Maybe at the moment she didn't need to hear other people's woes. She had enough of her own. Actually, standing in a chip shop not really having to talk to anyone would be okay just at the moment.

For the second time that morning she took a deep breath and wondered why her heart was banging on her ribcage.

'Hello,' she said, striding up to the counter. 'I'm here about the job.'

'What job?' asked the spotty youth slouching behind the counter who could barely raise his eyes from his phone.

'The one in the window,' replied Kim. She stepped aside so he could see the back of the sign behind her.

He looked at her blankly.

'Is the manager around?' she asked.

'Max,' he hollered at the top of his voice, staring at Kim.

There was no response.

'Max,' he shouted again.

'What?' came the reply from somewhere out the back of the shop.

'There's a woman here asking for you,' he shouted.

Kim could feel herself go bright red. All this felt so uncomfortable. She'd forgotten that she'd dropped chips on the floor just a few days ago. How embarrassing. She prayed Max had forgotten her.

Max came bustling out. He was short for a man, maybe five seven, the same height as her, and had a shiny face. He wore a blue and white striped apron over a plain white T-shirt. He was frowning. She got the impression he frowned a lot.

'Yes?' he demanded. There was no hint of recognition on his face, thank goodness.

'Err, I'm here about the job,' she said. 'The one in the window.'

His eyebrows immediately flared up and she could see him taking in her wedding-ready updo and pristine makeup.

He swallowed. 'Are you having a laugh? Did someone send you in? Was it that idiot Binky that I fired last week? You can go back and tell him that he was fired for thinking it was funny to deep fry the card reader.

Are you his mum? Is that who you are? Has he sent you to get his job back, because I can tell you your son is a useless waste of space.'

'No, I'm not Binky's mum,' said Kim. 'I'm Harry's mum but you won't know Harry, he's just moved in down the road, I mean I know he's been in here; he wears gaming T-shirts but I'm not sure you would remember him, not that it matters. I've come for the job.'

The man stared back at her.

'It says very clearly no time wasters,' he replied.

'I'm not a time waster, I promise. I just need a job. An easy one.'

Max was staring back at her. 'You think working in a chip shop is easy, do you?' he demanded.

'God, no, that's not what I meant at all.' Why did this have to be so hard? 'It's just that I've just moved to the area and well, I need something quick. I'm actually a hairdresser by trade but I asked next door and well, the old bat there kicked me out so I saw your sign and I just thought, well, you sound desperate so I thought you might give me a chance.'

'She kicked you out next door?' Max asked.

'Yeah. Sorry, shouldn't have called her an old bat, I mean you are probably friends.'

'No,' he said reaching forward and pulling up the partition. 'She is an old bat. Why don't you come through to my office and I'll talk you through the gig.'

Kim scuttled through before Max could change his mind.

She followed him through the tight space, past a

rotating kebab spinner and some deep freezers. He showed her into his office which was really just an alcove under the stairs. He shifted a large cardboard box off a seat and indicated for her to sit down. He took his chair behind the desk facing a computer. Despite his short stature he had to bend so he didn't bump his head. He reached up to take a form out of the rack on the wall.

'Name?' he asked.

'Kim,' she said. 'Kim Jacobs.'

'Age?' he said next. 'Actually, don't worry about that. That's just for the kids. We get some sixteen-year-olds here which affects the wage. But I don't expect you're sixteen, are you?'

'Err no,' she said. 'What is the wage by the way?'

'Minimum. If you last a month it goes up by ten per cent but you'll have to remind me because, well, no one seems to last more than a month so I never have to remember. I get all these promises from these students that yes, they are committed. They won't let me down and then you ask them to work a couple of Friday nights on the trot and commitment goes right out of the window. Committed to the drink more like. But you being more mature, now I'm sure that won't be a problem, will it?'

'No,' said Kim shaking her head. 'Not at all. I've no social life, zip, none, you can work me all the Friday nights you like.'

'Good,' he said, nodding and studying her as though properly for the first time or perhaps he was trying to work out why she had no social life. 'You say you're new to the area?'

'Yes, I've, err, moved down here with my son because . . . well let's just say it's complicated. I really, well, I really don't want to talk about it.'

'Brilliant,' replied Max. 'Suits me down to the ground. If I have to listen to one more lightweight student moaning about how hard their life is I might put the next one in the deep fat fryer.'

'Mmm, tasty,' she quipped.

'What?' he asked.

'Deep fried student,' she said.

'Right,' he said slowly. He clearly wasn't a man of banter or lightweight conversation. He looked down again at his form. He asked for a phone number and an address.

'On the same street,' he nodded. 'Always helpful. I can come and hammer on your door when you don't turn up or when you say you're sick and then when I ring the doorbell you don't answer.'

'I'll turn up,' she said. 'I'll be here.'

He nodded.

'Tomorrow night then. Be here for 5.30. Wear flat shoes, rubber soles ideally so you don't slip on the fat. Wear old clothes because they will stink by the time you get home and you don't need to do anything fancy with your hair. Just up and out of your face.'

'Yes chef,' said Kim, 'Absolutely. I can be here tomorrow, chef.' She smiled at her sudden remembrance of how to address the person in charge in a commercial kitchen. She'd seen them do it many times on *MasterChef*.

'You are not coming to work in a Michelin restaurant,' said Max. 'You will be mostly trying to put stuff in hot oil without burning yourself and shaving rotating dead meat. Understood?'

'Understood,' nodded Kim. 'Thank you. I won't let you down.'

Max openly sighed and waved her away. She made her way past the rotating meat and spitting fryers. The spotty youth was nowhere to be seen so she lifted the counter and let herself out. She walked out onto the street and gulped in the fresh air. Fresh air never tasted so good. She reached up to touch her hair and it already felt slightly sticky from the grease-filled atmosphere. Still, it was a job, it was a start, it would get her out of everyone's way and give her something to do. That had to be progress.

Chapter 11

Kim knew she had to talk to Harry.

It was overdue. In fact, she had a mental list of things in her head that she wanted to talk to him about and she had no idea how she was going to broach them. Her being here with him had changed the dynamic. She could no longer play the role of caring parent who had a right to know how her son was. That had all got messed up. She didn't feel like she had a right to ask anything of him anymore. He was sharing his new home with her. She didn't have a right to ask him more than that.

And yet there was stuff she needed to know. She required reassurance as to what was going on in his head. And so she had to talk to him. Or at least try.

She decided she would have to deploy the tactic that seemed to spark their best conversations in the past. When they weren't facing each other, when there was no eye contact. When they were together for another reason other than to talk.

She knocked tentatively on his bedroom door then popped her head round when she heard a 'yeah' grunted.

'I've got five minutes,' she said. 'Do you want your hair cutting?'

He was sitting at his desk staring at a computer screen. Joystick in hand. Many shots were being fired.

He shrugged. 'Fine,' he replied. He made no indication of movement, just carried on with what he was doing.

She was about to ask him to come downstairs and sit in the kitchen because then the hair would be easy to brush up. He didn't really think it was okay to cut hair in a carpeted room, did he? That would be stupid. But she bit her tongue. Asking him to move might lead to a refusal and she couldn't risk it. So she went back to her room, picked up her scissors and black gown and re-entered her son's room. Thank goodness Vicky had thought to bring her hairdressing gear with her when she came, although Kim suspected that was only so she could get a cheeky haircut whilst she was here.

She tried to ignore the still packed boxes littering the floor and the suitcase splurging its contents all over the carpet in front of the wardrobe. Harry had made no attempt to organise his room at all. It was almost as if he didn't expect to be staying. She felt dismayed that he cared so little about his surroundings but perhaps now was not the ideal time to bring it up.

She put the gown round his neck as he continued to play his game and laid a towel on the floor surrounding his chair, hoping that would capture most of the hair.

She took a deep breath and set to work.

'So I got a job today,' she began. 'I'll be out of the house a lot more. Took your advice. You were totally right.' She knew she was jabbering but she was nervous.

'Great,' he said.

'It's at the chip shop at the end of the road,' she continued. 'It's not much, I know. I mean it's nothing very special or anything for your mum to be doing.'

He shrugged again. 'Sounds great,' he said, like he hadn't even registered what she'd said as he stared into the screen in front of him. 'Do we get free chips?' he asked. So he was listening.

'No idea,' she replied. 'I'll have to see. Max doesn't strike me as the overly generous type but I would have thought he'll be wanting to get rid of leftovers at the end of the night.'

Harry nodded.

Kim gulped.

'So, are you sure you are all right with me staying?' she asked. 'I mean, I know this is all such a mess and it wasn't meant to be for long, but is it okay for you? I'm just so grateful, I really don't know what to say.'

She swallowed and looked up to see his reflection in the screen. He looked grim.

'It's fine,' he said. 'Fine. As long as you stick to the rules and as long as it's okay with Angus and Sonny. If either of them comes and says they've changed their minds though then I'll have to take their side. You understand that, don't you?'

'Yeah. Of course. Totally.'

Harry looked at her reflection in the screen. 'And don't expect me to talk about what's going on with Dad or anything. I can't do that. I don't want to be caught in the middle of it.'

'That's fine,' she said, pulling up the strands of hair

on the top of his head and snipping in with her scissors. 'Absolutely, totally understand that. But just so you know, if you want to talk to your dad it's okay by me. I won't be offended or anything. If you want to talk to him, talk to him. He is still your dad is all I'm saying.'

Harry nodded. 'I know,' he said.

'Angus and Sonny have been really kind to me,' she continued, deciding to change track. 'I'm really glad you are sharing with them. Are you?'

Harry shrugged. 'Sure,' he said. 'They're better than the guys on my course. Thank goodness I'm not sharing with chemistry students.'

'Why? What are they like? Did you meet them today? Did you have your first lectures today? How did it go?'

Harry gave her a look. She'd clearly exceeded the limit of how many questions a mother can ask a teenager in any one go.

'Everyone is so brainy,' said Harry, looking back at the screen. 'They all looked like they understood everything the tutor said.'

Kim felt her heart sink. When was Harry going to stop being so insecure about how smart he was?

'I'm sure they didn't,' she said. 'They're all bound to be pretending. You're not going to say you don't understand on day one, are you? I bet they all felt exactly the same as you.'

'Maybe,' said Harry.

'It's all bound to be really strange at the beginning. But you'll get used to it. And to them. I'm sure you'll come home in a few weeks' time and they will all be your best mates.'

'I doubt it,' said Harry, slumping further down in his chair. He was at an awkward angle, making it difficult to get the scissors in the right position, but she didn't think a 'sit up straight, will you' would go down very well.

'I just want you to know that I'm so proud of you. I know I keep saying it, but it's true. At least you will never end up working in a chippy at the end of the road like your old mum, eh?' She let out an awkward laugh.

'There's nothing wrong with working in a chippy, Mum,' he said. 'Nothing. Most people have normal jobs like that, you know. Not everyone wants mega brainy jobs like Dad. It's not the be-all and end-all to do something really important. Working in a chippy sounds great.'

Kim felt quite taken aback. That was quite a speech from her son. She wasn't entirely sure where that had come from.

'Of course,' she replied. 'You're right. Not everyone can be like your dad. Career wise, I mean. I'm just saying that I wish I'd worked hard like you and gone to university. Don't get me wrong, I like hairdressing, but it would have been nice to have had options like you have.'

'Do you think?' said Harry. He was looking at her reflection intently now in the computer screen.

'I do,' said Kim. 'Just make the most of it, hey?'

Harry said nothing and resumed shooting.

She took a deep breath. She had just one more subject to cover.

'And how are things going with Suki?' she asked as innocently as possible.

Harry got up abruptly and shook the black cloak off his shoulders.

'What is this, the Spanish Inquisition?' he said. He didn't look very happy. 'I said she's not my girlfriend, didn't I? So don't ask me about her or anything in fact. If this is going to work, you staying here, then you cannot be bombarding me with a million questions every time you get the opportunity. Don't ask me about Suki and don't ask me about my course. Okay? That's another rule. Do you understand?'

She swallowed and nodded.

He headed out of the door.

'But you've got a wonky left side,' she muttered as he left. She sank onto the bed and put her head in her hands. She'd not played that very well. She should have kept quiet. Laid low. Too many sensitive subjects. She was forgetting that it wasn't that long ago that Harry was fretting that he might not even get into university, given his disappointing results, and now she was giving him the third degree. And he was clearly sensitive about Suki. Why hadn't she kept quiet? And why was it that the people you were closest to were the hardest ones to talk to? Particularly your children. Your words got all tangled and mixed up. She should learn to keep her mouth shut for a while when it came to her son. She needed to give him his space, at least whilst they were sharing the same house.

Chapter 12

Kim had to ask Angus if he had a full-length mirror to check her appearance before she started her first shift at the chippy as she didn't have one in her own room.

'Be my guest,' he said as he stood aside at his bedroom door and waved her in. His room was surprisingly tidy, a far cry from Harry's. Clothes were out of sight and his desk showed neat piles of books rather than the jumble of cables and computer paraphernalia that cluttered her son's. She tried not to look round for fear of being accused of being nosy so headed towards the wardrobe on the back wall and the full-length mirror on its front. She felt her shoulders sag as soon as she caught sight of herself. She'd scraped her hair back into a bun, knowing it was likely that she would have to encase it all in a blue nylon net. She wore a black long-sleeved T-shirt which totally washed her pale skin out, her 'Fat days' jeans so she would feel comfortable but made her thighs look as wide as the M6 and her black and pink trainers. She reckoned the look aged her by at least ten years but there was nothing she could do about it. Max had said to dress down and she feared seeing his face if she arrived in anything fancy.

'You got a date?' asked Angus with a smirk. 'Looking smoking.'

'Very funny,' she replied, walking past him.

'Don't forget to bring us free chips back,' he shouted after her as she left the room. She couldn't believe the excitement that the potential of free chips had caused in the house. When she'd told Sonny and Angus they both had reacted in exactly the same way as Harry. 'Do we get free chips?' was the most they could say about her new job and she wasn't at all hopeful that she would be able to deliver.

When she arrived in the chippy ten minutes later she was surprised to be greeted by one of the most glamorous young ladies Kim had ever seen, stood behind the counter. She looked around, confused. Where was Max in his greasy apron and who the heck was this?

'Sorry,' the girl said grinning at her. 'Not open yet.'

'Actually, I'm Kim. I'm supposed to be starting work here.'

'Shit, yes, sorry. So sorry,' she gasped. 'Dad said we had someone new coming in. Sorry. I'm Annie. His nib's daughter. Sorry, it's just me until Dad gets back from the wholesaler. Shouldn't be long. Won't you come through?' She lifted the hatch and stood aside to let Kim through. As she brushed past her she felt even more underdressed. For under her work apron Annie had on a full forties-style tea dress complete with a full net underskirt. It looked at odds with her apron which strained over her generous curves but totally fitted in with her elaborate curler-set dark hair and full red cupid's bow lips. She looked like she was about to walk onto the set of a World War II film. Kim was itching to know how she had done her hair like that, but the bigger question had to be what on earth was she doing dressed like that working in a chip shop.

'Did I get the dress code wrong?' asked Kim. She had never felt so dowdy.

Annie looked at her confused for a moment, then laughed. 'God no,' she said. 'Not you. It's me. I pride myself on getting the dress code wrong. Unless it's forties, of course, then I'm bang on the money. You look wonderful, you really do, perfect. I'm just, well, a forties nut and I like to dress like this.' She shrugged, still grinning. 'I'm at art college if that explains it any better. You know that place where you go if you are a bit mental and want to live a bit crazy by pretending you live in a different era? I can thoroughly recommend it actually. Keeps me amused, I can tell you. Now, Dad told me to show you round so let me give you the guided tour.'

Kim followed Annie to the back of the shop, not knowing what to say. This was not what she had been expecting.

'So, let's start with the absolute essentials,' Annie said. 'See this chair?' she asked, pointing at a rickety wooden chair wedged between two fridges.

Kim nodded.

'This is the staff room. Where you get to go on your break. Dad keeps promising to stop one of the legs wobbling but you know, other priorities.'

'Now, the toilet is through there,' she continued, waving at an open door which housed the toilet as well as a mop and bucket. 'Fire exit is through that door but it sticks a bit so you need to shove it with your shoulder if you really want to escape. What else?' she said, pausing to think. 'Oh yes, the first aid kit. Really important for new starters. You will become very good friends with the first aid kit, believe me. Burns cream is in there. Just slap it on, works wonders. Now there is an accident book which you must fill out, nudge, nudge, wink, wink, know what I mean.'

Annie winked at her, giving Kim a chance to take in her gloriously thick false eyelashes.

'Oh, and in case you're wondering, this is where the magic happens.' She pointed at Max's office under the stairs.

'Yes, I know,' said Kim. 'I had my interview there.'

'Really,' said Annie wide-eyed. 'You had an interview and you still came back. That old misery guts didn't put you off?'

'Err, err . . . ' Kim didn't know how to answer that one.

'It's all right,' said Annie. 'You don't need to be nice about him. I tell him to his face that he's a misery. He just needs to get out more. Period. Actually, you don't have any single friends, do you? It's a never-ending task trying to set him up. Jesus, there must be someone out there who can put a smile on his face.'

'Err . . . err . . . I'm new to the area so I don't know anyone, sorry,' said Kim.

'No worries. Husband's job, was it, brought you here?'

'Err, not exactly, no. No, we split up actually. That's kind of why I'm here.' Kim felt herself wince. Is that what she was now? Husbandless? She didn't know. Her entire life felt in this very weird suspension where she wasn't sure of anything.

'I assumed with the wedding ring that you were married,' said Annie, looking down at Kim's hand hanging by her side.

Kim looked sharply down at her hand. She'd forgotten all about her wedding ring and its significance. It was so familiar to her. Yet now as she looked at it, it looked like something totally alien had attached itself to her finger.

'I'd forgotten I was still wearing it,' she said, forgetting Annie was there.

'Was it quite recent then?' asked Annie. 'Sorry, I'm so nosy. Tell me to shut up.'

'It's okay,' replied Kim. 'Like a week or so ago, I think. Time has sort of run away with me.' Kim suddenly had an urge to take the ring off. Right now. The sight of it made her want to cry and she didn't want to cry. She needed it off. So in front of Annie, standing in the back of the chippy, she pulled her wedding ring off for the first time in twenty years.

'What should I do with it?' she asked Annie, as if she should know.

'What do you want to do with it?'

Kim shook her head. 'Throw it in the deep fat fryer?'

Annie shook her head. 'Might not comply with health and safety, I'm afraid. We've got a safe that Dad uses for cash. We could put it in there?'

She nodded and then followed Annie to the back of the shop and to Max's office under the stairs. Annie scrabbled under the desk and opened the safe then held her hand out for Kim to hand her ring over. And that probably would have been fine had Max not chosen to return from the wholesalers at that very minute.

'What's going on?' he asked. 'The front door is wide open, the fryers are not on yet and you're stealing cash from the safe?'

Kim swallowed. This was not a good start.

Fortunately, Annie reappeared from under the table.

'We were just putting Kim's wedding ring in the safe so that she didn't throw it in the deep fat fryer,' she announced, as though that were perfectly reasonable.

Max glanced between the two of them, clearly not knowing who to blame for these shenanigans.

'I need help unloading the van,' he said eventually, turning his back and heading towards the back door.

'And get those damn fryers sparked up,' he shouted over his shoulder.

Kim helped Annie get out from her awkward spot under the table.

'He's a cuddly bear really,' said Annie. 'Honestly. He just needs to get out more.'

Kim didn't think it would be possible but her shift went from bad to worse. She started off on the fryers with Max, watching carefully when the right time was to cook and for how long and how to manoeuvre the heavy baskets and dump the contents without causing yourself damage. She thought she was getting the hang of it until she dropped a basket, spilling chips all over the floor. Horrified, she bent to pick the basket up, grasping the hot metal with her hand and giving herself a burn. Max looked at her as though he had seen the same charade played out a million times. He asked his daughter to show Kim how to use the first aid kit. Annie tended to her wounds and told her to take time out in the staff room/rickety chair for five minutes and then go on the till in the front of the shop.

Kim watched in awe as Annie dealt with the steady stream of customers with speed, efficiency and a massive smile on her face. After a while Annie got her wrapping chips in paper which she got the hang of quickly, her dextrous hairdresser's hands helping her out. She could, however, soon feel sweat pouring down her back and pimples literally breaking out onto her face. All was going better until Annie got her taking the orders at the till whilst she stood by her side. An old man in a trilby and a raincoat came in and Kim asked him what he would like.

'My usual,' he said.

'And what would that be?' she asked.

He stared at her. 'I've been coming in here for ten years – surely you can remember what I have.'

Kim looked nervously over her shoulder. Annie appeared to have disappeared, right when she needed her.

'I'm sorry,' she said to the man. 'It's my first day. Could you tell me what your usual is?'

The man frowned, clearly displeased his usual order wasn't up in lights somewhere for all to see. He was just about to speak to hopefully share this apparently top secret information when Sonny came running into the shop completely breathless as though he was being chased by aliens.

'Kim, Kim,' he gasped, doubling over in order to try and get his breath back. 'You need to come home.'

'Why? Is it Harry? What's happened?'

'No,' he said, rearing up. 'It's your husband. He's here. He says he wants the keys to the house. What should we do? I offered him a cup of tea but Angus told me off. Said you wouldn't like that.'

Kim stared at Sonny. The old man was also staring at him. Sonny was wearing a bright orange sweater that Kim suspected his mother had knitted for him, red cargo shorts and black workmen's boots. A look that was not easy to carry off.

'We've called Harry,' continued Sonny, 'but he's not answering and now your ex has gone up to Harry's bedroom and we can hear him going through his drawers. Angus said to come and get you.'

Kim was trying to grasp what Sonny was saying. The thought of Richard being in such close proximity sent a chill through her bones. Anger was also rising up inside her. He couldn't just arrive out of the blue. And he definitely had no right to be going through Harry's things. What was he playing at?

'It's battered sausage, a fresh one mind, small chips, mushy peas and gravy. Large peas, small gravy,' said the old man looking at her. 'You got that?'

She hadn't heard a word of it and looked at him blankly.

'Annie!' exclaimed the man as she thankfully re-appeared. 'There you are. This new woman here won't take my order.'

'She's new, Bill, give her a chance. Now what do you want?'

'My usual,' he replied.

'No, let's not play this game,' replied Annie. 'You know you don't have a usual. You change your mind most weeks.'

'Battered sausage, small chips, large peas, small gravy,' said Sonny, beaming at Annie. 'That's what he wants. I heard him. Didn't mean to interrupt or anything. Just trying to be helpful because I interrupted his order, you see. I came barging in because Kim's husband is at our house turning the place upside down. I'm Sonny by the way.' He continued holding his hand over the counter for Annie to shake. 'Sonny Benjamin Wallace. I'm from Devon. It's wonderful to meet you.'

Even Annie was lost for words at Sonny's introduction. Sonny was grinning like he'd set eyes on the greatest thing he had ever seen. She took his hand and smiled back. 'Great jumper,' she said.

'I knitted it,' replied Sonny.

Everyone's eyebrows shot up including the old man still patiently waiting for his chip supper.

'Really?' asked Annie. 'That's so impressive.'

'Really,' replied Sonny. 'We were snowed in once for five days so Mum taught me to knit and me and Dad rewired the house. There are some amazing similarities between house electrics and knitting.'

Everyone was still lost for words. Including Annie. For a moment.

'I've always thought so,' she finally agreed with a grin.

'Do you knit?' asked Sonny.

'Of course,' replied Annie. 'Absolutely.'

Kim watched as Sonny blushed bright red and suddenly became awkward.

Bill rapped his pound coin held in his hand hard on the counter. 'Have you got my order then?'

'Sorry, what was it?' asked Annie, still looking at Sonny.

'Battered sausage, small chips, large peas, small gravy,' murmured Sonny.

'Fresh cooked sausage, mind,' demanded Bill. 'Don't want one that's been hanging around in that cupboard for a few hours.'

'Right,' said Annie, finally turning away to pull together the order. 'Can you put that through the till, Kim?' she asked.

'Of course,' said Kim still in a daze, still trying to process what was happening right in front of her and what was happening back at the house. What should she do? She couldn't just leave on her first shift but she couldn't let Richard wreak havoc over the road either. Likewise, it wasn't fair on Sonny and Angus to have to sort her mess out. Albeit Sonny appeared to have completely forgotten the reason for being here as he gazed doe-eyed at the back of Annie's head.

It would all come back to him immediately when Richard appeared at the door.

Kim looked up from the till and there he was. Her husband standing in the doorway of the chip shop where she now worked. Where she now stood sweating and pimply with greasy, pulled back hair. Richard on the other hand looked good. He had a new coat on!

He must have had to go shopping without access to his own clothes. She wondered if Alison had taken him. Certainly the coat was of a modern style that he would not have chosen himself. Kim had often tried to gently steer him towards slightly more fashionable attire as she knew it would suit him but he had always refused, appearing to be desperate to stick to the safety of plain, unobtrusive items. This coat he was sporting was pretty cool and sophisticated, deep blue with dark green stitching. Clearly Alison had succeeded where she had failed in bringing Richard's look into the twenty-first century.

He hovered at the door clearly not sure what to do. Eventually he joined the now oddly forming queue of Bill and Sonny.

Sonny turned as he approached and caught sight of him. He gasped and turned back to Kim.

'I didn't tell him where you worked,' he gasped. 'Honestly I didn't. You've no right to come here,' he said, turning back to Richard. 'No right at all.'

Richard looked at Sonny like he had no right to talk to him.

'Just go away, Richard,' said Kim. 'Just go away.'

'I came for the house keys,' he said. 'Since you couldn't send them to me. You left me with no choice.'

The sound of his voice cut through Kim like a knife. So familiar and yet so strange to hear it, here in these strange surroundings in utterly bizarre circumstances.

'Battered sausage,' Bill shouted at Kim. 'You've not put it in the till yet. Do I need to tell you the order again?'

'Battered sausage, small chips, large peas, small gravy,' said Kim, not taking her eyes off Richard. 'I'm just serving this gentleman,' she said to him. 'You'll have to wait.'

'Do you know what,' said Sonny. 'I'll have what he's having too. Can you do one of those for me as well?' he said to Annie as she turned round to wrap Bill's supper.

'Sure,' she smiled.

'That's four pound eighty-two,' Kim said to Bill. Bill looked at her aghast.

'It can't be,' he said. 'It's normally four pound thirty-eight. What have you done?'

'Me?' said Kim. She looked down at the till as though it was an enigma machine and she had no idea how to work the code. She had no idea what she had done.

'Put it through again,' said Bill. 'You must have put it in wrong.'

Kim was staring down at the till but tears were now swimming in front of her eyes. She couldn't see anything. She couldn't think straight.

'Battered sausage, small chips, large peas, small gravy,' repeated Bill. 'You put large gravy in, didn't you? I bet that's what happened. You can't do that, you know. I asked for small gravy for a reason.'

'For goodness' sake,' Kim heard Richard mutter.

Annie gently pushed her aside and cancelled the previous order and set up a new one.

'Four pound thirty-eight, please,' she said to Bill, holding out her hand. 'Give her a break, eh? She's new,' she added.

Bill grumped and handed over his accurately counted out money and shuffled out of the door.

'Are you going to come and get me the keys?' Richard asked as soon as Bill had left.

Kim looked at him open-mouthed. 'No,' she said. 'I'm at work.'

'Really?' he said, looking round. 'This is what you call work. I know you were only a hairdresser, but seriously, frying chips? What are you doing?'

'I'm trying to earn a living so I can pay my rent,' replied Kim.

'She has to,' chipped in Sonny. 'We've told Sammy, who was going to live with us but went to work in an Amazon warehouse instead, that we've found someone to take her place so Kim is going to pay Sammy's rent. And now that Kim has stopped getting drunk and throwing up on Angus and we've set some house rules for her then it's all going to be fine, really it is.'

Richard looked at Sonny in the same way again. Like he had no idea why he was speaking to him.

'Are you just doing this to make me look bad?' he said, turning back to look at Kim, a look of total confusion on his face. 'Why on earth would you want to work here?'

'Hey you,' said Max, suddenly appearing from behind the fryers. 'There's nothing wrong with working in a back street chippy. It's an honest living and can you stop distracting my workforce. And no, Kim cannot do what you want her to do, right this minute, because as she said at the very beginning, she's at work.'

'You've not exactly got them queueing out the door,'

pointed out Richard. 'Surely you can spare her for ten minutes.'

Max appeared to consider the request. He glanced at Kim. Kim gave him a look that she hoped conveyed that she needed him on her side. He turned back to Richard.

'She's at work. Now if you don't want to buy any chips I suggest that you get out.'

Richard blinked at him. Kim held her breath. Richard was used to winning arguments. Whenever she argued with him, he was a master at expressing extreme logic in a calm and precise manner, making it impossible to win. It drove her mad sometimes. He never lost it. Never reacted emotionally, never appeared to be irrational. Unlike her who was the opposite. Emotion always beat logic when push came to shove for her. Always. Kim could see Richard formulating any number of rational reasons why Kim should go and get the keys but Max had overridden him. Max had played the boss card and he couldn't beat that.

'I'll be in the pub on the corner unless Harry shows up,' said Richard. 'If he does, I'll ask him for his keys. But then he won't be able to get in, of course, if he wants to.'

Richard looked at her calmly.

She reached into her jeans pocket and pulled out a set of keys. She unclipped a single Yale key then handed a green jelly baby key ring with three keys attached to it, to Richard.

'Are those your house keys?' gasped Sonny as Richard took them.

Kim nodded.

'Are you sure about this?' said Sonny. 'I mean, you said the other day that you would give him your keys over your own dead body?'

'I'm sure,' nodded Kim.

'And Angus's dead body, I believe,' Sonny told Annie and Max who were watching. 'He's our housemate. His godfather owns a vineyard in France.'

'You had them in your pocket the whole time?' asked Richard, incredulous.

Kim nodded.

He looked back at her, speechless, as if he didn't know what to do now. Like he wasn't done yet but didn't know what his next move was. 'I thought that we would have the opportunity to talk,' he said eventually.

'Talk about what?' asked Kim glancing awkwardly over at Max and Annie. She was very aware that your errant husband turning up in the middle of your first shift was not ideal.

'About what has happened. I thought that you might find that helpful,' said Richard.

'Helpful?' asked Kim. 'You don't really mean that, do you? You mean helpful to you. You want to have the opportunity to explain it all rationally so that I have absolutely no reason to be upset with you. Well you don't get to do that. You don't get to explain to make yourself feel better. Nothing you can say can make me feel better, so go away. Take your keys and go away.'

Richard stood for a moment not moving.

'I think you'd better do as she asks, don't you?' said Max. 'You got what you came for. Now you can go.'

Richard gave Max his best confused look. He wanted to dispute Max's opinion on the matter but something stopped him.

'We will have to talk at some point,' said Richard, turning his gaze back to Kim.

'It is good to talk,' added Sonny. Kim glanced at him. 'But only when you are absolutely ready,' he nodded vigorously. 'Not before.'

'Okay,' Richard swallowed. 'Bye then.' He shrugged, not knowing how to sign off his departure. Kim hoped he wouldn't try.

'I'll show you to the door,' said Sonny completely unnecessarily. 'Here, it's this way.' Sonny strode the five yards to the clearly positioned glass door and held it open for Richard. 'You be on your way,' he continued. 'It's a long drive back up north. Oh gosh, I've gone all Jane Austen,' he said, giggling to himself.

Richard turned and walked out the door. Kim watched as he pulled his new designer coat around him and walked off into the darkness.

'Well,' said Sonny, coming and leaning on the counter. 'Interesting turn of events, I feel. You okay, Kim? Do you need a hug?'

'What she needs is ten minutes in the staff room and then back to work,' said Max sternly. 'I think your home life has caused enough drama for one evening, don't you? I'm hoping every shift won't be like this. Leave it at home next time – okay?'

'Of course,' said Kim, feeling stunned and out of sorts, the image of Richard walking away into the darkness burned onto her brain. Seeing him again in the flesh had for some reason brought flashbacks of the early days of their relationship into her mind.

'I'm not sure he's your type,' Vicky had said when she'd first introduced him all those years ago.

The truth was she was sick of her type. Bad boys who constantly let her down. She was done with her type. It had never been heart palpitations and over-excited fumblings in the backs of hatchbacks with Richard. This was a grown-up relationship, she'd told Vicky. One born of mutual respect and trust and that was the type of relationship she wanted now. Richard was her keeper. He had been the one who she had thought would actually mean it when he stood in church and committed to her until death do us part.

However, a relationship built mostly on respect and trust doesn't have much left to hold it up when someone destroys that by sleeping with the next door neighbour.

Chapter 13

Kim got home at the end of her shift wanting to totally collapse. She staggered in weighed down by leftover chips and a couple of pies (turned out that Max was only too pleased to get rid of food that was left over at the end of the evening). The hallway was cluttered with all manner of trainers and sports shoes scattered where they had been left and a hockey stick stretched from one side of the narrow hallway to the other as if to barricade any visitors out of the building. She entered the living room to find Angus and Sonny watching *Captain Marvel* so loud it was all she could do to grab the remote and turn it down. They were both spread-eagled across the two couches with kebab boxes spilling their debris on the murky brown carpet and several bottles of lager upended on the floor. There was also a tub of Ben and Jerry's ice cream at Angus's feet. Half-eaten and melted to a sticky goo.

Kim realised that Richard may have seen this. This absolute domestic chaos. He may have smelt it as well. Lamb meat, mint sauce, grease, feet and some gases that had clearly been released into the air via the two lumps reclining on the sofas.

It was all Kim could do not to gag.

She caught sight of herself in the mirror above the gas fire. Her hair was limp and dejected, her face was flushed with the heat coming off the fryers, and her mascara had smudged under her eyes.

'Is that free chips I can smell?' asked Angus, leaping up and grabbing the bag from her.

Kim was surprised he could smell anything above the odours they had accumulated during their evening.

Angus delved into the bag and chucked a packet of wrapped up chips at Sonny.

'How did it go?' asked Sonny. 'I mean apart from your husband turning up and all that.'

'Epic,' said Angus, stuffing his face with chips and peering round Kim to continue watching the film.

'Just peachy,' said Kim. 'I think I'll just get a cup of tea and go to bed,' she said, not willing to rake over the evening's events with two of her housemates. 'Is Harry in?'

'Shagging the neighbour,' replied Angus, nodding towards the front of the house vaguely in the direction of where Suki lived.

'Is he?' asked Sonny, turning sharply to Angus. 'Is he really? Has he told you? Are they shagging?'

Kim turned to look at Angus. Angus looked at her out of the corner of his eye.

'Well if he isn't shagging her he's wasting a hell of a lot of time over there,' he said with his mouth full of chips.

Kim bit her lip. She couldn't comment. Not on any level. She'd been warned off that department very clearly.

'I think they just like hanging out,' said Sonny, nodding vigorously at Kim. She smiled at him gratefully.

She sighed and went into the kitchen.

Carnage.

Once again, breadcrumbs, sugar, coffee granules and milk littered the work surface. A damp tea bag sat on the side next to the bin. Not in the bin. Next to the bin. Pizza boxes were piled high next to the bin. Not in the bin. Next to the bin. Salt and ketchup stained the table. Dirty pots attempted to approach the sink without actually reaching it. She'd tidied up before she went and did her shift but it didn't take long in a house of three boys for it to get in a state again.

All she could think was that Richard had seen this. Seen how they were living. And that actually Harry's room was the worst of all. Richard in his lovely new coat had observed all this.

Kim couldn't get it out of her mind that Alison and Richard had bought a coat together. And it was a really nice coat. And that really bothered her. She knew they must have bought it together because there was no way on this planet that Richard would have bought a coat like that on his own. It showed taste and skill in the clothes shopping department which Richard didn't have but she knew that Alison did have as they had been shopping together many times. Their annual trip to Manchester had been a treat that Kim had really looked forward to. Alison had lived in Manchester so knew all the cool boutique shops and best coffee houses and great little lunchtime eateries. Kim had loved it. She'd felt so cosmopolitan with her worldly-wise companion. It was a far cry from trawling the high street chains in Lancaster then popping into Greggs for a sausage roll.

Consequently, Kim could picture the entire scenario of Alison and Richard buying a coat together. With lack of access to his wardrobe, Kim had given Alison the golden ticket to revamp Richard's look. There would have been no option but to suggest that Richard buy new clothes because heaven knows how long Kim would take to send him a set of keys. She had given Alison free rein to pull out all the stops and take him on a joyous trip to Manchester. There would be a quick stop at Foundation Coffee House with its cool intellectual vibe then a cruise down Cathedral Street leading to Harvey Nichols where they could peruse the designer labels before a leisurely lunch on the second floor overlooking the city. The distressing thing was that Kim knew that had she suggested to Richard such a day out he would have turned his nose up. Said he wasn't interested in shopping. Told her to go but he had better things to do, implying that spending time shopping and eating was not for someone of his intellect. He wouldn't have said that, of course, but she would have most definitely felt it. Rather than shopping and eating he would have suggested a good solid walk in the Lake District, which she really enjoyed to be fair. It would involve a 6.30 a.m. departure from Lancaster to beat the crowds swarming to the national park. Then there would be a bacon butty at a roadside café before stomping up a massive peak with a sandwich stop at the top. Then back to Lancaster for a late lunch cooked by Richard. He did do a fantastic roast.

They were good days. Great days in fact. But it would have been nice to intersperse that type of leisure activity suggested by him with the odd day of fancy shopping in Manchester. She occasionally could persuade him into a sale in an outdoor clothing shop in Keswick but she knew that never in a million years would he have agreed to frequent the designer shops that adorned the streets of Manchester.

But Alison had clearly managed it. Convinced him it was a necessity and then she would have made the experience so lovely and enjoyable that Richard would be left wondering why he had never partaken of the pastime before.

It would have been a dream day for her to spend with her husband.

And Alison had stolen it. Along with her husband.

The image of Richard in his lovely coat was absolutely burned on her mind and the whole backstory of how he got to purchase the coat kept rotating over and over in her head, causing her sleepless nights and a near total disappearance of appetite.

For the next couple of weeks she moved around like a zombie as she attempted to set herself some kind of civilised lifestyle.

She bought fresh fruit and vegetables and put them in the fridge, fearing for their safety amongst the aggressive bottles of lager and industrial sized butter and cheese and half-eaten cans of beans.

She set about keeping the house clean and tidy, in gratitude for them letting her stay and in accordance with the rules set by the boys. It soon became clear that the task was in some ways similar to the painting of the Forth Bridge. When she got it all shipshape it unravelled again the minute they all got home. But she never complained. Never ranted in the way she would have at home. How could she?

In truth she barely saw her housemates. Partly through consciously trying to avoid them so as not to get in their way and partly due to the fact that their timetables totally clashed. When they were getting back from university she would be heading out to work. When she came home late in the evening they would be either out or barricaded into their rooms. She slept in in the morning purposefully getting up late to avoid any kind of awkward chat. She was relieved to work pretty much every night. Sadly, however, she was reminded every time she approached her place of work of the altercation with Richard when he arrived to retrieve the house keys. The image of his lovely new coat rotated round and round in her head along with some of the things he had said that kept coming back to haunt her.

'I know you were only a hairdresser, but seriously, frying chips? What are you doing?'

She'd not thought much about it at the time but as she raked over and over the evening, day after day, that short statement was sending her into all kinds of confusion.

'*Only* a hairdresser.'

The more she thought about it, the more it stung like Richard had slapped her. Was that what he really thought of her all along? She couldn't decide if she was angry or disappointed. Angry that that was Richard's view of her profession. Disappointed in herself that she had married such a man. That she had believed all along that Richard did not look down on her, that he respected her job, but with that one word, Richard had stuffed her way down below him. That word had confirmed all her fears that she had fought so hard throughout their entire marriage to deny. All along he had thought she was '*only a hairdresser*'. His polite enquiries about her work and how her day had been were just that – polite. Not genuinely interested, not concerned over what was happening in a major part of her life.

It felt like he had made a mockery of her entire existence. She loved being a hairdresser. Sure, maybe if things had gone differently, she may have gone down a different path, but she genuinely enjoyed it and besides it worked for the family. Her being flexible in her career had afforded them the type of family life they both wanted. The ability to spend time with their son.

Knowing Richard saw her as 'only a hairdresser' made her question entirely how he saw her and even why he had married her.

She was contemplating all this as she spent yet another depressing afternoon watching gameshows and marvelling at a man from Colchester not knowing where the 2012 Olympics were held when her phone rang. Her heart leapt and she realised with dismay that she hoped it was Richard calling. Calling to help her make sense of the thoughts that were circling her mind. Had he ever really loved her? Why had he married 'only a hairdresser'?

Unfortunately for Kim she could see from her phone screen that it wasn't Richard calling. It was her mother. This was bad, really bad. Kim's mother never called her. She always waited for her to call then complained that they hadn't spoken in so long. Kim had called her the week after she'd left Lancaster, to be met with utter disbelief and lack of any understanding. In the end Kim had rung off, not being able to cope with her mother's lack of support for her leaving her beautiful four-bedroom house to move to a terrace in a strange city. Kim couldn't really explain it to herself, never mind her mum, and so she had ended the call, promising to call back another time.

'Hello, Mum,' Kim said when she picked up the phone.

'Hello,' said Janice. 'Just ringing to see how you are. You've not been to see us. Your dad's just said you've not been to see us since Richard's party.'

'I'm still in Nottingham,' she told her.

'Oh. Why? Shouldn't you be back by now?'

'I'm going to stay a bit longer than I thought,' replied Kim.

'Why's that then?'

'Still trying to sort myself out, Mum.'

'Can't you do that back here?'

'Not really. I can't really face anyone at the moment.'

'But what about your job?'

‘I’ve called them all. Told them I’m taking a break for a while. Given them Sheila’s number.’

‘I could do with you coming to do my roots.’

Kim paused. ‘Sheila will do it. She’s on Park Road. She’ll fit you in.’

Janice stayed quiet for a moment.

‘Who’s looking after Richard?’ she asked eventually.

‘What?’

‘Who’s looking after Richard whilst you are away?’

‘I don’t know, Mum,’ she replied. She figured she could say Alison but she really didn’t think that Alison would be looking after him. Alison wasn’t that type of woman. Her and Neil had had a strict cooking and cleaning rota that Kim had thought was a bit unfair on Neil if she was honest given that he travelled so much with his job. She figured that Alison wouldn’t be taking up all the domestic chores that she had, at the time, happily taken on. Richard, for the first time since they’d been married, would probably be having to look after himself.

‘Perhaps he’s looking after himself?’ she told her mother.

There was another silence at the end of the phone.

‘He’ll never manage that big house on his own. Though I suppose there’ll be less cleaning without you and Harry there. How’s he eating? I hope he’s not living on takeaways. I’m not sure leaving him to manage that house on his own is wise, Kim. Not with his big job and everything. He’ll need to get someone in, I imagine. Until you come back.’

Kim stared at the phone in disbelief. What planet was her mother on? She sounded like she was feeling sorry for her husband.

'You were listening, were you, when I told you that Richard had an affair? With Alison next door.'

'Yes, I heard you. Of course I did. But you'll get him back. He'll see sense. They always do. But you won't get him back whilst you are down in Nottingham. You need to get back here. Look after him. Make him realise what he is missing.'

'Is that what you think I should do, take him back?'

There was a pause. 'Of course you should, Kim. That lovely house and those lovely holidays you go on. I couldn't believe it when you brought him home. I thought, my Kim is set for life here. Now he's made a mistake. I understand it would have been a shock, but don't dwell on it too long, hey, or else you may have missed your chance. He might think you don't care. You get back up here, Kim. That's my advice. You can't get back together if you're not there.'

Kim felt all the energy sap from her. This was her mother talking. Her own mother. Telling her to go back to a lying cheat because he gave her a nice lifestyle and he had a good job. She wondered if Richard had been a bin man she would have reacted in the same way. Janice had always been in awe of Richard and it was the only time Kim could remember her mother talking about her daughter with any pride, when she'd overheard her tell their neighbour that she was engaged to a professor. Her voice dripped with delight that day. Was it any wonder that Janice was desperate for Kim to stay married to a man with such an esteemed profession?

'I've got a job in a chip shop,' Kim told Janice, wishing to change the subject. She couldn't quite process the level at which her mother was hurting her right now.

'A job where?' she asked.

'In a chippy,' replied Kim. 'It's just at the end of the road. Just temporary so I don't have to rely on Richard for money.'

'A chippy?' her mother questioned.

'Yes.'

Her mother sighed. 'And you with a son at university. It's hardly setting him the right example, is it? And I'm sure Richard doesn't want to see you working in a chip shop.'

'He already has. He came down to get his keys.'

'He saw you working in a chip shop? Heavens, Kim. What would he have thought?'

Kim shook her head. Her mother's morals clearly had taken a hike somewhere whilst she'd been away. Or maybe they had always been this wayward; it was just that this situation had brought them out in a bad light.

'Look, I'll have to go, Mum,' she said. 'I need to go to work soon and I need to eat before I go or else I'll end up eating chips again.'

'Now don't go letting yourself go and put weight on,' chipped in Janice. 'That won't impress Richard either.'

'Right, thanks Mum,' said Kim, feeling close to tears. 'Gotta go. Bye then. Say hi to Dad.'

'Bye love. And come back soon. Just you think about what I said.'

* * *

Kim spent another hour thinking about it and the more she thought about it the more she felt depressed. It seemed like her biggest achievement in life had been marrying Richard, according to her mum.

How was that supposed to make her feel?

And so now she wasn't with him, was she worth nothing? Should she be trying to get him back?

But he'd bought a new coat, with Alison. And she was pretty sure that after that there was no turning back. She wouldn't be able to get him back even if she wanted to.

Chapter 14

Three weeks went by and she found herself wandering into the kitchen to find the Ryvita and low-fat cream cheese as she did every lunchtime. It was easy, required no preparation and she could kid herself that she was being healthy. She was just spreading the last of the Philadelphia over a cracker and wondering if she had the energy to go and buy some more when Sonny came barrelling into the kitchen.

'Will you cut my hair?' he gasped, bursting into the kitchen.

Kim had been dying to cut Sonny's hair ever since he arrived. It was too long, curls bouncing over his collar and on the top of his head like an overexcited crowd at a Harry Styles concert. It was the perfect reflection of Sonny's personality, bouncy and cheery, a bit in your face and a bit quirky. Totally unique, it just needed a decent stylist like her to pull it into order.

'Of course,' she said, happy to have something to focus on. 'Shall we do it now? My kit is upstairs.'

‘Oh, would you?’ gasped Sonny. ‘You are such a lifesaver.’

‘Why don’t you go and give it a wash and I’ll set up in here. I’ll be ready as soon as you are.’

‘Brilliant, just brilliant,’ he said, walking up to hug her. ‘Absolutely brilliant.’

Kim felt a tiny sigh of contentment as she unrolled her cloth case surrounding her scissors and combs. They gleamed at her as if to say, ‘welcome back,’ and she felt a tinge of regret that she hadn’t gone further afield to try and find a job in a salon. Still, she was committed to the chip shop now so would have to content herself with perhaps being on hand to do the boys’ hair whenever they needed it.

Sonny bounced in, wet hair dripping on his T-shirt, blue towel clutched in his hand.

‘Wow,’ he said, stopping in his tracks. ‘You have a cape and everything. So you are actually like a real hairdresser?’

Kim laughed. Sonny really was the best person. Even when he was half insulting you, you couldn’t take offence.

‘Yes, I am a real hairdresser,’ she said, indicating for him to sit down. ‘I had over fifty clients back home.’

‘Mum kind of cut mine,’ said Sonny. ‘Well I told her what to do whilst I watched in a mirror. I was kind of going through a whole New Romantics thing, you know, a bit Spandau Ballet and Duran Duran. I even dyed it once. That was fun.’

Kim draped her black cape around his shoulders and picked the blue towel up from his lap and lightly dried his hair with it as he carried on with the history of his hair.

'I put some highlights in,' he giggled. 'Dad went mad. Said I looked like an idiot.' Sonny shrugged. 'But I thought they looked dead cool.' He looked up at Kim. 'You would have been horrified at them, I would imagine. I'm sure I did them all wrong.'

'Not at all,' said Kim, grinning back. 'I bet you looked a knock out. Now, tell me,' she said, running a comb through the curls on the top of his head. 'What brings you to the salon today?'

'Well,' said Sonny, with a sigh. 'It all needs to go. I think I need it super short, you know, sharp, like super tidy. Make me look more grown-up. Make me look like an honest, hard-working student, make me look . . . make me look . . . well, make me look more "geography student",' he said, holding his fingers up in quote marks.

Kim paused her combing, listening to Sonny's request. He was being very specific but she wasn't quite sure what motivation lay behind the drastic change he was requesting. She had a slight taming in mind whereas he seemed to want a total identity change.

'And may I ask what is motivating this change of style?' she asked.

Sonny didn't answer immediately. She couldn't see his face but she sensed a frown; certainly his shoulders were frowning. His body language was always so up but now it was most definitely down.

'I just . . . ' he hesitated. 'I just . . . I just think I need to grow up a bit, you know. I'm at university now. I need to show some maturity. Make an effort to fit in.'

'Fit in?' asked Kim. She looked at Sonny's particular ensemble today. He was wearing a bumble bee striped sweater which was possibly knitted by himself. Underneath was a wing collared shirt, the type you'd wear with a dicky bow, and he was wearing red cargo shorts with Timberland style boots. It was all way too much and he may have got away with it on a more creative course packed with students trying to stand out, but Kim imagined he was three colours over the allotted accepted number for geography students.

'You want a geography student haircut to try and fit in?' she asked him.

Sonny nodded vigorously. 'Yes,' he said. But all the joy had gone out of his voice. When he'd talked about his home styling efforts he'd spoken of fun and laughter. His request did not strike her as coming from a place of joy.

She raised her scissors to start and then paused mid-air.

'Has something happened?' she asked.

'What do you mean?' he said, turning to look at her sharply with a look that said he knew exactly what she meant.

'Well, I just wondered what had sparked this sudden decision, that's all.'

'Nothing,' he said with a shrug, turning his face away.

But she knew there was more to it. She carried on combing.

'You know you have a lovely wave in your hair,' she said.

Sonny nodded, his shoulders still slumped. Kim brought her scissors up to begin to cut but something stopped her. She knew it wasn't right. This hair did not want to be cut. She needed a change of tack. She carried on combing, pretending to look at lengths. Stalling for time.

'So how was uni today?' she asked.

Sonny shrugged again. 'So, so,' he said.

'Right,' replied Kim. 'You meet anyone nice on your course?'

'Not really,' he answered. 'They all seem so . . . so . . . serious. We had a tutorial the other day and they were talking about maps and I made a joke about how much I love maps and I'd be lost without them and nobody laughed. Nobody. They just stared at me. So I don't really say anything in tutorials anymore.'

'Doesn't sound like you,' said Kim, pretending to snip but not taking anything off.

'Just easier that way,' he sighed. 'But . . . ' he paused.

'But what?' she asked.

'Well, we had to split into groups to work on a project and well, no one wanted to work with me, which you know I should be used to by now, I mean it's not like it's not happened to me before, but I just thought coming to uni would be a fresh start away from all that, you know?'

'So you didn't get picked and now you want to look like them so you get picked next time?' stated Kim.

Sonny shrugged. 'Guess so,' he muttered. 'Thought it was worth a try.'

Kim sighed. This was heartbreaking. Sonny was one of the most genuine, unique people she had met in a long time. And the idiots around him were going to ruin him. Just because he was different, then he was feeling the need to conform. But Sonny different was good. Sonny different was an absolute breath of fresh air. Sonny different brought a smile to her sad face pretty much every day. Why couldn't everyone else see that was special? Why couldn't Sonny see that that was special?

She continued to comb and part hair, trying to work out what to say, but no words came. She made to try and start cutting but she just couldn't do it.

'I worked with Annie yesterday,' she said casually. 'She asked after you.'

She hadn't, but Kim was desperate to divert Sonny in any way possible.

He spun round. 'Did she?' he asked, his eyes lighting up.

She nodded. 'She had another amazing look,' she continued. 'She looked like Elizabeth Taylor. She's dyed her hair jet black and blow dried it out. She looked brilliant.'

'I bet she did,' said Sonny, nodding.

'I so admire her,' Kim continued. 'I mean she's eighteen and I've never seen someone more comfortable really standing out in a crowd than her. She rocks up to the fish and chip shop with the biggest smile on her face and serves pie and pea suppers in diamanté earrings for goodness' sake.'

'She's a legend,' sighed Sonny.

'She totally is,' said Kim, shaking her head. 'I wish I'd have worked out at such a young age that the only thing that matters about how you look is that you feel good. Not how it makes others feel. She's totally nailed that.'

'Well I think she looks brilliant too,' said Sonny. 'Like the most amazing person I have ever seen.'

'So if you could look like anyone, who would you want to look like?' asked Kim. 'What would be the look that would make you feel great?'

Sonny shook his head. 'I'm not sure,' he said. Then he laughed. 'I dressed up as Elvis Presley once,' he said, his eyes shining. 'I had the moves and everything.' He stood up and did the perfect Elvis style hip thrust. 'It was the best night ever. My mate Cassie's sixteenth birthday. It was so cool.'

'Did you have a quiff?'

'Oh yeah. I so looked the part. Sequinned jumpsuit and everything.'

'Right,' said Kim. 'So let's do a quiff then.' She raised her scissors. 'If it's a quiff that made you feel good then let's do a quiff. That's much more suited to the Sonny I know than the boring geography look.'

Sonny stared at her open mouthed. 'Do you think?'

'Of course I think. You haven't the face for short hair. Just won't work. Whereas a quiff? Wow, that's going to knock them dead. And imagine how Annie is going to react. It's going to blow her mind.'

'Do you think?' said Sonny again, starting to look excited.

Kim nodded. 'I do. She's going to see someone with some fun and imagination, not someone who can only muster up a dull, boring, uninspiring look. She is going to see a kindred spirit is what she is going to see.'

'Do it,' said Sonny, nodding vigorously. 'Just do it.'

Kim set to work. She started by trimming the untidy sides, cutting his hair close to his head whilst leaving a hint of sideburn. Then she gave the same treatment to the hair on the back of his head before getting to work on the top. She thinned it out, giving it shape and texture before creating a cool-looking contemporary quiff, using some wax and gel then finally adding a touch of hairspray. She stood in front of him and smiled. It suited him. Gave him attitude, enhanced his out-there personality.

'Go and have a look,' she said.

He went into the lounge to look in the mirror above the gas fire. He came back grinning from ear to ear.

'I feel great,' he said in wonder.

'And that is what matters,' said Kim. 'Oh and you look great by the way.'

He nodded. He stepped forward and put his arms around her. 'Thank you,' he said. When he stepped back she thought he might have had a tear in his eye.

'My absolute pleasure,' she replied. 'And by the way, you will get picked. But by the people worth picking you. You'll see.'

He nodded then bounded back into the lounge to take another look.

'Isn't this just like going to the real hairdresser's? he shouted through to Kim. 'You go in, determined to ask for what you want and come out with something entirely different.'

Kim laughed. 'You're right,' she said. 'Just like a real hairdresser's.'

Sonny bounded back in again and hugged her. Kim could feel a tear spring to her eye. She was so touched but all she could think of was that she wished her son would hug her like that.

'Would you like to share one of Mum's frozen meals with me?' he asked.

'No, I couldn't do that,' said Kim. 'They're yours.'

'No, really. You would be doing me a favour. I can't remember how to defrost them so I'm behind on eating them. Please help me eat them, Kim. Please. And show me how to defrost them again. Please,' he pleaded.

Kim looked at him for a moment. She thought about the packet of mince she'd bought that she was going to turn into spaghetti bolognese and freeze in one-person portions in an entirely depressing way. The thought of it made her want to cry. Eating alone was something that she just wasn't getting used to. There was nothing lonelier than cooking for yourself and then sitting down at a table with your Hotmail.

'Tell you what,' said Kim. 'How would you like it if I taught you how to cook a meal, then you can go home to your mum at Christmas and cook for her?'

Sonny's eyes grew wide. 'Would you?' he asked. 'Wow, if I went home and cooked my mum a meal she would so think the university fees were worth it.'

Kim laughed. 'Well come on then. Let's show your mum you are really being educated.'

After Kim had got Sonny to wash his hands and don an apron she announced the first rule of successful cooking. Picking the right music to cook to.

‘Is it really?’ asked Sonny, wide-eyed and innocent as usual.

‘Well technically, no. Actually the first rule of cooking is to pour yourself a glass of wine but it’s perhaps a bit early for that so let’s stick with the music first and I’ll introduce wine at our next cookery lesson. Now what are you going to ask Alexa to play?’

‘Oh God,’ said Sonny, putting his head in his hands. ‘The pressure. The pressure. I don’t want to get it wrong. Wow, so much pressure.’

Kim was already starting to think this was a bad idea. They could be here some time. ‘How about some Queen. Can’t go wrong with Queen and we could start with “Under Pressure”?’

‘Oh that’s brilliant. Of course. Great idea. Let’s start with that.’

Once the music had been lined up, Kim told Sonny to find a knife and a chopping board whilst she hunted down the carrots and onions she had bought earlier. Sonny successfully produced a chopping board but arrived at the kitchen table with a cutlery knife. Kim managed to find a sharp knife which was of course dirty having been used to butter toast sometime in the last week. She scrubbed it clean whilst also digging out a vegetable peeler which of course hadn’t been used in the month since they had all moved in. She handed Sonny the peeler and told him to peel four carrots. It soon became apparent that Sonny had never peeled a carrot in his life and she was forced to take the carrot and the peeler off him and give him a close-up demonstration.

‘How come you have never peeled carrots before?’

asked Kim, trying hard to keep the judgemental tone out of her voice.

Sonny looked at her. 'I have two older sisters,' he replied with a shrug. 'They are going to be busted to know I can peel a carrot, I cannot tell you. Totally busted.'

It took Sonny some time to get the carrots done and Kim was already feeling a knot in her stomach thinking about how she was going to show him how to dice an onion. In the end she did half then handed the knife over as she hardly dared watch as he totally butchered the other half.

'It just takes practice,' she said. 'Remember I have been doing this for what . . . nearly forty years. You'll get the hang of it.'

'Wow, forty years cutting onions,' said Sonny, shaking his head. 'There is a frightening thought.'

It was a good job that Kim was actually starting her shift later on that night or else they would have needed to pause the bolognese cooking and resume it the following evening. As it was it took nearly an hour before the bolognese sauce was bubbling gently on the stove top with Sonny staring at it as though he had just invented a cure for the common cold.

'I did that,' he said, pointing at it in glee.

Actually I probably did most of it, thought Kim but she wasn't going to discourage him.

'What's going on in here?' boomed Angus as he walked in the kitchen door. 'Do I smell grub?'

'I cooked, I cooked!' said Sonny, bouncing up and down. 'Look at it, Angus. It's real food. And I did it. Can you believe that?'

Angus peered into the pot and sniffed. 'Frankly no,' he replied. 'Looks way beyond you.'

'Kim helped, of course, told me what to do, but I actually did it, didn't I Kim?'

'He did,' agreed Kim looking cautiously at Angus, worried that she had overstepped her position in the household. She was trying to be 'insignificant' and here she was teaching Sonny how to cook.

'Wow – your hair,' said Angus, pointing at Sonny's head. 'Where did you get that done? You actually look like you might get a girlfriend with that hair.'

'Really?' gasped Sonny, his eyes wide. 'Do you think so? Kim did it. I wanted a geography haircut but she convinced me to go with something more . . . more . . .'

'Suited to your excellent personality,' added Kim.

Sonny beamed at her. 'Yes,' he replied. 'That's it. Hit the nail on the head.'

'So when is it ready?' asked Angus.

'What?' said Sonny.

'When will it be ready? When are we eating?'

'You are going to eat my food?' questioned Sonny.

'Well you're not going to eat all that, are you? So when are we sitting down for dinner? I could do with a quick shower. So shall we say fifteen mins?' He looked at Sonny then at Kim. Sonny looked at Kim.

'Perfect,' said Kim. 'Sonny can put the spaghetti on and I'll set the table.'

'Great,' nodded Angus. 'Spag bol, is it? A nice glass of red will go down well with that, I reckon. See you in fifteen.' He turned and left the room.

Kim thought she might faint, so excited was she by

the thought of sharing a meal with two other people. And with her two new housemates at that. How she had missed sitting down and eating a meal with someone. Eating alone should be banned.

She talked Sonny through cooking the pasta step by step as she cleaned up the table and set three places. She wondered if she should text Harry to see if he was around to join them but didn't dare given during their last conversation he had been very clear. She needed to stay out of his way.

Angus arrived back in the kitchen with a bottle of red wine in hand, just as Kim was showing Sonny how to drain the pasta. She wondered if Angus was actually missing shared meals as much as she was. She hurriedly got three wine glasses out and put them on the table and filled three glasses with water. She really shouldn't arrive at the chip shop for a shift a bit drunk – that would never do. Max would not be impressed.

'So,' she said to Sonny. 'Why don't you put both pans on the mat and perhaps we can help ourselves or shall I be . . .' She stopped herself short. She was about to say 'Shall I be mother,' before realising that would perhaps not go down well.

Angus instantly rose from his chair and grabbed some utensils and started serving out spaghetti expertly. No mean feat. My, she'd like to meet his mother. There really was some excellent breeding there underneath all the macho type stuff. He knew how to handle himself in many a situation including doling out pasta.

It wasn't long before they all had full plates in front of them and Angus had poured them all a large glass of delicious-looking red wine. Kim thought this might be the first time she had felt anything close to happiness since she had left the family home. The only thing that was missing was Harry. She wished with all her heart he was there and smiling like the rest of them.

'To spag bol,' said Angus, raising his glass.

'To my spag bol,' said Sonny, beaming.

'Cheers,' said Kim, raising her glass and digging in.

There was a companionable silence as the three of them tested the food followed by some mmms and then Angus announcing that it wasn't half bad.

'Picture!' said Sonny suddenly, bouncing out of his chair and grabbing his phone off the side. 'Need to take a picture. This will send my friends wild back at home. Come on, lean in for a selfie.'

Sonny put his arm around Kim's shoulders and extended his arm out to take a photo. Kim instinctively leaned in the opposite direction.

'Come on, Kim, I can't get you in,' said Sonny.

'You don't want me in your student photos,' she cried. 'Your mates will just want to know who the old bat is.'

'Oh they know all about you already,' said Sonny.

'Do they?' asked Kim. 'What have you told them?'

'Well, the truth, I guess. That your husband is a twat and you're staying here a while. Oh, they loved the chip shop stand-off by the way. Kept them all mightily entertained.'

Kim wasn't sure that she was comfortable being the gossip amongst Sonny's circle of friends from Devon.

'Don't worry,' said Angus. 'I've not breathed a word

about you to anyone outside the house. Not since the whole thing with that girl I brought home. No one knows you exist.'

Kim stared at Angus, equally horrified. Just about summed up her life. No one really knew she existed.

She heard the front door slam and her heart lifted. It had to be Harry. Great, he was home to hopefully join in the fun, but she wasn't exactly sure how her son was going to react to her sat down for a meal with his two housemates. She had, of course, consciously made sure that there was enough spaghetti cooked and bolognese sauce left for him to join them. She was his mother after all.

'Harry!' cried Sonny as soon as he walked in. 'Your mum is the best. She taught me how to make this food. I cooked a meal; can you believe it? I used the cooker and everything. Come and have some. There's so much left. It's good, isn't it, Angus? Tell Harry how good it is.'

'It's well edible, mate,' agreed Angus.

Kim looked at her son. She'd not really been able to scrutinise him recently. He looked pale and drawn. Like he wasn't getting nearly enough sleep. His clothes, whilst appearing clean (thank goodness) – albeit dark clothes hide a multitude of sins – looked crumpled as though they had been repeatedly thrown on the floor and picked up again the next day to wear. She wondered how he would smell if she ever got close enough.

He slung his bag on the floor and sauntered over. She jumped to her feet and got him a dish. Shc just couldn't help herself. She piled on the spaghetti and then the sauce and placed it in front of him. She noticed immediately that all the cheese was gone to sprinkle on the top. She knew there was none left in the fridge. They'd used a whole slab of parmesan. She felt herself start to panic. She knew of course that Harry always had a heap of parmesan on his bolognese. Always. She'd have to go and buy some. There was no way he was going to eat that without his customary huge pile of parmesan that he would definitely stir in until the dish became almost half parmesan/half bolognese.

'I'll pop to the corner shop and get more parmesan,' she said in a high-pitched voice. 'We ate it all. I'm so sorry, Harry.'

Angus bellowed with laughter. 'Parmesan,' he said. 'The shop won't have parmesan. Dairylea maybe, but not parmesan.'

'Oh,' said Kim sitting down suddenly. 'I'm so sorry, Harry. Can't believe we ate it all.'

Harry shook his head. 'It's fine,' he said, speaking with his mouth full, spitting shards of mince and pasta. His breeding clearly wasn't half as good as Angus's and that was all her fault, of course. And he was eating like he hadn't had a decent meal in days. And that was all her fault as well, of course. She was here. Right under his nose and she couldn't even feed her son.

There was an awkward silence that Kim felt the need to fill. This was an occasion to celebrate. Them all sitting and having a meal. She hoped very much they could do this more often.

But then she ruined it.

She uttered the immortal words no child ever wants

to hear and no parent should ever utter. The phrase should be absolutely banned the world over. But she just couldn't help herself. It just came out.

'Have you had a good day?' she asked her son.

'Jesus, Mum,' he gasped, sweeping his dish off the table and getting up whilst still shovelling hot food into his mouth. 'I told you not to ask.' He turned and left the kitchen.

Kim was mortified.

'Teenagers,' said Sonny, shaking his head sadly.

Chapter 15

By the time Kim arrived for her shift at the chippy she thought she had got herself back together after Harry's outburst. Harry being upset with her brought into sharp focus what a mess her life was in and how her mess was encroaching on Harry's life. She didn't know what to do about that but she had a shift to do and so even though her face was puffy with tears she had to gather herself enough to function as a normal human being. Thankfully it was just her and Max on today so as long as she kept her head down, she should be okay.

Of course emotions don't listen to firm instructions. Serious talks about not escaping at inopportune moments seem to somehow go unheard. 'Do not cry in front of the least appropriate person during this difficult time,' somehow is a command that tear ducts take very little heed of and so it only took Max asking her to help him unload some stuff from out the back of the van for that simple request to inspire a tsunami of tears. She tried to hide the turmoil as she hauled a pack of Tango through the door but the tears were flowing so freely that even the most unsympathetic man on the planet – i.e. Max – had to comment.

'Your husband been visiting again?' he asked as they passed in the backyard.

'No,' she gulped. 'No, actually. Just ignore me. I'll be all right.'

And so he did. They passed each other several times marching in and out of the shop with goods piled high. Kim continued to sniff hard in a desperate hope to suck her tears back in whilst Max looked stony faced as he handed her a six-pack of ketchup bottles.

'Is he begging you to come home?' Max asked eventually when it was clear ignoring the tears wasn't going to make them go away.

Kim looked at him agog. 'No!' she said. 'They bought a coat together.'

She didn't elaborate, assuming it was obvious that the fact they had bought a coat together meant her husband had no intention of wanting her back.

'Who did?' asked Max.

'Richard and Alison.'

'Who are they?' he asked, furrowing his brow.

Jesus, thought Kim. How can he not know the key villains in her story?

She sighed. 'Richard is my husband, the guy who came to get the keys . . . '

'Right, yeah. Of course. So who is the other person?'

Kim shook her head. Richard and Alison occupied so much of her thoughts that it was impossible to believe that her main work colleague did not know them intimately as well.

'Alison,' she said. She still hated saying her name. 'Is my next door neighbour who my husband Richard is currently shacked up with and is out on the town buying coats with.'

Max stared at Kim, still looking confused.

'Why is he living with her and what's the big deal about buying a coat? It's just a coat.'

Now Kim was confused. What the hell did Max think was going on here?

'He's living with her because they were having an affair.'

'They were having an affair?' he asked.

'Yes,' said Kim. 'Of course they were. What did you think was happening?'

Max shook his head looking totally flummoxed. 'Well I assumed you had left your husband because you were having an affair.'

'I most certainly wasn't.'

'Right, I'm sorry about that. Erm . . . err . . . '

'How could you think that?' Kim was starting to feel angry.

Max was still looking startled and confused.

'Err . . . err . . . because that seems to be what normally happens. Good-looking woman like you and a not so good-looking chap like your husband. I just assumed you had a better offer. It often happens like that, doesn't it?'

'No!' cried Kim. This altercation had certainly dried up her tears. Nothing like a bit of discord to stop yourself wallowing in your own self-pity.

'Oh,' said Max. 'Right. Well, best get the rest of the soft drinks out the van.' He turned round and headed outside.

'I'm totally the injured party, here,' she said, running after him. 'None of it was my fault at all. The night he told me he was having an affair I'd thrown him a surprise fiftieth birthday party and said in front of everyone there how much I loved him and how he'd made my life complete. I very nearly quoted bloody *Jerry Maguire*. You know, "you complete me". The only reason I didn't was because he's never watched a romcom in his life.'

'He's never watched *Jerry Maguire*?' said Max, turning round and looking almost as horrified about this revelation as about the fact Richard had an affair.

'No, none of them,' she confirmed. 'Not one. Not *Pretty Woman*, not *When Harry Met Sally*, not *You've Got Mail*, not *Sleepless in Seattle*, not one of them. Zilch.'

Max hauled a massive cannister of oil out of the back of the van and strode back towards the back door. But Kim wasn't finished with him. Her anger at being assumed the perpetrator of her own sorry destiny was providing great relief to her sadness.

'So none of it is my fault, you see,' she said, striding after him. 'He's totally put me in this position. He's humiliated me, forced me out of my home, meaning I've had to move in with my son in his student house share and now, not only is my relationship with my husband totally ruined, my relationship with my son is because he hates me and won't talk to me and I have absolutely no idea what to say to him.' She paused, breathing heavily. 'And you assumed it was me who got me into this mess?' she said, standing in front of him with her hands on her hips.

Max turned to look at her. She wasn't sure if he'd

zoned out and not even heard her tirade. He wrinkled his brow.

'I still don't get the coat,' he said.

Why were some people so dense? 'Because Richard didn't have the keys to the house he didn't have any clothes, so him and Alison went clothes shopping together, which Richard always flatly refused to do with me, and bought this lovely coat that makes him look great and he never would have done that with me so . . . so . . .'

'It's definitely over?' asked Max.

'I think so,' said Kim.

'Because they bought a coat together?'

'Yes!' said Kim, feeling even more exasperated.

'I think there is probably more to it than that,' stated Max.

'Of course there is,' she said. 'I'm just saying that buying a coat together is like another level in a relationship.'

'More so than having sex?' he asked bluntly.

That knocked the wind out of her sails. She audibly gasped.

'Yes,' she said eventually. 'It is. Anyone can shag someone. Taking someone on a successful shopping trip is an entirely different ball game.'

Max stared at her. 'It was Annie's birthday present for me,' he said, nodding.

Now what is he talking about? thought Kim.

'My ex – Rachel – came home with this massive Lego set for Annie's tenth birthday. I knew we couldn't afford it. We'd agreed a smaller set but this massive *Harry Potter* themed kit arrived. She reckoned she'd been saving her tips and it was in the sale. We'd just bought this place and we were really strapped for cash. She was working as a receptionist in a hotel. I couldn't believe it. I knew it was a fancy hotel, but tipping the receptionist? Anyway, I took the box out of the bag to have a look and the receipt fell out. I thought I'd see how good a deal she'd got which is when I noticed it hadn't been paid for in cash. It was on someone's credit card. Not ours. I asked her what card she'd used and she just crumbled. She told me Mr Paul Hargrave had bought the Lego on his card. He was one of the partners in the hotel. I've since learnt that hotels are a hotbed of affairs apparently. Must be all those empty bedrooms you have access to. It had been going on for six months and they were waiting until after Annie's birthday to tell me. Do you know what she said? She wanted to make sure we all had one last happy birthday together. One last happy birthday? They went shopping together and bought my daughter's birthday present. It still blows my mind.'

'See, shopping,' sighed Kim. 'So intimate!'

Max nodded grimly. He'd stopped charging from the van to the shop now.

Kim didn't know what to say. Her anger had been dissolved by Max's sorry tale. Then it struck her. No wonder he'd been so unfriendly. He'd assumed she was just like his ex-wife. He'd assumed she'd cheated on Richard just like his wife had on him. She looked up at him. He was still clearly in pain, even after all these years. Christ, is that what she had to look forward to eight years from now? Still reliving the whole coat purchase story?

'Is your ex still with him?' Kim asked.

Max shook his head as if he was trying to get rid of some awful image in his mind. Probably a Lego model of Hogwarts, she thought. 'Yes,' he said. 'They live in West Bridgford in a big old Victorian mansion whilst I'm above the chippy. No wonder she left me really, is it?'

Kim didn't reply. They both stood in silence for a moment.

'You are meant to say that you have absolutely no idea why she left me as I'm such a charming bloke and what's wrong with living above a chippy,' said Max, raising his eyebrows.

Kim wasn't sure if he was joking. And it was all a little bit close to home.

'I know why Richard cheated on me,' she said gloomily.

'Why's that then?'

'Because I'm just a hairdresser.'

'Why? What does he do that's so clever?'

'He's a university professor.'

'Oh right. Pretty smart then.'

Kim nodded.

'I'm sure there were other factors,' said Max. 'Having said that, I reckon Rachel definitely ditched me for the glamorous lifestyle that money can buy. I mean, I know I'm no oil painting but Mr Paul Hargrave is no Adonis.'

Kim didn't know what to say. It wasn't often you heard a man show insecurity in his looks. Sure, he was on the short side for a bloke but he had a nice face atop his slightly cuddly body. He was no showstopper, but when he wasn't frowning he came across as your average decent guy. She wasn't sure that was what Max needed to hear right now though.

'Amazing how a bottomless credit card can make the ugliest men suddenly wildly attractive,' said Kim.

'Exactly,' agreed Max.

'Alison has bottomless stimulating conversation,' sighed Kim.

'Yeah, I'm sure that was it,' agreed Max, raising his eyebrows.

'Well, can I just say, you've done a brilliant job with Annie,' Kim told him.

Max smiled. Possibly the first time she'd seen him genuinely smile. 'She's made my shitshow of a marriage worthwhile. I have no idea what I would do without her.'

Kim nodded. 'How long did it take her to kind of get over what happened, do you think?'

'Years,' said Max. 'But we screwed it up to start with. Battled for custody, the whole shebang. Rachel claimed that living above a chippy was no fit place to send a child so didn't want her to stay over. I guess you've got none of those worries with your son. You've taken full custody of him in every sense.'

'Oh don't,' said Kim, burying her head in her hands. 'I should move out. I know I should move out but . . .'

'You are still in a mess. You don't know where you should be?'

Kim raised her head and nodded.

'Has he asked you to move out?'

'No,' she said.

'I reckon if he wanted you out, he would have said,' said Max. 'Kids are selfish like that. Annie made me shave off my beard, and I loved my beard. The little minx.'

'Maybe you're right.'

'After Rachel left me I spent two years only talking to Annie about Justin Bieber,' Max told her. 'What I don't know about Justin Bieber is not worth talking about. And I hate Justin Bieber. Anyway, all I'm saying is you need to find some neutral ground with your son, something uncontentious to talk about. Just to take the pressure off.'

'I'm doomed. He only loves computer games and I am utterly shit at computer games.'

Max looked at her. 'Yep, doomed,' he agreed. 'Something will come up. Just be patient.'

'Annie doesn't look much like a Justin Bieber fan now,' commented Kim.

'She certainly doesn't,' said Max, raising his eyebrows again.

'Well, I think she's brilliant,' said Kim. 'And so confident in her look. Amazing at her age.'

'Oh I reckon that's all to defy her mother.'

'Really?'

'Yep. It may surprise you to know but Rachel is like mega glam, skinny, always on some faddy diet and Mr Paul Hargraves is definitely funding some high-end plastic surgery. Last time I saw her she looked proper trout-faced and her forehead, you could have used it as a chopping board to cut chips on. Rachel basically wants to be Kim Kardashian and wants her daughter to be another Kardashian. When we first split she was forever taking Annie to Bridlesmith Gate and buying her designer clothes because she wanted to show off she had a rich boyfriend who bought her daughter two-grand leather coats.'

'Shopping has so much to answer for, doesn't it?'

Max nodded.

'But Annie wasn't keen on all that kind of gear. And because she's never been a beanpole, I think it made her feel even worse about her curves. But her mum couldn't see that. Thought she was being kind dressing her up in these fancy clothes when actually she was being cruel.'

'So she rebelled,' said Kim. 'Found a different way to be glamorous that your ex-wife doesn't get.'

Max nodded. 'You know, all her clothes are from charity shops. Makes me laugh so much. Rachel begs to take her shopping but Annie's having none of it. She's found her way. And she did it all on her own.'

Kim thought about Harry at home in his room on his own in his dark hoodies and sweatpants and his unwillingness to have any conversation with his mum whatsoever.

'Should I move out?' she asked Max.

'Out of where?'

'Out of Harry's house. I'm not sure our relationship can survive.'

'It will and as I said, something will come up. You'll find some mutual ground somewhere that will force a conversation and then you are away. Mark my words. Your Justin Bieber is just around the corner.'

They were just about to shut the fryers down at the end of the night when Sonny came dashing in like the little ray of sunlight he always was.

'Hey Sonny,' said Kim. 'Everything okay?'

'Is Annie in tonight?' he asked. 'Thought I'd come and show her my new haircut.'

'Sorry, no,' replied Kim. 'Just me and Max tonight.'

Sonny nodded thoughtfully. 'It's okay. No problem. I also came in to ask you a question. Do you like quizzes?'

'Well, I guess so,' replied Kim. 'I mean the amount of daytime TV I'm watching you'd think I was obsessed with them.'

'Perfect,' said Sonny. 'Want to join our quiz team at the pub next Monday night?'

'Oh,' replied Kim. Wow. A night out? Well, yes, she could really do with a night out. Not that she was any good at quizzes of course and Sonny must be mad to invite her, but a night out was a night out after all. And the chip shop happened to be shut on a Monday so no worries there.

'Well, yes I guess so,' said Kim. 'Well, of course. I'd love to come to a quiz. But I have to warn you that I'm pretty rubbish. I mean, I have zero general knowledge. Are you sure you want me to be on your team?'

'Oh, I've not invited you for your general knowledge,' he said. 'Do you think Annie would like to come?'

Kim had to smile. Of course, she wasn't being invited for her knowledge, she was being invited because she worked with Annie and Sonny fancied Annie and inviting Kim allowed him to invite Annie.

'I don't know,' replied Kim. 'You'd better ask Max.'

'Ask me what?' shouted Max. 'Sorry, no jobs at the moment. I for once have a fully competent and reliable workforce.'

'No, I don't want a job,' said Sonny. 'I haven't got time for a job.'

'But aren't you a student?' asked Max.

'Exactly,' said Sonny.

'Then I'd have said you have all the time in the world but there you go. So what did you want to ask me?'

'You know that girl who works here? The really pretty one who dresses like a Hollywood starlet?'

'You mean my daughter?' replied Max.

Sonny's jaw dropped. 'You didn't tell me that,' he mouthed at Kim.

'I'm sorry . . . I-I-I didn't realise,' stuttered Sonny. 'But now you have said, I can see the family resemblance.'

'You think I look like a Hollywood starlet?'

'No . . . no, just you have the same . . . the same . . . hairline.'

Max was wiping his hands and coming out from behind the counter. Kim noticed Sonny go pale.

'So what did you want to ask her?' he said.

'I wanted to ask her if she would like to join our quiz team next Monday night at the pub. Kim's coming, aren't you Kim, so it'll be, you know, like a family, fun thing, not like a . . . a date or anything.'

Max nodded. 'So you won't mind if I come too then,' he said, 'if it's not like a date thing?'

Sonny's eyes flared wide. 'No, of course not, if you want to come that would be just brilliant.' He looked at Kim in a panic.

'I happen to be partial to a quiz,' said Max. 'So I'll come and see if Annie wants to come too. If not it will just be me. I assume that's okay?'

'Of course, Annie's dad,' Sonny replied.

'You can call me Max,' he said. 'What time is it?'

'Starts at seven,' said Sonny, 'although me and my housemates are going straight from uni so we'll be in there from about six.'

'Is Harry coming?' asked Kim.

Sonny turned to her almost as if he had forgotten she was there.

He nodded. 'And Suki, but Angus said not to tell him I'm inviting you; you know after his outburst earlier. We thought, well, we thought he might not come if we told him.'

Kim nodded.

'Just a lovely fun family evening then,' said Max.

'That's the plan,' said Sonny. 'That's the plan.'

Chapter 16

Kim had spent all day feeling anxious about the pub quiz. She realised she was only really invited in order to get Annie there, but knowing that Harry and Suki were also going to be there, she didn't want to screw it up. This was a social occasion where she might just get the chance to have an easy-going conversation with her son. How amazing would that be? After a day binge-watching *Tipping Point* in the vain hope a question might come up and she might look vaguely intelligent, at 6.45 p.m. she pulled a clean T-shirt over her head, zipped up her hoody and headed off to call on Max so they could arrive together.

Max hadn't confirmed if Annie was coming too so Kim was pleased to see her waiting outside the chip shop with her dad and even more pleased to see that she hadn't followed Kim's dress code. Her hair, as always, was beautifully piled up on her head complete with a green bow perched on the front. She wore a very smart green forties style dress coat and was sporting some funky winged glasses. She also, as ever, wore a smile that never failed to make Kim smile back.

'You been revising?' asked Annie, blowing on her hands to keep warm.

'Might have watched a few episodes of *Tipping Point*,' said Kim. 'So I'm really hoping that counts.'

'We're in the midst of twentieth-century cubism at college,' she replied. 'I reckon there will be a few questions on that so I'm feeling pretty smug.'

'I've read all the back pages of the paper today, so I'm all over that sporting category,' said Max. 'I reckon we'll give those university nerds a run for their money. Shall we go, team?' he said. Kim couldn't help grinning. It felt so good to be part of something even if it was just a pub quiz team.

The rest of their team members were already a couple of pints ahead of them when they arrived. Thankfully Sonny had already let the cat out of the bag as to who was joining them. Harry nodded at his mum when she walked in and rose to shake Max's hand when Sonny did his introductions.

'This is Annie,' he said excitedly. 'The girl I told you about. Here, sit next to me, Annie, here. And this is Max, Annie's dad, although I didn't realise he was Annie's dad until last week, but then when you look at them you can see they have the same hairline. And you all know Kim, of course you all know Kim. And this is Suki, she's err, Harry's friend. Have I got that right, Harry? You are friends, right?'

'Yes,' said Harry through gritted teeth.

'You met Suki, didn't you, Kim, or did you? Can't remember.'

Kim felt herself go red. She could remember vividly meeting Suki. Just before she'd thrown up all over Angus's shoes.

'We've met,' said Kim, nodding at Suki. 'And I'm so sorry, still, I mean, I hope Harry apologised for my behaviour that night. It was totally out of character and . . . and it's never happened again and never will . . .'

'What happened?' asked Max, sitting down.

Oh no, thought Kim. She'd didn't want to drag that all up now.

'Of course, that's when Kim threw up all over the floor,' said Sonny, slapping his forehead. 'But we have set some rules up since then, haven't we? We said if Kim wanted to stay she had to not treat the house like a hotel, buy her own food and drink . . . what were the other ones?'

'I believe we said she couldn't talk to any women who came to the house?' added Angus, arching his eyebrows at Kim.

'Oh no,' said Suki. 'I hope that wasn't because of me, was it? I mean it was fine, honestly. Harry told me what you had been going through.'

'It wasn't because of you,' said Sonny. 'It was because she told a girl that Angus bought back to the house that he already had a girlfriend, when he didn't.'

'Wow, you really made an impact in that house,' said Max, grinning.

'Not since,' said Kim. 'Ever since I have abided by the rules and tried to stay out of everyone's way. That's what

I have been doing.' She looked at Harry. He gave her a glimmer of a nod. She allowed herself to heave a very small sigh of relief.

'Well it's good to have you on the team tonight,' said Suki.

Kim could have hugged her. 'I hope I won't let you down,' she said. 'I mean, Harry's probably told you that I never went to university or anything so I hope you are not expecting too much?'

'Aah, I reckon that's all bollocks,' piped up Max. 'I reckon us non students will turn out to be a lot more switched on than these so-called clever people. Now, can I get a round in as the only full-time earning person here actually contributing to the economy?'

'Yes please,' piped up all the students round the table.

Sonny handed Kim the picture round that had been circulated to all the teams prior to the quiz starting. On it were a number of photographs of celebrity faces, some well known and some not so well known. Each team needed to write underneath each picture who they thought it was. The sheets would be marked at the end of the quiz then the number of correct answers added to their final score.

Kim looked at the sheet. Many of the answers had already been filled in by those who had been there earlier. She looked through them, some she recognised, some she didn't, until she spotted one that she thought might be incorrect. Someone had written William Shatner of *Star Trek* fame, but looking closely after she had dug her reading glasses out of her bag she was pretty convinced it was Lee Majors who actually starred as the Six Million Dollar Man back in the seventies.

She looked up wondering if she dared contest the answer. She wasn't sure who had written it down. If it was Harry it would be a bad move. He wouldn't want her showing him up. But it didn't look like his writing, it was far too neat. She peered at the picture again. Yes, it was definitely Lee Majors, she thought. No doubt about it.

'You know, I reckon this one is actually Lee Majors,' she said to the group. 'I don't think it's William Shatner.'

'Oh,' said Suki, taking the sheet back off her. 'Are you sure? I grew up watching *Star Trek* with my dad. It was our thing. I was sure it was William Shatner.'

Now Kim felt really bad. She'd dissed Harry's girlfriend's/not girlfriend's answer.

'Well I'm sure you're right then,' said Kim. Happy to step back but then instantly worrying about Suki if she was humiliated when they found out it was actually Lee Majors.

'Who's Lee Majors anyway?' asked Angus. 'Never heard of him.'

'Oh, he was in a big TV show in the seventies, I think, called *The Six Million Dollar Man*,' said Kim.

'So was it the *Billions* then of the seventies? Was he super rich?' asked Sonny. 'God, I love that show.'

'No,' said Kim. 'No, he had like bionic implants so he had superpowers. He could run super-fast and he had super long vision and bionic hearing, I seem to remember.'

'So like a Marvel hero?' asked Suki.

'Well no. Not really. I mean, he didn't have a costume

or anything and I don't think he could tell anyone he had these superpowers. And I seem to remember he finished every episode in the bath outside his ranch. Or was that *The Fall Guy*?'

'*The Fall Guy*?' asked Sonny.

'Another show Lee Majors was in. I think. It was a long time ago.'

'Well we should put Lee Majors on the sheet,' said Suki. 'I'm sure you must be right. I mean, I wasn't even born then.'

Thanks for pointing that out, thought Kim.

'No, you should leave William Shatner on,' said Harry. 'You were really certain when you said it and Mum, well her memory isn't that great.'

'But your mum is of that era,' protested Suki. 'She must be right.'

Oh God, thought Kim. *Please don't force him to choose between his mum and his new girlfriend/not girlfriend*. That would be a nightmare. Maybe it had been a bad idea to come. A pub quiz was guaranteed to cause arguments between the closest of friends and family.

Max arrived back at the table with Annie and a trayful of drinks. As they were handing them round, Sonny came up with the bright idea of asking Max.

'As one of our older teammates,' said Sonny to Max. 'Do you think that's William Shatner?' he asked, pointing at the picture.

Max squinted, then got his glasses out of his pocket and looked again.

'Sure,' he said with a shrug. 'I reckon so.'

'Well there you go then,' said Kim. 'Must be him.'

'Why, who did you think it was?' asked Max.

'Well I just thought it might be Lee Majors,' said Kim. 'You know, the Six Million Dollar Man?'

Max took a long drag of his pint before he looked again.

'I think you might be right,' he said. 'I'd forgotten all about that show but now you've said it, I think it is.'

'Think, or sure?' asked Angus.

'Erm,' said Max, taking another look. 'I think it is Lee Majors. Yes, definitely Lee Majors.'

'Is that your final answer?' asked Angus.

Max looked slightly scared but stuck to his guns. 'Yes, final answer,' he confirmed before taking another long drag of his pint, giving Kim a quizzical look.

'Sorry, Suki,' said Angus, taking the pen and putting a line through her answer and writing Lee Majors. 'You guys had better be right,' he warned Max and Kim.

She looked at Suki apologetically. She looked unfazed but Harry was frowning. Kim prayed they were right as well.

Kim spent the rest of the evening trying to only interject to confirm someone else's answer or to offer a guess when there was clearly nothing else on the table. She didn't want to put herself in the firing line to be responsible for another answer. Oh no.

She almost sighed with relief when they announced a science and nature round. She could totally sit this one out and be excused of any responsibility.

'I'm useless on anything to do with science,' she said,

holding her hands up before a question had even been asked. 'I'm not the scientist in our family. Harry's the one doing the science degree. This is your round, Harry.'

Harry reluctantly took the sheet off Angus in order to be in charge of writing the answers down.

'Not my thing either,' said Suki. 'Not much call for science in an art degree.'

'Are you doing art?' asked Annie, turning to her. 'Do you like it? I've applied for next year after I finish my foundation.'

'Oh really?' said Suki. 'It's a really good course. I love it. But I wish I'd done a foundation though. That's so smart. The foundation undergrads are so much better prepared than the rest of us who came straight from school.'

'I honestly can't wait,' said Annie, her eyes shining. 'As long as I get in, of course.'

'Harry says you're a hairdresser,' said Suki to Kim to try and include her in the conversation. 'That must be so interesting.'

Crikey, this girl was absolutely lovely. Kim prayed that Harry would make a move and marry her.

'It is, really,' said Kim. 'But I am a bit jealous listening to you all. I do sometimes wonder what would have happened if I'd have thought it possible to spread my wings a bit. Can you believe this is the first time I've lived outside of my home town my entire life?'

Suki shook her head. 'I couldn't wait to get out of Kettering,' she said.

'I miss Devon,' said Sonny. 'But you don't get YO!

Sushi in Devon and now I don't know how I've survived without it.'

'Nottingham's a bit shit compared to Edinburgh,' said Angus. 'But only because there's too many English about.'

'My dad really wanted me to go to Durham,' said Harry. 'That's where he studied chemistry, but I'm glad I ended up here,' he said. Kim noticed him glance at Suki. That was a good sign.

'You are way too thick to get into Durham,' piped up Angus.

'Cheers, mate,' said Harry with a sigh. 'You are not wrong.'

'And they are all arseholes,' continued Angus. 'Poppy went for an interview there. She said they were all English wankers. She might not have said wankers but that's what she meant.'

'Did you go to university, Max?' Sonny asked.

'God no,' said Max nearly spitting his beer out. 'What do they call it? The University of Life. That's where I went.'

'Oh,' replied Sonny. 'Where is that?'

Max stared at Sonny in disbelief. 'All around you, my friend,' he said. 'All around you.' He grinned at Kim. 'Reckon education is wasted on the young, don't you?' he asked.

'Not at all,' she replied. 'I think I just wasted being young.'

They were a few drinks down by the time they got to the last round. Kim had started to relax a little although her contribution to the quiz had not improved. She was relying on Lee Majors to come through for her at the end. But her ears pricked up when they announced the subject of the final round. Music! Maybe now she could add some value.

The quizmaster played intros to famous songs. The first few were ones she had never heard of but all the younger ones seemed to have. She gave a sad look to Max. They actually stood no chance in this round whatsoever.

But then Max pricked his ears up. It was vaguely familiar to her but she could not have said who it was or the name of the song. The rest of the table also looked perplexed. Apart from Annie. Annie was grinning from ear to ear looking at her dad. They both stood up and started doing a little jig as the intro built before they collapsed into giggles at the end.

'Wow, that was amazing,' said Sonny. 'Will you teach me that routine?' he asked Max.

'Err no,' said Max. 'Absolutely not.'

'So what's the song?' asked Harry who was still holding the pen.

'Go on, Dad,' said Annie, grinning. 'You tell them.'

'It's Justin Bieber,' said Max, 'and it's called "Love Yourself".'

'Hell yeah, Dad,' said Annie, giving him a high five.

'I have to admit it's a great track,' said Max.

'You will never regret the time you spent with me and Justin,' said Annie.

'Never,' said Max, smiling back at his daughter.

Kim watched jealously as Max and Annie shared a special moment. The sooner her and Harry found their

Justin Bieber, Kim thought, the better. She would put some serious thought into working out what, or who it could be, next week.

The quiz was coming to a close and the quizmaster had announced the scores on the doors prior to revealing the results of the all-important picture round. 'The Oldies and The Goodies', the team name that Angus had conjured up for them, were doing very well, sitting right up near the top of the leaderboard, mainly thanks to a blinding sporting round which Max had totally nailed and a remarkably flawless music round given the breadth of ages in their team.

Now it all hung on the picture round.

Kim felt a knot in her stomach. She prayed that Lee Majors was not going to let her down.

They swapped sheets with the next table who were their main rivals, a table of locals who had given the young students the odd dirty look when they got over-excited. Max had glared back at them on their behalf.

Harry marked their sheet as the answers were called out by the quizmaster. Annie was delighted with her correct identification of Greta Garbo and Angus did a fist bump when the grainy portrait of Robbie Burns gave them another tick where their neighbours had failed.

Kim was annoyed when she realised she hadn't spoken up and made a guess at an eighties soap opera actress. She hadn't been absolutely sure and was also embarrassed in this esteemed company to admit that she used to watch the soaps. Sadly, it lost them the lead as their neighbours drew level, and so it inevitably all came down to Lee Majors or William Shatner.

'They put William Shatner,' Harry announced, nodding his head at the table next to them, his pen poised over their paper.

'I'm so sorry if I'm wrong,' Kim said to the team. She felt physically sick.

'It's all right,' said Suki, touching her arm. 'It's just a quiz.'

Was it though? This could be her totally showing her son up in front of all his friends.

'And so for the final answer of the night,' announced the quizmaster. 'Sometimes trips people up, this one. The last picture on the sheet is . . . '

Kim held her breath.

'It's actually Lee Majors. How many of you wrote down William Shatner?'

The table erupted. Sonny leapt out of his seat, taking the opportunity to fling his arms around Annie. Angus raised both fists in the air in the direction of the table next to them. Harry ceremoniously put a cross on the paper and handed it back to the next table. Max raised his glass in congratulations to Kim.

Kim had never been more relieved in her life. Thank goodness for all those hours wasted watching telly in her youth.

'It's a good job you were here,' Suki said to her.

'Damn good job,' said Angus, clinking her glass. 'What a team! What a team! Damn good job you were here.'

Kim grinned. For the first time in a while she felt like it was.

Chapter 17

It took another week for Kim and Harry's Justin Bieber to arrive on the scene. However, it wasn't quite the Justin Bieber she was envisaging. Turned out she was going to be forced to engage with her son on a much more serious level.

It all started when Richard's name flashed up on her phone screen. She didn't know if she wanted to answer it. The triumph of the pub quiz had successfully blurred away her thoughts for a while on Richard. She didn't know if she wanted them back in focus.

The ringing stopped. She'd dithered over answering for too long. Then it immediately started again. She sighed and tapped the button responding with a non-committal, 'Hello.'

Richard was breathing heavily as though he were trying to calm down or had been for a run, which was extremely unlikely.

'I've just had a message left for me,' he said without any introduction. 'It was John Sinclair from Harry's university. This is really very serious, Kim. What the hell is going on down there?'

He paused like she should understand instantly what he was getting at. All she could muster was that he was criticising her in some way which was unfathomable and extremely uncalled for in the circumstances.

'I have no idea what you are talking about,' she replied.

'John said that Harry isn't turning up,' said Richard.

'Isn't turning up where?'

'At uni. He's not been to any tutorials since the start of term and he suspects he's not going to any lectures. John also said he hasn't turned in any work.'

'Who's John?' she asked, struggling to keep up.

'Harry's tutor.'

'Right.' How was she supposed to know that? Was a mother supposed to know the name of her son's tutor? Was that a thing? Was it yet another thing that she didn't know about university life? And what was going on then? She couldn't understand. Harry was leaving the house every day.

'Have you just let him wallow in bed every day?' accused Richard. 'I'd have thought the least you could do if you insist on living with our son during his first term at university would be to make sure he actually goes?'

Kim was speechless. When would Richard realise it was his fault they were all in this situation, not hers?

'He leaves the house every day,' she protested. 'What am I supposed to do? Take him up there and hold his hand until he walks into the room?'

Richard was quiet for a moment. Kim's mind was whirring. What was going on? Where was he going if he wasn't going to uni? Why wasn't he going to uni? It was all her fault. Of course it was all her fault.

'Have you not asked him how's he getting on?' said Richard. 'How's his course going? Basic questions like that?'

Kim shook her head. 'Of course I have,' she snapped. 'Well I've tried but . . . but . . . he snaps my head off. Says I'm interfering so I've backed off. It's . . . it's complicated. The last thing I want to do is crowd him right now. Come over as the overbearing mother.'

'You are living with him during his first term at university. If that isn't the definition of overbearing mother I don't know what is,' replied Richard.

'But I'm not living with him to keep an eye on him, am I?' protested Kim. 'I'm living with him because I have no choice. Because my husband cheated on me with my next door neighbour.'

Richard's heavy breathing returned. 'But you didn't have to move in with Harry. You didn't have to do that. Why didn't you go to one of your friends, or your family?'

Kim swallowed. Did Richard not think she went over this a million times a day in her own head?

'Because I couldn't face them. I couldn't face any of them. Not after that speech I made at your party. Not after you made such a fool of me.'

Richard was silent.

Kim didn't fill the gap.

'I'm sorry,' he said.

Kim thought she had misheard.

'My timing wasn't great,' he added.

Inexplicably, the image of him wearing *that* coat popped up in her head. The coat he had bought with Alison on his amazing shopping trip to Manchester. Was he wearing it now? She wanted to ask him but didn't want to know the answer.

'They could chuck him out,' stated Richard when Kim didn't say anything. 'They'd be well within their rights to chuck him out if he doesn't show up.'

'They can't do that, surely?' said Kim. She felt herself start to panic. She couldn't let that happen to Harry. She would never forgive herself. 'What was the tutor's name again?' she asked.

'John Sinclair.'

'And you've tried getting hold of him?'

'Yes. But the number just rings which is pretty poor. Not even an answerphone. Mind you, I read his last research paper and I can't say it was very inspiring. Not sure he's actually got a good grasp of his field.'

'I'll go and see him,' said Kim, ignoring Richard's comments on the quality of John Sinclair's tutelage. Richard probably could have been condescending about Stephen Hawkins' brain power. 'I'm here so I'll go and find him, explain what's been happening. Tell him to cut Harry some slack.'

'You are going to tell him what exactly?'

'I don't know. That he's got PTSD or something? Anything to stop this John Sinclair bloke throwing him off the course.'

'Harry doesn't have PTSD,' said Richard.

'He might do. His father sleeping with the next door neighbour is enough to give someone PTSD, isn't it?'

Richard gasped on the other end of the line. 'I think you'll find that there are far more serious incidents that trigger PTSD. Like being on the front line of a war or prolonged abuse. I hardly think our affairs would be seen as a big enough trauma to cause Harry to have PTSD.'

'What do you mean "our affairs"? Only you had an affair. Not me.'

'Oh, you know what I mean. I meant our circumstances. Our position.'

Kim could sense Richard getting exasperated with her. She could feel her anger rising.

'Okay then, I won't say he has PTSD. I'll just say his father had an affair and so that's why he's all over the place and that he needs help and support rather than getting chucked off the course.'

'That's totally unfair to blame me. I don't want my name dragging through the mud in the faculty. These things get round. Can't you just explain that you are living with him and this is causing him some distress and affecting his ability to turn up to his lectures.'

'Ooh, that sounds good,' said Kim. 'I'll write that down, shall I? Now just tell me how to spell lectures?'

'L . . . E . . . '

'I was joking,' raged Kim. 'I will go down there and explain Harry's circumstances and ask John Sinclair for help and support.'

'But you won't tell him about . . . about . . . ' hesitated Richard.

'Damn right I'll tell him you had an affair with another member of staff at your university, so is it any wonder that Harry has a slight phobia of setting foot on any kind of campus at the moment.'

She pulled her phone away from her ear and pressed the end call button.

Her phone immediately lit up with Richard's name, trying to call her back. She rejected the call and put her phone on silent, throwing it on the sofa and heading to the kitchen to make a strong coffee and to think.

After her anger at Richard had subsided she tried to put her contempt aside and work out how to tackle the problem at hand.

She needed to talk to Harry. But . . . she was fearful that he wouldn't tell her anything and zero progress would be made. Worse, he would be angry and it would further damage their fragile relationship. She needed intervention from another angle. Perhaps she should ask Sonny or Angus. See if they could have a word with him. Find out what was happening. Yes, that was a good idea.

No, it was a rubbish idea, she decided sometime later. She couldn't use Sonny or Angus as a go-between. Not fair on them or Harry. What if it soured Harry's relationship with them? He clearly got on well with them. She couldn't do anything to jeopardise that. No, she should go through the official channels. Keep it all above board. She'd go and see Harry's tutor, John Sinclair, and get to the bottom of it. See if he could help. That was the sensible thing to do.

However, calling clearly didn't work. Richard had failed there. She had no choice but to go in and see him.

Track him down before they made a decision on Harry's future that they couldn't pull back from.

She would venture onto campus and find John Sinclair. It was a prospect that filled her with horror. The few times she had ventured onto the campus at Lancaster City University for functions with Richard she felt like she had a massive sign over her head saying 'No degree', and that everyone was looking at her as though she wasn't clever enough to be there. She absolutely knew that she would feel exactly the same at Nottingham. Whilst some people feared hospitals and the way they made them feel, Kim had exactly the same feeling about university campuses. Like she wanted to get away as soon as possible.

She googled 'John Sinclair, Chemistry, Nottingham Barton University' and soon tracked down where the science faculty seemed to be based on the campus. She knew that there was a bus that went from the end of the road several times a day. She went upstairs, had a shower to calm her nerves and then contemplated her wardrobe. She wanted serious, intelligent, confident. Sadly when Vicky had come up and brought her extra clothes she hadn't deemed any such outfits useful for her current situation. Vicky delivered only party gear and outfits to have fun in. Kim didn't think the backless sequined dress would send the appropriate signals to Harry's tutor. After much contemplation she settled on a silver cardigan which she tried to tone down with a white fitted T-shirt and some smart black trousers. It was more Christmas drinks after work with your colleagues than meeting with your son's university tutor but it was the best she could do. She picked up her bag and left the house, hoping she wasn't going to do something that she would later regret.

The minute she boarded the bus she regretted the silver cardigan. Everyone was dressed in dark, serious colours and looked a bit scruffy. They were also all student age. She'd never felt so old and overdressed in her life. Sadly the only shoes to go with the smart black trousers were some black patent court shoes which contrasted horrendously with the practical boots and flat shoes that adorned every other person on the bus.

She practised what she was going to say to John Sinclair over and over in her head, staring out of the window, not wanting to catch the eye of any of her fellow travellers, fearing their puzzled looks as to why on earth someone who looked like her was on her way to a higher education establishment.

She followed everyone's lead when they poured out of the bus at the entrance to the campus. She looked around, bewildered. She'd studied the map online of the layout but in the flesh it looked entirely different and she couldn't see any signs or handy maps. What they needed was one like they had at theme parks, she decided, with intelligence restrictions for each area rather than height restrictions. She knew she would have to ask for help which filled her with no joy at all.

'Excuse me,' she said to a group of girls heading down some steps towards her. 'Could you tell me where the science block is? Block, I mean err, faculty?' Christ, she sounded like she was at a local comprehensive.

She was sure universities didn't call their buildings anything as basic as a block.

'So it's past the new theatre,' a very smiley girl piped up. 'You go all the way down this path and turn left at the end and you'll be in an open quad next to the library, and science is next to the library. I can take you if you want?' she grinned.

'Oh God, no,' replied Kim. 'That's really kind, but I'm sure I'll be okay. Thank you.'

'No worries,' said the girl and went to catch up with her friends.

Kim thought she must look like a total imbecile if the girl was worried about her getting from one side of the campus to another.

She continued down the path indicated by the girl and soon found herself in front of the library and confronted by the space age-looking structure of the science faculty. The building sported brave and funky architecture with statuesque pillars and soaring glass windows. Nothing like the grubby sixties science block she remembered from her school days. This was a building to inspire the next generation of scientists if ever she saw one rather than inspire them to use a Bunsen burner to set light to a wooden stool in order to stay warm.

She spotted that people were using access cards to get into the building. Well, some were. She realised that if she just joined onto the back of a crowd entering at the same time then they would hold the door open, allowing as many people to glide in unannounced as desired. She joined onto a gaggle of male students and smiled gratefully as one at the back held the door open for her. She suddenly panicked thinking what if Harry saw her here. He would go absolutely ballistic – until she realised the reason she was here was because he wasn't coming here so she was very unlikely to bump into him.

The grand foyer of the building was awash with indoor plants and funky seating where students were gathered, no doubt discussing scientific things. It was so lovely. Not what she was expecting at all. She couldn't imagine why Harry would not want to spend his time here.

She spotted a large sign with pictures of all the staff on it. She walked towards it and gazed up, searching for Mr John Sinclair. She soon spotted him. He was older than she expected. Maybe late fifties, early sixties. Grey hair, glasses (of course), he was smiling at least, which was more than could be said for some of them. He looked fairly normal for a lecturer. But then she supposed that Richard looked normal until she started talking to him and you realised he had one massive brain.

Now what?

She noticed a sign at the bottom of a staircase and quickly located that chemistry appeared to be on the first floor. Maybe she would find Mr John Sinclair there, or at least some kind of reception or secretary that might track him down for her.

She headed up the stairs and turned right following further signs. Through another foyer with funky seating and a botanical tribute to life on earth but sadly no reception or administration type person to guide her on her way. She wandered down a corridor reading out plaques on doors. Kitchen, Storeroom, Faraday, Einstein, Pasteur until she started seeing full names, not just the surnames of famous scientists. She wondered if, when they made their amazing discoveries, they dreamed of having their names on doors in universities the world over. She kept following the doors of full names hoping that these were the offices of the lecturers and if she kept going, she might just chance upon John Sinclair. And she did. Suddenly she was stood in front of John Sinclair's door, her heart beating wildly as she wondered if she dared knock, totally unannounced. She'd be hoping it might be a bit like going to A&E. You'd arrive, give your name and your problem and then you'd be sent to triage to ascertain the best way to solve it. Once through triage you'd get to your final destination fully prepared and ready to present your problem to the exact person who would make it go away, that person having already been briefed on exactly why you were there.

Meeting the person who you wanted to solve your problem totally cold, with them having no idea who you were or why you were there was terrifying. She wanted someone to introduce her first. Do the preamble and then she could dive in. Her doing the introduction was not what she had planned for.

She took a deep breath and knocked. She couldn't walk away. Her son's future depended on it.

There were a few seconds' delay before the door was pulled open. There was John Sinclair but he was not alone. Two students were perched on chairs next to a low table behind him. Oh my goodness. Had she just interrupted some terribly important conversation? She felt herself go red.

'I'm so sorry,' she said. 'So sorry, really, I'll go. I'll come back another time. Really.'

'Are you Steph?' asked John Sinclair. 'Don't worry, they said you would pop in today. Come in, sit down.' He stood to one side and gestured for her to go in. 'We were actually just discussing the law of conservation of mass. No doubt you'd have some interesting comments to make on that one.' He chuckled as though he'd executed a fabulous in-joke of the highest scientific level. 'Come on in, Steph. This is Joshua and Louis. Two of our finest second years. This is Doctor Steph Albon, a visiting lecturer from Cambridge.'

'No, no,' cried Kim, now feeling herself shaking. 'I'm not Doctor Steph, I'm Kim Jacobs, I'm, I'm a visiting hairdresser from Lancaster,' she blustered. What did she have to go and say that for? Probably desperation that she wouldn't get caught up in some heavyweight conversation about the conservation of something.

John Sinclair's eyes were wide, as were Joshua's and Louis's, sat behind him.

'And pray tell what can I do for Kim Jacobs, the visiting hairdresser from Lancaster?' said John Sinclair with a smile emerging on his lips. 'I have absolutely no doubt you would also have some interesting views on the law of conservation of mass should you like to join us?'

'Oh crikey no,' she cried. 'No idea, not a clue. Nothing. I have nothing to say on conservation whatsoever. I just was hoping to, err, catch you and talk to you about my son Harry Jacobs, but I'll come back another time. If that's all right, of course.'

'Your son?' asked John Sinclair, screwing his face up. 'Oh yes, of course, I know who you mean. First year.' He looked at Kim in astonishment. 'Have you come all the way from Lancaster this morning? I only left your husband a message a few hours ago.'

'Err, no,' she said. 'No, actually I live in Nottingham, kind of, sort of, it's complicated, you see. That's what I wanted to talk to you about. About my son and well . . . ' she glanced nervously over at Joshua and Louis who were openly staring at her.

'Yes, right, okay, yes,' said John Sinclair, scratching his head. Clearly the penny had just dropped as to why she was there, despite the confusion of her introduction. She knew she'd needed triage.

'How did you find me?' he asked.

'I err, I err, googled you and then just sort of came looking,' she replied.

'Fair enough,' he said, nodding. 'Right, okey dokey, what to do?' He looked Kim up and down. Kim yet again regretted her sparkling silver cardigan.

'I'll come back another time,' she said. 'If that's okay. I'm sorry to just turn up. I just didn't know what to do.'

'No, no,' said John, clearly not used to his students' mothers turning up at his door. 'Right, why don't you give me your number and I'll call you and we'll work out what to do, how's that?'

'Really? Is that okay?' she asked.

'Really,' nodded John Sinclair, grinning. 'Write it on here and I'll call and we can talk then.'

'Brilliant,' said Kim, grasping the pen and paper from him. 'That's really so kind of you. Really.'

'The pleasure's all mine,' he said, taking the paper from her and smiling warmly. 'Now I'd better get back to teaching these knuckleheads something.' He nodded at Joshua and Louis.

'Of course,' she said, backing away. 'So sorry to interrupt.'

'Speak soon,' John Sinclair said, waving and closing the door with a broad smile.

Well, that could have gone worse, she thought to herself as she exited the building. Progress had been made and he'd been very smiley. Yes, she had definitely done the right thing coming. Even though parts of it had been quite humiliating. If it saved Harry's place here then it would be all worthwhile.

Chapter 18

Kim felt a bit shell-shocked sitting on the bus on the way home. Stepping into Harry's world had been unsettling. But then again she had no familiar environments at the moment. None whatsoever. Being in the university felt just the same as everywhere else. Unusual, unfamiliar and as though she didn't belong. As she wistfully looked out the bus window she wondered if she would ever feel like she belonged anywhere ever again.

It would be wrong to say that she didn't feel just a bit tearful, just a bit emotional when she turned her key in the door of the house. She could hear voices coming from the kitchen as she pushed the door closed behind her. A deep voice. A man's voice. Not one of the boys. She was tempted to just go straight to her room but she supposed she had just better check they hadn't been invaded by a chatty burglar.

When she stepped in the kitchen she immediately regretted it. There was a man there. Pacing up and down the kitchen on his mobile phone, talking in a concerned voice. A woman was perched on a chair at the table. Immaculate in a two-piece suit. She'd clearly just had an excellent blow dry and her makeup was perfect. Natural but you knew it was there. And then leaning against a countertop stood Angus, chewing his nails, looking slightly nervous. Which was new. She'd not seen that look on him before. When she walked in he looked up at her in horror. He gave her a pleading look and then turned to his mother.

'So err . . . ' he faltered. 'I forgot to mention. This is Kim. She lives with us.' He gave Kim another pleading look that Kim had no idea how to fathom. What did he want her to do or say? 'This is my mum, Lorraine, and my dad, Duncan,' he continued, nodding at the man still on a mobile phone pacing up and down.

'Oh,' said Lorraine, standing up. 'Are you a mature student?'

Kim glanced at Angus. He shrugged. What did a shrug mean? She had no idea.

'No, actually,' she said. 'I'm Harry's mum. Harry who also lives here.'

Lorraine looked at her son with a quizzical look. Angus offered her nothing by means of explanation so Kim was forced to plough on.

'I'm staying in the spare room for a while. Not for long. Just until Christmas. Just until I get myself sorted out.'

Lorraine's eyebrows flew up.

'Sorted out of what?' she asked.

'Just, erm . . . ' Kim sighed. She really didn't want to be going into the detail. 'Just a tricky domestic situation.'

Oh goodness, thought Kim, now this woman would think she was being abused or something. She couldn't bear that. 'Me and my husband split up and I'm staying here temporarily.' She hoped that covered it.

Lorraine had sat back down in her chair looking a little pale as she gazed around the kitchen, perhaps trying to make sense of the situation.

'I realise that perhaps it's a shock to see me here and I'm sorry about that, especially if Angus hadn't mentioned it.'

Lorraine turned to look at her, her eyes still like saucers. 'What I absolutely don't understand,' she said in her gentle Scottish accent, 'is how you let them live like this.' She cast her hand around the room. Kim turned her gaze to what she was indicating. The kitchen was in its usual state of chaos. It was completely tidy the day before. She'd seen to it, as agreed, but it only took a day for dirty pots to be piled everywhere, the butter to be open and out on the counter and a Chinese takeaway carton left on the table behind Lorraine spewing chow mein over its edges. It was disgusting but Kim knew none of it was her mess. It was all down to the three boys and their hideous habits in just twenty-four hours.

'Duncan is on the phone to an industrial cleaning company right now,' said Lorraine. 'To fix this mess.'

She got up from her chair and strode over to Duncan and tapped him on the shoulder. 'Duncan. You can get off the phone. We don't need them anymore.'

'What?' said Duncan, pulling the phone away from his ear.

'Look,' said Lorraine, pointing at Kim. 'We don't need them to come now.'

Duncan shrugged and made his excuses on the phone before stepping forward and shaking Kim's hand vigorously.

'So there is a cleaner, brilliant,' he said. 'Right. Can we take you out for some lunch now then, son, now that that crisis is over?'

It was time for Kim's eyes to be like saucers. 'No, no, I'm not the cleaner.' She looked at Lorraine, bewildered. 'I'm Harry's mum, Kim. I live here. That's what I do. Just like the rest of them. I do clean as part of the agreement for me staying here and I can assure you that this place was tidy yesterday, but this is what happens in a student house with three boys over twenty-four hours.'

Lorraine looked back at her, still confused. 'Yes, but how have you let it get in this state?' she said. 'How can you live like this?'

'I haven't let it get in this state,' said Kim. 'They have.' Kim looked at Angus for some admission of culpability or for help in explaining the simple fact to his mother that he didn't clean up in the kitchen.

'But I just don't see how a woman of your age could live in a kitchen in this state,' said Lorraine. 'Surely you would have to do something about it?'

Kim didn't know what to say. She felt indignant that Lorraine could not see the unfairness of what she was saying. That her son Angus was let off all accountability for his actions because there was a female in the house who would of course clear up after him.

'Why didn't you tell us that someone's mother was living in the house?' Lorraine said, turning to her son.

'Harry,' interjected Kim. 'His name is Harry, and I'm Kim.'

'It never came up, did it?' said Angus. 'And it's no big deal,' he shrugged.

'You may have already covered this,' said Duncan, 'but can I ask why you are living in your son's student house share?'

'My husband had an affair with the next door neighbour, if you must know,' said Kim, exasperated. 'So I'm staying here just for a while until I get myself sorted.'

'Oh,' said Duncan, looking Kim up and down like she was a piece of furniture. 'Shouldn't we have been informed of that or something? Is that allowed?'

'Jesus,' said Kim under her breath. 'I'm a middle-aged woman. You could have had a whacked-out weirdo studying an ology who deals drugs in his spare time.'

Lorraine blinked at her then looked over at Angus. 'Tell me there has been no drugs in this house.'

Angus sighed. 'Of course not, Mother,' he said.

'Or anywhere else?' she asked.

'No!' said Angus firmly. 'I mean, there are drugs around, like everywhere, but I haven't done any.'

Lorraine shook her head. 'I knew we shouldn't have let you go to an English university,' she said.

Angus shook his head. 'You think there are no drugs at Scottish universities?' he said. 'Seriously?'

'If you'd got your results you could have been at St Andrews, not here,' she said looking around at the mess.

'Living in this squalor.' She looked at Kim again as though it was all her fault.

'Well,' said Duncan, clapping his hands together. 'As long as the whole cleaning debacle is sorted then it must be lunchtime. Where are we going, son? Let us give you a good feed, shall we? Tell you what, let's all go. How about it?'

He flashed Kim a smile. Well actually Kim noticed he flashed her chest a smile. She swallowed. Perhaps she was wrong. Perhaps he didn't. No, he can't have done.

'I reckon we need to get to know Kim, don't you?' he said, looking at his wife. 'If she's living with our son.' He moved across and put his arm around her shoulders. She instantly froze.

'And,' he said squeezing her shoulders, 'she can fill us in on all Angus has been up to. I bet there are some stories, aren't there?' he said. 'I bet my lad has been up to some shenanigans, hey? How many girls have you had back here then, son? Come on, tell us the truth. I bet you've had to turn a blind eye to some goings-on, hey Lynn?'

'It's Kim,' she said, stepping to the side. 'We all keep ourselves to ourselves, don't we?' she said to Angus as she extricated herself from Duncan.

'Right, right, of course you do,' said Duncan, laughing. 'Of course you do. If he's anything like me at university then he's having a right old time of it,' he said, giving Angus a punch on the arm.

'Doing my best,' said Angus, grinning. 'Doing my best.'

'That's my boy. You make sure you have some fun now, get it out of your system.'

'Duncan, please just shut up,' said Lorraine, looking embarrassed for the first time. Kim was relieved that her disdain was no longer focused on her.

'Just making sure he doesn't waste this opportunity,' said Duncan. 'Now are we going to the pub or what? Come on, we are wasting valuable drinking time here! You coming, Lynn?'

'It's Kim,' she repeated. 'Err, no thank you. I have to go to work.'

'Work?' asked Lorraine. 'You've got a job here?'

'Yes,' nodded Kim. 'At the fish and chip shop. So I can pay the rent. Though I'm actually a hairdresser by trade.'

Lorrainc looked unimpressed by anything she had said.

'That reminds me,' said Angus. 'The landlord at the pub says he wants his hair cutting just like Sonny's. Will you do it for him?'

'Well, I suppose so,' said Kim, taken aback.

'Don't worry, he'll pay. I told him you worked at a really flash salon and so you were really expensive. He's loaded so he can afford it. I'll just take a ten per cent commission. Seeing as I know you.'

'That's my boy,' laughed Duncan. 'Millionaire by thirty, I reckon.'

Angus nodded. 'I reckon the lads on my course would be up for a cut too, you know. They are starting to look a bit shabby. I'll sow the seed,' he said, tapping his finger to his nose.

'I've got you booked in to see Maurice at Christmas, remember,' said Lorraine. 'You'll wait to have your own hair cut, won't you? Maurice would be so disappointed if you let anyone else touch your hair.'

'Kim's brilliant, Mum,' said Angus enthusiastically. 'She gave Sonny an Elvis cut and he actually looks cool. Which is nigh on impossible. He's half a chance of losing his virginity now, thanks to Kim.'

Lorraine's eyebrows shot up. Again.

'That's not why I cut his hair,' Kim tried to explain.

'Well I think it's time we went,' said Lorraine. 'Get some decent food inside Angus,' she added as though it was also Kim's fault that he was living on takeaways.

'Oh, I've been using those food box things,' said Angus. 'All the time. It was just Sonny's birthday yesterday so we treated ourselves to a Chinese, didn't we, Kim?'

Such a blatant lie. She nodded and smiled.

They heard the front door go. Kim looked at Angus, hoping it wasn't the 'birthday boy' arriving, for Angus's sake.

Harry and Suki appeared in the kitchen. Kim scrutinised her son now she had the knowledge that he was living a completely different life to the one he was supposed to be. He looked a little dishevelled. He looked like he didn't care. His black joggers were crumpled and his green hoody had the saggy look of something that hadn't been washed in some time. He clearly took no pride in his appearance and Kim couldn't take any pride in her son's appearance either.

'Hi Harry,' she said. 'This is Angus's mum and dad, Lorraine and Duncan.'

He nodded and said 'Hi.'

'And this is a friend of Harry's,' said Kim. 'Suki.'

'Nice to meet you,' nodded Suki.

Kim watched as Lorraine looked the crumpled mess up and down. Angus by contrast was, as always, looking sharp in his designer gear.

'So this is your son?' said Lorraine, looking at Kim.

'It is,' said Kim. She wanted to wipe the judgemental look off Lorraine's face.

'Well, we really should go,' said Lorraine to Angus. 'I think we are done here.'

'Sure,' replied Angus. 'See you guys later.' He turned to leave.

'It was good to meet you,' said Kim, sticking out her hand to Lorraine.

'Yes, it was,' said Lorraine. She gave her a thin smile and walked out the door.

'Good to meet you too,' said Duncan, stepping forward and giving Kim a full-on hug. 'You take care now,' he said as he released her. 'Goodbye,' he nodded to Harry and Suki.

They waited until they heard the front door close before any of them spoke.

'Angus looks just like his dad,' said Suki.

'Doesn't he,' agreed Kim.

'What was with all the hugging?' asked Harry.

Kim sighed. 'That kind of bloke, I guess,' she said. 'I can see why Angus feels like he should be chasing women all the time if that's the example he has.' She shook her head.

'Err, Mum,' said Harry. 'Suki was wondering if you would cut her hair?'

'Of course, ' said Kim. 'I can do it now if you want?'

'Well, if it's not too much trouble. I really just want the ends cutting off, that's all. I mean, I can come back another time if that's more convenient.'

'No, no, take a seat. Now is perfect.'

She was just about to offer Suki a cup of tea when a cunning idea came to mind.

'We've run out of tea bags, Harry,' she said to her son. 'Would you go to the shop and get some? I'm sure you'd like a cup of tea, wouldn't you, Suki?'

'Well, that would be great if that's okay.' She looked nervously between Harry and Kim.

'Erm, are you sure?' asked Harry, also looking nervous. Kim thought she knew why. He didn't want to leave his mother alone with Suki.

'Go on, Harry,' interjected Kim. 'I could really do with one. It'll only take five minutes.'

Harry sighed. 'Okay,' he agreed. 'I won't be long.'

Kim had already got the gown around Suki's shoulders and was combing through her hair by the time she heard the front door shut behind Harry.

She felt bad. She had been warned about talking to any girls in the house. It was one of the rules after all. 'No talking to any girls that we bring into the house.' But this was too good an opportunity to miss. Maybe she would be able to find out something from Suki about why Harry wasn't going to university. But she had to be quick. He'd be back really soon.

'So how's your course going?' asked Kim.

'Oh it's brilliant, honestly. I'm so glad I came here.

They really do push you to try so much. Totally next level to A level art. And the facilities are amazing.'

Right, that was enough about Suki's course. Could she jump straight to asking about Harry? She would have to. She had no choice.

'I hope Harry's enjoying his course as much as you,' she said. 'He doesn't really talk much about it much. Has he said anything to you?'

Too direct perhaps. She would just have to see how that landed. She'd said it now. She felt Suki's shoulders tense. She didn't reply immediately.

'I think . . . I think . . . ' she stumbled. 'I think you'd better ask him.'

'Oh,' said Kim. 'Sorry. I didn't mean to put you in a difficult position. Is he okay?'

Suki turned to face her, her usual smiley countenance evaporated.

'Not really,' she replied. 'But I've not told you that. He's begged me not to say anything to you. So please don't say I've said anything. Please? Seriously?' She was panicking now, making Kim feel terrible. She'd put the poor girl in a horrible position.

'Of course not,' said Kim. 'I won't say anything.'

Suki turned back to face forward. Kim bit her lip. But how could she not say anything? What on earth was wrong?

'Thank you,' she said to the back of Suki's head.

'For what?' said Suki, still facing away.

'For being there for him.'

She didn't reply, just nodded her head ever so slightly.

They both jumped as the front door banged. Harry

was back. They both had their backs to the kitchen door so weren't facing him as Harry walked in.

'Hiya,' said Kim overly cheerfully, not wanting to give away the tense atmosphere in the room. 'That didn't take you long.'

'Well, I didn't want to leave poor Suki exposed to your haircutting chat for too long,' he replied, raising his eyebrows at his mum as he put the kettle on.

'Suki's been telling me all about her course, haven't you Suki?' said Kim. 'Sounds amazing.'

'Yep, it is,' nodded Suki. 'I'm really lucky.'

Harry looked over at them both suspiciously.

'You getting that kettle on or what?' asked Kim quickly. 'Mine's white, no sugar, in case you have forgotten. Now Suki – what were you telling about print making?'

Chapter 19

When she got home from her shift later that night the house was quiet. Goodness knows where they all were. The kitchen was still in the state that she left it in. She sighed and poured herself a cup of tea and listened to her voicemail messages that had landed whilst she was at work.

There was one from John Sinclair. *Damn it*, she thought. How had she missed that call?

'Hello, it's John Sinclair here. Calling for Kim, visiting hairdresser from Lancaster.' Kim heard him chuckle. She hoped this meant he had a good sense of humour. 'Sorry I couldn't talk earlier but well done you for tracking me down. Universities are designed to keep their staff well-hidden so top marks for ingenuity there. So give me a call back and we'll organise something so we can talk properly. Speak soon. It's John by the way, John Sinclair.'

Too late to call him now, she thought, looking at her watch. She'd give him a ring in the morning. He sounded friendly, cheery in fact. She hoped that was a good sign.

She then listened to the message from Richard.

'Hello, it's me. Any news? What happened? I've carried on trying to contact John Sinclair but to no avail. Let me know if you have spoken to him. Bye.'

Kim put the phone down. It was too late to call Richard too. She couldn't help wondering what he would be up to. Cosying up on the sofa with Alison watching an intellectual documentary? She could picture the scene vividly. Red wine open on the coffee table. Maybe some cheese and crackers out. They were probably wearing matching Arran jumpers bought on the amazing shopping trip to Manchester when they bought Richard's new coat.

The next morning she decided to call John Sinclair first and then she could inform Richard of the progress she had made where he had failed.

She felt nervous dialling his number. Any conversation with him seemed so important, like the slightest word out of place could ruin her son's entire future. She rehearsed her opening lines in her head, hoping to give herself some confidence.

'Hello, John, it's Kim, Harry's mum, thank you so much for calling me back last night. I'm sorry I couldn't take the call. When would it suit you for us to get together?'

Yep – sounded okay. She was good to go. She finished dialling the number and took a deep breath.

'Hello, Kim, visiting hairdresser from Lancaster, how the devil are you? Thank you for calling me back. Sorry to disturb your evening.'

'No, err, it was fine. No, great. I'm sorry I didn't pick up. I was at work and must have been in the middle of an order.'

What was she doing? Already too much information.

'An order? What kind of order at that time of night?'

'I don't know. I was probably up to my armpits in Gordon's fish and chip supper. He likes his curry sauce on the chips but not on the fish. He's very particular about that so I would have had to concentrate.'

Shit, shit, John Sinclair does not need to know about Gordon's curry serving preferences.

'Well of course,' said John Sinclair. 'And may I say Gordon is absolutely right. Curry sauce on fish, not good.'

'So he tells me,' agreed Kim. 'Erm, so, thank you for calling me and it would be great to come and talk to you about Harry. I had no idea he wasn't turning up.'

'No, no, I'm sure,' said John Sinclair. 'Parents are always the last to know. There's normally some underlying problem that needs to surface.'

'Well that's what I wanted to talk to you about. His life is a little complicated at the moment.'

'Well, sounds like we need to have a chat and see what we think the best course of action is. We never want to remove students from a course, but something has to change here so let's meet up.'

'That's unbelievably kind of you,' gushed Kim. She couldn't believe he was being so understanding.

'So how about we meet at Lillie Langtry's?' he asked.

'Where on campus is that?' she replied.

He laughed heartily. 'I forgot you are visiting from

Lancaster. It's a lovely pub with excellent beer in the centre of Nottingham. Really. It's an institution. How about 7 p.m. tomorrow night?'

Oh, thought Kim. She hadn't been expecting that. A pub. Well, she supposed that would be less formal. Allow them to have a relaxed chat.

'Well that would be great but I'm working tomorrow night.'

'Of course you are. So what night do you get off?' he asked.

'Mondays and Wednesdays,' she said.

'I have department meetings on Mondays so how about next Wednesday? Seven p.m. in Lillie Langtry's. Looking forward to it. See you there, Kim, visiting hairdresser from Lancaster.'

'Okay. See you there.' She ended the call and stared at the phone.

Not what she had been expecting. Wednesday was a whole five days away. A long time in a crisis. Which is what she felt this was. Five whole days to continue to worry about Harry's fate. Not ideal. And in a pub. She was confused. Was this how lecturers normally dealt with this sort of stuff? In the pub? She had been expecting a formal chat in John Sinclair's office whilst she pleaded her son's case and promised to do better. Not a chat over a pint in a pub.

She sighed and searched for Richard's number. Better inform him of her progress before he started pestering her.

'In a pub?' said Richard when she had relayed the events of the previous day and her visit to the university and her conversation with John Sinclair that morning. 'He asked you to meet him in a pub?'

'Yes,' she replied. 'He said it was a Nottingham institution.'

'The university is an institution, not a pub,' he replied.

'Is it okay to meet a parent of a student in a pub?' she asked.

'Well, I guess it's highly unusual to meet a parent of a student full stop. Can't say I've ever met anyone's parents the whole time I've been lecturing.'

'Right,' said Kim.

'Did you suggest the pub?' asked Richard.

'No!' exclaimed Kim. 'Of course I didn't.'

'What does he look like, this John Sinclair?'

'I don't know. Early sixties maybe. He was quite jolly actually. Kept calling me the visiting hairdresser from Lancaster because he got me mixed up with some Doctor Steph someone or other, a visiting professor from Cambridge.'

'Doctor Steph Albon?'

'No idea. Could have been.'

'He got you mixed up? She's like the leading lecturer on conservation of mass in the country.'

'Well, he was expecting her and it all got a bit confused.'

'Are you sure he's asked you for a drink and not Doctor Steph Albon?'

'Of course I am. We are meeting to talk about Harry. That was very clear.'

'Mmmm, well I suppose there is nothing else we can do except wait for this pub meeting. God, I wish I was down there. Come and talk to Harry myself. Maybe I would get something out of him.'

'No,' said Kim. 'Trust me. It will make matters worse.'

Richard went quiet for a moment. 'We're really screwing this up, aren't we?' he said.

She didn't correct him over the 'we', he sounded so dejected. She did of course blame him but she was only too aware that her being here in Nottingham was probably not helping matters.

'I know I can't stay here forever,' she said. 'I know I shouldn't be here at all but the thought of coming back . . . I just can't face it, not yet.'

Richard didn't reply. The silence fell heavy. She didn't know what to say.

'Can I ask you a question?' he said.

'Yes.'

'Which compartment on the washing machine do you put the liquid in? There are three – why are there three? I'm worried I've put it in the wrong one because my clothes aren't getting very clean.'

Kim couldn't believe what she was hearing. She had no idea how to respond.

'Why don't you ask your girlfriend?' she spat out eventually.

Richard didn't respond.

'No need to be like that,' he said eventually.

'There is every reason to be like that.'

'Alison has got her daughter staying so I can't ask her.'

'Why not?'

'Because Olivia won't speak to me. She's taken it all really badly.'

'Shocking. I mean, just rude of her to be upset with you for splitting her mum and dad up.'

'It's really upsetting Alison,' continued Richard.

'And you are telling me this, why?' asked Kim.

'Sorry, sorry. You're right. Sorry. I guess I'm just used to talking to you about stuff. I'm an idiot. Ignore me.'

The comment made Kim sad. It bought back memories of late night chats over bottles of wine when Richard would open up about problems at work. She missed those chats too. It was probably when they were closest, if she was absolutely honest.

'Right. I'd better go,' said Richard. 'Well done with tracking down John Sinclair. And do you know what, I'm sure you talking to him will make all the difference. You'll know exactly what to say. I know you will.'

She swallowed.

'Well, I'll do my best.'

'Of course. Well, say hello to Harry and call me after Wednesday. The fact he's happy to wait until then hopefully means they are not on the verge of chucking him out anyway.'

'Hopefully.'

'Bye, Kim.'

'Bye, Richard.'

Later Max arrived at the door with his hair wet, having just washed it ready for a haircut. He'd shyly asked her the previous evening if she wouldn't mind cutting his hair as Sonny had been so evangelical about her skills at the pub quiz.

'Wow, I nearly didn't recognise you without a greasy apron and a hairnet,' she said to him as she opened the door to let him in. He was wearing a smart striped shirt tucked into dark denim jeans and he smelled amazing, nothing like the weird usual mix of gravy and curry sauce.

'Well, I like to make an effort outside the shop. You do get a bit sick of looking and smelling like you run a fish and chip shop,' he replied.

'Apologies for the obstacle course and the tip-like nature of the household,' she said, kicking a random trainer out of the way. 'I do live with three teenage boys, don't you know.'

'I'm surprised it's this tidy, to be honest,' he said, looking round the kitchen which actually wasn't looking too bad as she had just had a tidy up.

'Right, welcome to my salon,' said Kim. 'Take a seat and we will see what we can do.'

Max sat down and she took a closer look at his hair. It was very dark with some flecks of grey. Good condition. He looked after it well or he was just lucky. She ran her fingers through it, immediately knowing he needed some layers putting in and the sides and back shaving into his neck. Then it needed thinning a bit. That would take some of the grey out. It could take years off him.

'What are you after then?' she asked.

'I'm in your hands,' he said. 'Whatever you think. I normally go to the barbers where you queue up and wait. Cheap as chips. Ha, ha, do you get it? Actually I think my large chips might cost more than my haircut there so it's even cheaper than chips.'

She didn't like to say she could tell it was a cheap haircut.

'I can't remember the last time I had, you know, a proper hairdresser cut it. Always been a bit intimidated by them. And you have to talk, don't you? Discuss your holidays and all that.'

'Well you don't have to talk if you don't want to. If that's what puts you off hairdressers.'

'Oh no, it's fine talking to you. I know you. I don't see you as a hairdresser.'

'Right, I'll take that as a compliment.'

'I did want to talk to you about something actually.'

'Oh really,' said Kim, snipping away. She was all ears. She hoped he would open up a bit. She realised that she knew nothing about what he did outside of the chippy. She'd be really interested to know what else he got up to.

'So I'm thinking of introducing tofish to the menu,' he said. 'What do you think?'

'Tofish? What the hell is tofish?'

'It's a vegetarian alternative to fish.'

'Right. Well I don't know,' said Kim. 'What does it taste like?'

'Absolute shit.'

'Oh,' replied Kim.

'It's just that, well, everyone's doing it, aren't they?' said Max.

'Doing what?'

'Going veggie. Especially the students. Well, they've been going that way for years if I'm honest, but it always felt like there were enough meat-eating drunkards to keep me in business, but I think the balance is shifting. I think I need to do something. Move with the times. Attract a new audience.'

'Do you think you'll ever get the vegetarians in when you've got a rotating hunk of lamb on full display?'

Max turned to look at her. 'Good point,' he said.

He turned back to face the front, his shoulders sagging. 'I don't think I can get rid of the kebab. It's still a good seller.'

'I think you're right,' agreed Kim. 'I don't think you'll ever sell as much tofish as you do kebabs. I see what you're saying though. You've no vegetarian option at all, have you? Apart from chips. What you need to be doing is getting the vegetarians who are coming in to spend more than what they spend on just chips. What about a halloumi kebab? You can charge a fortune for them. Me and my mate Vicky went to see Inspiral Carpets in Williamson Park last summer and they had loads of street food there and I spent ten quid on a halloumi kebab.'

Max turned round to look at her in total awe.

'I know,' she said, feeling embarrassed. 'It was a festival atmosphere. My common sense on how much to spend on a filled pitta bread went totally out of the window. What can I say?'

'You went to see Inspiral Carpets?'

'Yes.'

'I *love* the Inspiral Carpets.'

'Really? You like your music then?'

'I do,' he said. 'It's how me and Rachel met. Well, our mutual appreciation of Shed Seven actually.'

‘Shed Seven? Now there’s a blast from the past. Remind me of what they did again.’

‘“Chasing Rainbows”, “Going for Gold”, “Disco Down”.’

‘“Chasing Rainbows”, I remember that.’

‘You should hear it live. Everyone chanting. It’s amazing. It really is the best concert moment I think you can have.’

‘Wow. That is some recommendation.’ Kim had never seen Max so animated. ‘So when did you last see them then?’

She sensed Max’s shoulders tensing. ‘Not since December 2014,’ he replied.

‘Oh, how so? Do they not tour anymore?’

‘Oh yeah, they come to Rock City here in Nottingham every other year.’

‘So why have you not been? If they are that good?’

‘Well, me and Rachel met at a Shed Seven concert, you see. It was our thing.’

‘And now it’s ruined. That’s terrible.’

‘I know. She denied me my marriage, my family and the joy of seeing Rick Witter giving it some to “She Left Me on Friday”. Do you remember that one?’

‘Oh I do. That’s a great song.’

‘Well, ironically she left me on Friday and ruined my weekend. Well, she pretty much ruined the rest of my life actually.’

Wow, thought Kim. Sounded like Max had never really recovered from his wife’s affair.

‘Does it ever get easier?’ she asked.

He paused. ‘Eventually,’ he said. ‘I think I’m nearly

at the stage where I miss Shed Seven more than I miss her.'

'You should go and see them, Shed Seven. It might help,' offered Kim. 'Closure and all that. Especially if you loved them that much.'

Max shook his head. 'Funnily enough they are in Nottingham around now,' he said. 'They always tour near Christmas, but no. I couldn't. It does still hurt.'

Kim carried on cutting in silence and thanked her lucky stars that her split with Richard hadn't involved any of her favourite music. That would be unbearable.

Kim's phone suddenly rang, making them both jump. She glanced over to it sat on the table and she saw that it was John Sinclair calling again.

'Sorry, Max,' she said, putting her scissors down. 'I'd better take this, it's Harry's tutor.'

'Hello,' she said. 'Is everything okay?'

'Hi Kim,' he responded cheerily. 'Everything's fine. I just wanted to let you know that I've had a meeting cancelled so I can get out earlier next week. Would 6 p.m. be okay?'

'Err, of course, that's absolutely fine.'

'Jolly good. See you next week then. Lillie Langtry's, you got that?'

'Yes, Lillie Langtry's. See you there.'

She put the phone down.

'Everything all right?'

'Yes – well no – well,' she sighed. 'Turns out Harry isn't turning up at uni so I've arranged to meet his tutor to have a chat with him.'

'At Lillie Langtry's?'

'He suggested it. It's not a strip club, is it?'

Max laughed. 'No, it's a decent pub actually. Why aren't you meeting up at the university?'

She shrugged. 'It was his idea to meet there.'

Max looked at her. 'Does he know your circumstances?' he asked.

'What do you mean – my circumstances?'

Max squirmed in his seat. 'Well, that you are, you know, single, as it were.'

'I have no idea,' replied Kim. 'What does it matter anyway?'

'Well, it sounds a bit like a date to me,' he said.

She gasped. 'No way,' she replied. 'No way. It's not. Honestly.'

Max turned round to face her. 'You are a single woman now. A man wants to meet you in a bar. Just be careful, that's all I'm saying.'

Chapter 20

Kim was still sat at the kitchen table pondering Max's assertion that her 'meeting' with John Sinclair was actually a date when Angus poked his head around the door.

'I've got a sort of date tonight,' he said. 'Can you cut my hair?'

'Err, okay,' she replied. She hadn't cut any hair in weeks and now several on the trot! 'Take a seat,' she said.

Angus dumped his bag on the floor and sat down on the chair that Max had vacated less than an hour ago.

She looked down at his dark red mop, worrying about the fact his mum had been very clear that she would not encourage Kim cutting his hair. She ran a fresh comb through it to assess the situation. She needed to go carefully. He certainly didn't need a radical change like Sonny. Angus needed entirely different handling to his housemate.

'So just a tidy up then?' she asked. 'Just needs sharpening up, yeah?'

'Yep,' agreed Angus. 'Nothing radical. Just been noticing a few stray ones when I put the gel on in the morning.'

'Sure,' she replied. 'Not a problem. We'll soon get you ready for that date of yours.'

'Like I said, not really a date,' pressed Angus.

'Of course,' replied Kim. 'Of course.'

'Just getting together to discuss coursework, that's all. Well that's what she thinks but you know she's pretty hot, so you never know, do you? Always best to be prepared is what I always say,' he laughed. Kim didn't.

'Of course,' she replied.

Angus took his phone out and looked down at it and Kim couldn't help but notice the picture of a very attractive girl on his home screen.

'So have you heard from the girl in Edinburgh?' she asked. 'Poppy, was it? Is it definitely all over? Just so I know. Don't want to put my foot in it. Not that I will talk to this girl, of course, if you bring her over. I know the rules. Sorry, didn't mean to pry.'

Kim watched in fascination as the back of Angus's neck grew bright red.

'Well, yes, I mean, I don't know really, it's sort of in the air. I mean we message each other all the time but we haven't actually talked about us really. And she's up there, I'm down here, so it's not worth carrying on with really, is it? I'm sure she feels the same.'

'Clippers?' Kim asked.

'What?'

'Clippers? Does your hairdresser normally use clippers on the back?'

'Oh yeah. Right. Yes, he does. Number four, I think.'

'Sounds about right. So will you see her when you go home at the end of term?' she ventured. It felt like he wanted to talk about it.

'Course, yeah. I'm hoping we'll be hanging out. Won't be the same being back in Edinburgh and not seeing her. That's if she wants to see me, of course, and hasn't shacked up with some brainy cretin who likes to name all the bones in the body. Jeez, what a boring bastard. Why would she want to spend time with someone like that?'

'So has she met someone then?'

'No idea.'

'Have you asked her?'

'No. I just know she's been out partying a lot so she's bound to have met someone, hasn't she? How could she not? I mean she's stunning. Have you seen her? Here, look at a picture.'

He lifted up his phone to show Kim the picture of the girl on his screen.

'Look at her. There's no way she hasn't been snapped up by some boring twat of a doctor, is there?'

Kim peered at the photo. Indeed she was a beautiful girl. A stunning girl in fact, but in a natural way. Dark brown curls surrounded a smiling face with a cheeky grin. She looked fun, she looked smart. She looked like an absolute catch.

'She's gorgeous,' agreed Kim. 'You've got her as your background still?'

'Well, yeah, you know, not got round to taking it off.'

'So tell me about this girl you're meeting tonight.'

'Well, she's on my course. And we have to do a project in teams and well, I can tell she's really smart and will do a ton of work and so I picked her. And as I say, she happens to be quite hot.'

'What's her name?'

'Err, not sure. Ellie, I think. Or Evie? Something like that.'

'And she's worth getting your hair cut for?'

Angus shrugged. 'Might as well, seeing as you are here. And Poppy's going to FaceTime me over the weekend too and I don't want her to think that I'm letting myself go. There's some uni ball she's going to. Wants to show me her dress or something.'

'She wants to show you her dress?' questioned Kim.

'Yes.'

'What's Poppy like?' asked Kim.

'What's she like? Well, she's gorgeous as I said. But she's also really smart and funny. She's just like great, really.'

Kim nodded.

Angus went quiet.

'So does she have a date for this ball?' asked Kim.

He shrugged. 'I don't think so. It's a medical school thing, I think. She hasn't mentioned going with anyone. But like I said, I'm sure she's not short of offers. She must have guys falling round her.'

'How long were you seeing each other before you came to university? If you don't mind me asking.'

'Not long at all. We actually hooked up at our high school graduation dinner. So like a few months. Nothing really.'

Kim nodded slowly.

'And she wants to FaceTime you to show you the dress she is going to wear to a ball this weekend?'

'That's what she said in her text, yeah. Look.'

Angus tapped on his phone then held it up to show Kim.

HEY – HOW ARE YOU? NERVOUS ABOUT THIS DRESS I'VE BOUGHT TO GO TO THE MEDICS BALL. CAN WE FACETIME TO SEE WHAT YOU THINK? HOW WAS HOCKEY TRAINING? P XX

Kim took it in.

'So you can see why I need to get my hair cut?' said Angus. 'She'll be looking amazing and I'll be looking like a right scruff if I'm not careful.'

'I thought you were getting your hair cut for Evie?'

'Who's Evie?'

'The one who you are meeting later to talk about your project?'

'Oh yeah. Sure. Yeah, for Evie.'

Kim carried on cutting.

'So your dad's a bit of a card,' said Kim. 'Sounds like he enjoyed himself at university.'

Angus laughed. 'Oh yeah, he sure did. He was a bit of a lad at uni. Let's just say that.'

Kim watched him glance down at his phone and the picture of Poppy. Kim was convinced Angus thought he should be playing the field like his dad had done in his university years. Trouble is that playing the field is all well and good as long as you own your own heart. If someone has stolen it then the field actually is not that much fun.

They both heard the front door open and voices in the hall and they were soon joined by Sonny and Harry in the kitchen.

'Wow, amazing. You're cutting Angus's hair,' said Sonny, stating the obvious. 'So cool.'

'I've got a hot date tonight,' he said, winking at Sonny.

Kim shook her head in despair.

'What! Who with?' said Sonny, looking at him in awe.

'A girl on my course. She's so hot. I can't tell you.'

'How do you do it? I mean, what do you actually say? I mean, what do you actually do to get these women?'

'Just part of my natural charm,' said Angus, winking at Sonny again.

'But tell me the actual words,' pressed Sonny. 'I need to know how you do this.'

'I just walked over to her and said do you want to do this eco study project together. I reckon we could do a decent job between us. And she said yes so I said let's meet at the Student Union at 7 p.m. and she said yes and there we are. Voila!'

'So much easier if you have a shared interest like a degree, I guess,' sighed Sonny. 'The trouble is I have no idea what our shared interests are.'

'Sex,' said Angus. 'That's the shared interest, matey boy.'

'Angus!' exclaimed Kim.

'What?'

Kim shook her head. She knew she had promised not to get involved with any women the boys brought back to the house but she simply couldn't stand here and listen to Angus treat her sex so carelessly.

'This girl, Evie, is it? Well, don't forget to treat her like a human being. You know, like a person with feelings. Treat her like . . . well, like Poppy if she was here, or like you would want Poppy to be treated.'

'If anyone screwed over Poppy I would absolutely deck them,' said Angus, looking angry. 'No one would get away with treating her badly. I would kill them, I swear.'

Kim had to take a step back he shook his head so violently. It was so clear that Angus had really deep feelings for this Poppy. He just didn't know what to do about it.

She looked down and Angus was staring at his phone screen again.

'Have you shown Harry and Sonny the picture of Poppy?' Kim asked.

He looked up sharply. 'Err, no.'

'You've got a picture of Poppy?' said Sonny, immediately leaping forward and peering at Angus's phone. 'Let me see.'

Angus handed the phone over and Sonny peered at it.

'Really?' he said, looking back at Angus in wonder. 'That's the girl you've got back home?'

'Well, not really. I mean, we weren't going out for long.'

'Look at this hubba, Harry. Would you be cheating on that?' asked Sonny.

Harry gave the screen a cursory look. 'Guess not,' he shrugged.

'Who is this date tonight, Beyoncé or something?' asked Sonny. 'She cannot be any better than that. And if she is then – just wow – wow is all I can say.'

Sonny sat down next to Harry looking in complete shock.

'I can't bring myself to ask anyone out and you . . . you . . . ' said Sonny. 'My mind is blown. I mean, I've hovered outside the chippy so often to see if Annie is working that Max thinks I've permanently lost my key and I'm coming to check if you are there, Kim. But every time I see her, just absolute drivel comes out of my mouth. I told her she was wearing nice socks the other day. Nice socks! Best chat-up line known to man. I'm such an idiot.' Sonny hit himself on his forehead with the palm of his hand.

'You invited her to the pub quiz,' said Kim.

'That was different. That wasn't a date,' said Sonny. 'I wasn't inviting her to spend time with just me. I was inviting her to spend time with all of us. I knew she would be up for that. But just me? I'm not so sure. How did you get Suki to like you?' Sonny asked Harry, nudging him on the arm.

Harry glanced up at his mum.

'We're just friends,' he said firmly. 'We both like *Tomb Raider*. That's all.'

'You like her though, don't you?' said Sonny. 'You'd like her to be your girlfriend? You know, if she asked.'

'We're just friends,' said Harry again, looking back down at his phone.

Maybe they were just friends, thought Kim. But maybe Harry wanted more and he didn't know how to go about it. Or maybe he didn't want more and was fed up with the pressure. Or maybe not going to uni was stopping him wanting to get too involved in anything? Perhaps he was a commitment-phobe. Unwilling to commit to a girlfriend or his course?

Jesus, life was complicated as an eighteen-year-old boy. And she thought that being a forty-eight-year-old woman was bad. She looked round at her three housemates. What a crowd. Angus trying to live up to his father's misguided reputation when what he really wanted was right under his nose. Sonny just desperate to have a girlfriend and trying to emulate Angus when all he really needed to be was himself. And Harry. Struggling with goodness knows what that was stopping him living his life.

If only she could find a way of helping them.

She caught sight again of the beautiful, fun-loving girl on Angus's phone.

'Do you have a dinner jacket?' she asked him.

Angus turned sharply to look at her. 'Of course I do,' he said.

Kim knew he would have. He was just the type to be used to attending functions that required a dinner jacket.

'Why don't you wear it when you take Poppy to the ball?'

'What?! I'm not taking her to the ball.'

'But you could. You could go and see her and take her to the ball.'

'Are you serious?'

'Sure,' she shrugged, trying to act casual. 'Do you want to take her to the ball?'

Angus paused for a moment. 'Of course I do. I mean I'd love to. But I've no idea if she would want to go with me and I don't even know if someone else is taking her. I mean, what if she said no?'

'Why do you think Angus should ask Poppy to the ball?' asked Sonny. 'I don't understand.'

Kim took a deep breath. 'Because Poppy wants him to ask her to the ball.'

All three boys stared at her.

'How can you know that?' asked Harry, looking sceptical. 'You cannot know that.'

'Yeah,' said Angus. 'There is no way you can know that.'

'Well,' began Kim. 'She said she wants you to FaceTime her so that she can show you the dress she's planning to wear, yeah?'

'Yeah,' nodded Angus, looking very confused.

'Now if that is not a plea for you to take her then I don't know what is. Why else would she be showing you her dress? For goodness' sake, Angus, take her to the damn ball! Because if you like her, and I think you really do like her, then you need to do something about it, rather than assuming the worst and acting as though it doesn't matter by messing around with all these other poor girls.'

Angus stared back at her.

'I'm not sure you giving me relationship advice was in the rules we drew up?' he said.

'Okay,' she said, putting her hands in the air. 'I take it all back. I apologise. I've overstepped the mark. Ignore everything I said.'

She moved round to the back of his head and resumed her snipping.

'Do you really like Poppy?' asked Sonny, his face agog.

Angus said nothing. Even Harry was waiting for an answer.

Slowly Angus nodded his head.

'But . . . but . . . why all these other girls?' he asked.

Angus looked to the floor and shrugged.

Kim squeezed his shoulder. 'Fear of rejection,' said Kim. 'Just the same as you, Sonny. We all fear rejection when it's someone we really care about.'

Sonny had never looked more stunned. 'Even Angus,' he whispered.

'Even Angus,' replied Kim.

'You have to ask her to the ball,' said Sonny, suddenly jumping up and down. 'Just ask her. If you love her you have to ask her. Doesn't he, Kim?'

'No one said anything about love,' said Angus, looking stern.

'No, they didn't,' said Kim. 'But if you do really like her, then you should ask her to the ball.'

'Oh my God, this is so romantic,' said Sonny, clutching his heart. 'It's like Prince Charming asking Cinderella. Come on, Angus, we need the fairy tale ending. Ask Poppy to the ball. Tell you what, if you ask Poppy to the ball I'll somehow grit my teeth and ask Annie out. Which is way harder as she will say no but, you know, anything for you, mate.' He put his hand on his shoulder.

Angus eventually turned to look at Kim.

'Well?' she asked.

'Will you iron my dinner shirt for me?' he asked.

'Hurray!' said Sonny, jumping up and down. 'You go get her, man!'

'I'm not ironing your shirt,' grinned Kim.

Even Harry had a small grin on his face.

'I'd offer to iron your shirt,' said Sonny, 'but I don't know how. Anything for romance.'

'You don't know how?' said Angus. 'Have you done, Kim?'

'Yes,' said Kim.

'Then, follow me, Sonny, and I will show you how to iron my shirt.'

'Will you?' gasped Sonny. 'Wow, thanks Angus. And thank you, Kim. You know, for helping Angus realise he loves Poppy.'

'No one said anything about love,' repeated Angus. 'Now get up those stairs and iron my shirt.'

They exited the kitchen leaving Kim and Harry alone together. How she ached to solve his problems in the same way but she didn't know where to start. She didn't really know what his problems were.

She hadn't realised that she was looking at him intently until he looked up at her and met her gaze.

'Don't you dare start trying to matchmake me,' he said, getting up. 'I'm not Angus, I'm not Sonny. Just leave me. Me and Suki are just fine.' He picked up his phone and walked out of the room.

Chapter 21

Kim was feeling particularly churned up as she began her shift at the chip shop the following week. Sonny had decided that tonight was the night that he was going to ask out Annie. They'd discussed his strategy at length the night before. He'd asked her question after question about what to say and what to wear and how to do it and whilst Kim had been tempted to give advice, she felt like he needed to be confident in himself and what he thought was the right thing to do. After all his personality was his biggest asset and he needed to be true to himself. As she told him, it was his personality that was going to secure the date, not hers. He needed to let it shine.

'What's your gut feeling about her?' she asked. 'How do you think she would like to be treated? What first date would appeal to her?'

He looked back at her, bereft. Panicked.

'You can do this,' she told him. 'Come on. You promised Angus. You need to have at least tried before he gets back from Edinburgh.'

That was the other reason why she was feeling nervous. Angus had left for Edinburgh in a flurry on Friday after deciding he was just going to surprise Poppy. Turn up on her doorstep in his dinner suit and ask her to the ball. He was hyper. Totally excited. Which was great. Kim just prayed that her hunch had been right and that actually Poppy wanted to be with Angus and was not off shagging every medical student in sight. They'd heard absolutely nothing from him since he left which could be a good or bad sign. He was having such a good time that he had forgotten to report back to base, or it hadn't gone to plan and he was wallowing in misery somewhere. Possibly even gone back home to lick his wounds with his mum and dad whilst his father told him he was an idiot for trying and he should get back to Nottingham and get back in the saddle so to speak. She really hoped that she had given Angus the right steer because if she hadn't then it was sure going to make life difficult in the house again.

She gave the chips a good shake in the fryer. She couldn't believe how quickly she had got to grips with everything after her initial poor start. She actually felt quite at home there. It was almost her refuge. Her chance to escape her everyday worries around Harry and his future and her own future come to that.

She was just putting a new batch of chips in the fryer when she caught sight of something bright out of the corner of her eye. She looked up and the bell over the door went and in walked Sonny. She swallowed. 'Wow,' she mouthed to him. This was either genius or catastrophic. Maybe she should have offered more guidance, she thought.

Sonny had gelled his hair to a stiff peak and was wearing a shiny red bomber jacket with white jeans. She couldn't see his face as it was obliterated by an enormous bunch of flowers in all the colours of the rainbow.

'Wow,' she mouthed again.

He moved the flowers away from his face so he could cover his mouth as he coughed. An anxiety rash was spreading up his neck to his face. She wanted to go over and hug him. She wanted to go over and hold his hand but she knew that would be wrong. All she could do was watch.

He stepped towards her and cleared his throat again.

'Is Annie working tonight?' he asked.

He knew full well that Annie was working as that was the sole reason for him being here.

Kim nodded, keeping up the charade of this not being completely planned and manipulated.

'Yes,' she said. She turned round and shouted, 'Annie!'

Annie and Max were behind the counter behind her, both staring open-mouthed at Sonny.

'Oh, there you are,' said Kim. 'Err, Sonny would like to, err, talk to you?' she stumbled. Christ, she was more tongue-tied than Sonny. What a shambles. She scurried to join Max, allowing Annie free rein at the front counter.

Annie glided forward, looking a little bewildered. Today she had on a pink fifties ensemble, complete with black netting underskirt underneath her apron. Her hair was tied up in a polka dot scarf and her makeup was as immaculate as ever. Bright red rosebud lips and a fake beauty spot on her left cheek.

Kim stood next to Max and held her breath.

'Hello Annie,' said Sonny. 'I err, hope you don't mind me dropping into your place of work like this?'

'Of course not,' replied Annie. 'I mean, you drop into my place of work quite often.'

'Well yes,' said Sonny. 'I suppose I do. But your dad's fish is my favourite. It's even better than the Codfather down in Devon. Have I ever mentioned the Codfather? It's right on the seafront. It's amazing.'

'You have mentioned it actually,' said Annie. 'I almost feel like I've been there.'

'Oh, you would love it. You would so love it. They have these benches outside but you have to be careful of the seagulls because once a seagull swooped down and just took a chip right out of my hand.'

'Wow, really,' said Annie. Kim knew for a fact that Sonny had told Annie this story before during one of his many trips to the chippy to see her.

'Nothing like as good as this place though, of course. I mean, this must be the best chippy in Nottingham, mustn't it – at the very least.'

'Dad doesn't do awards,' replied Annie. 'Doesn't believe in them. I've told him he's an idiot but there you go. The older generation, hey?'

Kim felt Max was about to speak up and she put her hand on his arm to stop him.

'So did you want your usual?' asked Annie. 'Fish, chips and gravy?'

'Err, no, I mean yes, I mean I do but I wanted to ask

you first, I mean I wanted to give you these first,' he said, thrusting the flowers over the counter into Annie's face. So much so that she had to take a step back.

'Oh wow,' she said. 'Wow. That's lovely. Thank you. Is this what you do in all your favourite chippies? Has the Codfather got a steady flow of flowers coming from you down in Devon?'

'Oh no,' gasped Sonny. 'No, I've never given someone who works in a chip shop flowers before.'

'Right,' nodded Annie.

Get to the point, thought Kim.

'What I mean is that I've actually never given anyone flowers before, apart from my mum on Mother's Day but only the ones you get free in church, it wasn't like I bought them or anything, so that doesn't count, right?'

'Still nice though, to give your mum flowers.'

'Yep.' He coughed again and took an envelope out of his inside pocket. 'I also wanted to give you this,' he said.

Oh goodness, thought Kim. What the hell was in there? She and Max exchanged a nervous look.

'Err, do I open it?' asked Annie.

'Yes, yes please. I need an answer now. So yes, open it.'

The chip shop was suddenly deafeningly quiet as Annie tore open the envelope and extracted a card. She appeared to read it and then looked up to Sonny.

'The pleasure would be all mine,' she said.

Sonny literally jumped in the air and did a swirl on the ground.

Kim gripped Max's arm in delight.

'Ow,' he said, leaping away.

'Sorry,' she said.

'What just happened?' he asked.

'Sonny just asked your daughter out.'

'What!'

'Don't worry, he's going to treat her like a princess.'

'He'd better,' mumbled Max.

Kim decided it was safe to return to the front counter as she really wanted to know what was in that envelope. 'Do you want me to put those flowers in the staff room?' she asked Annie.

'Yes please,' said Annie, handing them over. She was beaming, thank goodness.

'You okay?' she said, looking at Sonny.

Sonny nodded. 'She said yes,' he said, looking slightly shocked.

'Lovely,' smiled Kim, trying to sneak a look at what was written on the card.

'Afternoon tea,' said Annie, showing the card to Kim. 'Can you believe it? I've always wanted to go to Josephine's for afternoon tea. Did you suggest it?' she asked. 'Was it your idea?'

'No,' said Kim, holding her hand up. 'Nothing to do with me, I swear.'

'Kim just told me to be true to myself,' said Sonny, still grinning from ear to ear. 'She didn't tell me what to wear or what to do. She just said be me because that was enough.'

'Of course it's enough,' said Annie, putting her hand on his arm. 'More than enough.'

Sonny looked like he might cry.

Hold it together, thought Kim. Crying at this point might not look good.

'Brilliant on the afternoon tea,' said Kim. 'How on earth did you come up with that?'

Sonny grinned. 'Two things,' he said. 'I'm from Devon. Devon is me. And what else is from Devon?'

'Cream tea?' said Kim.

'Exactly. And then I thought, well I thought, Annie always looks so amazing and pretty and I thought it would be great to take her somewhere pretty to, you know, show how pretty she is and every time I pass Josephine's I always think it looks so pretty so it was obvious really, wasn't it? A pretty place for a pretty lady.'

You smooth-talking bastard, thought Kim as she watched Annie literally melt in front of Sonny's adoring gaze. Now that was how to sweet-talk a lady. She looked up at Max who had heard every word of Sonny's reasoning around taking Annie for afternoon tea. He was looking at Annie's face that was literally glowing with the full-on compliment. Kim didn't think that Sonny would have any problems with Max now.

Max cleared his throat. 'Well, I'm sorry to break up this little interlude but we do have a chip shop to run, so can we all come down off cloud nine and get back to work?'

'God, sorry, sorry,' gasped Sonny. 'Didn't mean to interrupt. I'll go. Just need to do this.'

He jumped up onto the counter and enveloped Kim in a massive hug.

She laughed and hugged him back. 'What's all this for?' she asked.

'Thank you,' he said. 'Thank you for not doing what my mum asked, for teaching me how to cook spaghetti, for cutting my hair, for . . . for . . . for being my friend. You may have just changed my life.'

Kim shook her head. 'I didn't do anything of the sort. You did. You did it all.'

'Not without you though.' He gave her a cheesy thumbs up and then turned to go just as Angus chose that moment to burst through the door.

'I'm back,' he roared, literally beating his chest.

'Yey,' said Sonny. 'Angus is back.' He ran at him and jumped into his arms.

'What the hell,' Kim heard Max mutter.

They hugged then Angus released Sonny to the floor.

'I'm king of the world,' declared Angus, quoting Leonardo DiCaprio's famous line.

Kim felt herself relax slightly. The weekend must have gone well.

'Did you take her to the ball?' asked Sonny, literally jumping up and down. 'Did you, did you?'

'Oh yes,' grinned Angus.

'She said yes?' asked Kim urgently.

'Oh yes,' said Angus. 'Like so happy to see me. And we went to the ball and I showed all those doctor pimps that this is my lady. It was epic.'

Max was staring at Angus bug-eyed. Suddenly his chippy had been turned into teen romance central.

'He does tend to trash talk when he's overexcited,' Kim said to Max.

'Are you taking the piss out of my Scottish accent?' asked Angus.

'No,' said Kim. 'Just not sure you should be calling doctors pimps.'

'Doctors *are* pimps,' said Angus.

Kim sighed. She had some work to do there.

'That's so amazing,' said Sonny. 'I'm so happy for you. No need to chase after all those other girls any more then?'

'Oh no. One woman man, me now. Poppy has it. Now I know she wants it, she can have all of it.'

'So you were right then,' said Sonny to Kim. 'Angus loved Poppy all along.'

'No one said anything about love,' said Angus firmly.

Kim looked at Sonny and raised her eyebrows.

'You are the best,' declared Sonny, pointing at Kim. 'You are so clever!'

Kim shook her head. 'No I'm not,' she said. 'You're the ones studying at university, not me. You just remember that. I'm just a hairdresser who works in a chippy.'

Sonny shook his head. 'You are so much more than that.'

Kim looked back at him. He really was the sweetest guy.

'And by the way there is nothing wrong with being a hairdresser who works in a chippy,' shouted Max. 'But at this precise moment she needs to get back to being a hairdresser who works in a chippy rather than the world's greatest matchmaker. We have chips to serve, guys, so isn't it about time you ordered some food and then cleared off?'

'Wow, yes, forgot, sorry Max,' said Sonny.

'Mr Lawrence to you,' said Max.

'God yes, of course yes, sir I mean, Mr Lawrence, I'll have fish, chips and gravy, please.'

'Large or small?'

'Excuse me?'

'Large or small?'

'Oh, erm, small actually, is that okay? I can order large if you want me to.'

'Annie, serve the lad what he wants, will you, and then get rid of him.'

'Yes Dad,' grinned Annie.

'I'll go large,' said Angus.

'Of course you will,' sighed Max, returning to his station behind the fryers.

When they were clearing up after the shop had shut and Annie had cranked up the radio and was dancing as she swept the floor, she asked Kim to tell her the whole story of why Angus had cantered off up to Edinburgh to invite a girl to go to a ball.

'It's so romantic,' she sighed, leaning on her broomstick. 'But how could you be so sure she would say yes? How did you know?'

Kim shrugged.

'I could tell by the way Angus talked about her that he really cared about her. He just didn't know what to do about it. Then he showed me that text from her where she wanted him to see her dress and I realised that was his opportunity. It was a pretty clear signal from her. I might have read it wrong but I knew that whatever way it went then at least Angus would have got it out of his system and then he could move on either way.'

Annie was staring at her. 'Wow. That is so insightful. Like really. You should do this sort of stuff for a living.'

'What do you mean?'

'Listening to people and helping them sort out their problems.'

Kim shrugged. 'It's just what I do when I'm cutting people's hair really. Just listening.'

'But you're really good at it. You should be like a counsellor or something.'

Kim wrinkled her nose. 'No one is going to pay me to listen to them. They pay me to cut their hair.'

'But you are so easy to talk to. People would pay for that. And you listen, you *really* listen. That's kind of rare.'

'Not really, is it? It's just what I do. And in any case you need qualifications for proper counselling, don't you?'

'Sure,' said Annie. 'Of course, but you'd sail through that.'

Kim laughed. 'I don't think so. I've not studied for nearly thirty years. No chance. Studying is for young people like you. I'm way too old for that.'

Annie raised her eyebrows. 'Not too old for dancing whilst sweeping though,' she said, handing the broom to Kim.

Kim laughed. 'Never too old for that.' She took the broom from her and spun around just as a familiar track from the nineties came on. That reminded her of a thought she had had. She looked round to make sure that Max was out of earshot.

'You bought your dad a Christmas present yet?' she asked Annie.

'No,' sighed Annie. 'He's such a nightmare. I never know what to get him.'

'I could give you an idea. Something that really he would only accept from you and you would absolutely need to go with him. That would be really important. But I think he might absolutely love it.'

'Wow, tell me, tell me,' begged Annie.

Annie leaned in to hear Kim whisper to make doubly sure that Max wouldn't hear. A grin spread across her face.

'Kim,' she said when she had finished. 'You are a genius.'

'Second time I've been called that tonight,' she said. 'You'll have to watch me. I'll be getting too big for my boots.'

Chapter 22

Exactly the right person called when Kim was staring at her wardrobe in despair. It was taxing her for no apparent reason as to what to wear for her meeting with John Sinclair. It was probably the juxtaposition of having a meeting with her son's tutor in a pub that was giving her such angst, and Max's whole assertion that it was in actual fact a date that John Sinclair had set up. She had absolutely no idea how to dress for a meeting that she needed to be clear about was not a date but was also in a pub. However, she knew that there was one person who just might have the answer.

'Hi Vicky,' said Kim, picking up her phone. 'You have called at just the right time.'

'Really. You not about to head off to fry some chips then?'

'No. Now listen carefully, this is a tricky one.'

'I'm all ears.'

'So I heard via Richard that Harry hasn't been turning up to any of his lectures.'

'Ah yes. Richard told me.'

'You've seen Richard?'

'Yes. That's why I rang. I was just coming out of Greggs yesterday. I was mortified. No one needs to see a qualified baker coming out of Greggs with a steak bake. It's not good for my business.'

'Was Richard going into Greggs?'

'Yes,' gasped Vicky. 'Can you believe it? Never would have thought he was a Greggs man.'

'And he told you about Harry?' asked Kim.

'He asked me to go and have a coffee with him. I'm sorry, mate. He looked awful and kind of desperate. What could I say? And he said he needed to talk and I thought I might learn something that might be useful to you so I said yes.'

'So did you go for a coffee in Greggs?'

'God no. I made him take me to Costa. If he was paying then I wanted a large cappuccino in a proper mug and chocolate on top.'

'Fair play. I would have done the same.'

'Thought so. I also took him for a lemon muffin. Hang the calories. Anyway, so we sit down and you will never guess what he told me.'

'What?'

'Him and Alison are no more.'

'What!'

'Yes. It's over.'

Kim sat down hard on the narrow single bed. She felt totally winded. This was the last thing she was expecting.

'Why? When?' she asked.

'Well of course I asked a gazillion questions. Knew you'd want to know all the gory details.'

Kim wasn't so sure.

'But I'm not quite sure if even he understands what happened to be honest. But from what I could gather it all started falling apart the minute they moved in together.'

'I guess I did kind of force their hand on that.'

'Yep. Good move as it turned out. Moving out and taking the keys so he had no choice but to move in. Genius. Anyway he was mumbling on about grapefruit at breakfast and . . . '

'He always has a bacon butty. I know it's bad for him but look at him, he's as skinny as a rake,' interrupted Kim.

'And then he said she sent him to the supermarket and he'd come back with the wrong stuff and she'd told him off.'

'Richard hasn't a clue about food shopping,' replied Kim. 'He'd come back with a week's worth of ready meals and twelve packets of biscuits.'

'And he kept going on about some shopping trip to Manchester to buy clothes and she made him buy all this designer gear that he hates and traipse round all these shops that he had no interest in at all and he just couldn't understand what she was trying to do.'

Kim went quiet, her mind swirling. For so long she had built up Richard and Alison's clothes buying trip into something magical. In fact she had already visualised in great detail Richard and Alison's forthcoming Christmas shopping trip to Manchester where they would buy the perfect gifts for all the family whilst sipping mulled wine at the German market and share warm fuzzy hugs and kisses under the sparkling Christmas lights. It was so lovely in her head it was like something out of a Richard Curtis film. It made her so jealous she wanted to scream. But it sounded like the fantasy Christmas shopping trip was not going to happen because actually Richard didn't like that sort of thing whether it was Kim he was going with or Alison.

A bizarre sense of relief at the realisation flooded over her. It wasn't her that put him off such experiences. Alison hadn't succeeded where she'd failed at all.

'So . . . so,' said Kim, trying to gather herself following the relief of being able to pop the fantasy shopping bubble. 'What else did he say?'

'Well it sounded like it all came to a head when Alison's daughter came to visit. She didn't want anything to do with him apparently. Totally understandable if you ask me. Anyway, so he moved back into your house and he said he realised that he was relieved to be home. That it made him realise that was where he wanted to be and, get this, Alison comes over and says she's managed to talk her daughter round and he needs to go back next door and talk to her and make nicey-nicey and get the daughter on side and he said he realised he didn't want to. He didn't want to go back and he didn't want to have to suck up to Alison's daughter. He just wanted to be home. Which of course went down like a bag of sick with fancy pants Alison, so I imagine there was a big bust-up and they split up.'

'Really?'

'I made the big bust-up bit up actually. He didn't say that. He just said that they decided that clearly it wasn't right and they should part ways.'

'I was going to say. Richard doesn't do big bust-ups. It's not his style.'

'He probably wrote a hypothesis on why he thought the relationship was no longer tenable and then handed it to her and asked her to mark it,' said Vicky.

'Probably so,' Kim agreed. 'I don't know what to think. I mean I'm glad it's over. I didn't want it to work out. Of course I didn't but . . . but where does that leave me and Richard?' she asked. 'I mean, I don't know who he is anymore after all this. Oh, I don't know what to think.'

'Well, don't think anything. Just let it sink in. You must be a bit shocked, I imagine. This is a twist in the tale no one saw coming.'

Kim sighed. 'Too right. Talk about blindsided.'

'Do you want me to come down?' Vicky asked. 'Take you out again.'

'Not sure my liver or my housemates can take that again,' said Kim. 'I'll be okay, I should probably talk to him, I guess. I don't know. Did he say anything else? Anything about me?'

She wasn't sure why she was asking that. Not sure at all. She was so confused it was untrue.

'Well he told me he'd talked to you about Harry and him not turning up at uni. What's going on there then?'

'I don't know,' admitted Kim. 'Harry won't talk to me at all. He's so defensive. I can't get anything out of him and you know living here complicates it which is hard. But I went to see his tutor to see if I could learn anything, but he was busy so I'm seeing him tonight actually.'

'Oh yeah, Richard mentioned something about that. He was rattling on that he wasn't sure you were doing the right thing seeing him and then he said he didn't rate the tutor and he was a bit of a ladies' man so he'd heard when he'd done some digging. But he was rambling so I had no idea what he was talking about.'

Kim bit her lip. So Richard had done some digging. What had he done that for? Now she was even more confused.

'So this tutor has asked to meet in a pub in the centre of Nottingham,' Kim told her friend.

'Oh yes. Does it sound like a lap dancing club?'

'Yeah, it does. Lillie Langtry's. But it's like a proper ale pub, I think. That's what John said anyway.'

'John?'

'Harry's tutor. The guy I'm meeting tonight.'

'Is he hot?'

Kim sighed. 'Not really. In any case, it's irrelevant. Not interested. This is all about Harry. And sadly when you brought my clothes down all you brought was pulling gear which gives off totally the wrong impression, which is why I'm sat here scratching my head wondering what to wear. Any ideas?'

'I see your dilemma,' agreed Vicky. 'I had not factored such a scenario in when I was selecting from your wardrobe. Look, you know what we say?'

'If in doubt go glam.'

'Exactly. It will give you confidence and it's not an invite to a man to come on to you just because you have made an effort.'

'I hope you're right,' said Kim. 'I hope you're right.'

In the end Kim decided she would stick with exactly what she wore when she went to the university to see John Sinclair. Even though the ensemble included a silver cardigan she hoped it would communicate that she had made no more of an effort for this evening's meeting than she had for a casual trip to campus.

She was ready by 5.15 p.m. and was attempting to vacate the building without any of her housemates spotting her. She didn't need to be asked any awkward questions by any of them, least of all Harry. She felt bad enough about seeing his tutor behind his back as it was. She waited until it all seemed quiet outside on the landing, hoping they were all downstairs.

She tiptoed out and got downstairs to the first floor just past Sonny's door when he flung it open and called her name.

'Is that you, Kim? I wanted to ask you if green jeans are too much for afternoon tea – ooh, where are you off to? You look ace. Loving the shiny jumper thingy.'

Kim stopped in her tracks and turned round slowly.

'Green jeans – fine,' she said. 'Whatever you think. Annie will love it.'

'Thanks,' nodded Sonny. 'So are you going to the chippy like that?'

'Err, no. It's my night off. I'm just off out.'

'Where?'

'To meet someone.'

'Who? Is your friend Vicky back in town? I love her. Can I come with you?'

'No. It's not Vicky.'

'Oh. Who then?'

'Just someone I'm meeting for a drink, that's all.'

At that point Angus came running up the stairs from the ground floor and screeched to a halt outside the bathroom looking up at Kim.

'Wowser – where you going?' he asked. 'Hot date, is it?'

'No!' screeched Kim. 'I'm just meeting someone for a quick drink, that's all.'

'Like who?' he asked. 'You don't know anyone. Oh I get it. You been on the apps, haven't you – you sly devil.'

'The apps?' asked Sonny. 'What do you mean, the apps?'

'Dating apps, you mongoose. You know, Tinder, Grindr, Plenty of Fish or whatever the old persons' version is,' said Angus.

'Excuse me. I'm not old and I haven't been on Tinder,' said Kim.

'Good,' said Sonny. 'If you're meeting someone from Tinder then we would be forced to accompany you. You can't trust anyone on there. Did you know people lie about their age, their height, about everything. You think you're meeting a six-foot-tall carpenter from Stevenage and it turns out they are a five-foot-two Cornish winkle picker and believe me, you don't want to date a five-foot-two Cornish winkle picker.'

'So, who are you meeting then?' asked Angus.

'An old friend from way back who happens to be in Nottingham,' she mumbled.

Kim clearly was doing a very good impression of a rabbit in the headlights. Angus didn't look convinced at all.

'Oh how lovely. Are you going to bring her back here to meet us all? I like meeting your friends,' he said sarcastically.

At that point of course Harry came out of his room. Of course he did. She attempted a warm smile at her son which he didn't return.

'Tell your mum to bring her friend back to meet us,' said Sonny.

'What friend?' asked Harry.

'Err, I'm, err, just going into town to meet an old friend who happens to be in Nottingham,' explained Kim. Her heart was thudding by now. She was not a natural liar.

'Who?' asked Harry.

'Err, you've never met her,' said Kim. 'We were at primary school together. Then she moved to, err, Derby aged ten and she heard I was in Nottingham and got in touch, see, and said we should meet up. So we are. Tonight.'

She bit her lip.

'Are you meeting Dad?' asked Harry.

Blimey, where did that come from?

'No,' said Kim, shaking her head. 'No, of course not.'

'He's split up with Alison,' he said, looking her right in the eye.

Wow. How did Harry know? Had Richard told him?

Kim nodded. 'Yeah, actually I knew. Vicky rang to tell me.'

'What, so . . .' said Sonny, his head swivelling between the two of them. 'So your dad isn't shagging the neighbour anymore?' he asked Harry.

Harry nodded slowly, still staring at his mother. 'Looks like it,' he said.

'Shiiiit,' said Sonny slowly. 'What does that mean?'

Kim didn't have an answer to that question. She had absolutely no idea.

'It means he's still a jerk,' said Angus. 'You can't go around treating women like he does.'

Kim thought she wouldn't point out that Angus had been treating women appallingly up until very recently.

'Did he call and tell you?' Kim asked Harry, wishing they weren't discussing this on the landing that really needed hoovering, in front of Angus and Sonny. However this was the longest conversation she'd had with her son in some time and so she was loath to walk away.

Harry nodded. 'A few days ago.' He swallowed. 'He wants to come and see you,' he continued. 'He wanted to know what I thought.'

'He wants to come and see me?' she said, surprised. 'I'm sure it's you he wants to see really,' she said.

Harry shrugged.

'What if he wants you back,' Sonny gasped. He had his hand over his mouth and his eyes were swivelling between all three of them.

Kim kept her gaze on Harry. She couldn't read him. Was that what Harry thought? What exactly had Richard said to him? Did Harry want them to get back together? She had absolutely no idea and no time to work it out. If she didn't leave now she'd miss her bus and that would look bad for her meeting with John Sinclair.

'Look, I've got to go or else I'll miss my bus,' she said. She put her hand out and touched her son's arm. 'I'm glad you spoke to your dad. Would you like him to come and see us?' she asked.

He shrugged. 'Not bothered,' he claimed.

'I'll talk to you later,' she said.

He nodded. Like in agreement. She would talk to him later. She made a promise to herself. She'd talk to John Sinclair and then she'd talk to Harry and get him back on track. And then maybe she'd talk to Richard and find out what the hell was going on. Wow, she had a busy evening ahead of her. Little did she know that none of that was going to go to plan.

Chapter 23

Lillie Langtry's turned out to be an attractive-looking pub in an old building in the heart of Nottingham opposite the Theatre Royal. To Kim's relief it appeared to be frequented mainly by a more local, older crowd rather than by students who all seemed to be roaming the streets in fancy dress that evening. She had already bumped into a Spiderman and a Robin Hood as well as a hen party out in full cowgirl gear. She walked through the door and looked around, relieved to see it wasn't crammed and noisy, so she wouldn't be forced to shout her family's woes into John Sinclair's ear as they were squashed together in some tiny corner. She was, however, ten minutes late due to her getting slightly lost on her way from the bus stop so she felt somewhat flustered as she scanned the interior of the pub.

'Visiting hairdresser from Lancaster,' she heard a cry from behind her. That joke was beginning to get old now, she thought. She turned round and John Sinclair had secured a small table for two in a cosy corner and had a nearly drunk pint in front of him. He also had a massive grin on his face.

He stood up and beckoned her over.

'I'm so sorry I'm late,' she gushed.

'What can I get you to drink?' he asked. 'The beer is excellent but please feel free to have what you want.'

'Err, gin and tonic would be great. Thank you. Would you let me get them?'

'No, you sit down,' he said, grabbing his pint to take with him to the bar. 'I won't be long.'

Kim watched as John Sinclair went to the bar and leaned across it smiling warmly at the barmaid behind the counter. They appeared to know each other, that or else John Sinclair came here a lot. She watched as he sank the rest of his pint and put it down on the bar only for a new one to arrive immediately. He lifted it to his lips to drain the top off before putting it down and handing his credit card over to the barmaid to pay for the drinks, chatting away. He was wearing jeans and a blue checked shirt under a navy jumper. The standard uniform for a man of his age out meeting his mates for a night in the pub. Kim had been hoping that he would be wearing similar to what she'd seen him in on campus. What she had been hoping for was a man in smart trousers and open necked shirt and jacket. What she had been hoping for was a man who looked like he'd just left work from being a lecturer at university and he was just calling into a pub for a quick chat with a concerned parent. John Sinclair looked like he was ready to settle in for the night. This did not bode well.

He walked towards her, grinning, and settled his pint on the table before placing her gin and tonic in front of her. Then he sat down and took a long swig of his drink. Kim sipped hers and launched into her carefully rehearsed story.

'Thank you so much for this, Mr Sinclair,' she said.

'John, please call me John,' he responded, putting his hand on her arm.

'Err, okay, John,' she said.

He took his hand away.

'So err, I just wanted to explain what's happening with Harry and see if there is anything we can do to get him back on track, because you see it's not his fault, none of it, and I think if you knew what he's been going through then that might explain his lack of attendance and maybe we can do something about it.'

John Sinclair leaned back in his chair and smiled. She noticed that his cheeks were slightly rosy. Like he may have had time for more than one pint whilst he was waiting for her.

'Well, fire away,' he said grinning. 'Let's see what we've got, shall we?'

Kim wasn't sure if he was taking her seriously. He was smiling too much. But what could she do? All she could do was plough on.

'So, you see, erm, Harry's not had the greatest start to university life because, well he found out, well we all found out that his dad, Richard, was having an affair with the next door neighbour, the day before he was due to come to Nottingham.'

John Sinclair nodded. 'Well, yes, I had heard on the grapevine that there had been some sort of scandal up in the science faculty at Lancaster,' he admitted.

'Really?' gasped Kim.

'Well, these things get round, you know, and well, a good friend of mine is a physics lecturer there and people talk, I guess, and also your husband had been in touch to let us know his son was coming and to keep an eye on him so, you know, I guess it meant that Richard Jacobs was on my radar, as it were.'

'Right,' nodded Kim, trying hard to keep up. Richard had never said he'd contacted Nottingham before Harry went.

'You'll understand then that Harry was having to deal with finding out about his father's affair just as he was leaving for university, which was tough enough, but then you see there was a spare room in his student house and I needed to get away so I came with him, to Nottingham. So just at the point where he thought he was getting away from his parents, Mum came too.'

'Hence the visiting hairdresser from Lancaster?' smiled John.

Kim nodded. 'Only not so visiting. I didn't mean to stay for long but I just couldn't go back and now I've got a job here so I kind of ended up staying longer than I thought I would. But you see the point is that it's been incredibly difficult for Harry and neither me or Richard have made it easy for him, and I think he just needs someone like you to talk to him and tell him it doesn't matter that he hasn't been to any lectures and that he can start getting back into it now and that he just needs to turn up and do the work and it will be okay. Would you . . . would you be able to do that?'

John Sinclair nodded. 'Of course,' he said. 'If, of course, he will come and see me. I can't make him, you need to understand that. But if we can get him in then I will of course talk to him and try and see how we can get him focussed. Sometimes freshers arrive and are just intimidated by the whole thing and so it's a case of welcoming them in. Making them feel comfortable. Perhaps Harry is feeling that he just can't face it all at the moment given what is going on in his home life so he just needs to understand that actually coming into university is a safe space and actually an escape from other things he may be dealing with.'

Kim nodded vigorously. 'That could be it,' she agreed. 'That could so be it. I can imagine he's just thinking he can't face it. That sounds like him. He can get overwhelmed. He did when he did his A levels which is why he didn't get the grades he needed to get into the university he wanted to and ended up here instead. Last minute.'

'Well, I'm sorry to hear that we were second choice,' said John Sinclair.

'No, no, that's not what I meant,' said Kim, getting all flustered. 'It's like I said at the time, there is a reason you're meant to go to Nottingham.' She looked at John thinking that maybe he was the reason. That actually Harry needed to be somewhere with compassionate tutors like John who would look after him, not write him off as a no-hoper. 'Thank you,' she said to him. 'I can't tell you how grateful I am that you have agreed to help us. Really. I so appreciate it.' She smiled and felt herself relax for the first time that evening. If John could help Harry then that would be such a load off her mind.

John Sinclair took another sip of his drink and licked his lips. 'It's surprisingly common,' he said, shaking his head.

'What is?'

'Affairs in a university setting. I think it's to do with dealing with the same pressures and stresses of work. There's some kind of connection there that can lead in the wrong direction.'

Kim looked at John Sinclair. What was he talking about? It seemed quite straightforward to her. It was to do with weak men wanting a shag. That's really what it was to do with but perhaps she shouldn't say that right now.

'But of course that's no consolation to you, is it?' he continued. He patted her arm again. 'I'm so sorry this happened to you. It must have been devastating. How long had you been married?'

'Twenty years,' she replied.

'Wow,' said John. 'A long time. Would you mind me asking how you met?'

'I cut his hair,' replied Kim, not wanting to go into the full detail. It made her too sad.

John Sinclair laughed. 'Of course you did. Is that what you are doing here, cutting hair?'

'No. I'm working in the chippy at the end of the road.'

'Of course you are. You did tell me,' said John, looking bemused.

Kim nodded. 'They've been really good to me actually. Given me something to do,' she said with a shrug. 'And I'm keeping my hand in with hair cutting. I do the boys in my house share and the guy who owns the chippy. So you know, I'll go back to it someday.'

'Incredible,' said John. 'You are an inspiration.'

'Not really,' she replied.

'You are. What you have been through and you keep going. I mean, being left by your husband after twenty years. That's a blow. That's horrendous. And you seem to be picking yourself up amazingly.'

Kim didn't actually feel like she was picking herself up at all. She suddenly felt tears spring to her eyes. She wished she could control when the unhappiness of her situation overwhelmed her. Now was not the time, but being reminded that your marriage had dissolved after twenty years was enough to tip her over the edge.

To her utter mortification she felt a tear slip down her cheek.

'I'm sorry,' she said, whisking it away with the back of her hand. 'I didn't mean to get emotional.'

'It's okay,' John Sinclair said, putting his arm over her shoulder. 'It must still hurt. I mean, what he did to you. What a terrible thing to go through.'

'It was. It is,' she agreed, scrabbling for a packet of tissues out of her bag. 'Not sure I'll ever get over it,' she mumbled, blowing her nose. A fresh set of tears found their way down her cheeks.

John Sinclair squeezed her shoulder blades.

'You will get over it,' he said firmly. 'Look at you,

you have everything going for you. You look amazing. You are beautiful. You won't be alone for long.'

Kim wanted to point out that she wasn't actually bothered about being alone. She was still grieving for her marriage.

'You don't need to be lonely, you know,' he said, turning in his seat to look at her. His face was quite close to hers now. She could smell beer fumes. She felt herself lean back. He was too close.

'And well, I was wondering if you might like to cut my hair one night?' he asked as he put his hand on her knee.

Kim scraped her chair back super-fast. Unfortunately there was a wall behind her so she did not have far to go.

John Sinclair was leering at her and still had his hand on her knee.

'What the hell do you think you are doing?' came an all too familiar voice as she blinked at John Sinclair.

The next moment Richard had appeared at John Sinclair's shoulder and was pulling him away from Kim. This did nothing to relieve Kim's confusion. What was Richard doing here, out of nowhere? John had staggered up out of his chair, thankfully taking his hand away from Kim's knee, and was now facing off against Richard.

'Who the hell are you?' he demanded of Richard.

'Richard Jacobs, Kim's husband, Harry's father, Director of Chemistry at Lancaster University.'

Not sure the last bit was necessary, thought Kim. Perhaps that was how all lecturers greeted each other. With their full intellectual credentials.

'And your point is?' asked John Sinclair, his eyes wide.

'My point is that you need to get off my wife.'

John Sinclair laughed in his face. 'The wife that you cheated on with a colleague?' he asked. 'Hardly qualifies you to still call her your wife.'

'And nothing qualifies you to come on to her,' said Richard. 'And in any case. You have no room to talk. I hear you've had that many affairs with students there is practically a whole Mills and Boon series dedicated to you.'

Kim gasped. He'd seemed so angry on her behalf that Richard had done the dirty. And yet . . . and yet . . . he was just as bad. What was it with these professors?

'Well,' said John, 'I didn't see the lady protesting too much,' he said, turning to address Kim. 'She was just offering to cut my hair, weren't you?'

'No,' said Kim, shaking her head. 'You were asking me to cut your hair. I never offered to cut your hair.'

'Good job I arrived when I did,' said Richard.

'Erm, what are you doing here?' asked Kim.

'I was worried about you meeting John alone,' explained Richard. 'Thought you would need some moral support.'

'You mean you didn't think I was capable of having the right conversation?'

'No, no, not at all. I just thought, you know, since I'm more aware of the university system then I should be here with you, to help. And when I heard of John's reputation then I thought that perhaps you are a little vulnerable right now, that perhaps I should be here.'

Kim shook her head. None of this made any sense. She'd come for a meeting to sort out her son's future and ended up with a letch trying to come on to her and her two-timing husband turning up to defend her honour.

Maybe it was time to leave.

'I think it's time I went,' she said, 'I mean, we've discussed what we needed to, haven't we John? So, no need for me to hang around. I'll be going home. Maybe the two of you can stay and have a drink or something,' she said, trying to sidle around them to make her escape. 'Talk about science type stuff or something.'

'But I thought that perhaps we could go out to dinner,' said Richard, catching her arm as she tried to squeeze past them.

'What?' she asked.

'Go out to dinner, talk, you know?' he said. He furrowed his brow. She noticed he wasn't wearing the designer coat. Just an old walking jacket he'd had for years. One she suspected she'd bought with him just after they first got married.

John Sinclair threw back his head and laughed heartily. 'My, Jacobs, you want to have your cake and eat it, don't you? Do you seriously think this fine woman has any time for you since you did what you did? Now Kim,' he said, leering into her, so close she could smell beer fumes again on his breath. 'I know this lovely little Italian round the corner. I booked a table. You'll love it. Only the locals know it. You come with me and have a good old moan about Jacobs here and get it out of your system.'

For the third time that evening she felt herself leaning back to try and get away from John Sinclair.

'Is everything all right?' came the most welcome voice of the night. Kim swivelled her head around. It couldn't be. It was. She had never been so relieved to see anyone in her life.

'Max!' she shrieked, shaking Richard's hand off her arm and side-stepping John Sinclair. 'What are you doing here?' She flared her eyes at him in what she hoped portrayed a strong message of 'help me'.

'Annie's just getting a drink,' he said. 'We're off to see Shed Seven.'

'Really!' said Kim, unable to help herself. 'She got you tickets for Christmas then? That's brilliant.'

'Who's this?' asked Richard.

'Hello,' said Max, glaring at Richard. 'We met before. I own the chip shop.'

Richard looked back at him blankly.

'Where Kim works,' he added.

'You actually work in a chippy?' asked John Sinclair, incredulous. 'I thought you were just saying that to add to the sob story. To get me on side. But you actually do work in a chip shop?'

'I actually do,' said Kim. 'Max's Fish.'

'Oh yes, I remember,' said Richard. 'You were stood in the back somewhere, slicing a big sausage thing.'

Max ignored him and turned to Kim.

'Are you okay?' he asked again.

'She's fine,' said Richard. 'I got here in time.'

'I didn't ask you,' Max said to Richard. He turned back to Kim. 'Do you want to come with me and Annie?' he asked.

'Yes!' declared Kim. An escape route from the hell brewing in Lillie Langtry's. It was all so confusing. She still didn't understand why Richard was here and she had no grasp of what the hell had just happened with John Sinclair. She just needed to get out and have time to think.

'Have you got a spare ticket for Shed Seven, then?' she asked.

'Where's Shed Seven?' asked John Sinclair. 'Is that a new place?'

'It's a band playing at Rock City,' said Max to John Sinclair as though he were the greatest dullard to walk the planet.

'Oh,' said John Sinclair. Clearly the chippy owner had made him feel like a total dullard too.

'I'd really like the chance to talk to you,' said Richard, looking at her imploringly.

Kim didn't know what to think. She looked to Max. He shrugged. 'It's up to you – do what you need to do. But you are very welcome to join us.'

'And there is always my offer,' said John Sinclair. 'A little pasta alfredo and candlelight rather than a sticky club floor and deafening music or time with your cheating husband.'

'Will you stop doing that?' said Richard to John Sinclair angrily. 'This is nothing to do with you.'

'I'll come with you,' Kim said to Max. 'If that's all right?'

'Of course,' said Max. 'Let's go and find Annie.'

'Tomorrow,' said Kim, looking at her husband. 'Let's talk tomorrow?'

'But . . . ' he began.

'Tomorrow,' she said firmly. She turned to John Sinclair.

'I'll talk to Harry,' she said to him. 'Find out what is going on. I'll get him back into uni.' She suddenly didn't want this lecherous oaf helping her son. She would do what she should have done in the first place. She'd talk to him.

'Let's go,' she said to Max. She brushed past her son's tutor and her husband and headed straight for the door where she gasped for fresh air. Gulping it in. Max and Annie soon joined her on the pavement. Annie put her arms around her excitedly.

'I can't believe you are coming with us,' she said. 'This is so brilliant. Dad said he had to rescue you from two arseholes. Are you okay? Lucky we were in there, hey?'

Max shook his head. 'She rescued herself,' he said. 'I didn't do anything.'

Kim smiled at him gratefully. She had to wonder if Max had called in just to check she was all right. Whatever, she was glad she was out of there.

'Are you sure you can get me in?' she asked Annie.

'My mate's dad, Felix, is on the door. I've already texted him. We are good to go.'

It was hard to say which were her highlights of the concert. Rock City was a smallish club holding about two thousand people with a sticky floor for moshers and dancers and an enormous balcony for chanters and cheerers.

The three of them chose the sticky floor option. Bouncing up and down furiously to 'Going for Gold' and 'Disco Down' and laughing their heads off to the lead singer's expletive-ridden banter as he read out a tweet from someone who couldn't make the gig due to having to have a triple heart bypass. He also found the time to take the mickey out of a fourteen-year-old who had been brought along by his nineties-music-loving parents. He was the envy of everyone present, however, when the singer handed over his maraca to the lucky boy as the crowd cheered in delight.

Kim caught Max's eye as they launched into 'She Left Me on Friday'. He gave her a wry smile. Kim nodded at Annie who was belting out the lyrics in complete abandonment and watched as Max joined her, holding her hand high in the air and punching the air with his other hand. Shouting the lyrics at the top of his voice.

Before too long it was encore time and the unmistakable first few bars of 'Chasing Rainbows' filled the room. Every single person had their hands in the air and were soon chanting the chorus back to the lead singer as he stood back in awe. This middle-aged crowd joining him in the shared admission that they had all just been chasing rainbows all their lives.

It was a euphoric crowd that streamed out of Rock City. Not a downhearted one. They had all travelled back to their youth for a couple of hours, sung their hearts out, punched the air and jumped up and down. Felt as one as they remembered who they had been and who they were now. And gained reassurance from the feeling that they were not alone. That many people felt just as they did. Many people had had someone leave them and hurt them and almost all of them felt they had just spent their lives chasing rainbows.

Kim sat behind Annie and Max on the bus as they talked excitedly about the gig. Max was full of it. She was relieved. It could have been high-risk telling Annie to take him to get over his vivid memories with Rachel. But it looked like all that was banished. He'd had a great time with the product of his happy meeting with Rachel all those years ago. Thank you, Shed Seven, she mouthed silently to the sky.

Max and Annie insisted on walking her to her door.

'Thanks for suggesting this Christmas present,' said Annie before they left.

'Best one I've ever had, I reckon,' said Max, looking at his daughter adoringly,

'Will you be okay?' Max asked Kim.

She nodded. She'd seen that Harry's light was on upstairs. He must be in. She'd go and talk to him now.

'I'll be fine,' she said. 'And thanks again.'

'What for?'

'Rescuing me in the pub.'

'I didn't do anything,' he said. 'Have a good night.'

As she closed the door behind her she hoped the rest of the night panned out just as well as she climbed the stairs towards Harry's bedroom.

Chapter 24

Kim knocked on the door. She could tell by the flickering of the lights under the door that he was in there playing computer games. She couldn't hear voices so she hoped that Suki wasn't in there with him.

'Yeah,' came a shout from inside.

'Can I come in?' she asked.

There was a pause then a quiet, 'Yep.'

'Hiya,' she said cheerily. 'Just thought I'd let you know I'm home.' She walked into the room. No sign of Suki although it looked as though she had been there earlier as an empty chair was positioned right next to Harry. 'Had such a good night,' she said, sitting down in the empty chair.

Harry continued playing.

'How was your *friend*?' he asked with emphasis on the friend as though he knew she had lied. She decided to embrace it.

'Oh, well, that was a little lie. I actually went to meet Max and Annie. We went to a concert. We went to see Shed Seven at Rock City,' she continued.

'Who?'

'Shed Seven. Band from the nineties.'

'Never heard of them.'

'Well you're not middle-aged, are you? They were brilliant. The place was buzzing.'

'You didn't dance, did you?' he asked.

'God yeah. We were moshing and everything. It was just a big sweaty crowd of middle-agers trying to grasp hold of their youth.'

'Sounds delightful.'

'It was,' she replied. 'It really was.' She paused. 'Do you know, it's the first time in ages I felt like I wasn't alone, that there were a million other middle-aged people out there alongside me jumping up and down wishing we could do it all again, wishing that we could have our youth back, wishing that crap hadn't happened to us during the course of getting older.'

Kim gave Harry a sideways glance. He was listening, she knew he was.

'For the first time since we moved here I almost felt like I belonged.' She looked at Harry again. 'Do you feel that?' she asked him. 'Do you feel like you belong?'

She watched him swallow and then a tear slid down his face. She gently took the controller out of his hand and wrapped her arms around him and let him sob on her shoulder. Her heart was breaking. What on earth was wrong? She just prayed that this release of emotion would lead to him telling her what was going on.

The sobs gradually abated and Kim tried to wipe her own eyes without Harry noticing. He leaned back in his chair, shoulders slumped.

'I'm so sorry, Mum,' he gasped. 'I'm so sorry.'

'Why? What on earth have you to be sorry about? I'm the one who should be sorry. I'm the one here screwing up your life. You have absolutely nothing to apologise for.'

He gave a deep sigh and looked up at her, shaking his head.

'I've not been going to uni, not to anything,' he said. 'No lectures, no tutorials. Nothing.' He looked down at his hands clutched in his lap.

'But why haven't you?' she asked gently. Maybe too gently. This was supposed to be a surprise after all. She held her breath.

He looked back up at her. 'Because I can't do it,' he said. 'I . . . won't get it. I won't understand it and then you'll be disappointed and Dad will be mad and I'll disappoint everyone.'

'Of course you can do it,' said Kim. 'Of course you'll understand it. You are so smart. You take after your dad, you're so clever.'

Harry was shaking his head firmly now. 'I don't take after him. I really don't. He just gets it. He doesn't have to work at it. He just knows. Whereas I have to bust a gut and I still don't get it. I don't get it, Mum, and . . . and the truth is, I don't really want to get it.'

'What do you mean?'

'I thought I was interested in it; chemistry, I mean. But I don't think I am. Not at all. In fact I think the only reason I'm here at all doing chemistry was because everyone assumed I would be great at it and I never found anything that I was interested in more. So it was just easier to do chemistry. But I went to the first lecture and realised what a huge mistake I'd made. I hate it, Mum. I really do.'

The tears started to slide down his face again and Kim lunged forward to hold her son.

'Why didn't you say something before?' she said into his hair.

He pulled away. 'You had enough going on. And you are so proud of me for getting to university. I'm so sorry I'm letting you down,' he said, breaking down in tears yet again.

'You could never let me down,' she said, wiping away her own tears. 'I let you down. I should have spotted you weren't happy. You should have been able to talk to me. I shouldn't have put any pressure on. Christ, I shouldn't even be here. I've so screwed everything up.'

'I'm glad you're here,' said Harry, taking her hand. 'Really I am.'

And now she was gone. Sobbing on her son's shoulder. The pain and the heartache clutching at her as well as the absolutely unbridled love for her son. They held onto each other tight until they had both let go of some of the multitude of emotions running through them. Kim was glad she was here too.

They sat in silence for a couple of minutes, both processing and recovering from what had just happened. Both trying to find the words to take the first steps into the aftermath.

'So we need to get you out of this course then,' said Kim. 'Is that what you are saying? You need to leave?'

Harry looked at her and nodded. The tears started to spill again. 'I'm so sorry.'

'No more sorrys,' she said. 'Been there done that. You have nothing to be sorry for.'

'But what do we tell Dad?' he asked. 'He'll be so upset.'

Kim shook her head. 'We'll explain. He'll just have to deal with it. And he will. He loves you, you know, whether you carry on his legacy or not. It might take him a bit of time but he will get his head around it. I'll make sure of it. You leave your dad to me.'

'But you are barely talking to him,' said Harry.

'Not your problem,' she said firmly. Then she suddenly remembered. 'He's here, you know?' she told Harry.

'What do you mean, here?'

'In Nottingham. I bumped into him earlier. He wants to talk to me about something. Not sure what. I said he could come round in the morning. So, I'll talk to him then.'

Harry nodded. He looked absolutely drained, but also relieved. He was actually looking her in the eye which he hadn't done for so long.

'Do you have any ideas as to what you would like to do instead?' she asked.

Harry shook his head. 'No,' he said. 'I just don't know. That's really terrible, isn't it?'

'Not knowing what you want?' she said. 'No, Harry, that's absolutely normal, believe me. I can guarantee there are a cagillion people out there feeling exactly the same as you do now. You are not alone.'

Harry looked at his mother. 'You know that cagillion is not a real number, right?' he said.

She smiled. 'See, you really are smart. Now I reckon I've got some jelly babies in my room that are begging to have their heads bitten off in agony if you are up for it?'

Harry smiled back.

'You've not got a bottle of vodka stashed in there, have you? That's what I could really do with.'

Kim cuffed him over the head with her hand. 'No, I haven't, and that is the last thing you need. I am still your mother, you know, even if we are housemates.'

'And a lousy example of a housemate when you have been stealing other people's stuff, including vodka!'

'Good point,' agreed Kim. 'I reckon Angus owes me since I got him together with the love of his life. Shall we go and raid his wine rack and see if there is any leftover pizza in the kitchen?'

'Now you are talking,' he replied and stood up out of his chair. He towered over her and took her in his arms.

'Love you, Mum,' he muttered into the top of her head.

'Love you more,' she said into his chest.

Chapter 25

It was 9.30 the following day when Richard knocked on the door. Even though she had been expecting him she still nearly jumped out of her skin. She was extremely tired. She'd spent half the night tossing and turning going over the events of the previous evening in her head. From the chaos of her meeting John Sinclair in the pub to Richard arriving out of nowhere and then Max and Annie's rescue mission to take her to the utter shared joy of music and dance. And then to of course the grand finale when she finally got out of Harry what was wrong.

What a night. What a night indeed.

How to explain all that to Richard? She told Harry to get up early and go out. Let her talk to him first. Sonny and Angus were both already at lectures so she was confident they had a good chunk of time to themselves.

She showered and scraped her hair back ready for her shift later on that evening in the chippy. She put on a touch of lipstick. She wanted Richard to think that she was holding it together and hadn't totally fallen apart.

'Hello,' she said to Richard when she opened the door. 'Come in.'

She watched as he picked his way past the usual obstacle course of footwear. She guided him into the kitchen where an empty bottle of Angus's wine, that she'd shared with Harry the night before, was still on the table. She whipped it away quickly thinking she'd have to confess later and hope that his union with Poppy still had him in a good mood.

'Coffee?' she asked, automatically putting the kettle on.

'Sure,' said Richard, looking around nervously as she peered into mugs to try and find one that was clean.

'How was the concert?' he asked.

'Brilliant,' she replied. 'Do you remember Shed Seven? "Chasing Rainbows"? "Going for Gold"? Big in the nineties.'

'Err, no,' said Richard, 'Can't say that I do.'

'My feet are killing me,' she continued. 'Moshing for two hours solid.'

'Right,' said Richard.

She wondered if Richard knew what moshing was.

She plonked two mugs down on the table and sat down. 'Did you stay and have a drink with John Sinclair?' she asked, trying not to smirk.

'No,' said Richard firmly. 'No, I just went back to the hotel. We had nothing to say to each other.'

Kim nodded and took a deep breath. She needed to talk about Harry. Best get it over with.

'We need to talk . . . ' they both said at the same time.

'Oh,' said Richard. 'Go ahead. You first.'

'Okay,' she said, taking another deep breath. 'It's Harry. I came home and managed to talk to him last night.'

'I thought you said he wasn't talking to you?'

'He barely was but after the whole thing with John Sinclair I wasn't confident he was going to help so I decided I just needed to tackle him.'

'And?'

'Well, turns out, how do I put it . . . ' she faltered.

'Go on,' urged Richard.

'Turns out he hates chemistry.'

'What?! How? I don't understand.'

'Look, we've been pushing him in the wrong direction all along. He said he used to like it and he actually does quite like it, hate is probably too strong a word, but my point is he doesn't like it enough to study it at university and he doesn't think he's smart enough for it and basically he wants to quit his course.' Christ, she wasn't handling this very well at all. She was talking drivel.

'Quit his course!' exclaimed Richard, standing up. 'He can't quit his course. What do we tell John Sinclair?'

'Who gives a damn about John Sinclair? It's your son you need to worry about. He's been so busy trying to live up to our expectations that it's sent him on entirely the wrong path. He was doing what he thought he should be doing, not what he wanted to do.'

'So, what does he want to do?'

'He doesn't know.'

'He doesn't know?'

'No. He just knows he needs to get out of this course. Give him room to breathe. He'll work it out. He just needs time, that's all.'

Richard took his chair again. He was pale and shaking his head.

'But I always thought he loved chemistry. I had no idea.'

'Look, I know it's a lot to process,' she said, laying her hand on his arm hoping to calm him. 'It's a shock but he needs our help to get him through this. We need to be understanding. We need to be there for him.'

He nodded his head slowly, putting his hand over hers.

'Does he blame me for pushing him in that direction?' he asked.

'I don't think he blames anyone, but we are both guilty of putting too much pressure on him.'

'Why didn't he say something before?' he asked her.

She gave a deep sigh. 'Too much going on. Us splitting up. There was a lot happening.'

Richard looked deep into her eyes. He was wearing an old Pringle jumper she'd bought him for Christmas in 2012. The light blue triangles matched his eyes.

'Me and Alison split up,' he said. 'That's what I came to tell you.'

'I know,' she replied.

'What? How?' For the second time that morning he looked totally shocked.

'You told Vicky. Do you really think she wasn't going to get on the phone as soon as you'd spoken to her?'

He looked surprised.

'I told her not to tell you. That I wanted to tell you,' he said.

'Of course she was going to tell me, Richard. She's my friend not yours.'

He nodded.

'What happened, then?' she asked. She felt herself instinctively pull away. She leaned back in her chair and removed her hand from underneath Richard's.

'I just . . . I just . . . realised that it wasn't right.'

'It sounded pretty bloody right when you allowed it to destroy our marriage,' she said.

'I know, I know,' he said, putting his head in his hands. 'I can't believe I've been so stupid. I just, I don't know, I got carried away with the thrill of it all somehow.'

'The illicit sex, you mean?' demanded Kim.

He looked up at her in shock. Then nodded. 'Yes,' he said. 'I suppose yes, you are right. But then after a while, after you left and we moved in together, well there was nothing else. It was weird. There was just nothing and she kept trying to fill it with . . . with stuff like shopping trips and weekends away and visits to meet her old school friends but there was just nothing. I *felt* nothing. I felt like I was on some weird vacation the whole time with someone I didn't know that I had to make polite conversation with and do what they wanted to do when all I wanted was to go home. I just wanted to go home and . . . and . . . and talk to you.'

Kim stared at him. The irony of ironies. It had just been about sex with Alison all along. Alison the university scholar, whereas he needed Kim the hairdresser for conversation.

She didn't know what to say. She didn't know how to articulate the thoughts running through her mind. She was still so angry with him for what he did. But then she was so relieved to see him and to hear that it was all over. That Alison hadn't succeeded where she had failed. She hadn't made him happy.

Richard looked up at her and took her hand. Fully in both of his.

'I'm so sorry,' he said. 'I've been an absolute fool. I have no idea what got into me. I'm a prize idiot. And I know I have no right to ask your forgiveness but I have to. Because I can't not. I have to ask you if there is any way you can forgive me and if there is any way you would consider coming home.'

Kim was speechless. And in shock. She had absolutely no idea what to say. On the one hand she was desperate to go back to her life. Back to where she was a few months ago. But she wasn't sure if she could forgive her husband. She wasn't even sure who her husband was anymore. So much had happened, so much had been said that had totally thrown off how she saw him that she wasn't entirely sure there was a road back. In short, she didn't know what she wanted. Just like her son.

'I just don't know,' was all she could say. 'That's a hell of a lot to take in after all that has happened.'

He nodded. 'I understand,' he said.

Kim swallowed. Her head was swimming. She heard the door go. Shit. That was Harry back.

'That's Harry,' said Kim, standing up and withdrawing her hand.

'Right, okay,' said Richard, gathering himself and standing up. He straightened his pullover as if he was about to meet someone's parent.

Harry poked his head around the door. He looked like he hadn't had much sleep either or perhaps it was the unusually early start for him.

'Harry,' said Richard, striding towards him. Kim watched as Richard flung his arms round their son. She had never seen him do that before. Richard was not the most tactile of people. Clearly his affair had brought out the nurturing side in him.

She watched as he released Harry and held his shoulders at arm's length. 'It's fine,' he said. 'It's all going to be fine.'

'I'm so sorry, Dad,' said Harry, his face crumpling.

'No need,' said Richard. 'Your mum has explained it all. You don't have to be sorry. I realise that chemistry is not the be-all and end-all. Well I'm just starting to realise that, actually, but it's fine. We'll get you off that course and then . . . well, plenty of time for all that. But it's good, excellent. We'll work it out.'

Harry stared at his father as though he had turned into an alien.

'Are you sure?' he asked.

'Of course, son,' he replied. 'We'll get through this. I'm right behind you.'

'Thanks, Dad,' said Harry falling into his arms again. 'I can't believe you are taking it so well.'

Kim walked over and put her hand on her son's back. She smiled at Richard. He really had taken it surprisingly well.

'So you are welcome to come home, if you want to,' said Richard. 'I'll speak to the university, sort all that out and you can come home with me if you like?'

Harry looked at his father. 'Well, I don't suppose there is much point in me staying here,' he said. 'And I can't expect you to keep paying my rent when I'm not doing the course.'

'Well no,' said Richard. 'That would be a waste of money. And it would be rent free in Lancaster. Gives you time to figure out what you want to do. Take all the time you need.'

Harry glanced over at his mum. 'What do you think, Mum?' he asked.

Kim didn't know what to think. She felt sick at the thought of Harry leaving but it did make total sense. Richard was right. They couldn't justify paying rent on his room here and being at home would give him time to rethink his future.

'You could come too,' Richard said to Kim. 'Come home with Harry and let's just see what happens. No pressure. Separate rooms, whatever you want.'

Now Kim really didn't know what to think.

'What do you want to do? she asked Harry.

Harry shook his head. 'It's the only option really,' he said. 'So back to Lancaster it is.'

He was right, of course. Now he had decided to quit university he did need a roof over his head, and a job quite frankly. She certainly couldn't afford to pay his rent here as well. It made sense to go back home. Of course it did. But where did that leave her?

She looked at Richard. His cool blue eyes reflected in the Pringle jumper. The one that he'd worn every Christmas Day since 2012. It was his jazzy jumper as he called it. For special occasions. And he'd chosen to wear it today. Christmas was looming. Did she picture herself in their home on Christmas Day, the three of them and Richard in his jazzy jumper, reserved for special occasions?

Yes, she did, she thought. She could see herself at home on Christmas Day. It was a nice thought. Surrounded by all that was familiar. All back to normal with her husband and her son.

'Let's go home,' she said.

Richard pulled her in for a group hug. His eyes closed tight.

Kim felt stunned. This was big. She was going home.

'Just to see,' she said to Richard, pulling back. 'Not promising anything. But let's see.'

Richard nodded enthusiastically. 'Of course,' he said. 'Of course. However you want to play it.'

She wasn't sure. She wasn't sure at all. But she felt she owed it to her family to give it a go. See what it felt like. Going back home.

Chapter 26

Soon afterwards Richard left to go back to his hotel. They agreed that he would come back to the house that evening and pick up Harry and his stuff and they would drive home together. No point in hanging around and they'd never get all their stuff in Kim's car again. Not now that Kim had kitted out her room. In any case she had to go and hand her notice in at the chippy and she was due to work that night. She couldn't just leave Max in the lurch. She said she'd go and talk to him and see how soon he could replace her and then she would travel back to Lancaster after her last shift.

After Richard left, her and Harry sat at the kitchen table.

'You okay?' she asked.

He nodded. 'Just relieved that you and Dad are fine with it. Me giving up uni. Can't believe how well Dad reacted to be honest. What did you say to him?'

She shrugged. 'Said we had to take responsibility for not spotting sooner that you were unhappy. And I guess

I used the affair card. He really has no right to be angry with you given what has happened over the last few weeks.'

Harry nodded. 'It's going to be weird,' he said. 'Going home.'

'Sure is,' she replied. She glanced around the, as usual, wrecked kitchen. 'Imagine being in a clean kitchen!'

He grinned. 'I'm going to miss Angus and Sonny,' he said.

She nodded. 'Me too. We'll tell them when they get back from uni, shall we? At least our rent is paid up until Christmas. And I was always supposed to be out of here by then anyway. We'll need to look into finding them some new housemates ready for the new year.'

'Yeah,' said Harry. 'Guess so.' He got up suddenly. 'I'm going to go and see if Suki's in,' he said.

'Of course,' said Kim. 'Good thinking. I'll go and see if Max is at the shop. Let him know he needs to find a new worker. See you back here later?'

Harry nodded and Kim noted for the first time that morning that he looked sad again. Clearly the prospect of saying goodbye to his 'gaming buddy' was not a happy one.

Kim put her coat on and walked towards the chippy, hands deep in her pockets, shoulders hunched against the cold. She wasn't sure quite what she was going to say to Max. After all, she had said in her 'interview' that she was fully committed and would not let him down and now she was heading over there to hand her notice in. She could see his resigned face already that told her she was just like all the others.

She headed round to the back door, hoping that Max was in there early prepping for the day ahead. She pushed the door open and could see that he was in his office under the stairs staring at a spreadsheet on his laptop.

'Hiya,' she said cheerily, walking in. 'Am I disturbing you?'

'No way,' he said, looking up, a big smile spreading over his face. 'Come to complain about how sore your feet are after all that moshing last night?'

She sat down in front of him gratefully, realising that yes her feet were really sore. 'I haven't danced like that in ages,' she said, grinning at the memory.

'Me neither,' he replied. 'It was so amazing. I just can't believe I avoided it for this long and Annie, oh my God, she absolutely loved it. She's already looking at what festivals they are playing next year. She wants to go to a festival with me, Kim. Her dad. How cool is that? You did that,' he said, pointing at her. 'You made that happen, suggesting Annie took me.' He shook his head again. 'You really are a smart lady. You have given me, what do you call it . . . closure?'

'Maybe,' said Kim.

'Yep, that's it's, closure, after how long? Not only that, you have given me a new Justin Bieber to share with my daughter which is just brilliant seeing as it's my favourite band. And . . . and . . . I've seen what you've done for Sonny and Angus. Christ, you haven't half sorted them out. Different kids from when they arrived.'

'I didn't really do anything,' she said. 'All I do is listen really. Years of being a hairdresser, you see. You've heard it all.'

'Yeah well, I can't thank you enough and I'm so glad you could come with us. That worked out great.'

Kim looked at him. 'Were you really just in Lillie Langtry's for a pre-concert drink?' she asked.

'Sorry,' he said. 'I just kind of heard alarm bells and I know you are more than capable of looking after yourself but I just wanted to check you were okay. Sorry. Didn't mean to be overbearing or anything.'

'No. I'm glad you came. Really. And it meant I got to see Shed Seven, so you know, brilliant. Wouldn't have missed that for the world.'

'You should come with us to this festival Annie's banging on about. You'd love it, I reckon. Next May, I think it is. Go on, come with us, then I won't feel like the only geriatric.'

Kim swallowed. 'Might be difficult,' she said, shifting in her chair. 'That's why I've come over actually. You see, erm, I've come to tell you that I'm going back to Lancaster.'

'What?! When? Why?' He looked truly shocked. 'I thought you were here until the end of term?'

'Well, the truth is that Harry is dropping out of uni. He hates it, you see. That's why he wasn't going to any of his lectures. He was only doing it because he thought that was what we wanted him to do.'

'I see,' said Max. 'That's a shame.'

'It's all been agreed with his dad this morning. So Harry's going back with him tonight and I'll follow as soon as you can replace me.'

Max's face returned to a totally confused look. 'Why do you need to go back?'

'Err, well, so it turns out that it's all over with Alison and . . . ' Kim was now really sweating. 'He wants me back, so what's happening is me and Harry are going back to Lancaster because Harry can't stay in the house because it's pointless carrying on paying his rent if he's dropping out, and I'm going to go back too, to kind of see what happens. Give it a go . . . ' she said, trailing off under Max's increasingly confused glare.

'You are going back to him even though he cheated on you?'

That was so the question she didn't want him to ask. The question she had been desperately trying to shove out of her head all morning.

'Like I said,' she replied. 'I'm going to give it a try. See how it feels. See if I can forgive him.'

There, that sounded reasonable, didn't it?

Max said nothing, just blinked at her.

'You would have given it a go too, wouldn't you?' she asked. 'If Rachel had come back to you, if it had all gone wrong with the other bloke?'

He didn't reply.

'For Annie? You'd have at least tried for Annie?'

His eyes flickered. He was going to say yes, she thought. She needed him to say yes.

'Depends on whether I wanted to go back to being that person I was before she left me.'

Interesting answer, she thought. Did she want to go back to being the person she was before all this happened? She thought so. Lovely life, lovely family, lovely home. What wasn't there to like?

'Well it's your decision,' he said, getting up quickly

as though he suddenly had better things to do than talk to her. 'I take it tonight will be your last shift then?'

'Well, err, well I can stay until you find a replacement. I don't want to leave you struggling.'

'It's fine. I've been there before. Normally people just leave without telling me at all, so this is actually great. I'll put a notice up now. I'll have some penniless student being trained up by tomorrow lunchtime. No bother. Now, better get on. I need to go to the wholesaler.'

'Right, sure,' she said. 'I'll get out of your way. Err, but I just wanted to say how sorry I am, Max, to be leaving. Really sorry.'

He finally looked at her, eyes glistening. 'Not as sorry as me,' he said and walked off into the front of the shop.

It was her cue to leave which she did, a little bewildered and confused and strangely upset.

Chapter 27

Kim turned her key in the door of fifty-one Leopold Street with a heavy heart. The fact that Max clearly didn't approve of her decision had unsettled her. She thought he would be supportive. After all he had been in her position. But no. It was very clear that he thought she was doing the wrong thing. She hadn't even realised she wanted his approval until she didn't get it, and now she felt incredibly alone and the thought of facing him tonight was not appealing.

She picked her way over the obstacle course of boots and trainers and went to make herself a cup of tea in the kitchen. She didn't know quite how she was going to fill the rest of the day until Richard arrived to pick up Harry and she needed to go and do her shift. She supposed she should start to pack her stuff up. After all she could leave for Lancaster tomorrow now that Max had made it clear that he didn't want to see her after tonight.

She wandered upstairs with her cup of tea and sat down on her bed. She looked round her tiny little room and thought about what she could pack up that Richard might be able to fit in his car. Maybe the cheerful curtains she had bought from a charity shop all those weeks ago. The ones that had felt so impossible to hang but she'd done it and without injury! No, she would leave those here for the next tenant. Make them feel at home. She'd leave the mirror that she'd bought as well. The house in Lancaster had an abundance of mirrors so no need to take this one away. Hopefully Angus and Sonny would be able to find two other students to take their rooms. Angus had mentioned that often students came back from placements in January and so he was confident that they would get someone for Kim's room, so they should be able to replace Harry too. She hoped that they would be good to Angus and Sonny. That they'd get them, understand them. She hoped they would be good friends to them. The last thing they both needed was a horror story moving in. She'd keep her fingers crossed for them.

She could pack up her clothes, she figured. Especially the party dresses. Unlikely to need them before tomorrow. Yes, Richard could take those back with him. Oh and Bjorn the cheese plant, of course. Bjorn needed to go back with Richard and Harry. He would never fit in her car. Yes, she could gather some stuff together for Richard to take back. That would be sensible. She sat staring at her room that had been so transformed from when she moved in. She'd definitely put her mark on it and made it her own. She took out her phone and took some selfies of her there in her own student house share. Just so she wouldn't forget.

Perhaps she'd get her stuff together later. She couldn't face it quite yet. She'd perhaps just have a quick nap. It had been a late night last night and she could just do with a little snooze.

She had no idea how long she had been asleep when she heard the front door bang. She woke up with a start. She reached for her phone to see what time it was. Three o'clock already! Christ, she'd better go and see how Harry was getting on with his packing.

There was no sign of him in his room so she carried on downstairs to see if that had been him coming in.

She found him in the lounge on the sofa, his head bowed over his phone.

'Hi,' she said. 'Do you need some help with packing your stuff up?'

'Suppose so,' he said, not looking up.

'You okay?'

He shrugged.

She took a seat next to him. 'How was Suki?'

He shrugged again. 'Okay,' he said flatly.

'Tough saying goodbye?'

He didn't reply but she watched as a single tear bounced on to his phone screen.

She put her arm around him. He leaned in and sniffed hard.

'I didn't expect her to be upset,' he mumbled.

'Well that is generally what happens when you care about someone and they leave.'

'I know but I didn't think she cared that much.'

'Of course she did. You're good mates, aren't you?'

He nodded. 'She said she'd miss me,' he said as though he couldn't believe what he was saying.

'Of course she will. You'll miss her, won't you?'

He nodded. 'She's the only thing that has kept me here this long really. I never thought that I would meet someone like that. You know, in freshers' week and everything. Didn't think that sort of thing would ever happen to someone like me. I might have quit a lot sooner if it hadn't been for her and her being here.'

'Will she come and see you?' Kim asked.

'She says she will, but it won't be the same, will it? Not the same as living opposite each other.'

Kim squeezed her son tight. 'It won't, I'm afraid, but you'll find a way – if you really care then you always find a way.'

They heard the front door slam and the arguing tones of Sonny and Angus come bursting through the door.

'I am not helping you put a blow-up Santa on the roof,' they heard Angus say. 'No fucking way. You will kill us both and you are not doing it either, do you hear. I'm not spending the next day in A&E with you because you fell off a roof putting a stupid fucking blow-up Santa there.'

'But it might make Kim and Harry stay if we make the house look all Christmassy and cosy and lovely. How can you leave a house with a blow-up Santa on the roof? Just not possible.'

They burst into the living room.

'Thank God you are still here,' said Sonny. 'Please stay,' he said, falling to his knees in front of Kim and adopting the praying position. 'You can't go. You are both the best housemates in the entire world. You cannot leave. Please don't leave.'

Sonny was virtually crying.

'Oh get up, man,' said Angus brusquely, sitting down on a lounger. He turned to Kim and Harry. 'So what the fuck,' he said, raising his arms in surprise. 'A WhatsApp message saying Harry's dumping his course and you are both going back up north. What the actual fuck?'

Kim was taken aback. This wasn't the reaction she had been expecting.

'I WhatsApped them,' explained Harry. 'Thought they should actually know as soon as possible.'

Kim nodded. 'Look, I'm really sorry, guys,' she began. 'But with Harry giving up his course then there is really no reason to be here any longer.'

'I hear Harry's excuse. If I hated my course I would get the chuff out of here too but what about you?' Angus said, pointing at Kim accusingly.

'Well,' said Kim, swallowing. 'I was going soon anyway. Remember the rules? And err, Richard has ended his affair with the neighbour and so . . . '

'You are going back to him? What the . . . !' exclaimed Angus. 'What the actual hell?'

'I don't understand,' said Sonny. 'You're getting back together?' Sonny looked like he had been physically wounded. He'd recoiled from her as though he had just learned she had an infectious disease.

'Well yes, well sort of, well it's like I'm just going to move back in and see how we go.'

'Bullshit!' said Angus. 'Utter bullshit. You'll move back in and he'll have you back in that bed shagging him in no time and then he'll think you've forgiven him just in time for him to start another affair.'

Kim stared at Angus, shocked.

'Richard's not like that,' she said. 'He's genuinely sorry. He really wants it to work.'

'You think?' said Angus. 'It's what they all say.' He paused. 'It's what my dad says. Every time he has an affair. He says he's sorry, oh so sorry, and then a couple of years later it happens again.'

'I cannot believe he's like that,' said Sonny, shocked. 'He seemed so nice when I met him. He bought me a McDonald's. And he got my order right. I asked for no salad and he got it perfect. He really listened to me. I still can't believe he cheats!'

Angus shrugged.

'And your mum, she seems way too smart to get cheated on,' continued Sonny. 'She's smart, like really smart. She wears matching clothes and everything. I bet she wears matching underwear as well.'

'Sonny,' said Angus. 'If I didn't know you better, then I would think that comment came from a very bad place but I know that it doesn't at all. But please, Sonny, think what you are saying, mate.'

'Sorry,' said Sonny, looking deeply confused.

'And in any case, you are wrong. No one's too smart to get cheated on,' said Angus grimly, looking sideways at Kim.

Sonny turned back to Kim and Harry. 'Please don't go,' he said. 'I don't want you to go.'

'I really don't have any choice,' said Harry. 'If I could stay I would. I really would.'

'But it makes me so sad to think of this place without you both,' said Sonny.

Kim felt her heart swell. She was so going to miss this pair.

'It's the right answer,' she said now, having to fight back the tears. 'We have a life up there. In any case I can go back to my hairdressing, back to my friends, my family.'

'You have a life here,' said Sonny.

'Do I?'

'Yes! You have a job in the chippy, you have friends, Max and Annie, and you have family, me, Angus and Harry. But we need Harry to stay too. We are a family now; we have to stick together.'

'But the rule was I had to be out by Christmas – it's what we agreed?'

'Sod the rules,' said Sonny sulkily.

Kim was beyond touched. She looked at Sonny and then at Angus. She couldn't believe they were so desperate for her to stay. She couldn't believe they thought that this odd little household had become a family. She'd been here less than three months. How life could change in such a short time.

'Look Sonny,' said Kim, putting her hand on his shoulder. 'I cannot tell you how grateful I am that you have put up with me for the past few months. I will honestly never, ever forget it.' She swallowed. 'But I have to go back,' she said. 'I have to go back and see if I can pick up the pieces of my old life.'

'You were more than happy to leave it behind a few months ago,' said Angus.

Kim turned to look at him sharply. 'I had no choice, because of what Richard did, did I? But now it's all over with Alison then it has to be worth a shot.'

'If you say so,' he shrugged.

'It's the right thing to do,' she said, getting up. She couldn't take any more of this. 'Thank you,' she said earnestly. 'I can't tell you how much it means to me that you want me to stay. Seriously. Especially considering how I behaved when I first arrived. I am going to miss you, you know.'

'Yeah, whatever,' said Angus, getting up and thrusting past her towards the door.

'You coming, Sonny?' he said, turning round at the last minute.

'Where to?'

'The pub. I think we need a drink.'

'Yeah, right, okay,' said Sonny, getting up. 'What time are you leaving?' he asked Harry.

'Dad's coming to pick me up about 5 p.m.,' he replied.

Sonny nodded. 'I'll make sure we're back to say goodbye,' he said. 'But I think that Angus needs me right now. He's very upset. I know he hides it well but he's devastated that you are both going.'

Harry nodded. 'You go,' he said. 'Hopefully I'll see you later.'

Sonny nodded. 'You will,' he promised.

* * *

Kim and Harry packed up his room mostly in silence, both lost in their own thoughts as they dragged out rucksacks and suitcases and bags for life to pile all of Harry's worldly goods into. Kim noted that he hadn't accumulated anything in the nine weeks he had been here. No books, no clothes, no trinkets to make it home. It was almost as if he always meant it to be temporary.

They shifted everything down into the lounge and Kim left Harry to find all their crockery in the kitchen whilst she went and packed all her party dresses ready to put into Richard's car. She'd only worn one of them after all. The black sequined backless number when Vicky had come down and she had thrown up all over the floor.

Goodness she was a mess back then. She realised she had behaved so badly. Getting drunk all the time, stealing Angus's wine and cold pizza. She had been so utterly lost. She had no idea what to do with herself. What a long way she had come since then. Got herself a job, actually managed to fit into the household pretty well in the end, to the point where they were begging her to stay. She couldn't believe it. It brought a tear to her eye when she thought of Sonny sat at her knees pleading with her. And the look on Angus's face. She'd felt wanted, really wanted.

Yes, things hadn't turned out too bad in Nottingham after all. Something to be proud of. But it was time to go home. Time to go back to see if she could recapture the remnants of her old life that she had been so devastated to leave.

* * *

She opened the door to Richard at 4.55 p.m. Despite the cold he still wasn't wearing the coat that Alison had bought him. Kim wondered where it was. Would she find it on the coat rack when she walked in the door? Her stomach lurched at the sudden thought that she would have to face Alison at some point. And all her family and friends. All eyes would be on her as she returned home. That wasn't going to be easy but she figured she had nothing to be ashamed of. It was down to Richard to smooth the way and do the explaining and not her.

Richard thrust an enormous bunch of red roses in her face.

'I know this is not enough, nowhere near enough,' he said, 'But I need you to know I'm going to do everything I can to make you happy again. This is just the start. I promise.'

She smiled back. She didn't think Richard had bought her flowers since their very first date. They were daffodils, she remembered, and she thought they were the most beautiful flowers she had ever seen.

She wondered if Richard had bought Alison daffodils. She shook her head trying to dispel the thought.

She walked back towards the kitchen to put them in water before realising they didn't have a vase in the house. There had not been much call for one during their first term. She found a jug and filled it with water and put the roses in there. She'd work out what to do with them later.

She walked back into the lounge to find Richard and Harry already relaying to and from the car with

Harry's belongings. She spotted Bjorn the cheesy cheese plant in the corner of the lounge and picked it up and carried it out to ask Richard if he could fit it in.

She dumped it on the path outside the house, huffing and puffing slightly. It was heavy. Richard and Harry were busy reorganising boxes and bags to try and get more in.

'Can you fit Bjorn in?' she asked.

Richard turned round to look. 'How did that get here?' he asked in surprise.

'Vicky brought him down in her van with her when she came to visit,' said Kim. 'She decided I needed company. That I was missing my dancing partner. Did you not notice he was gone?'

Richard shook his head. 'I'm not sure how we will get it in. It's big.'

Kim was inclined to agree. They already had the seats down in the back of Richard's car and the plant was tall. But she also knew that there was no way Bjorn was fitting in her car. It was far too small.

But there was no way she could leave Bjorn behind. No way.

'It may have to stay behind,' suggested Richard.

'I can't leave him behind,' stated Kim.

'Well, I don't know what we are going to do then,' said Richard.

'We've got an idea,' came a voice from behind them.

Kim whizzed round faster than a spinning top, her heart racing. But she wasn't prepared for the sight that greeted her.

She'd recognised Max's voice immediately. But she wasn't prepared to see him there alongside not only Annie, but also Angus, Sonny and Suki.

'Wow,' she cried, delighted to see them all. 'So glad you all came to say goodbye,' she said.

'We haven't,' said Max. 'Like I said, we've got an idea.'

She felt confused. Max looked pretty grim, as did Angus. Annie was grinning, Sonny was jumping up and down as though he was bursting for a pee and Suki was gazing imploringly at Harry who had stepped to her side.

'What do you mean?' she asked.

'Yeah, what's this all about?' said Richard, stepping forward alongside Kim.

Kim's heart was beating so fast now she could barely breathe.

'Well,' said Max, glancing at Richard and then turning his eyes back to Kim. 'So we have had a meeting,' he started.

'In the pub,' added Sonny, grinning. 'I've had a couple of pints so apologies now if I have to dash off to the loo.'

'No problem,' said Kim. 'Carry on,' she urged Max.

'Yep, so we had a meeting . . . '

'It was all my idea actually,' said Sonny, putting his hand up. 'Thought we might be able to think of something between us.'

'Shut up, Sonny,' said Angus, punching him on the arm. 'We agreed that Max would do the talking.'

'Sorry, yes, sorry,' said Sonny.

'We really need to be getting on the road,' said Richard, checking his watch.

'This won't take long,' said Max. 'If Sonny lets me get a word in edgeways. Now we had a meeting and we have come up with a plan, an option as it were, that would mean you could stay here.'

'It's brilliant,' said Sonny. 'Genius.'

'Look . . . ' said Richard.

Kim put a firm hand on his arm. 'Let them speak,' she said.

'Continue,' she said again to Max.

'So, Annie wants to cut her hours in the chippy,' said Max. 'She's been offered a job in a vintage dress shop.'

'I wasn't going to take it because I didn't want to let Dad down,' she said, 'but . . . but . . . well, I'll let Dad tell you.'

'So I was wondering if Harry would like her job, in the chippy, and then he can afford to stay and earn some money whilst he decides what he wants to do.'

Kim felt Richard let out a deep sigh. She looked over at Harry who was blinking at Max, trying to grasp what he was saying. She noticed that Suki had taken his hand in hers.

'I should be able to give you just enough hours to cover your rent and food,' said Max. 'The job's yours if you want it.'

Kim glanced at Richard. He clearly could not understand what was happening.

'You can't stay here,' Richard said Harry. 'Come home and you can live rent-free and you won't need to work in a chippy. And I can help you decide what course to apply for next year. I can help you with your application. Have you thought about biochemistry? I was thinking that might be right up your street. I was going to get the lecturer at Lancaster to talk to you about it. See what you thought because you'll need to apply soon. Applications will need to be in by the end of January.'

Harry looked at his dad. Then he looked at Suki. Then he looked back at his dad.

'Thanks, Dad, but . . . but . . . ' he looked at Suki and Max again. Then back to his dad. 'But I think I'd like to stay here. If I can afford it, then I'd like to stay. Have a complete break from study. Do something completely different. Whilst I decide what I really want to do.'

Richard clearly could not comprehend his son. 'You want to stay here and work in a chippy?' he asked.

'Yes,' said Harry. 'If Max is all right with that?'

Max nodded. 'You work hard, you can have a job as long as you like,' he said.

'So you'll stay?' said Sonny, barely able to contain himself. 'You'll stay? Just say it. I need to hear it. Will you stay?' Sonny was clutching onto Harry's shoulder jumping up and down.

Harry looked around him, a small smile on his face. 'I will,' he said.

Sonny and Angus exploded, jumping up and down, slapping Harry on the back. Suki grinned and held tight onto his hand then leaned forward and kissed Harry square on the lips.

'You kissed, you kissed!' exclaimed Sonny. 'Are you together now? Like a couple?'

'Of course they are, you numpty,' said Angus. 'Always have been.'

'But no one told me, no one said!' said Sonny, totally aggrieved. 'I thought you were just playing games?'

'You actually fell for that one?' said Angus. 'It was as clear as day, from day one.'

'Sorry, Dad,' said Harry, turning to his father. 'But I really would like to stay. Is that all right with you, Mum?' he said before Richard had the chance to comment.

'Of course it is,' she said. 'As long as you earn the money you can do what you like. You are eighteen now after all.' She paused. 'I'm proud of you,' she said, flinging her arms round her son. And she was. He was making his own decisions and he looked happier than he had since he arrived. And that was all that mattered.

Richard was left looking bewildered stood by his car. 'So I guess I will be able to fit your plant in,' he said to Kim, going to pick it up.

'Hang on a minute, we haven't finished quite yet,' said Max, turning to Kim. 'You see, I've still got your job to fill, which I could do without quite frankly as I'll need someone to be training up Harry here and I think you'd be good at that, and so we were wondering if you would consider staying too. But I would have to cut your hours to give Harry enough, so we were thinking that you could do with something else so we came up with another idea.'

'It was Annie's idea this time,' said Sonny. 'And it's absolutely *amazing*. Like the best idea anyone has ever had since the beginning of time.'

Annie took her phone out of her pocket and showed Kim a screenshot from the Nottingham Barton University website. 'We think you should apply for one of these at the university,' she said. 'Look, it's an apprenticeship-style degree in counselling. It's part-time so you'd be able to earn money at the same time, and it's a much cheaper way of doing it, and we all think you are brilliant at listening and helping people so maybe . . . maybe you should do it professionally?'

Kim couldn't take in what she was saying or what she was showing her. She must have been looking totally stupid in front of Annie who changed her expression to one of concern.

'But only if you want to,' Annie stumbled. 'We also thought you might want to go back to hairdressing and we were all going to go round the hairdressers in town for you and see if we could get a job for an excellent hairdresser, but we thought . . . well, we thought that actually you might want to go to university. That this could be your chance to go, if you wanted to.'

'I don't understand,' said Kim, struggling to take it all in. 'I can't go to university. I'm not clever enough.'

'Of course you bloody are,' said Angus. 'You're smarter than any person I know. You've helped all of us one way or another since you moved in. That's why Annie found this course at the university to be a counsellor so you could help people all the time.'

'Me, go to university?' repeated Kim.

'Yes,' said Angus. 'You. We'd help you apply. Look, if I can get in, anyone can. Believe me.'

'It's a great idea, Mum,' said Harry. 'They're right.

You would be brilliant at it. You really would. And that's the pressure off me then, isn't it, if you're at uni?' He grinned.

Kim was still in shock. She just couldn't take in what they were suggesting, it seemed so improbable. She never in her wildest dreams thought that she would ever get to be a student . . . at university.

'We checked the qualifications,' said Annie. 'You did A levels, right?'

Kim nodded. 'Not very well,' she admitted.

'Well, they are desperate for mature students on this course. Life experience they want, not just some green eighteen-year-olds like us who know nothing.'

'That's right,' nodded Sonny. 'I knew nothing until I moved in with Kim. She even taught me to cook spag bol.'

Kim still couldn't comprehend. 'Me, go to university?' she said again.

'Look,' said Richard, putting his hand on her shoulder. She jumped. She'd forgotten he was there. 'It's a lovely idca really but I bet you want to get back to your hairdressing, don't you, Kim? Back to your clients. I'm sure they have really missed you and you love hairdressing, don't you? You always have.'

Kim looked at Richard, trying to work out what he was saying. Sounded like he wanted to erase what had happened and have his old life back. Where she was conveniently 'just a hairdresser'.

She could see that Richard was starting to panic that she wasn't instantly dismissing this crazy idea that Annie had come up with.

'In any case,' he said. 'You don't want to be scraping by just working in a chippy, do you, living in student digs? Come home, Kim. Come home. Call your old clients, they'll be delighted to hear from you, you know they will. You'll be able to pick up just where you left off. You were born to be a hairdresser, you know you were.'

Kim screwed her nose up at him. 'When you last came down you called me "just a hairdresser",' she said. 'Like it was an unworthy career.'

'No, I didn't.'

'Yes, you did,' said Max, Annie and Sonny in unison.

'And you just said that it was "just" a chippy, like that was an unworthy place of work.'

'No, I didn't,' said Richard.

'Yes, you did,' said Max, Annie, Angus, Sonny and Suki.

Richard looked away under their glare. 'I didn't mean that,' he said.

'Yes, you did,' said Max, Annie, Angus, Sonny and Suki.

'You so did,' muttered Max.

'Are you sleeping with my wife?' Richard suddenly blasted at Max, losing his cool. 'Is that what this is really all about?'

'What!' screeched Kim and Max.

'No,' said Max firmly.

'So, what is it then?' demanded Richard. 'Do you want to sleep with her, is that it? All this nonsense about going to university. Kim doesn't want to go to university. She's a hairdresser. Always has been, always will be. She loves it, don't you Kim? She doesn't want to be working in a chippy and studying all hours. That's not her. You don't know her. That's not her at all.'

'Well why don't you ask her?' said Max. 'I think it's about time you let Kim speak about what she wants, don't you?'

'Of course,' swallowed Richard. He looked at her. 'Tell them, Kim. That them you want to come home,' he said.

Kim looked back at him then round at the rest of the group. At Max, her boss and friend, Annie, possibly the daughter she never had, Sonny, the wonderful amazing ray of light that was Sonny, Angus, her troublesome mate who perhaps just really had a heart of gold, Suki, her son's girlfriend who was her own woman through and through, and Harry, her amazing, brave son who'd just made some really tough decisions.

'I already am home,' she told Richard.

Epilogue – New Year's Eve

So here she was wrapping napkins round cutlery again. It brought back the memory of Richard's surprise fiftieth birthday party so sharply that she couldn't help but wince. What a party that had been in more ways than one. This evening's celebration would be dramatically different, she was sure. For a start she was using serviettes from the chip shop instead of the thick cream squares embossed with the birthday boy's age. The thin crispy paper would barely clean up a little finger but she knew that none of this evening's guests would give a monkey's. She put the six sets of wrapped cutlery into an empty pint glass and put it in the middle of the table. There, party preparations were done.

She'd arrived back in Nottingham earlier that day, having spent Christmas up in Lancaster with her parents. It hadn't been the best Christmas, she couldn't lie. Her mum was still struggling to understand any of the decisions that Kim had made in the last few weeks, most of all her decision to stay in Nottingham and not return to her hometown.

'But this is your home,' Janice never tired of reminding her.

'It is,' Kim told her. 'It will always be. But I'm just doing what I should have done at eighteen. Gone away. Tried something new. Experienced more things. Found out who I wanted to be. Chased some rainbows.'

'Chased some rainbows?' asked Janice, never having looked more confused by her daughter.

Kim shook her head and smiled. 'Nothing,' she said. 'Aren't you at least pleased that I might be going to university?'

'You had a perfectly good job and a husband who provided well for you. I have absolutely no idea why on earth you need to go to university.'

Kim sighed. She daren't mention the rainbows again.

Seeing Richard had been difficult, of course. He was even more confused than her mother, albeit he recognised he had no right to be since his actions had been the catalyst for changing the course of Kim's life. She'd gone over to the house two days after Christmas to collect some things to take back to Nottingham with her. It had been weird knocking on the door of her previous home. Even weirder walking in. It felt empty and echoey. Far too big for a man living on his own. And dusty! Clearly not much cleaning had gone on since she left. There were no Christmas decorations evident either, but then he had spent Christmas down in Cornwall with his parents and Harry. So no need to deck the halls here but it made her feel a little sad that he'd made no effort when she had always totally gone to town on making sure that the house looked magical and festive. Maybe he'd never cared? Maybe he'd actually never noticed?

They'd sat and drunk an awkward coffee whilst they mainly discussed Harry. Richard had at least appreciated seeing his son over Christmas and bridges seemed to have been built. Kim was relieved about that. Richard also appeared to have stopped harassing him about his future. No mention was made of the need for Harry to decide on alternative course options or make university applications. He appeared to be letting him be for now. However, disappointingly, Richard didn't ask about her future either. She was desperate to talk about it to him now, sat in the kitchen of her old home. Just like they used to before all the mess came. They would sit at that island and talk through what was going on in their lives. But he never asked. He clearly didn't want to know if she had successfully pursued the crazy idea of getting herself to university.

And so it wasn't with sadness that an hour later she loaded her car with clothes and a few personal items to take back to Nottingham. It was with relief that she had made the right choice. This really wasn't where she belonged anymore. Everything had changed. Most importantly she had changed.

As she drove away she stole a glance at Alison's house. It looked empty and cold. She noticed no Christmas decorations there either. Perhaps she had gone away. Perhaps she was avoiding spending New Year in the house where last year she had spent it with her husband, her lover and her lover's wife, as it turned out.

It was clear from the outset that this New Year's Eve celebrations were going to be very different to last year's for Kim. Sonny had insisted that they begin their celebrations with pre-dinner drinks and so Kim, Max, Annie, Sonny, Harry and Suki were all gathered in the lounge drinking sherry. That was what Sonny deemed to be the drink of choice for such an evening. He then proceeded to give them an early rendition of 'Auld Lang Syne' on the ukulele that Annie had given him for Christmas. It was so bad they were all very relieved to hear a knock at the door.

'Who's that?' asked Sonny, pausing his tune and cocking his head. He leapt up and dashed for the door before anyone could get there first.

The next minute Angus walked through the door followed by Poppy, the gorgeous girl from his phone background.

'Oh my goodness,' cried Kim, leaping up to embrace him. 'What are you doing here? We thought you were celebrating in Edinburgh with your family.'

'What happened?' Harry asked Angus.

'Dad screwed up and mixed up his Christmas presents,' he explained. 'Gave Mum a box with see-through size six underwear in, clearly meant for his mistress. All hell let loose. And I mean *all hell*. It's been grim ever since so we decided to ditch the fancy meal in the hotel in the middle of Edinburgh and join you guys.'

'Bloody hell,' said Sonny. 'Size six, you say? Your mum is at least a twelve.'

'Again, Sonny,' said Angus. 'It's a good job I know you. Poppy, this is Sonny. Ignore everything he says.'

'Good to meet you,' grinned Poppy. 'I hope you don't mind me tagging along.'

'Of course not,' said Sonny, wide-eyed. 'I've got a girlfriend,' he announced.

'He means me,' said Annie, getting up. Annie had really dialled it up for the evening's celebrations in their humble abode. She'd gone full on Marilyn Monroe with a figure-hugging soft pink dress and a blonde wig. 'You look incredible,' said Poppy, grinning. 'I feel like I should change.'

'She always looks amazing so I wouldn't bother if I were you,' said Sonny. 'You won't look better than her.'

'As I say,' said Angus to Poppy. 'Ignore everything he says.'

'No. I think he speaks a lot of sense,' laughed Poppy.

'Oh wow,' said Sonny, suddenly jumping up and down and waving his fingers at Poppy. 'You are a doctor, aren't you? My fingers really hurt with all the ukulele playing I have been doing since Christmas. What do you suggest?'

'Sit down and shut up,' said Harry, getting up and holding his hand out to Poppy.

'I'm Harry,' he said. 'Angus's other housemate. Don't worry, I'm the sane one, well almost sane. And this is Suki. She's my, well, she's my girlfriend,' he said, beaming with pride.

'Hi,' said Suki, waving. 'Glad you are here. Please tell me you can play the ukulele better than Sonny?'

'Sorry, no,' said Poppy.

'It's my fault,' admitted Annie. 'I thought it would be good for Sonny to have somewhere to focus his energy.'

'I'm this idiot's father,' said Max to Poppy, indicating Annie. 'I've clearly brought her up really badly for her to have decided to inflict Sonny on the world of music.'

'Max is a big Justin Bieber fan,' Kim told Poppy with a smirk.

'I love Justin Bieber!' exclaimed Poppy.

'Really?!' said both Angus and Annie with entirely different levels of enthusiasm.

'Alexa, play Justin Bieber,' shouted Annie.

'This is your fault,' Max whispered to Kim as the sound of Justin Bieber filled the room.

Kim laughed. 'Do you want to come and help me sort the food out whilst these kids listen to young people's music?' she asked.

'What can I do to help feed these extra mouths?' asked Max as he walked into the kitchen. 'Do you need me to go and fire up the fryers and get some fish and chips on?'

She looked over at the enormous pan of bolognese.

'I think we are all good for food,' she said. 'Sonny went a bit overboard chopping carrots now he's learnt how to do it, so there's plenty.'

'Good old Sonny,' said Max, shaking his head. 'Listen, I've been meaning to ask how your meeting went at the university before Christmas,' he asked. 'I kind of didn't want to mention it in case it went badly but did it go okay? I've been dying to know.'

Kim looked at him gratefully. Finally someone asking her who clearly wanted her to succeed in pursuit of this crazy plan. She gave him a full update on her meeting with the course leader for the apprentice counselling degree course at Nottingham Barton University.

Martha Bennet could not have been more encouraging, she told him. Although quite rightly she had been very honest about the challenges that going into counselling would present.

'Being a counsellor is an extremely difficult role to have; however, the rewards can be enormous. You need to think very hard as to whether you can deal with the very difficult situations you will be faced with,' she'd said.

Kim had thought about barely anything else. She knew that the situations she had helped her clients with, and indeed her housemates, would be nothing compared to the situations people might come to her with as a counsellor. But the thought of being able to help people who really needed it, well, it gave her a real sense of purpose, something she had never really felt before, and she felt so drawn to it, so fired up that people actually thought she might be able to do it. She had never in her life felt more motivated to do something and her meeting with Martha had only helped confirm that. She had written her application with help from the seasoned application writers, Angus, Sonny and Harry, and hoped to hear early in the new year if she had been successful. Martha had reassured her that she saw no reason why she would not be accepted if that was what she really wanted to do and was prepared to put the work in.

'I can't wait for the day I next visit as a real bona fide university student,' Kim said to Max, her eyes shining. 'I still can't quite believe it.'

He was smiling at her as he leaned against the worktop.

'Believe it,' he said. 'It's happening.'

'But just a few months ago I was dropping my son off to be a student and now he works in a chip shop and *I'm* going to be a student.'

'You both work in a chip shop,' pointed out Max.

'Correct,' said Kim, grinning. 'And I could not be prouder.'

'Of who?' asked Max.

'Both of us,' said Kim. 'We've both come out of the year happy. We've both found ourselves really, haven't we?'

'Found a better rainbow to chase?' suggested Max.

Kim looked at him. Boy was she grateful they had met, for so many reasons.

Max raised his glass to hers, 'Here's to chasing better rainbows,' he said.

She grabbed her sherry glass off the counter. 'Exactly,' agreed Kim, clinking his glass with her own. 'To chasing better rainbows,' she said.

Acknowledgements

First of all, big thanks to Hannah Todd of the Madeleine Milburn Literary Agency who excitedly exclaimed 'that's it' when I first gave her a vague idea of the concept behind this book. This was after I'd told her that after turning fifty all I could think of writing about was murder! Her tales of her fellow students during her university days also inspired the character of Sonny, who I am very fond of, so thank you for him, Hannah.

Thank you Kate Bradley for your very positive response after you read the first draft. I always appreciate your honesty and so I know that it was genuine and heartfelt. Your support as always is so appreciated. Also many thanks to everyone else at HarperCollins who I know work really hard behind the scenes. And special thanks has to go to Susanna Peden who is an absolutely fantastic publicist. The exposure you have got for me so far has been brilliant – you are truly excellent at what you do.

I'd also like to thank some amazing women in my life that inspire me every single day. Without meaning to show off (well maybe a little bit!), I wrote this book whilst training for the London Marathon and many people were amazed and impressed that I managed to complete the challenge! However, I am privileged to know three brilliant women, Helen, Rosie and Anouk, who all face marathon-scale challenges every single day of their lives and deserve far more praise than me. You are all utterly amazing and I am so proud to be able to call you my friends.

Thanks must go to my book group who are a constant source of knowledge on many things but most importantly for this book, on having teenagers at university. Extremely useful intel, and if I have got anything wrong it is purely my fault and not theirs. Thank you Beth, Claire, Debs, Helen, Jo, Nicky, Nicola and Vix.

Writing this book has reminded me of the time many years ago when I started university. I just want to thank my mum and dad for never pushing me in any direction and having faith that I would find my way. I've been lucky enough to have some great jobs over the years, including being a writer, and I have you to thank for that.

Finally – as always – thank you readers for reading. Without you I wouldn't be doing this, so thanks to you, every single one of you. I really do appreciate it.

If you loved *The Time of Her Life*,
don't miss Tracy's other funny
and uplifting novels . . .

'Filled with fun'
FABULOUS

'Pure Joy!'
Katie Fforde